CABINET REFORM IN BRITAIN

1914-1963

CABINET REFORM
IN BRITAIN
1914-1963

Hans Daalder

STANFORD UNIVERSITY PRESS
STANFORD, CALIFORNIA
1963

To Mau

This work originally appeared in The Netherlands
in 1960 under the title *Organisatie en Reorganisatie
van de Britse Regering, 1914–1958,* Van Gorcum &
Comp. N.V., Assen. The present edition has been
translated, revised, and expanded by the author.

Stanford University Press
Stanford, California
London : Oxford University Press
© 1963 by the Board of Trustees of the
Leland Stanford Junior University
All rights reserved
Library of Congress Catalog Card Number : 63–14127
Printed in the United States of America

PREFACE

Ever since World War I, the structure of British central government has come under severe pressure, as government tasks have increased and become considerably more complicated. Simultaneously, the structure of the Cabinet has become the subject of critical discussion. Whereas some regard constant piecemeal adjustment to new administrative demands as the only realistic answer, others have argued for a more drastic overhaul, whether by what they have called a "rationalization" of the interdepartmental structure or by the establishment of a non-departmental Cabinet, dedicated, above all, to the consideration of long-term policy.

In matters of Cabinet reform, complacency and concern seem to have alternated in a curious cycle, which recurred during the preparation of this book. I first became interested in the problems of British Cabinet structure in 1951, the year of the "Overlords controversy." Most research for this book was done in more serene days between 1954 and 1959, and the Dutch edition was published in the Netherlands in 1960. The suggestion for an English translation came from some British colleagues in the still quiet period of early 1961, before Macmillan's political fortunes began to slip. By pure accident, it will now come out at a time when uncertainty about policies and considerable political excitement have stimulated a new crop of administrative innovations and have provoked demands for further reform.

It is not my intention to enter into this renewed debate. The purpose of this book was, and is, merely to give an account, seen through the eyes of a foreign observer, of certain typical trends in British thought on British central government. To this end it offers, in Part I, a description of the evolution of the Cabinet since 1914, indicating at every point what demands there were for Cabinet reform. In Part II is given a more detailed description of the actual changes and demands for reforms in the organization for defense and economic policy. Many ideas about Cabinet reform originated in the defense field, but their translation into the civilian field, particularly the field of economic policy, revealed the serious shortcomings of any organizational "models" derived from defense experiences. Finally, in Part III, chronological description gives way to analysis. After a summary of the changes that have taken place since 1914, the problem of Cabinet organization is tested against three distinct schools of thought put forward by a number of leading British politicians and academicians seeking to ease the difficulties of government at the top. This scheme, inevitably, implies some repetitious argument. But, after considerable reflection, I thought this preferable to a sacrifice of clarity or completeness.

This study concludes that specific (and too narrow) views of politics underlie each of these schools of thought. It does not offer any "solutions" of its own, for the simple reason that it queries their existence. The workings of central government in any country are the result of a complex interplay of institutional traditions, the ever-changing forces of personality, party, interest groups, and bureaucratic organizations, and the rise of intractable problems demanding government action. In this situation a priori solutions seem neither relevant nor adequate. Unfortunately, it is often forgotten that public-administration theory can be applied to the Cabinet only if all these disparate forces are taken sufficiently into account. It is policy, not machinery, that counts. Too often, new administrative devices even obscure a continuing absence of clear policies.

In writing this book, I have been in the interesting position of using the works of British authors on the subject, both as source material and as objects of study. It goes without saying that I have not attempted to rival such excellent studies on the working of the Cabinet as Sir Ivor Jennings' *Cabinet Government,* A. Berriedale Keith's *The British Cabinet System,* Lord Morrison's *Government and Parliament,* the various important writings of D. N. Chester, F. M. G. Willson, and W. J. M. Mackenzie, or John P. Mackintosh's more recent *The British Cabinet.* Unlike those studies, this book does not attempt an exhaustive study of the institutional arrangement of the British Cabinet; nor does it pretend to be a comprehensive analysis of the political history of successive Cabinets. It centers rather on the problem of Cabinet reform, both as a theoretical and as a practical proposition. But since I wrote this book for foreign readers, and since institutional norms and political factors obviously have a considerable bearing on the specific character of Cabinet-reform proposals, I have inevitably included considerable descriptive material.

Readers might note the timing of the writing of this book. It was well under way when D. N. Chester and F. M. G. Willson published *The Organization of British Central Government, 1914–1956;* the Dutch edition was published before F. A. Johnson's *Defence by Committee: The British Committee of Imperial Defence, 1885–1959*; and I had already finished a rough translation of the present edition before I was aware of Mackintosh's recent opus. If the earlier publication of these studies preempted some of my findings, it also enabled me to check my text at various points. On balance, I am decidedly grateful to their authors.

The manuscript proper was delivered to the publishers in January 1963; the Postscript in October 1963, immediately after the exciting political events that culminated in the replacement of Mr. Macmillan by Lord Home (as he then was).

Even in these days of rapid communications, writing about the politics of a foreign country presents very peculiar problems. It is not easy to keep *au courant* of changing moods and events, and it is often difficult to locate very specialized or new books in time. As will be evident from the text, I have in the main relied on written sources, and I have not hesitated to quote from them frequently, both to reproduce the arguments of others and to convey the special atmosphere of British politics. For those who find my use of quotations too liberal, let me reply with a quotation from Montaigne: "I make others say what I am not able to say so well myself, now for want of words, now for want of understanding. I do not number my borrowings, I weigh them." Footnotes and bibliography will show my indebtedness.

In addition, I am glad to express my thanks to the Passfield Trustees and to the Librarian of the British Library of Political and Economic Science, London, for allowing me access to some of the papers left to this library by Mrs. Beatrice Webb; to the Warden and Fellows of All Souls College, Oxford, for allowing me to publish some unpublished material from the late G. M. Young; to the late Lord Hankey for permission to quote certain passages from his testimony to the Haldane Committee in 1918, as well as some lines of his letter to me of 10 November 1957; to Lord Attlee for giving me permission to use a lengthy abstract from his book *The Labour Party in Perspective*; to Lord Beaverbrook for similar permission to use material of his various writings, in particular his *Politicians and the War*; and to the authors and publishers of the following works, who kindly allowed me to quote some rather lengthy abstracts: L. S. Amery, *The Forward View* (Geoffrey Bles); Sir Arthur Bryant, *The Turn of the Tide, 1939–1943* (William Collins); D. N. Chester, *Lessons from the British War Economy* (Cambridge University Press); Sir Winston Churchill, *The Second World War* (Cassell and Co.; Houghton Mifflin); Colin Cooke, *The Life of Richard Stafford Cripps* (Hodder & Stoughton); the Earl of Avon, *The Eden Memoirs* (Cassell and Co.; Houghton Mifflin); Patrick Gordon Walker, "On Being a Cabinet Minister," *Encounter* (April 1956); Sir Harold Nicolson, *King George the Fifth* (Constable); the Earl of Ronaldshay, *The Life of Lord Curzon* (Ernest Benn); J. A. Spender and C. Asquith, *The Life of Herbert Henry Asquith* (Hutchinson); (Lord) Francis Williams, *The Triple Challenge* (Heinemann).

I have had the benefit of a British Council Scholarship in 1954, and of a modest travel grant from the Dutch *Organisatie voor Zuiver Wetenschappelijk Onderzoek* in 1957. I am most grateful to the Warden and Fellows of Nuffield College for allowing me a glimpse, in May 1962, of that high-powered intellectual kitchen, in which so many excellent studies are brewed. I learned a great deal from all of them in conversation, and particularly from Mr. D. N. Chester, who kindly read a considerable part of the manuscript. I only wish that I might have had the benefit of his well-grounded suggestions at a more embryonic stage of the manuscript, so that I could have done more justice to them. On the basis of the slightest acquaintance, Professor K. B. Smellie magnanimously gave me access to his private collection of newspaper clippings. In this book, as in other things, I owe much to Professor W. A. Robson, under whom I had the good fortune to work at the London School of Economics and Political Science in 1954. Mr. J. L. Roberts of Victoria University, Wellington, New

Zealand, and Miss Mary Leonard of Stanford University Press introduced me to the excellent and subtle standards of Anglo-Saxon book editing. Mr. D. N. Bhalla and Mrs. Jean Kleinegris-Sanders deserve praise for their ability to turn poor manuscript into excellent typescript.

To these I must add a list of those who were most helpful to me at various times: the late Lord Hankey; Lord Bridges; Professors Max Beloff and K. C. Wheare (Oxford); Professor Philip W. Buck (Stanford); Professor Herman Finer (Chicago); Professor S. E. Finer (Keele); Professor Wilfred Harrison (Liverpool); Professor W. J. M. Mackenzie (Manchester); Mr. C. H. Wilson, Chancellor of Glasgow University; Mr. Donald Tyerman, Editor of *The Economist*; and Miss V. M. Carruthers, Librarian of the Treasury Library. Custom forbids me to name individual civil servants. One of them, in particular, did a great deal more than even the bond of close friendship owes. All these helpful persons would be poorly rewarded if any reader were to conclude that this book is launched in any sense under their auspices. The faults it has are typically my own.

My family has suffered the writing of this book twice, and they have been more than patient (even though one of them thinks this is the last book I ought to write). The Dutch edition was dedicated to my parents. It seems fitting that this new version should be dedicated to someone whom I have learned to regard as "my English mother."

H. D.

UNIVERSITY OF LEIDEN
1 NOVEMBER 1963

CONTENTS

PART I
The British Cabinet

PART II
The Central Organization for Defense and Economic Policy

PART III
Cabinet Reform in Britain

[PART ONE]

THE BRITISH CABINET

ONE

THE CABINET IN THE BRITISH POLITICAL SYSTEM

Ministers "are parliamentarians first and for the greater part of their public life, Ministers of the Crown at intervals," wrote L. S. Amery, a parliamentarian of long standing and a minister of wide experience.[1] In a similar vein, Walter Bagehot has spoken of the British Cabinet as "a committee of the legislative body selected to be the executive body."[2] Such statements do not imply that the Cabinet is merely an executive agent of Parliament. Amery, for one, used to lay considerable stress on the fact that the Cabinet occupies a distinct place, having functions and a history separate from Parliament's; he criticized Bagehot on that score.[3] Herman Finer has therefore qualified Bagehot's definition: ". . . except that the process of selection is not express choice by the legislature and is indirect and complex, while the articles of delegation are rather vague and elastic."[4] The essence of the statements quoted is, however, that the Cabinet is more than an agency of executive coordination. It is, above all, a body composed of parliamentary leaders. This circumstance has had definite consequences for its structure and place in the British political system. This introductory chapter will deal, therefore, with certain basic features that characterize any British Cabinet, whatever its composition, whatever its political tasks, whatever the political situation.

The British System as Cabinet Government

The Act of Settlement (1701) sought to exclude ministers from Parliament, but the attempt failed within a few years. Since the passage of the Reform Bill of 1832, the House of Commons has become more representative and more effective in enforcing ministerial responsibility. But the development of the earlier "factions from interest" or "factions from affection"[5] into tightly knit parties following the extension of the franchise has nevertheless made for a very special relationship between Cabinet and Parliament. Usually, a Government is fairly certain of its forces in the House of Commons. This has enabled it to acquire a decisive influence on

[1] Amery, *Constitution*, p. 10. For complete titles and publication data of books or articles that are cited more than once, see the Bibliography, pp. 340–53.

[2] Bagehot, p. 9.

[3] Amery, *Constitution*, pp. 13–14; Amery, *My Political Life*, III, 72–73.

[4] Finer, p. 576. See also John Stuart Mill, *Representative Government* (1859), Chap. 5, Everyman's ed. (1948), pp. 228–41.

[5] This terminology is from David Hume, "Of Parties in General," *Political and Literary Essays*, World's Classics ed. (1903), p. 54ff.

parliamentary proceedings. The Cabinet virtually dominates the legislative process. It determines the main lines of policy. It formulates the budget, and hence controls both the over-all level of taxation and the specific direction of Government outlays, insofar as these have not been determined by previous Acts of Parliament. Because the Cabinet and the leadership of the majority party are one, for all practical purposes, the House of Commons has become an arena for public debate between the Government and the Opposition, rather than a distinct organ of legislation and control. Parliamentary government has in fact become Cabinet government.

But Cabinet control of Parliament can easily be exaggerated. Some have spoken of "Cabinet dictatorship," of a "new despotism," of "the passing of Parliament"; in short, it is claimed that Parliament has shrunk from an "efficient part" into a mere "dignified part" of the Constitution.[6] These views neglect many characteristics that make Parliament a truly effective body and give substance to both individual and collective ministerial responsibility. They do little justice to the very special atmosphere of Parliament, and to the very real control that the Opposition and the electorate exercise over any government. They overestimate the rigor of party discipline and underestimate the political influence of Government backbenchers. Above all, they forget that Parliament provides the testing ground for future members of the Government, and that these members, in turn, continue to think and act as parliamentarians long after they have become ministers. In other words, whereas the critics of Cabinet government correctly draw attention to the potential conflict of interest between the Cabinet and Parliament, they underestimate the substantial identity of outlook between the two bodies. Indirectly, they therefore underestimate the influence that parliamentary life tends to have on the executive in all its branches.[7] In effect, the concept of "Cabinet government" means merely that the Cabinet is the activating and leading part of Parliament.

In the constant contest between the Government and the Opposition, each party tries to probe the weakest spots in the armor of its adversary, while itself maintaining a closed front. Each party knows that it must form a debating team whose arguments will win votes for the party at the next election. This has considerable effect on ministerial recruitment. The Government's choice of a spokesman for a particular debate is based not only on considerations of formal or even factual ministerial responsibility,

---

[6] See Bagehot, p. 4. Two of the phrases are book titles: Lord Hewart of Bury, *The New Despotism* (1929); G. W. Keeton, *The Passing of Parliament* (1952). "Cabinet dictatorship" is attacked in Sidney and Beatrice Webb, *A Constitution for the Socialist Commonwealth of Great Britain* (1920), pp. 71–72, 171–73; and in Ramsay Muir, *How Britain Is Governed* (1930), pp. 41–80, 87–106; cf. *Parliamentary Reform*, pp. 157–59. On 17 May 1950, Lord Cecil of Chelwood introduced a motion in the House of Lords holding "that the growing power of the Cabinet is a danger to the democratic constitution of the country" (167 H. of L. Deb., cols. 327–35).

[7] For a comprehensive discussion of such ideas, see Jennings, *Constitution* and *Queen's Government*; Laski, *Parliamentary Government* and *Reflections*; Morrison and Richards, *passim*.

but also on its calculation of how best to weather an expected parliamentary storm. If the passage gets really rough, senior ministers with high standing in the House of Commons may have to be called in to succor less fortunate colleagues in defending the Government's case. This, in turn, affects the ministerial hierarchy.

The close relationship between Government and Parliament is further evident in the existence of two kinds of special offices: that of Leader of the House and that of the whips. Both in the Lords and in the Commons, one Cabinet minister acts as Leader of the House. According to Gladstone, the Leader of the House "suggests, and in great degree fixes, the course of all principal matters of business, supervises and keeps in harmony the actions of his colleagues, takes the initiative in matters of ceremonial procedure, and advises the House in every difficulty as it arises."[8] This description is perhaps somewhat exaggerated (and was even in Gladstone's time, when the Prime Minister generally occupied the post in the House in which he himself sat). Yet the supervision of day-to-day Government strategy in Parliament, and, conversely, the representation of each House in the inner Councils of the Government, are of such importance that in each House a very senior minister must give them his close attention.

In trying to gear the parliamentary machine to the Government's benefit, the Leader of the House works in close contact with the Government whips. These officers (of whom there are a number in each House, some paid, others unpaid) seek to maintain liaison between the party leaders and the backbenchers, and to preserve the unity of the Government party in the House concerned. Government influence on parliamentary proceedings is also apparent in the regular contacts of the Government and Opposition whips ("through the usual channels," "behind the Speaker's Chair") for the discussion and determination of future parliamentary business.[9]

Government, Lords, and Commons

Although each Government must defend its policies in both Houses of Parliament, members of the Government can speak only in the House in which they have a seat. Great changes have occurred since William Pitt formed a Cabinet composed of seven members of the House of Lords and only one member of the House of Commons, Pitt himself. In 1942, Churchill could even refuse to include the Leader of the House of Lords (Lord Cranborne, later Lord Salisbury) in his War Cabinet, even though this meant that the Cabinet would no longer have a direct link with the House of Lords.[10] Normally, however, each Prime Minister must include representatives of both Houses in his Cabinet. Legislation, too, has in-

---

[8] From *Encyclopaedia of Parliament,* s.v. "Leader of the House."
[9] See especially Morrison, pp. 93–120.
[10] Churchill, IV, 76. Cranborne was a "constant attender" of Cabinet meetings, however (*ibid.,* p. 77).

directly guaranteed the inclusion of some peers in the Government.[11] *Ceteris paribus,* this increases the size and complexity of the ministry. Normally, the following Government members are drawn from the House of Lords: the Lord Chancellor, who presides over the House in both its political and judicial capacities; one or more occupants of a "sinecure" office, who can act as Leader of the House of Lords and Deputy Leader; perhaps one or two important departmental ministers, some junior ministers, the whips, and the Lords in Waiting.[12]

There is an important difference between the House of Lords and the House of Commons, however. The House of Lords has to be satisfied with whatever minister the Government charges with the defense of a particular matter. But in the House of Commons, each department has to be *directly* represented, whether by its minister, a junior minister, or (as is often the case) both.[13] The House of Commons, and particularly the Opposition, exerts a constant pressure to have ministers of important departments selected from among its members. Because the House of Commons has the final say in financial affairs, the Chancellor of the Exchequer, his junior ministers, and the Financial Secretaries to the War Office and the Admiralty, invariably sit in the Lower House. The norm has been posited that the heads of *all* large-spending ministries should sit in the Commons. But this assumed rule has rarely been put into effect; and it is no longer easy to interpret in view of today's large governmental expenditures in most fields.[14] There has also been strong insistence that the Foreign Secretary sit in the House of Commons. This has been the general practice since 1924, except for 1938–40 and from 1960 to the

[11] The Ministers of the Crown Act, 1937 (often amended since) divided ministers into four groups: the Secretaries of State and the other departmental ministers; the Lord President of the Council, Lord Privy Seal, Postmaster-General, and the First Commissioner of Works; the Ministers of State; and the junior ministers. It stipulated that only a certain number of ministers from each group might sit and vote in the House of Commons at any one time. As normally all offices are filled, those above these maximum limits must be chosen from the House of Lords. See Wade–Phillips, pp. 83–85; Jennings, *Cabinet Government,* pp. 70–71.

[12] Cf. Bromhead, pp. 99–109; Dogan–Campbell, pp. 320–21; Jennings, *Cabinet Government,* pp. 71–73; Keith–Gibbs, pp. 42–45.

[13] Jennings, *Cabinet Government,* p. 72. But this is not always possible. Some ministers—the Lord Privy Seal, the Chancellor of the Duchy of Lancaster, and the Paymaster-General (and, until recently, the Minister of Defence and the Lord President of the Council)—have no parliamentary secretary. If these ministers are given special tasks, and sit in the House of Lords, another minister must answer questions on their behalf in the House of Commons. In this way, the Minister of Works (not a member of the Cabinet) was at one time charged to answer in the House of Commons on matters of atomic energy. On matters of great importance, however, the Prime Minister himself will be answerable, as was Neville Chamberlain on foreign affairs from 1938 to 1940, when the Foreign Secretary, Halifax, sat in the House of Lords. Churchill answered when Lord Alexander of Tunis was Minister of Defence from 1952 to 1954. Since 1960, both the Prime Minister and the Lord Privy Seal have answered in the Commons for the Foreign Secretary, Lord Home.

[14] At different times between 1937 and 1951, the following ministers sat in the House of Lords: the Secretaries of State for Foreign Affairs, Air, Dominions, and India and Burma; the Lord Privy Seal; the Lord President of the Council; the First Lord of the Admiralty; and the ministers of Civil Aviation, Works, and Food; and the Paymaster-General and the Postmaster-General. Cf. Keir, p. 497, n. 1.

present.[15] Since 1923 it has been thought that the Prime Minister can sit only in the House of Commons. The number of ministers in Lords and Commons since 1945 is shown in Table I.

TABLE I

GOVERNMENT MEMBERS FROM LORDS AND COMMONS SINCE 1945

Government	Cabinet Ministers	Non-Cabinet Depart- mental Ministers	Other Ministers and Ministers of State	Junior Ministers	Whips	Total
ATTLEE (1945)						
Commons	16	9	6	31	12	74
Lords	4	2	–	2	5	13
CHURCHILL (1951)						
Commons	10	11	7	27	11	66
Lords	6	2	2	3	5	18
MACMILLAN (1957)						
Commons	13	7	8	30	12	70
Lords	5	1	3	3	5	17
MACMILLAN (1962)						
Commons	18	7	7	29	12	73
Lords	3	1	5	3	6	18

SOURCE: Dogan–Campbell, p. 316, and my own calculations. For figures of an earlier period, cf. Yu, pp. 24–26.

The division of ministers between Houses, in other words, strongly influences relations between ministers and between Government and Parliament, and will continue to do so unless Parliament adopts the proposal of Haldane and others that ministers be given the right to defend their policies in both Houses.[16]

The Ways of Ministerial Recruitment

As a rule, ministers are trained in the House of Commons, "the great University of Public Life."[17] There are two exceptions: peers who have never sat in the House of Commons, or have sat there only briefly before being called to occupy the family seat in the House of Lords; and a few ministers who obtain a seat in Parliament only after appointment to a ministry.[18] (See Table II.) Appointments of the latter sort have generally

[15] See the critical debate on the appointment of Lord Home, 627 H. of Deb. (28 July 1960), cols. 1973–2001.
[16] The number of peers in Churchill's Cabinet in 1951 was so large that Morrison nicknamed the administration the "Lords-Help-Us-Government" (493 H. of C. Deb. [15 November 1951], col. 833).
   For the proposal of Haldane and others, see Bromhead, pp. 99–100, and The Times, 14 March 1962.
[17] Haldane, Autobiography, p. 69.
[18] Many efforts have been made to escape elevation to the House of Lords. The best-known attempts after 1945 were those of Quintin Hogg (now Viscount Hailsham) and Anthony Wedgwood Benn (previously Viscount Stansgate). The Wedg-

TABLE II

PARLIAMENTARY EXPERIENCE OF NEW CABINET MEMBERS

Background	1868–1916	1916–58	Total
Members of the House of Lords without House of Commons experience before their appointment	10	5	15
Members of the House of Lords with House of Commons experience before their appointment	11	13	24
Members of the House of Commons	87	124	211
Members of the Cabinet without any parliamentary experience at the time of their appointment	1	28	29

SOURCE: Willson, *Routes of Entry.*

been unpopular with the House of Commons. They have been frequent in time of war, when a man's technical abilities are allowed to overshadow his political authority and experience. In peacetime, such appointees have often fit ill into political life and frequently have been honorably but quickly discharged.[19]

The House of Commons trains and tests future ministers according to its own norms and traditions, which have been powerfully affected by the ideals of the gentlemanly classes that for so long dominated British public life. It was only a few generations ago that, in Bagehot's telling phrase, "a differential duty of at least £2,000" was levied on the doorstep of the House of Commons.[20] The public schools, especially Eton and Harrow, and the great universities of Oxford and Cambridge, for a long time almost completely monopolized the schooling of future British rulers, thus inculcating their special values with lasting effect.[21] Not long past are the days when young men with ambition, adequate private means, and the right connections could go into politics as readily as the law, the Army, and, somewhat later, perhaps business and the civil service, living a life rather like the young Lord Halifax, "trying so to order . . . life as to reconcile the claims of the House of Commons with as much hunting as [they] could fit in, . . . [hunting] on Mondays, catching the evening train in time to vote if necessary in the House, and to return to Yorkshire Thursday night so as to be able to hunt Friday and Saturday."[22]

Since the middle of the nineteenth century, the social composition of

---

wood Benn case led to the appointment of a Joint Committee on House of Lords Reform, which in December 1962 recommended that peers and heirs to a peerage might have the right to renounce their titles, their peerages remaining dormant for the rest of their lives. When this book went to press the necessary legislation was being passed.

[19] For a review of such cases, see Willson, *Routes of Entry,* pp. 223–26. For a more critical appraisal, see also Addison, *Politics from Within,* II, 171–72; and Woolton, *Memoirs,* pp. 179ff, 371. Cf. *Life of Cripps,* pp. 110, 114ff.

[20] Bagehot, p. 152.

[21] Ross (*Parliamentary Representation,* pp. 52, 57, 74) found that between 1918 and 1945, Harrovians were eighteen hundred times, Etonians two thousand times more likely to find their way into Parliament than ordinary citizens. Cf. Matthews, p. 46.   [22] Halifax, *Fullness of Days,* p. 89.

the House of Commons has, of course, changed substantially. This process, already visible in the case of the Conservative and Liberal parties in the nineteenth century, was greatly quickened by the rise of the Labour Party.[23] Shortly before 1914, M.P.'s were awarded some financial compensation, and meals came to be served in Westminster Palace for half a crown.[24] But, considerable social reforms notwithstanding, the number of aristocrats in the House of Commons has remained relatively large.[25] In certain aristocratic circles political interest (not to say a sense of political vocation) continued unabated well into the twentieth century. Constituency parties often continued to live up to Gladstone's view that "the love of the English people for their liberties was equaled only by their love for the nobility."[26] By virtue of their early political training and expedient connections, young aristocrats could acquire a safe seat in the Commons, there to embark on the long years of training and probation that the House demands of future ministers.[27] During this period, they could hold less important offices without loss of prestige or dignity. They found the atmosphere of the House of Commons congenial. In particular, its style of debate—often the test case for a later career—suited the young aristocrat or the intellectual (whose training and outlook often corresponded with that of the aristocrat) better than politicians who entered Parliament late in life, after many years in another profession. According to Gladstone, a man who entered Parliament at forty-five had as much chance of becoming a successful minister as he had of becoming a successful ballet dancer.

There was accordingly a higher proportion of aristocrats in the Cabinet than in the House of Commons as a whole.[28] The figures for five eras from 1832 to 1935 are as follows:[29]

---

[23] Cf. J. A. Thomas, *The House of Commons, 1832–1901: A Study of Its Economic and Functional Character* (1939), *passim,* and W. L. Guttsman, "Changes in British Labour Leadership," in Dwaine Marvick, ed., *Political Decision-Makers: Recruitment and Performance* (1961), pp. 91–137.

[24] Richards, p. 232; Campion, *Parliamentary System,* pp. 12–15.

[25] Ross *(Parliamentary Representation,* pp. 77–83) calculated that between the two wars about two-fifths of the Conservative M.P.'s were of aristocratic descent.

[26] R. Michels, *Political Parties* (1959), p. 378.

[27] The aristocrats who entered the House of Commons between 1801 and 1924 were on the average ten years younger than the non-aristocrats (Laski, *Cabinet Personnel,* p. 13). The continuing importance of entry at an early age for a successful political career is apparent in the fact that those who were appointed to ministerial office after 1945 had entered Parliament at a younger age than those who remained backbenchers, and also in that the age at which senior ministers entered was, on the average, lower than those of other members of the Government (Dogan-Campbell, pp. 805–18).

[28] The first time the word "Cabinet" appeared in the order paper of the House of Commons was in an amendment to the Address of 1900, introduced by the Opposition against the Salisbury Government, popularly called the Hotel Cecil Ltd. The text of the amendment was: "We humbly express our regret at the advice given to Your Majesty by the Prime Minister in recommending the appointment of so many of his own family to offices in the Cabinet" (Low, pp. 28–29; *Life of Balfour,* pp. 237–39).

[29] From Laski, *Cabinet Personnel,* Tables III–VI, and Guttsman (1952), Table IV. Because Laski and Guttsman did not define "aristocrat" in exactly the same way,

Years	Aristocratic Ministers	Non-aristocratic Ministers
1832–1866	64	36
1867–1884	35	23
1885–1905	40	29
1906–1916	25	26
1918–1935	25	82

The rapid decline in the number of aristocrats after 1918 can be attributed largely to the coming into office of the first two Labour Cabinets, in 1924 and 1929. In the Conservative Cabinets, too, there was a decline, but it was relatively slight and reversible on occasion, as in the Eden Cabinet of 1956, when ten of the fourteen House of Commons ministers were directly related to the nobility and two others appeared in *Burke's Landed Gentry*.[30] The direct importance of an aristocratic background for the Cabinet is even more apparent when it is realized that the milieu of many non-aristocrats corresponded closely with that of the aristocrats. The non-aristocrats were generally trained in the same public schools and in the same colleges of Oxford and Cambridge. Many of them came from the professional classes, particularly from the Bar. Many were admitted readily to the highest London social circles.

The special background of Cabinet ministers did not necessarily lead to a conservative view of politics. Again and again, members of the governing class proved to be more radical than many commoners. But the ideal of the gentleman strongly influenced the atmosphere of the Cabinet.[31] It had a persistent impact on the Cabinet's code of honor and etiquette. It gave a special flavor to the ideal of a good minister. It united seemingly conflicting beliefs, such as a feeling of superiority and a readiness to subordinate oneself to hierarchical structures, a preference for the amateur in politics and a readiness to specialize, play and seriousness, fighting spirit and *esprit de corps,* individualism and group activity—qualities all that the public schools cultivate and Britons traditionally extol. When Baldwin received the King's commission to form a Cabinet, his first thought was that he ought to form a Cabinet of which Harrow would not feel ashamed.[32]

---

this tabulation should be considered an approximation rather than an exact indication of the developments.

[30] Bromhead, p. 42; cf. Ivor Jennings, *Party Politics,* I (1960), 228ff. Guttsman (1952) gives the following breakdown of the three political parties in the period 1918–35: Conservatives—19 aristocrats, 35 non-aristocrats; Liberals—3 aristocrats, 18 non-aristocrats; Socialists—3 aristocrats, 29 non-aristocrats.

[31] Lord Esher complained, however, of a deterioration in manners since the time of Gladstone and Disraeli. After seeing Asquith play bridge following an important dinner, Esher wrote in his diary: "Men and women in *their* presence felt a sort of moral reserve, which some people feel in church. There was a certain advantage to the State in having at the head of affairs men who necessarily drew the best of those they met. It kept order in the highest sphere of politics" *(Esher Papers,* II, 307–8). For a not-very-successful attempt to differentiate between the style of living and ambitions of aristocrats and non-aristocrats, see Guttsman (1954).

[32] Guttsman (1954), p. 17.

The Hierarchical Structure of the Government

The ministerial career of a British parliamentarian is strongly affected by his hope for advancement. Office is a standing temptation to most parliamentarians. Each new Prime Minister discovers, as the Liberal Asquith said, that there are always too many horses for the available oats, or, in another homely metaphor used by Lord Salisbury during the formation of a Conservative Cabinet, "The Carlton Club resembles nothing so much at this moment as the Zoological Gardens at feeding time." "I have had people in here weeping, or even fainting," said the Labour Prime Minister MacDonald in 1929 to a junior minister.[33] The political ladder of the Cabinet hierarchy has many steps, and the probationary period of a potential member is often long. M.P.'s who arrived at the threshold of the Cabinet between 1868 and 1916 had spent fourteen years on the average in Parliament before they were admitted to the inner sanctum. Since 1916, the period of apprenticeship has declined by about two years. But fewer than 10 per cent of the ministers who entered the Cabinet between 1916 and 1958 did so within five years of their entry into Parliament. In the same period, more than one-sixth of new Cabinet members had spent over twenty years in Parliament before being called to Cabinet office.[34]

Men who covet promotion usually concentrate on particular fields. They seek to play an active part in the debates of the many specialized committees of their parliamentary party or of Parliament itself.[35] They try to catch the Speaker's eye, not only for the sake of the debate, nor mainly to impress their electors with the activity of their M.P., but also to be heard by the leading politicians in their own party or by the whips, who have a substantial influence on ministerial appointments. They eagerly seek the unpaid and undefined post of Parliamentary Private Secretary, through whom ministers, Opposition frontbenchers, and (more rarely) junior ministers keep in touch with sentiment in Parliament. For a relatively small number, experience in such an office may lead to appointment as assistant whip or, preferably, as junior minister. Such appointments have disadvantages as well as advantages. Because the whips normally do not take part in political debate, a whip cannot build up a reputation by his public speeches. A junior minister works more in the public eye, but whether the office is so good a training ground as commonly alleged is doubtful. In the view of Duff Cooper,

It provides little in the way of training for the higher responsibilities to which it should lead. At the same time, it deprives the young politician of opportunities of distinguishing himself or of improving his technique in the House of Commons. He sees no Cabinet papers and remains therefore hardly better in-

[33] Asquith is quoted in Simon, *Retrospect*, p. 71; Salisbury in Finer, p. 582; and MacDonald in Dalton, *Memoirs*, I, 217.

[34] Willson, *Routes of Entry*, pp. 226–29. For the period after 1945, see Dogan–Campbell, pp. 320, 810ff.

[35] Cf. Richards, pp. 205–11; Willson, pp. 229–31.

formed on matters of high policy than his contemporary backbenchers. . . .
Nor is it open to [him] to enlighten his ignorance by asking questions in the
House of Commons. . . . Junior ministers are in fact put into cold storage,
and if they remain there too long their faculties may suffer from lack of employment and even become atrophied.[36]

Nevertheless, the junior minister has closer contact with leading politicians than most Members of Parliament. Sometimes his office provides
him with an opportunity for administrative training. The increasing burden on senior ministers also forces them to leave more things to their
juniors than was true in the more leisurely days of which Duff Cooper
wrote. The office is often the steppingstone for promotion as junior minister to a better department or, since the Second World War, to Minister
of State. Sometimes, a junior minister is directly called to head an im--
portant ministerial department or one of the sinecure offices.[37]

The senior ministers themselves are of course far from equal in importance.[38] A number of departments have traditionally been accorded
second-rate status. Their ministers have no prescriptive right to Cabinet
membership. This was true before 1914 for the Post Office, the Office of
Works, the Local Government Board, and various other ministries, and
between the two wars for the Ministry of Labour, the Ministry of Transport, and the Ministry of Pensions. Since 1945 numerous departments
established for new government tasks have had low prestige. Politically,
these ministries very often represent a dead end.

For the remaining few, an important portfolio and Cabinet membership may follow. Newcomers to the Cabinet generally occupy such lesser
offices as Secretary of State for Scotland, Minister of Education, Minister
of Agriculture, Minister of Transport, or Minister of Labour. In Morley's
words, "The Cabinet is very like a club in which as a rule new ministers
are to be seen and not heard."[39] Many rise no higher, but others arrive
at last at the main government posts: Foreign Secretary, Chancellor of
the Exchequer, Home Secretary, Commonwealth (and formerly Colonial)
Secretary, Lord Chancellor, Minister of Defence, perhaps Lord President
of the Council or Lord Privy Seal, and, above all, Prime Minister.

Almost all Cabinets have an inner group of some four or five persons,
men with whom the Prime Minister particularly consults because of the
importance of their office, their position in the governing party, or their
congeniality.[40] Both those who belong and those who do not—Whitehall

[36] Duff Cooper, *Old Men Forget*, pp. 161–62; Brabazon, pp. 120–22; Morrison,
pp. 66–69; Halifax, *Fullness of Days*, pp. 94–95. Ellen Wilkinson thought the fate of
junior ministers "less than the dust"; she advocated a "Parliamentary Secretaries'
Charter" (Morrison, p. 69).

[37] Willson (*Routes of Entry*, p. 228) calculated that between 1868 and 1916, ministers served on the average three and a half years, and between 1916 and 1958 four
and a half years in subordinate office before being admitted to the Cabinet.

[38] For a special study of the ministerial hierarchy and the numerous factors in-
fluencing it, see Heasman, pp. 314–30.

[39] *Holmes-Laski Correspondence*, I, 282; Laski, *Reflections*, p. 129.

[40] Cf. Lloyd George, *Memoirs*, III, 1042.

and Westminster, as well as Fleet Street—are well aware of these distinctions. The relations between members of the inner circle are not necessarily harmonious. "There is no love at the top," Lloyd George once said.[41] But at these dizzy heights, ministers know they are not only rivals but also dependent on one another. There is a noticeable reluctance to admit new persons to these exclusive circles: newcomers are on strict probation, and are finally accepted only with hesitation and reserve.[42] Not all parliamentarians look at this situation kindly, and many may well reiterate the words of one inveterate backbencher, Lord Winterton:

I believe that if all those who have held office or are in office were taken out in a ship, and if by some terrible misfortune the ship was lost, what would happen would be that our families would mourn us, there would be a service in Westminster Abbey, and foreign statesmen would shed their crocodile tears; but life would proceed as before, and the "man in the street" would probably say, "Well, the Old Gang has gone West at last, I feel sorry for the poor blanks, but I wish some of them had been drowned ten years before."[43]

The ministerial ladder, in other words, is steep, and only a few politicians reach the Cabinet. A recent study of the 1103 Conservative M.P.'s and 756 Labour M.P.'s who were first elected to Parliament in the period 1918–55 yields the data of Table III. (Five Cabinet ministers were appointed directly to a Cabinet post without previous ministerial experience: Ernest Bevin, Aneurin Bevan, Sir Walter Monckton, Sir John Anderson, and Oliver Lyttelton.)[44]

If few politicians are therefore ultimately successful, many have been, as was Sir John Simon, "very honorably but very strikingly ambitious."[45] Is this a general characteristic? Is this picture of constantly climbing and ever-dissatisfied politicians perhaps exaggerated? Obviously, there is the danger of an optical illusion: memoirs and biographies are published mainly of the successful. For many backbenchers a seat in Parliament is the end not only of their career, but also of their ambition—the apogee of a working life that was started and lived elsewhere. The House of Commons offers great opportunities for important work that is not affected by the "hidden hierarchy" of ministerial life.[46] For an adequate appraisal of the functioning of Parliament, this should not be forgotten. And yet, how many parliamentarians must have imagined what it would be like to possess

---

[41] Jennings, *Cabinet Government*, p. 264.

[42] For the view of Lloyd George in 1916, cf. *Life of King George V*, p. 274.

[43] Winterton, *Orders of the Day*, p. 182; cf. Amery, *My Political Life*, III, 79. Beveridge argued in 1954 that the road to the top was too long. He proposed introducing a new convention by which each Prime Minister would automatically be appointed a Marquess after seven years, and so be relegated to the House of Lords (*Power and Influence*, pp. 213–14). Cf. *Esher Papers*, III, 249.

[44] Data on total number of M.P.'s from a forthcoming book by Buck, *Amateurs and Professionals in British Politics, 1918–59*, Chicago (1963).

[45] *Life of Birkenhead*, II, 254, and below p. 25 n. 30; cf. the vignette by Earl Attlee, "The Attitudes of M.P.'s and Active Peers," *Political Quarterly*, XXX (1959), 29–33.

[46] Gordon Walker, p. 19ff.

TABLE III

OFFICE HOLDERS AMONG M.P.'s FIRST ELECTED BETWEEN 1918 AND 1955

Began as	Highest Office Reached				
	Parliamentary Private Secretary	Junior Minister	Minister	Cabinet Minister	Total
CONSERVATIVE					
Parliamentary Private Secretary	118	34	13	7	172
Junior minister	—	51	12	15	78
Minister	—	—	23	5	28
Cabinet minister	—	—	—	2	2
TOTAL	118	85	48	29	280
LABOUR					
Parliamentary Private Secretary	83	28	8	9	128
Junior minister	—	61	13	13	87
Minister	—	—	15	7	22
Cabinet minister	—	—	—	2	2
TOTAL	83	89	36	31	239

SOURCE: Buck, Tables 2, 3, and 4. Buck's figures exclude careers of politicians subsequent to their elevation to a peerage. Moreover, some young M.P.'s elected in the later years of Buck's study have since risen, and will rise, to higher posts than those they held at the time Buck's tables were compiled.

the key to 10, Downing Street. There is, after all, profound truth in K. C. Wheare's dictum that "the British Constitution is a frontbencher's constitution."[47]

The Relation between Ministers and Civil Servants

The urge for promotion has, as its corollary, a quick turnover of ministers in most departments. In the words of Tom Jones: "Playing musical chairs with Cabinet seats is an approved English game."[48] Bagehot and Sidney Low described the British political system as one of "government by amateurs." A British minister need not have a specialized knowledge of his department, so they argued. It is his task, in the famous phrase of Harcourt, "to tell the permanent officials what the public will not stand."[49] A minister should weigh the technical advice of his expert civil servants against his own common sense. He should give them political directives

[47] In a review of Morrison's *Government and Parliament* in *The Listener* (25 November 1954), p. 901.
[48] Jones, *Prime Ministers and Cabinets*, p. 784.
[49] A. G. Gardiner, *The Life of Sir William Harcourt* (1923), II, 587. Harcourt himself did not hesitate to adorn official memoranda with such epithets as: "unmitigated nonsense and feeble twaddle" (Kingsley, p. 273). Cf. Jennings, *Cabinet Government*, Chap. 5; Morrison, pp. 14–15.

and keep the bureaucracy within the limits of general Government policy. But he should not, according to British ethos, try to become an expert himself. This would detract from his usefulness as a minister, precisely because he would thus lose detachment. "I began to fear that I was becoming stale," Haldane wrote after six years at the War Office.[50] And, like Haldane, many ministers have wished for other work after several consecutive years in one department. Outside the Government, too, in Parliament and in the Press, there is constant pressure for change. It has even been argued that a regular change of parties in Government and Opposition is conducive to good administration. Too long a period of office by one party, the argument runs, leads to a certain sclerosis. A temporary period in opposition can do much to refresh the outlook of politicians. But if the period of opposition lasts too long, the Government *in posse* becomes a prey of uncertain theorizing.[51] Only a regular "swing of the pendulum" could thus guarantee that parties retain both their flexibility and their concrete orientation.[52]

There is a strong mystique in this reasoning. Its picture of an exact demarcation of functions between "amateur politicians" and "professional civil servants" is too neat—and in fact breaks down as the complexity of modern government comes to require specialization of politicians as it already does of civil servants. This is no reason to accept the conventional point of view, which holds that ministerial control of the bureaucracy inevitably suffers from a rapid turnover of ministers. It has been asserted that the power of the bureaucracy increases when a department sees "quite a number of embarrassed phantoms" come and go. This allegation is exaggerated. Rapid ministerial changes may often disturb the deliberate continuity that alone can give strength to a particular departmental policy. The consent of the Cabinet is required in important issues. Before this is obtained, the resistance of other departments and ministers may have to be faced. To be successful in the "Whitehall War," departments are highly dependent on the force a minister can develop in inter-ministerial controversy. A minister who pays only slight attention to his own department and clearly regards it as a mere steppingstone to higher office can demoralize his department. The same is true, however, if a weak minister is retained for years in a particular post. Ultimately, therefore, personal factors are more decisive than the length of tenure of ministers.[53] Some ministers are indeed run by their office. But many other ministers run their offices effectively from the first day they take over. Their influence is only enhanced by the fact that they move from post to post, and thus acquire a much wider experience than their official subordinates.

[50] Haldane, *Autobiography,* p. 236.

[51] Ernest Barker, *Britain and the British People* (1945), p. 40.

[52] The term "swing of the pendulum" owes its origin to Lord Salisbury, but see Mackintosh, pp. 483–89.

[53] Cf. Attlee, *Civil Servants and Ministers,* pp. 16–24; Morrison, pp. 311–26; Chester, *Machinery,* pp. 24–25; Smellie, p. 268ff.

Each minister can, moreover, always rely on the support of the Prime Minister and the Cabinet to overcome any signs of official insubordination, at least in the civilian field.

The high rate of mobility in the top echelons has one other important aspect: it strengthens the government machinery because of the close personal contacts that prevail between the more important ministers and senior civil servants. The people who are responsible for the most important decisions form a small, tightly knit group.[54] This group includes the more prominent ministers, a few military and scientific experts, some general administrators such as the Permanent Secretaries to the Foreign Office and the Treasury and the Secretary of the Cabinet, a few diplomats such as the Ambassador in Washington, and perhaps a few persons of exalted social position or of unusual value to one of those mentioned earlier. Many members of this circle have known one another since their youth. Many are close friends, or at least are on a first-name basis. They may have a common social life that cuts across party and personal rivalries. There is a very real cleavage between these people and those whose position depends on qualities other than their membership in the inner circle. For valuable insights into the making of policy on the higher levels of government, the rare publications of high civil servants such as Hankey, Tom Jones, Vansittart, Bridges, and Beveridge, and of high military men such as Fisher, Ironside, Alanbrooke, and Montgomery, are of as much importance as the memoirs and biographies of the more important statesmen and specialized studies in the field of political science or public administration.[55]

---

[54] Chester, *Machinery*, pp. 19–26. Esher wrote to Admiral Fisher in 1904: "When it comes to a change of Government, believe me it is six of one and half a dozen of the other. You will get plenty of sympathy now from Spencers and Edward Greys [members of the Liberal opposition], but wait till they are in office and *then* the roles are changed and you will get sympathy from Selborne [the Conservative First Lord of the Admiralty at the time], and you will have to fight his successors. All these people are really cyphers. Remember, not more than a dozen people in England count for anything (a large estimate) and you happen to be one of them" *(Fisher Correspondence,* I, 324).

[55] This is true, *a fortiori*, of the official biographies of King George V and King George VI, as well as of the diaries and other papers of an *éminence grise* like Lord Esher. See also Petrie.

TWO

THE CABINET BEFORE WORLD WAR I

The Origin of the Cabinet

The British Cabinet grew out of secret meetings of some important court officials: certain "Great Officers of State" and "Principal Secretaries to the King." In the course of centuries these offices moved out of the Court. When parliamentary power increased, it became essential for the Crown to fill them with persons who wielded sufficient influence with Parliament to secure its necessary approval for legislation and appropriations requested by the Crown. Ultimately, all the King's ministers came to be chosen from Parliament.[1]

Well into the nineteenth century, the King retained a considerable say in ministerial appointments, partly because he still had a strong influence on the composition of the House of Commons. But the increasing independence of the Cabinet dates from at least as early as the Hanoverian succession in 1714. George I, the first Hanoverian king, was indifferent to English politics and soon ceased to attend Cabinet meetings, thus in effect creating the necessity for a Prime Minister and paving the way for Walpole's long administration. Of greater consequence was the growth of Parliament into a truly independent body, as new classes in the British nation became politically conscious. This development culminated in the passage of the Reform Bill of 1832, which by extending the suffrage and other reforms destroyed the influence of the Crown on the composition of Parliament. The House of Commons displaced the House of Lords as the center of political influence. Collective ministerial responsibility became a political necessity rather than a credo to which lip service was paid. Electoral need and political survival forced a tighter organization of parties, both in Parliament and in the constituencies. If the center of power can be said to have shifted first from Crown to Commons and to Common Law courts, it now moved further to Cabinet, Constituencies, and Civil Service.[2]

In this process politics changed in content. State intervention became more intensive and posed new demands on government machinery. Until the middle of the nineteenth century, central administration in Britain had

---

[1] This section gives only a bare outline of a complex process. For more exhaustive studies, see E. R. Turner, *The Cabinet Council of England in the Seventeenth and Eighteenth Centuries, 1622–1784* (1930, 1932); Aspinall, *passim*; Anson, II, Part I, 108–22; Keir, pp. 243–426; Heasman, p. 307ff.; and especially the recent work of Mackintosh.

[2] This alliteration owes much to Low, p. 102.

been fairly chaotic. The few tasks the government performed were distributed among the Secretaries of State, certain committees of the Privy Council, and numerous more or less independent Boards. Administrative positions carried little prestige, and patronage and corruption were accepted as the natural order of things. With the new political developments, most government tasks came to be centralized under the effective responsibility of ministers whom Parliament could challenge directly on specific issues. The bureaucracy was taken out of politics and made into a career service, with recruitment by competitive examination and promotion by merit and seniority rather than by political jobbery. At the same time, many new links were forged between previously unconnected government offices.[3]

During the second half of the nineteenth century, the following new ministerial posts were thus established :[4]

The First Commissioner of Works (1851).—This minister was Chairman of a fictitious Board of Works, which was in charge of the construction and maintenance of palaces, parks, and public buildings.

The Secretary of State for Colonial Affairs (1854).—Between 1768 and 1782 there had been a Secretary of State for the Colonies who was simultaneously in charge of the Board of Trade. This post was abolished in 1782. Between 1801 and 1854, there was a Secretary of State for War and the Colonies. Criticisms of the defense organization during the Crimean War (1854–56) led to a separation between the War Office and Colonial Office, and they were subsequently put under separate Secretaries of State.

The Secretary of State for India (1858).—After the Indian Mutiny of 1857, this minister took over the control of India from the East India Company and its supervisory Board of Control.

The President of the Local Government Board (1871).— When this post was established, it consolidated into one department numerous Government functions, especially in the fields of the poor law and public health, which had previously been carried out by the Privy Council, the Home Secretary, and the Poor Law Board.

The Secretary for Scotland (1885).—There had been a separate Secretary of State for Scotland between 1707 and 1746, but afterwards Scottish affairs fell mainly into the hands of the Home Secretary. In 1885 it was decided—for both political and administrative reasons—to decentralize a number of administrative powers in Scotland and to put them under the general responsibility of a separate Secretary.

The President of the Board of Agriculture (1889).—The establishment of this post was a result of political and administrative pressures to put Government authority over agriculture under the control of a separate minister.

[3] Smellie, p. 56ff ; Finer, p. 755ff ; Willson, *Ministries and Boards, passim.*
[4] See Keir, pp. 419–22, 500–513 ; Willson, *Ministries and Boards,* pp. 44–45 ; and Anson, II, Part I, 156ff.

The President of the Board of Education (1899).—The Government's authority over education originally rested with a Committee of the Privy Council, which was presided over by the Lord President of the Council. In practice, however, the Vice President of the Board of Education came to have more and more authority. In 1899 a special Act of Parliament established a regular department for all education affairs.

Owing to these developments, the Cabinet grew considerably in numbers and became more formalized in structure. From five members in 1783 and ten or eleven in the first decades of the nineteenth century, it grew to fourteen or fifteen around 1850, seventeen by the end of the century, and more than twenty under Asquith in 1915.[5] This expansion was partly a matter of administrative need. The Cabinet was the only official forum for arbitrating interdepartmental disputes. Moreover, since tradition and the desire to keep discussions informal precluded the taking of minutes at Cabinet meetings, only those ministers who attended the meetings could be sure they were fully informed of Cabinet decisions affecting their departments. In addition, there were political considerations: the greater the number of ministers who shared in Cabinet deliberations, the more substance there could be in collective responsibility. As party strife heightened, difficulties were occasionally resolved by including potential opponents in the Cabinet.

Events also acquired a momentum of their own. Once the occupant of a particular office had been included—for whatever personal reason—it became difficult to exclude his successor. Numerous ministerial posts therefore came to carry a claim on Cabinet membership. In theory, each Prime Minister remained fully independent in choosing his Cabinet. But, except for some marginal cases, he actually had more freedom to choose persons for ministerial office than to choose which offices were to be represented in his Cabinet.

Asquith's Cabinet of 1914 was composed of nineteen ministers[6]: the Prime Minister, who was also First Lord of the Treasury; the Lord President of the Council; the Lord Chancellor; the Lord Privy Seal; the Chancellor of the Exchequer; the Secretaries of State for the Home Department, for Foreign Affairs, for the Colonies, for War, and for India; the First Lord of the Admiralty; the Chief Secretary for Ireland; the Presidents of the Board of Education, the Board of Trade, and the Local Government Board; the Postmaster-General; the Chancellor of the Duchy of Lancaster; the Secretary for Scotland; the First Commissioner of Works; and the Attorney-General. Only the Paymaster-General and the junior ministers were not included.

[5] Figures in Aspinall, pp. 145–52, and Yu, p. 148, n. 1. Figures for the period after 1900 in Chester, *Cabinet*, p. 32.

[6] In 1914 the Cabinet counted twenty portfolios but only nineteen ministers because Lord Crewe served simultaneously as Secretary of State for India and Lord Privy Seal.

The Formal Hierarchy in 1914

No member of the British Cabinet carried the title "Minister" in 1914.[7] The nomenclature of many ministerial offices reflected their ancient origin. Over the years, the functions of these offices had changed radically. Yet the historical origin of a particular office remained of some consequence, especially because London Society, which continued to dominate political life in 1914, still thought historical rank important. Various considerations—precedence, salaries, perquisites such as official residences, the control over ancient seals, or ceremonial rights and duties that might bring the occupant of a particular office into close touch with the Court— helped to create a subtle hierarchy among ministers.[8]

By 1914, British ministers could formally be divided into four categories: the Great Officers of State, the Secretaries of State, the Presidents of Boards, and some special ministers.

The Great Officers of State.—Of the twelve original Great Officers of the Realm listed by an Act of Parliament in 1539, three continued to fulfill functions that gave them a prospective claim on Cabinet membership: the Lord Chancellor, the Lord President of the Council, and the Lord Privy Seal.[9] The Lord Chancellor—Keeper of the Great Seal, Head of the Judiciary, and at the same time presiding officer over the House of Lords —continued to be the "highest gentleman in the Kingdom," taking precedence directly after the Royal Family and the Archbishop of Canterbury. His salary was £10,000 a year, twice as much as the Prime Minister received in 1914 as First Lord of the Treasury. Next in order came the Prime Minister, given precedence over all ministers but the Lord Chancellor by a Royal Warrant of 1905. Next came the Lord President of the Council and the Lord Privy Seal, whose duties had faded away to almost nothing.[10] The Lord President of the Council enjoyed a salary of £5,000, equal to that of the Prime Minister and the Secretaries of State. The Privy Seal did not carry any income; for that reason the office was sometimes left vacant or was combined with another ministerial portfolio.

The Secretaries of State.[11]—In principle, the office of Principal Secretary to the King has never been divided; to the present day, one Secretary of State can still transact the business of another without any formalities. The office of the King's Secretary was important because all contacts with

[7] Chester–Willson, pp. 24, 38.
[8] Cf. *Encyclopaedia Britannica*, s.v. "Precedence" and "Seals." The salaries given in these pages are from the Estimates for 1913.
[9] Cf. *Encyclopaedia of Parliament,* s.v. "Great Officers of the Realm." The Walpole Government of 1740 was composed of the Archbishop of Canterbury, the Lord Chancellor, the Lord President, the Lord Privy Seal, the Lord Steward, the Lord Chamberlain, the Master of the Horse, the Lord Lieutenant of Ireland, two Secretaries of State, the First Minister for Scotland, the Groom of the Stole, the Chancellor of the Exchequer, and the First Commissioner of the Admiralty (Anson, II, Part I, 111, n. 2). Only the last two ministers sat in the House of Commons.
[10] Cf. Hankey, *Diplomacy*, p. 49, n. 4; Heasman, p. 315.
[11] See also Newsam, pp. 19–26.

the Crown had to pass through it.[12] Often there was more than one Secretary, and the work was then divided *ad hoc*. In 1782, separate offices were established for Home Affairs and Foreign Affairs. In that year, the Home Secretary was a peer and the Foreign Secretary a commoner; ever since, the Home Secretary has taken formal precedence over the Foreign Secretary.[13] The Secretaries of State, as a group, occupied a special position in the Cabinet, of more weight than other ministers carried, with the exception of the Prime Minister, the Lord Chancellor, and the Chancellor of the Exchequer. Neither the Secretary for Scotland, who had a salary of only £2,000 in 1914, nor the Chief Secretary for Ireland was on a level with the Secretaries of State. Proposals to raise the ministers for trade and education to the status of Secretary of State were strongly resisted. Lord Esher, for instance, was of the opinion that this would undermine the position of an Inner Cabinet just when an increase in the number of ministers was making the existence of an inner group more desirable than ever.[14]

The Presidents of Boards.—These functionaries fell into two formal categories: the First Lord of the Treasury and the First Lord of the Admiralty on the one hand, and the remainder on the other. The former were the ministerial successors of two former Great Officers of State, the Lord Treasurer and the Lord High Admiral, both of which were placed in commission early in the eighteenth century.

The Treasury Board degenerated into a phantom board fairly rapidly.[15] But because the connection between politics and finance was so close in the eighteenth century, the First Lord of the Treasury had almost inevitably become the First Minister in the Cabinet. (The circumstance that Government whips continue to be Junior Lords of the Treasury still preserves the historical conjunction of Prime Minister, patronage, and party discipline.) Direct control over government finance came to rest with the Chancellor of the Exchequer. But as First Lord of the Treasury, the Prime Minister retains supervision of the civil service, as well as the right to recommend candidates to the Crown for high judicial office, the higher clergy of the Anglican Church, Regius Professorships, etc.[16]

Unlike the Treasury Board, the Board of Admiralty continued to function as a collegial body, and is still very much alive. In fact, the collective character of this Board had become so strong by 1914 that it placed very real restrictions on the First Lord of the Admiralty's control of the Navy. The political prestige of the Navy as the "senior service" was still

---

[12] Heasman, p. 311.

[13] Newsam, p. 19; cf. Morrison, *Autobiography*, p. 182.

[14] *Esher Papers*, II, 92–93; cf. Beaverbrook, 1917–18, p. 398; *Life of Austen Chamberlain*, II, 25; Hankey, *Control*, p. 43.

[15] Neither the Financial Secretary nor (since 1947) the Economic Secretary to the Treasury is a member of the Treasury Board; the Chancellor of the Exchequer exercises his duties not as a member of the Treasury Board but under a special patent.

[16] Cf. Morrison, pp. 326–27; Jennings, *Cabinet Government*, Chap. 14; Laski, *Parliamentary Government*, p. 104ff.

high in 1914. The First Lord's yacht and his official residence, Admiralty House, were a much coveted prize. But the status of the First Lord of the Admiralty was slightly below that of the Secretaries of State, and his salary was not made equal to that of the Secretaries until shortly before 1914.

The President of the Board of Trade ranked highest of the remaining Presidents of Boards. The Board of Trade had developed from a rather ineffective Committee of the Privy Council into a full-grown department; it had dwindled into a phantom board, all its business being transacted by its President.[17] The lower status of other Presidents of Boards, all of whom acquired the title of Ministers after 1914, was evidenced by their salaries, which normally did not exceed £2,000. They received even less than the Postmaster-General, who received £2,500 annually. (The salary of the President of the Board of Trade was raised to £5,000 shortly before 1914.)[18]

Formally, the Chancellor of the Duchy of Lancaster could also be placed in the category of Board presidents. But his office was of ancient origin, and he transacted his slight duties in close association with the reigning monarch. His status was therefore relatively high, as was his salary, which was partly paid out of the proceeds of the Duchy.[19] The post of First Commissioner of Works ranked low. Rosebery refused it in 1884, calling it "the least of all the offices, being only a sort of football for contending connoisseurs."[20]

Some Special Ministers.—The Postmaster-General directed an organization employing (in 1914) more civil servants than any other department except the Service Departments. The office was generally of managerial rather than political importance, however. Another special minister, the Paymaster-General, had no duties. All his work was done by a civil servant, the Assistant Paymaster-General. The political weight of the post depended on the personal prestige and power of its holder; he was rarely a member of the Cabinet. The Law Officers—the Attorney-General and the Solicitor-General, the Lord Advocate and the Solicitor-General for Scotland, and, in 1914, the special Law Officers for Ireland—acted as juridical advisers to the Crown, which they represented in legal proceedings. In 1914, the Law Officers did not yet receive a fixed salary, but instead received varying payments for the lawsuits in which they appeared.[21] The Attorney-General had considerable prestige as Head of the Bar. The post was often a direct avenue to the office of Lord Chancellor or Lord Chief Justice. But no Attorney-General was appointed to the Cabinet until 1912. When Haldane was appointed Lord Chancellor in that year, the then

---

[17] Llewellyn Smith, pp. 15–53.

[18] Cf. Beveridge, *Power and Influence*, pp. 72–73.

[19] Cf. Samuel, *Memoirs*, pp. 58–59; Woolton, *Memoirs*, pp. 402–5.

[20] Smellie, p. 162.

[21] Lord Birkenhead estimated the usual earnings of the Attorney-General at this time at £20,000 a year (Birkenhead [1960], p. 330). The present salary is £10,000.

Attorney-General, Rufus Isaacs (later Lord Reading) felt passed over; he was given compensation in Cabinet membership.[22]

The Political Hierarchy in 1914

The political significance of the various ministerial portfolios was not unrelated to the formal hierarchy. Ambition drove the most influential politicians to the offices with the highest status; this, in turn, influenced the political importance attached to certain Government functions. Still, there were some notable differences between the two hierarchies.

In 1914, ministers could be divided into five categories of political importance: the Prime Minister, ministers in charge of important departments, occupants of sinecure offices, certain marginal ministerial office-holders, and junior ministers.

The Prime Minister.—The office of Prime Minister developed later than many other ministerial posts. Formally, the fiction that the British Constitution did not recognize the office of a First Minister was maintained even longer.[23] But long before 1914, the Prime Minister had acquired a paramount position, as may be gauged from the various metaphors describing his position that were current before 1914: "the sun around which the other planets revolve," "the keystone of the Cabinet Arch," etc.[24] Four closely related elements could be distinguished in his position. He had become, in the first place, the main interpreter of the "King's pleasure." He nominated his ministerial colleagues, and could, with increasing freedom and self-confidence, advise the King to transfer or dismiss ministers from any office. More generally, he was the King's foremost counselor and controlled the main forms of patronage. In the second place, the Prime Minister guided the workings of Parliament. His appearances in parliamentary debates were the high points of political life. Before 1914 he almost invariably occupied the office of Leader of the House in the Chamber in which he sat, and therefore had a decisive influence on the arrangement of the parliamentary agenda. In the third place, he was Leader of his Party. This added a political dimension to his relations with his colleagues, Parliament, and the electorate. His actions largely determined his Party's political fortunes. His name became synonymous with a program, and his personal views directed political tactics and strategy to a high degree.

In the fourth place, he presided over the Cabinet, determining who was to be admitted to its sessions, when these were to take place, and what should be discussed. Cabinet meetings were held in his private residence, 10, Downing Street, the house Walpole had received as a sign of royal

---

[22] Simon, *Retrospect*, pp. 88–90.

[23] Cf. Low, p. 155ff.

[24] For a more elaborate analysis, see Jennings, Keith–Gibbs, and Carter. Interesting material is also found in Viscount Norwich (Duff Cooper), *British Prime Ministers* (1953) and Jones, *Prime Ministers and Cabinets*, pp. 788–89.

favor and had left to the nation to house future Prime Ministers.[25] The Prime Minister presided over Cabinet deliberations, directed the discussions, and formulated the decisions. He could not do without the Cabinet; but inside the Cabinet, his voice was weighed, not counted. He could threaten individual ministers with dismissal, and all ministers with his own resignation, which would force their resignation as well. In principle, his dominion was as wide as Government business itself. Other ministers were responsible not only to the Law and to Parliament, but also to him personally. Long before 1914, therefore, his position had become qualitatively different from that of his ministerial colleagues. Asquith spoke of an "unshareable solitude."[26]

The Main Departmental Ministers.—By 1914, the Foreign Secretary and the Chancellor of the Exchequer were undoubtedly the most prominent departmental ministers. Since the days of Palmerston, practically no politician had become Prime Minister who had not previously served in either or both of these offices. Unlike the Foreign Secretary, who until 1906 had generally been a peer, the Chancellor of the Exchequer was invariably a member of the House of Commons. He often acted as Leader of the House of Commons when the Prime Minister sat in the House of Lords. His prominent place was closely associated with the nineteenth-century view that large government expenditures were undesirable. He shared in the policy-making of nearly all departments, usually in a negative fashion. The importance of the Foreign Secretary needs little explanation in view of the fact that Great Britain was at the zenith of its power in the nineteenth century.

High in the hierarchy stood, in addition, the Home Secretary, the Colonial Secretary, the Secretary of State for India, and the two Service ministers. Then followed the President of the Board of Trade, an important position but one not admitted to Cabinet membership even under Disraeli. The remaining departmental ministers—the Chief Secretary for Ireland, the Secretary for Scotland, and the Presidents of the Local Government Board, the Board of Agriculture and Fisheries, and the Board of Education—were held in less esteem in the leading political circles. As *homines novi*, they had only recently and in some cases reluctantly been admitted to the inner sanctum, and generally were regarded as "minor members of the Cabinet."[27]

The Holders of Sinecure Offices.—The true sinecure offices were those of the Lord Privy Seal, the Paymaster-General, and the Chancellor of the Duchy of Lancaster. The Lord President had a few duties in connection with the Privy Council, but by 1914 his position, too, was largely honorific. The First Commissioner of Works also had comparatively little to do. Sometimes a sinecure office was left vacant or was combined with an

---

[25] Cf. "10, Downing Street: A Profile," *The Observer*, 1 May 1949.
[26] Asquith, *Memories*, II, 243, and *Life of Baldwin*, pp. 52–53; cf. Petrie, p. 172, and Hankey, *Supreme Command*, pp. 4–5.
[27] See the letter of Austen Chamberlain to Lloyd George in Beaverbrook, 1917–18, p. 398, and *Life of Austen Chamberlain*, II, 25, 51.

important departmental portfolio. The availability of these offices and their nuances in status offered the Prime Minister possible solutions to some of the personal and political problems he faced in appointing his Cabinet.

Because the Lord Presidency and the Privy Seal were high-ranking offices, the Prime Minister could offer these posts to politicians whose reputation and ambition made their inclusion in the Cabinet clearly desirable, but whose administrative talents were judged not, or no longer, adequate for the direction of an important department.[28] Sometimes these posts were occupied by persons who were charged with special tasks outside the normal departmental fields, such as the Leadership of the House of Lords, the preparation of new bills, the settlement of interdepartmental disputes, or the assistance of certain heavily burdened ministers. But however high their status in 1914, it nevertheless had declined since the eighteenth century. The importance of the departmental ministers had increased as the State extended its authority. In addition, Lords President of the Council and Lords Privy Seal were generally peers before 1914; this weakened their position when the House of Commons became more powerful than the House of Lords.

The Chancellor of the Duchy of Lancaster, the First Commissioner of Works, and the Paymaster-General ranked lower in the hierarchy. They were chosen in much the same way as the Lord President and the Lord Privy Seal, but they had less influence on policy and often were not admitted to Cabinet membership. Sometimes ministers without portfolio were appointed, but this practice met with strong resistance from the House of Commons, which felt that the existing sinecure offices offered the Prime Minister adequate flexibility.[29]

Certain Special Offices.—The posts of Lord Chancellor, Attorney-General, and Postmaster-General defied classification. The Lord Chancellor had remained an important member of the Cabinet, his juridical and parliamentary duties in the House of Lords notwithstanding. But his elevated and specialized position isolated him somewhat from the other ministers. Once or twice, ambitious politicians refused the post because they considered it a "political cul de sac."[30] As we have seen, the Attorney-General was not a member of the Cabinet before 1912; but the office was

[28] The Lord President has a slightly higher status than the Lord Privy Seal. Morley threatened to resign in 1910 if Asquith should appoint him Lord Privy Seal instead of Lord President of the Council. Even though such threats were common in Morley's case—"I have a drawer full of his resignations," Asquith said—he did have his way (see Chamberlain, *Down the Years*, p. 200; cf. Aspinall, p. 152, and Heasman, p. 308). Salisbury, however, was satisfied with the Privy Seal when he was Prime Minister between 1900 and 1902 (cf. *Esher Papers*, I, 268).

[29] Jennings, *Cabinet Government*, pp. 73–76.

[30] *Life of Birkenhead* (1960), p. 331. Sir John Simon, for instance, refused the offer of the Woolsack in 1915, notwithstanding the high salary, the pension, and the high esteem in which the office was held. One of the judges then greeted him as "the maddest lawyer in London" (Addison, *Politics from Within*, I, 59). Simon thought differently: "The prospect of leaving the House of Commons and becoming Lord Chancellor at the age of forty-two did not attract me," he wrote afterwards. He considered such an appointment "a removal at too early an age from the center of parlia-

attractive to ambitious lawyers because it was a promising step on the ladder to higher political or juridical office. The Postmaster-General's office was marginal, sometimes of Cabinet status but more often not. It was used on occasion to test the administrative ability of a promising young politician, and it was also used as a device for including an unpopular politician in the Cabinet without risking the opposition that might have been aroused by his appointment to a more politically sensitive post.

The Junior Ministers.—The Undersecretaries of State and the parliamentary secretaries ranked lowest in the ministerial hierarchy. Formally, they occupied civil service positions that had been opened to parliamentarians by special legislation. They served as spokesmen of their departments in Parliament and could speak from the Treasury Bench in the House of Commons.[31] But their place within the departments was not usually well defined: a junior minister could not routinely act for a minister in his absence, and was consulted or not by the minister at the minister's pleasure. High civil servants often cold-shouldered junior ministers, regarding them as parliamentary errand boys rather than political chiefs. As one Permanent Secretary is supposed to have said to another: "Do you tell your Parliamentary Secretary everything, or anying?" Junior ministers received lower salaries than the higher civil servants. They had no immediate or automatic access to either departmental or Cabinet papers. Their specific position depended chiefly on the attitude of their senior ministers.

A junior minister might be assigned special duties, or entrusted with preparing special bills; or he might head a special section of the department under powers delegated to him by his minister. The relative political importance of junior ministers also varied with that of their senior ministers. The junior ministers attached to the Treasury and the Foreign Office (the Financial Secretary to the Treasury and the Undersecretary of State for Foreign Affairs) occupied quasi-ministerial posts from which they might be called to head an important department.[32] Undersecretaries of State ranked higher in pay and position than the parliamentary secretaries of other ministers. Another important factor in a junior minister's

---

mentary life to a bourne from which no politician returns" (Simon, *Retrospect*, p. 103); cf. *Life of Birkenhead* (1960), pp. 112–14. From 1916 to 1931, Simon sat on the Opposition benches. But after 1931, he occupied the offices of Foreign Secretary, Home Secretary, Lord Privy Seal, and Chancellor of the Exchequer, as Leader of the National Liberal Party (which was in practice a satellite of the Conservatives). It was not until 1940 that "Sir John Simon signaled his abandonment of political ambitions by accepting at last the Lord Chancellorship" (A. Berriedale Keith, *The Constitution under Strain* [1942], p. 25.).

[31] Very occasionally, as in the cases of Grey in 1892–95, Churchill in 1908, and Lord Derby in 1916, junior ministers have been considered for Cabinet membership. But sufficient pressures militated against such a step, to prevent it from coming true in practice. See *Life of Derby*, p. 214. But see also below Chap. 4, n. 43.

[32] In 1914, the Financial Secretary to the Treasury received the same salary as the President of the Board of Education, £2,000 a year.

status was whether his minister sat in the Commons or the Lords. If the latter, the junior minister was the sole representative of his department in the House of Commons, and might have considerable opportunities to gain a reputation. But even this was only partly true in practice. When important affairs were under discussion, other Cabinet members might well replace them as parliamentary spokesmen.

The Volume of Cabinet Business in 1914

Originally, a Cabinet meeting was little but an occasion for high-ranking persons to deliberate in private. The rising influence of Parliament increased the political element in Cabinet discussions. As long as State intervention was limited, issues of parliamentary strategy, foreign affairs, and interministerial disputes—particularly between the Chancellor of the Exchequer and other ministers—dominated Cabinet business. But Parliament met only some hundred days per year, and its business was overwhelmingly transacted in plenary sessions; the extensive committee system of the present day had not yet developed. The pressure of government business was slight. Sir Robert Peel could still control the field of administration in great detail in the middle of the nineteenth century.[33] Peel's successor as Conservative Leader, Lord Derby, carried out his duties between July and February (when Parliament was not sitting) almost entirely from his country estate. "During those six months," one of his descendants said with envy, "he would pay one visit to London for a Cabinet, otherwise conducting the business of government by the aid of periodic red boxes at Witherslack."[34] Even under Rosebery, at the end of the century, a large part of a Cabinet session could be spent discussing the exact text of one of Juvenal's satires.[35]

But long before 1914 there were also many signs of change. "There was everywhere seriousness about State intervention."[36] Government business became more involved, and ministers were forced to occupy themselves with matters of increasing complexity. More departments meant more interdepartmental conflict. The burden of legislation and the pressure of parliamentary life became greater and the effective circle of politics became wider. Formal arrangements for consultation replaced the informal arrangements that London Society had earlier provided for political leaders. External pressure increased correspondingly. Politicians were forced more and more to pay attention to the reactions of the electorate and of vocal groups within it. Party matters and the need to consult with interest groups demanded an ever-increasing share of ministers' time.

[33] Jennings, *Cabinet Government*, pp. 177–78.
[34] Halifax, *Fullness of Days*, p. 157. Lord Derby divided his spare time between his horses and translating Homer's *Iliad* (cf. Asquith, *Memories*, I, 245). The phrase "red boxes" refers to the locked boxes in which important government papers circulate among ministers.
[35] Simon, *Retrospect*, p. 210.
[36] Haldane, *Autobiography*, p. 214.

But, as yet, these changes were not fundamental. Regulatory and military departments continued to take precedence over the government offices that were essentially of a service character.[37] Even in 1914, if not later, it was still possible to speak, as Auckland did in 1798, of "the dispersed and rusticated life of English politicians during the summer months."[38]

---

[37] Cf. Greaves, *Structure*, p. 98.   [38] Aspinall, p. 178, n. 4.

THREE

THE CABINET DURING THE FIRST WORLD WAR

The Cabinet under Asquith (1908–15)

The outbreak of war came as a surprise to most Britons, including a fair number of ministers. Asquith's Liberal Government, then in power, was in composition one of the most brilliant Britain ever knew. The rivalries between its many prima donnas—Lloyd George, Morley, Churchill, Haldane, McKenna, Simon, Samuel—made strong demands upon the Prime Minister's leadership.[1] At the same time, the Cabinet was one of the most controversial in British history. Since 1908, it had faced some of the most bitter political conflicts the country had yet experienced: the struggle over Lloyd George's budget in 1909, the issue of the House of Lords in 1910 and 1911, the introduction of social insurance in 1911 and 1912, and the conflict over Home Rule for Ireland, which brought England to the brink of civil war in 1914. Domestic policy naturally monopolized the attention of most members of the Government.

Certain preparations had nevertheless been made for the eventuality of war. Under the aegis of the Committee of Imperial Defence (C.I.D.), a network of expert committees had studied various aspects of a possible war. Admiral Fisher had been given the opportunity to modernize the fleet, and shortly before the actual outbreak of hostilities the First Lord of the Admiralty, Churchill, had on his own initiative directed the fleet to its war stations. Between 1906 and 1912 Haldane had drastically overhauled the Army. A small, well-trained Expeditionary Force was ready for action. Plans to mobilize the Services and to take other measures if war should break out had been prepared in minute detail in the famous War Book.[2] Since 1906 a series of secret consultations had been held with the French General Staff. Yet many ministers lived, like most Britons, "in perfect confidence and considerable ignorance."[3] On the few occasions before the war when ministers had become aware of the possibility of active British participation in a continental war, strong disagreement had arisen in the Cabinet. The Foreign Secretary, Sir Edward Grey, had been forced to inform the French Government that no staff consultations

---

[1] Cf. *Life of Asquith*, II, 131 and *passim*; see also Asquith, *Memories*; J. M. Keynes, *Essays in Biography* (1933), pp. 48–59; *Life of Haldane*, I, 163–64; Lloyd George, *Memoirs*, II, 1008; Samuel, *Memoirs*, pp. 87–90.

[2] Hankey, *Supreme Command*, I, 3–106.

[3] Churchill, *World Crisis*, I, 52.

could be held or commitments made without previous Cabinet approval.[4]
Even in August 1914, there was dissension in the Cabinet before war was
declared. Two Cabinet ministers, Morley and John Burns, resigned. Numerous politicians shared the illusion of the ordinary citizenry that war
could not last long.

Consequently, an air of improvisation predominated during the first
months of the war. "A rather motley gathering" of ministers and military
leaders met on 5 and 6 August 1914 to discuss sending the Expeditionary
Force to France.[5] Initially the Cabinet met almost daily, but this caused
serious personal and administrative strain.[6] Not all ministers could be
absent from their departments for long periods of time. The discussions
in a Cabinet of more than twenty members were often far from exact. The
time-honored absence of both agenda and minutes provoked uncertainties
about the precise nature of Cabinet decisions. Urgent matters were sometimes decided by small groups of ministers who happened to be together
or who could be reached on short notice. The less one could rely on
earlier plans, the more difficult the situation became. Numerous subgroups
and committees sprouted, and there was little coordination or organized
exchange of information. Seemingly minor issues developed into major
crises, and long hours were spent discussing relatively unimportant issues. As Hankey described the situation:

Behind each episode there lay a whole history of rumor, contradiction, conjec-
ture, planning, preliminary movement, discussion, decision, indecision, order,
counter-order, before the climax was reached, often in a welter of bloodshed and
destruction.[7]

In November 1914, Asquith decided to establish a special War Council.[8] Besides Asquith, the Council included the Secretary of State for
War, Kitchener; the First Lord of the Admiralty, Churchill; the Foreign
Secretary, Grey; the Chancellor of the Exchequer, Lloyd George; and the
former Leader of the Conservative Party, Balfour, who, as the godfather
of the C.I.D., had previously helped the Liberal Cabinet to formulate military plans. The Secretary of the C.I.D., Hankey, also attended the meetings of the new War Council. Following the precedent of the C.I.D., he
took minutes of the proceedings. (To guarantee secrecy, they were kept
only in manuscript.)[9] Asquith usually reported the War Council's decisions to the full Cabinet.[10] But Kitchener complained that he had no
time to cover the same ground twice, and in practice the War Council

[4] Cf. John A. Murray, "Foreign Policy Debated: Sir Edward Grey and His
Critics, 1911–12," in *Power, Public Opinion and Diplomacy: Essays in Honor of
Ebe-Malcolm Carroll,* Duke Univ. Press (1959), pp. 140–71; Mackintosh, pp. 316–24.
[5] Asquith, *Memories,* II, 25; Churchill, *World Crisis,* I, 231–32.
[6] Cf. Asquith, *Memories,* II, 47.
[7] Hankey, *Supreme Command,* p. 182; cf. Johnson, pp. 146–47; Cd. 8490 (1917),
para. 14ff.
[8] Asquith, *Memories,* II, 87–88.
[9] Hankey, *Supreme Command,* pp. 237–38, 325.
[10] *Ibid.,* p. 238.

therefore acquired a measure of executive authority.[11] Its decisions were circulated directly to the ministers concerned (not to the permanent heads of the departments, as had been done by the C.I.D.), and ministers were expected to take action accordingly.[12]

After the War began to interfere more directly with daily life, the Government was confronted with numerous problems for which its machinery was ill prepared. The establishment of the War Council did not bring about the expected improvements. The Council's plan to meet only "when serious questions involving new departures of policy or joint strategic operations arose" proved unsatisfactory.[13] The day-to-day fluctuation of war did not allow for a precise separation between "existing policy" and "new departures of policy." Moreover, the Cabinet was not prepared to delegate its authority to so small a body as the War Council, least of all when the Council wanted to depart from established policy. Consequently, the War Council grew from some eight to at least thirteen members, which hampered its secrecy and decisiveness, and its discussions were largely duplicated by the Cabinet.[14] Originally, the War Council played a rather important role, especially in the planning of the Dardanelles expedition. But although it met weekly at first, it became less useful as time went by. The number of Council sessions decreased, and between 19 March 1915 and 14 May 1915, it did not meet at all.[15]

Such developments were largely the result of personality and policy differences rather than theoretical defects in machinery. When hostilities commenced, Asquith had appointed Kitchener, a professional soldier, to head the War Office. Unlike most, Kitchener realized that the war was likely to last for years. He enjoyed widespread popularity in the country and immediately started a highly successful armed forces recruiting drive to man the greatly increased armies he knew were necessary. But as an administrator and Cabinet member he was less successful. He found it "repugnant to have to reveal military secrets," which he regarded as his exclusive concern, "to 23 gentlemen with whom he was barely acquainted."[16] His colleagues stood in awe of him, and initially allowed him considerable freedom. But there was never any real rapport between Kitchener and the Cabinet, a fact that was to have serious consequences when the developments of war took an unfavorable turn.

Relations in the Admiralty were also not free from strain. As First Lord of the Admiralty, Churchill took a very active part in determining strategy. Prince Louis of Battenberg, who was First Sea Lord when the war broke out, was forced to resign under a barrage of Press attacks on

---

[11] *Life of Kitchener*, p. 286.   [12] Hankey, *Supreme Command*, p. 238.
[13] Asquith, *Memories*, II, 87.
[14] Hankey, *Supreme Command*, pp. 237, 323–25.
[15] Cd. 8490 (1917) ; Fisher, *Memories*, pp. 81–83; Hankey, *Supreme Command*, p. 323.
[16] *Life of Asquith*, II, 124 ; cf. Hankey, *Supreme Command*, pp. 186, 324 ; Samuel, *Memoirs*, pp. 117–18; Grey, *Twenty-Five Years*, II, 240 ; *Life of Kitchener, passim.* See also Chap. 9 of this book.

his family ties with Germany. His successor, Fisher, whom Churchill had recalled from retirement, was most able but very obstinate. Kitchener's special position was an object of standing temptation to Fisher. Secrecy, to him, was dogma and hobby. Neither Fisher nor Kitchener was good at delegating authority, and both were temperamentally unsuited to work through an elaborate general staff. Consequently, the cooperation between the Army and the Navy was not well organized at lower levels, and at higher levels it became wholly dependent on the often strained personal relations between those singular men of war, Kitchener, Churchill, and Fisher. This became especially serious when in January 1915 the Cabinet authorized an attack by both Services on the Dardanelles.

By May 1915, the machinery of government had therefore fallen into a state of considerable disarray. Kitchener practically dictated war policy, but he showed no steady hand. Churchill and Fisher were at loggerheads over naval policy. Asquith gave Kitchener undivided support, reasoning that military policy should be determined first and foremost by the experts. Neither the War Council nor the Cabinet nor the Prime Minister exercised effective powers of scrutiny and coordination. At least one reason for this was a lack of information. There was little documentary reporting to the War Council or the Cabinet, and oral discussions were not a satisfactory substitute. Kitchener's taciturnity and Fisher's view that experts should only open their minds to their immediate ministerial superiors, not to the Cabinet as a whole, deprived the Cabinet of any direct advice by professional military counselors. As Fisher wrote, "When sailors get around a Council Board, they are almost invariably mute. The politicians who are round that Board are not mute; they could never have got there if they had been mute."[17] Or to quote from a contemporary appreciation of the situation by Balfour, neither Kitchener nor Churchill

would have tolerated for a moment the independent examination by any member of the Committee of experts belonging to their own departments. To describe that Committee [the "War Council"] as responsible for the decisions arrived at would be absurd, if "responsibility" for a decision is supposed to imply full knowledge and consideration of all the circumstances on which the decision should depend.[18]

Civilian ministers, in other words, frequently discussed war policy, but lacked adequate knowledge. Agreement among them was hard to find. Esher wrote in his diary at the time:

Arthur Balfour was there; he has been sitting on the Aulic Council, every member of which had a different plan; it is like a game of ninepins; one plan is knocked over, and in falling, knocks over the next one and so on until the board is clear; the result is a total want of initiative of any kind.[19]

Between military men and politicians a chasm appeared, providing opportunities for extensive intrigues. Disagreements were compounded

---

[17] Fisher, *Memories*, p. 61.   [18] *Life of Asquith*, II, 187.
[19] *Esher Papers*, III, 203.

rather than lightened by the fact that many politicians uncritically took the side of the military, while at the same time leading professional soldiers began to dabble in politics.

Home-front policy also presented difficulties. The C.I.D. had made no detailed plans to mobilize manpower or industry. The Government was reluctant to intervene too strongly in economic matters, and public opinion did not urge it to do so. Prices rose quickly. Labor unrest flared up. Serious shortages developed, most notably in the munitions and war-transport industries. There was no clear ministerial responsibility in these sectors, and *ad hoc* committees of the Cabinet were hardly effective. Conscription was still rejected; direction of labor and the requisitioning of industry were not even seriously considered.

Asquith's Coalition Government (1915–16)

The increasing dissatisfaction came to a boil in May 1915, when Fisher suddenly resigned his office; simultaneously, a serious shortage of munitions threatened. Asquith felt constrained to include members of the Conservative Opposition in his Cabinet. Some Liberal ministers lost their posts. Haldane was sacrificed to Press agitation seeking to foist pro-German inclinations upon him. Churchill—bête noire of the Conservatives for more than a decade—was removed from his post as First Lord of the Admiralty. Kitchener lost most of his powers over war production when Lloyd George accepted a new portfolio as Minister of Munitions.[20] A number of the most prominent and able Conservatives—including Balfour, Bonar Law, Curzon, Long, Selborne, Austen Chamberlain, Carson, and Lansdowne—entered the Government. So did Labour leader Arthur Henderson. The number of Cabinet members soon increased to 23.

Although the appointment of the Conservatives gave the Government a broader backing in Parliament, it created new problems within the Cabinet. A greater number of competent persons demanded their share of influence in directing the war. The so-called Dardanelles Committee, established to replace the War Council, started out with no fewer than eleven members, not including the Service Chiefs (who did not play a very important role at this time) and its Secretary, the ubiquitous Hankey.[21] Conflicts were constantly fought in two rounds, in the Dardanelles Committee and in the Cabinet. Continuous controversy poisoned the atmosphere. Moreover, not all ministers had enough to do. The Lord

---

[20] This was the first time that the terms "Minister" and "Ministry" were officially used in Britain (cf. Chester–Willson, pp. 24, 38). The official announcement read: "Mr. Lloyd George has undertaken the formation and temporary direction of this department, and during his tenure of office as Minister of Munitions, will vacate the office of Chancellor of the Exchequer." This statement implied that the new Chancellor, McKenna, held an acting appointment only, which could not but lead to political bitterness. The incident well illustrates the political importance of the Chancellorship in the political hierarchy; Lloyd George was clearly willing to shoulder the new tasks, but not at the expense of losing his rank in the list of ministers.

[21] Hankey, *Supreme Command*, p. 336.

Privy Seal, Curzon, for example, "moved restlessly hither and thither in quest of work which might prove of value to the state" and poured out his frustrations into long-winded memoranda.[22] Various ministers urged Asquith to take a stronger lead, but for reasons of temperament or expediency he thought it impossible to restrain his new Conservative colleagues too severely.[23] Opposition in the Cabinet increased. Notably, the Attorney-General, Carson, "a clever lawyer and a rebellious politician" with "an intensely emotional nature," became embittered.[24] "I find the Cabinet work not at all satisfactory," Carson wrote in August 1915 in a private letter. "It is hard to do anything that one would like to do, and the numbers are far too great. I should like to see a Cabinet of about seven with power by Order in Council to pass such ordinances as are necessary. We won't win this war under existing methods of organization, and that is what makes me ill."[25] He drafted a strong memorandum to his colleagues, whom he had called "twenty-three blind mice"[26] to their faces, and whom he had elsewhere described as "a Vestry meeting with the Vicar in the Chair."[27]

The situation came to a head in September 1915, when the Cabinet found it impossible to decide between the competing claims of the Western Front, the Dardanelles expedition, and Serbia. Kitchener's vagaries created more and more distrust. On 22 September, the Cabinet decided, in his absence, that the War Office should immediately form a competent General Staff "to guide and advise the Cabinet and its committees in matters of strategy."[28] Asquith further proposed to abolish the Dardanelles Committee, and to replace it with two small committees, one to deal with the actual conduct of the war and its problems, the other to concern itself with the financial outlook. This proposal led to "a fusillade of cross-criticism."[29] Balfour thought that no new committee structure would work effectively. He said that since Kitchener was neither by temperament nor by training a good man to work with a committee, he would inevitably regard it as "intended to control him in the exercise of what he conceives to be his proper functions." In addition, friction was bound to arise if persons like Curzon and Churchill should sit on a committee, on which they had obvious claims to serve.

Consequently, Balfour thought the Cabinet "should get on better as we are with the Cabinet system tempered by occasional and quite informal conversations such as those you [Asquith] have now and then arranged

---

[22] *Life of Curzon,* III, 127. Asquith considered Curzon a *mauvais coucheur* (*Life of Austen Chamberlain,* II, 24).
[23] *Life of Bonar Law,* p. 292; Churchill, *World Crisis,* II, 384; Chamberlain, *Down the Years,* pp. 111, 116.
[24] Beaverbrook, *1917–18,* pp. xiii, 149, 185.
[25] *Life of Carson,* p. 391.
[26] *Ibid.,* p. 389; cf. *Life of Dawson,* p. 122.
[27] *Esher Papers,* III, 280.   [28] *Life of Kitchener,* p. 350.
[29] Asquith, *Memories,* II, 23.

in Downing Street."[30] Lloyd George thought the proposal an improvement on "the sort of Duma"[31] that had hitherto been sitting, but felt that "unless there was a complete change at the War Office," the new Council would be "just as impotent as the Cabinet and the old Council had proved themselves to be."[32] Curzon argued that a War Council as proposed would be a very heavy burden on the Prime Minister, the Foreign Secretary, the Secretary for War, the First Lord of the Admiralty, and the Minister of Munitions. Lest the new body should in practice produce "little beyond an inter-departmental discussion without the benefit of independent points of view, fresh suggestion or outside experience," he suggested adding to the new committee "at least three other members who should be prepared to de-vote their whole, or at least the greater part of their time to the problem of the War."[33]

In other words, deadlock was complete, as policy divided ministers in a way no machinery could bridge. Carson, who had pressed for an execu-tive War Committee with full powers, resigned on 12 October because of the Cabinet's failure to agree to help Serbia and because of his dis-content with the way the war was being run generally.[34] On 19 and again on 21 October, the Cabinet met under Crewe (Asquith was ill) and after acrimonious discussion unanimously concluded that the existing machinery was ineffective, owing to the undue size of the Dardanelles Committee. "It was agreed that a drastic change was imperatively necessary" and that a new body, "quite small, and, so far as can be, departmental," should be introduced.[35] On 2 November 1915, Carson gave his resignation speech in the House of Commons. He publicly demanded the establishment of a small body of four or five members who would run the war and have powers binding on other ministers.[36] Asquith rejected the demand, argu-ing that there was not "any numerical specific against either want of fore-sight or want of good luck."[37] He instituted a new War Committee that initially had only three members: the Prime Minister, the Secretary of State for War (Kitchener), and the First Lord of the Admiralty (Bal-four). A few weeks later, McKenna and Lloyd George were added. Grey also attended frequently, and soon the official membership fluctuated be-tween nine and eleven, not including the Chief of the Imperial General Staff and the First Sea Lord.[38] The War Committee proved to be more decisive than its predecessors (once the thorny problem of the evacuation of the Dardanelles had been settled). It met often. The appointment of a new Chief of the Imperial General Staff, who replaced Kitchener as the

[30] *Life of Asquith*, II, 187.
[31] Lloyd George also spoke later of a Sanhedrin (Jones, *Lloyd George*, p. 94).
[32] *Life of Asquith*, II, 195.　　　　　[33] *Ibid.*, p. 188.
[34] *Life of Bonar Law*, p. 268.　　　　[35] Mackintosh, p. 335.
[36] 75 H. of C. Deb. (2 November 1915), cols. 532–35; cf. Amery, *My Political Life*, II, 77–78.
[37] 75 H. of C. Deb. (2 November 1915), cols. 525–26.
[38] Hankey, *Supreme Command*, pp. 441–42, 544 n.

main adviser of the Cabinet on matters of strategy, gave ministers more direct access to official expert advice, and cooperation between the Admiralty and the War Office improved somewhat. Asquith and Hankey, who was again appointed Secretary to the Committee, attempted to avoid duplicating business in the War Committee and the Cabinet by a new reporting system.[39] But the pressure of events and the need for secrecy made this little but a palliative. The Cabinet members not on the Committee were still unwilling to part fully with their share of influence and control. Since the Cabinet itself had no records and the information from the departments was inadequate, the Committee could never work with full knowledge and authority. If its executive authority increased at all during 1916, friction with the Cabinet increased *pari passu*.

Meanwhile, the political climate changed.[40] National warfare and coalition government weakened party ties. Rumor fed on secrecy, and power became fluid. The Northcliffe Press began a bitter anti-Government campaign in which it pushed the suggestion—not unwelcome to military ears—that the politicians should let generals and admirals direct the war.[41] Certain groups in Parliament supported Carson's campaign for a small War Directorate and publicly voiced the increasingly widespread feeling that Asquith was personally not suited to be a war leader. The nucleus of this agitation formed a small organization sometimes known as the Ginger Group.[42] Its members were Carson himself, who became more and more the actual Leader of the Opposition in Parliament; Lord Milner, the radical-imperialist former Governor of South Africa, who had considerable influence on the Conservative diehards; Amery, former *Times* correspondent, active admirer of both Carson and Milner, who may have brought the group together; Geoffrey Robinson (later called Dawson), whom Northcliffe had appointed Editor of *The Times* on Milner's recommendation; F. S. Oliver, a businessman who had written an exceedingly critical book about the first year of the war, *Ordeal by Battle*; and Waldorf Astor, owner of the *Observer*. Closely associated with this group were Sir Henry Wilson, later Chief of the Imperial General Staff; Sir Starr Jameson of Jameson Raid fame and Prime Minister of Cape Colony from 1904 to 1908; and Philip Kerr, later Marquess of Lothian. Lloyd George also participated occasionally in its weekly dinner meetings. Its members pleaded for a National Government instead of a Coalition Cabinet, for a War Directorate instead of a Cabinet of parties, for leadership by capable persons, and for action instead of any a priori program. The group enjoyed access to important sources of information and gained the increasing support of parliamentary backbenchers and influen-

---

[39] Hankey, *Supreme Command*, pp. 439–44.

[40] See also A. J. P. Taylor, "Politics in the First World War," *Proceedings of the British Academy*, XLV (1959), 67–95.

[41] The King tended to share this view (*Life of King George V*, p. 288). Cf. Churchill, *World Crisis*, III, 241–46, for a rather different view.

[42] Cf. Amery, *My Political Life*, II, 81–82; *Life of Carson*, p. 397; *Life of Milner*, pp. 305–7; *Life of Dawson*, p. 127ff; *Life of Henry Wilson*, I, 298–99.

tial Press organs to an extent it probably would not have achieved under normal party conditions.

The Reform Proposals of November and December 1916, Asquith's Fall, and the Formation of the War Cabinet under Lloyd George

Inside the Cabinet, too, dissatisfaction continued to mount as many ministers became increasingly critical of Asquith's leadership.[43] Certain factions having no connection with earlier party allegiances were formed in the Cabinet. The radical Lloyd George and the Conservative Party Leader Bonar Law developed a measure of cooperation that became apparent in their common attitude regarding the retreat from the Dardanelles, the forcing through of conscription in 1916, and the appointment of Lloyd George as Secretary of State for War to succeed Kitchener, who died in June 1916.[44] In the autumn of 1916, military reverses produced a certain amount of defeatism in political circles. Both inside and outside the Cabinet, a cleavage appeared between the more unyielding and the more cautious. Bonar Law became concerned about the increasing defection of Conservative parliamentarians, many of whom appeared to follow Carson rather than the Government whips. Lloyd George, in Bonar Law's graphic description, "at the same time the right-hand man to the Prime Minister, and the Leader of the Opposition," considered resigning to regain his freedom to plead outside the Cabinet for more dynamic war policies, and, if necessary, to force a general election on this issue.[45] Meanwhile the War Committee and the Cabinet faced a growing accumulation of unfinished business that even frequent meetings could not clear up.[46] Both Bonar Law and Lloyd George desired the formation of a compact body that would have full executive authority over war policy.[47] Under the active inspiration of Max Aitken (later Lord Beaverbrook), Carson, Bonar Law, and Lloyd George were brought together.

From that moment events developed rapidly. Asquith's Government was overthrown in December 1916, following a complicated process of political negotiation and intrigue.[48] It was succeeded by a practically non-

---

[43] Cf. Crewe in Asquith, *Memories,* pp. 129–30; Cecil, *ibid.,* p. 149; Austen Chamberlain, *Down the Years,* p. 116; Balfour in *Life of King George V,* p. 290; *Life of Lansdowne,* pp. 452–53; *Life of Reading,* pp. 251–53; *Life of Addison,* p. 157.

[44] *Life of King George V,* pp. 273–74; *Life of Lloyd George,* p. 320; Beaverbrook, 1914–16, II, *passim.*

[45] Hankey, *Supreme Command,* p. 557.

[46] *Ibid.,* pp. 551, 557–58.

[47] Lloyd George referred to Hankey as the inspirer of his new proposals (*Memoirs,* II, 962–63). Cf. Hankey, *Supreme Command,* pp. 562–63. Bonar Law stressed the importance of conversations with Carson and Jameson, both leading members of the Ginger Group (*Life of Bonar Law,* p. 304).

[48] The classical analysis of the downfall of Asquith's Government is given in Beaverbrook's *Politicians and the War, 1914–1916,* vol. II. This unconventional treatise has been accepted as basically correct by both Lloyd George and Carson (cf.

departmental War Cabinet of five members headed by Lloyd George. Before this Cabinet was formed, many meetings were held and numerous memoranda circulated in which a number of suggestions for reforms in central government organization were proposed. Because of the unexpectedness of the outcome, it is important to survey these exchanges in some detail.

Discussions began with a draft proposal that Bonar Law, Carson, and Lloyd George jointly sent to Asquith on 25 November 1916, asking him to announce the following decision:

The War Council has, in my opinion, rendered devoted and invaluable service, but experience has convinced me that there are disadvantages in the present system which render a change necessary.

Some body doing the work of the War Council should meet every day. It is impossible that the War Council can do this while its members have at the same time to fulfill the exacting duties of their departments. At the War Council, also, we have felt it necessary to have the advantage regularly of the presence of the Chief of the Imperial General Staff and the First Sea Lord. Their time is in this way taken up sometimes unnecessarily when every moment is required for other work. I have decided, therefore, to create what I regard as a civilian General Staff. This Staff will consist of myself as President and of three other members of the Cabinet who have no portfolio and who will devote their whole time to the consideration day by day of the problems which arise in connection with the prosecution of the war.

The three members who have undertaken to fulfill these duties are [at this point a blank space was left for later decision; the triumvirate had thought of themselves, and possibly of Henderson, as representative of the Labour Party] and I have invited Mr. Lloyd George, and he has consented to act as Chairman and to preside at any meeting which, owing to the pressure of other duties, I find it impossible to attend.

I propose that the body should have executive authority subject to this—that it shall rest with me to refer any questions to the decision of the Cabinet which I think should be brought before them.[49]

At first Asquith reacted to this memorandum only in a letter to Bonar Law in which he made some critical remarks about the personalities of Carson and Lloyd George and suggested that the proposal could not but create the impression that Lloyd George would in practice replace himself as leader of the Government. Meanwhile, the discussion was complicated by a memorandum from another Conservative minister, Lord Robert Cecil, who took up a proposal Asquith had made a year earlier and pleaded for the establishment of a Civil Organization Committee of the Cabinet. This body was to be composed of three members, one of whom would be a member of the existing War Committee, and its main task would be to

Lloyd George, *Memoirs*, II, 981). Later publications have not really challenged Beaverbrook's description. See also *Life of Asquith* and Asquith *Memories, passim; Life of Crewe*, pp. 181–90; Chamberlain, *Down the Years*, pp. 107–31; *Life of Lloyd George*, p. 332ff; *Life of Bonar Law*, p. 298ff; *Life of Derby*, p. 228ff; and Hankey, *Supreme Command*, p. 555ff.

49 Beaverbrook, 1914–16, II, 145–46.

report to the full Cabinet on short notice on civilian war measures that ought to be taken.[50]

On 29 November 1916, a special Cabinet meeting was called to discuss the desirability of changes in government organization. Agreement was reached in principle on the need to establish a "committee to deal with the domestic aspects of war policy," which, following the precedent of the War Committee, would have its own advisers. Lloyd George apparently was to be its chairman, while Runciman, Samuel, Austen Chamberlain, and Cecil were to be members.[51] Some Cabinet members received the impression that the entire task of the Cabinet was in principle to be divided between the War Committee and the proposed body. Crewe (who was in favor of the proposal), at least, concluded that "its complete acceptance in a practical shape involved the abolition of the Cabinet as a consultative body, though with no actual change in the position of ministers."[52] The proposal gained the approval of most Conservative ministers who met with Bonar Law on 30 November. During this meeting they opposed the scheme of Lloyd George, Bonar Law, and Carson, and suggested establishing a "War Council" composed of the "political heads of the fighting departments" and a "Home Council consisting of the principal ministers concerned with the Home Services."[53]

Next day, however, Lloyd George sent Asquith the following memorandum, couched in terms that strongly suggested an ultimatum:

Memo to Prime Minister. 1 December 1916.

1. That the War Committee consist of three members, two of which must be the First Lord of the Admiralty, and the Secretary of State for War, who should have in their offices deputies capable of attending to and deciding all departmental business, and a third minister without portfolio. One of these three to be Chairman.

2. That the War Committee should have full power subject to the supreme control of the Prime Minister to direct all questions connected with the war.

3. The Prime Minister in his discretion to have power to refer any question to the Cabinet.

4. Unless the Cabinet on reference by the Prime Minister reverses the decision of the War Committee, that decision to be carried out by the department concerned.

5. The War Committee to have the power to invite any minister and to summon the expert advisers and officers of any department to its meetings.[54]

This proposal differed substantially from the triumvirate's original memorandum of 25 November. It no longer spoke of the Prime Minister

[50] Asquith, *Memories,* II, 147–49.
[51] Hankey, *Supreme Command,* p. 564.
[52] Asquith, *Memories,* II, 130, and 30 H. of L. Deb. (19 June 1918), cols. 242–61. The proposal was criticized by Curzon (col. 278).
[53] Beaverbrook, 1914–16, II, 165. Austen Chamberlain (*Down the Years,* p. 142) rejected this scheme in later years.
[54] *Life of Asquith,* II, 252–53.

as President, although it still referred to his "supreme control." No longer
was the War Committee to consist of ministers without portfolio. Instead
there was to be a category of superior Service ministers. The memorandum still maintained the plenary Cabinet, but only the Prime Minister
would have the authority to refer questions to it; and it stipulated at the
same time that the Committee could summon other ministers *at its discretion*. It demanded that the new body have full authority "to direct all
questions connected with the war," and thus implicitly rejected the plan
for a co-equal "Home Council."

On the same day, Asquith sent Lloyd George a reply in which he referred to the generally acknowledged defects of the existing War Committee:

(1) that its numbers are too large; and (2) that there is delay, evasion, and
often obstruction on the part of the departments in giving effect to its decisions . . . ; (3) that it is often kept in ignorance by the departments of information, essential and even vital, of a technical kind upon the problems that come
before it; and (4) that it is overcharged with duties, many of which might
well be delegated to subordinate bodies.

Asquith, too, deemed reforms urgent. But he added two important reservations to Lloyd George's proposals:

Whatever changes are made in the composition of functions of the War Committee, the Prime Minister must be its Chairman. He cannot be relegated to
the position of an arbiter in the background or a referee to the Cabinet. . . .
    The reconstruction of the War Committee should be accompanied by the
setting up of a Committee of National Organization, to deal with the purely
domestic side of our problems. It should have executive power within its own
domain.[55]

Asquith ended his letter with the statement: "The Cabinet would in all
cases have ultimate authority."

On Sunday, 3 December, a conversation took place between Lloyd
George and Asquith. The latter felt that his position had been weakened
because he had just been notified of the Conservative ministers' intention
to resign. A measure of agreement was reached, which Asquith himself,
in a letter to Lloyd George on Monday 4 December, summarized as follows:

The suggested arrangement was to the following effect: The Prime Minister
to have supreme and effective control of War policy. The agenda of the War
Committee will be submitted to him; its Chairman will report to him daily;
he can direct it to consider particular topics or proposals; and all its conclusions
will be subject to his approval or veto. He can, of course, at his own discretion
attend meetings of the Committee.[56]

But on that morning, *The Times* carried a leading article, written by
Robinson under the active inspiration of Carson, which hinted (in agree-

[55] *Ibid.*, pp. 253–54.   [56] *Ibid.*, p. 264.

ment with Robinson's preference) that in practice Lloyd George would supersede Asquith. Asquith immediately reacted by letting Lloyd George know that he had begun to doubt the feasibility of Sunday's agreement, which opened the way to "infinite possibilities for misunderstanding and misrepresentation. . . . Unless the impression is at once corrected that I am being relegated to the position of an irresponsible spectator of the War," Asquith threatened, "I cannot possibly go on."[57] Asquith felt strengthened in his position by a number of factors on that particular Monday, and that evening he wrote Lloyd George yet another letter, informing him that the King had given him (Asquith) full powers to reconstruct the Cabinet. Asquith also repeated that Lloyd George's proposal for a "War Executive" was acceptable only if the Prime Minister were "its permanent President," no matter how much the pressure of other business might force him "to delegate from time to time the chairmanship to another minister as his representative and locumtenens."[58] He emphasized moreover that he alone would appoint the members of a reorganized War Committee and refused to accept Carson as a member. Carson himself had written to Bonar Law that same evening:

I am convinced after our talk last evening that no patchwork is possible. It would be unreal and couldn't last. A system founded on mistrust and jealousy and dislike is doomed to failure and in a crisis like the present it would really be disastrous on this account to the country. The only solution I can see is for the P.M. to resign and for L.G. to form a Government—a very small one. If the House won't support it he should go to the country and we could know where we are.[59]

When he received this letter, Bonar Law declared he would resign unless Asquith accepted the triumvirate's proposals. After receiving Asquith's latest letter, Lloyd George resigned. In a long, rather rhetorical letter, he informed Asquith of his conviction that it was his duty "to leave the Government in order to inform the people of the real condition of affairs." He argued that there had been "delay, hesitation, lack of forethought and vision" and that "unity without action is nothing but futile carnage. . . . Vigor and vision are the supreme need at this hour."[60]

Asquith then resigned as well. Bonar Law was unable to form a new Cabinet. A Buckingham Palace conference of the King and the main party leaders was equally unsuccessful. The King then charged Lloyd George to form a Government. Contrary to the expectations of many, he soon succeeded. His Cabinet had no more than five members, only one of whom, Lloyd George himself, was a Liberal. The other members were the Conservative Party Leader, Bonar Law; the leader of the pro-war section of the Labour Party, Henderson; the Conservative minister Curzon; and, finally, a man who fitted ill into the existing party divisions, a member par excellence of the Ginger Group, Milner. The Ginger Group also ob-

[57] *Ibid.*, p. 264.
[58] *Ibid.*, p. 265.
[59] *Life of Carson*, p. 410.
[60] *Life of Asquith*, II, 267.

tained considerable influence in other ways. Carson became First Lord of the Admiralty, and later was also a member of the War Cabinet. Amery, Philip Kerr, Waldorf Astor, and a close associate, Mark Sykes (who, like Carson and Amery, had pleaded more than a year earlier, on 2 November 1915, for a War Cabinet as now formed), were included in newly established Secretariats. "As a kind of informal brain trust," they were to have direct access to the members of the War Cabinet.[61] All leading Conservatives came over to the new Government. But all Liberal Cabinet members refused to take part for a variety of reasons, not the least of which was their loyalty to Asquith. Bonar Law and Lloyd George had invited Asquith to join the new Government as Lord Chancellor, but he "had declined to become a Merovingian ruler as Prime Minister, and as a subordinate member of the new Government . . . would not submit to the autocracy of the War Committee, of which there was no assurance that he would even be a member."[62]

The War Cabinet: Choice or Must?

From the viewpoint of Cabinet reform, these new developments raised two important questions: first, were Lloyd George's original proposals acceptable for a Prime Minister, disregarding the personal intentions that lay behind them, and second, what factors explain the unexpected outcome of a new type of Cabinet?

The Proposals of 1916

Churchill has argued that the suggested arrangement need not have been unfavorable to Asquith. As Chairman of the War Committee, Lloyd George would have been blamed for all setbacks of the war. He and the professional staff of both the Army and the Navy would certainly have quarreled. In such circumstances Asquith would have had the final word on all major and controversial issues. Ultimately, he would therefore have been in a better position to remove Lloyd George from office than he was in December 1916. As for the Cabinet, although it was to delegate much of its authority, it could still intervene decisively at any moment.[63]

Churchill's opinion was shared in principle by two members of the Ginger Group—Carson, as we saw, and Wilson, who wrote in his diary on 3 December: "Personally I don't like this proposal [of Bonar Law and Lloyd George], because it will leave the Cabinet to intrigue and bring down this trio, who will fall to a certainty if things go wrong, as they are sure to do for some time."[64]

---

[61] Amery, *My Political Life*, II, 92.
[62] Crewe in Asquith, *Memories*, II, 136; cf. Samuel, *Memoirs*, pp. 125–26.
[63] Churchill, *World Crisis*, III, 249–50. Churchill's son, Randolph, judged differently in his *Life of Derby* (p. 234): "Who can suppose that Asquith would not have been reduced in a very few weeks to a state of public *chaperonage* if he had stood by Sunday's bargain in the light of Monday's Press?"
[64] *Life of Henry Wilson*, I, 304.

Many others, however, shared Asquith's opinion that yielding to Lloyd George's schemes would spell "dishonor or impotence or both."[65] Austen Chamberlain, for instance, considered the clause under which Asquith would retain the right to attend all sessions of the War Executive and to refer its decisions to the full Cabinet as "plainly a face-saving device, the obvious result of which would be that the Prime Minister would become a *roi fainéant* with Lloyd George as Mayor of the Palace."[66] "In any case," Chamberlain wrote, "power and responsibility must go together, and the man who was Prime Minister in name must be also Prime Minister in fact."[67] Curzon spoke of a "protean compromise which . . . could have no endurance."[68]

Because the proposed arrangement was never tried, it is difficult to decide which of these conflicting judgments was correct. Lloyd George undoubtedly intended to separate the new War Committee from the Cabinet as much as possible. Such a divorce seems unthinkable in practice, unless an unassailable Prime Minister were to force the Cabinet to yield without murmur to the War Committee's views. Given the personalities at hand, it is much more likely that bitter conflicts would have arisen, which eventually would have led to a renewed subordination of the War Committee to the Cabinet, or, conversely, to the withering of the Cabinet under the impetuous drive of the War Committee, which would have become the Cabinet in all but name. Both results were possible, in practice and in theory.

It is more doubtful whether this might be said with equal confidence of the proposal to divide the Cabinet into two equally powerful committees, one in charge of warfare, the other of civilian mobilization. Such a proposal is based on the premise that these areas could easily be separated; in practice, war front and home front were becoming increasingly interrelated. Conflicts between these bodies would inevitably have flared up. Who would have arbitrated between them? The Prime Minister, as an infallible and politically unremovable dictator, guided only by wisdom? Or Parliament, which would have had to judge contradictory recommendations instead of agreed policies?

The Establishment of the War Cabinet

It is not easy to determine what factors were ultimately responsible for the establishment of a practically non-departmental War Cabinet. This kind of structure was actively canvassed in the circles of the Ginger

---

[65] Asquith, *Memories*, II, 159.

[66] Chamberlain, *Down the Years*, pp. 114–15. Crewe thought that "the veto of whatever Cabinet was left would not be seriously hampering, because it could not be exercised against a War Committee with all the knowledge and with their resignations in their pockets" (Asquith, *Memories*, II, 137).

[67] Chamberlain, *Down the Years*, p. 118.

[68] Letter to Lansdowne (*Life of Lansdowne*, pp. 452–53). For Balfour's views see Lloyd George, *Memoirs*, II, 999. For similar reasoning, leading Halifax to refuse nomination as Prime Minister in 1940, see Halifax, *Fullness of Days*, pp. 219–20.

Group. Carson and Milner had both publicly pressed for it. The Editor of *The Times,* Robinson, considered the establishment of the War Cabinet "a real triumph for the paper."[69] Austen Chamberlain mentioned as one of his conditions for staying in office that

the War Committee, necessarily having all real authority, should itself be in name as well as in fact the War Cabinet, and that there should not be a great body of Cabinet ministers without real influence on the general policy of the war and yet sharing the responsibility for decisions in which they were not consulted and exposed to constant criticism for acts of omission or acts of commission in which they had no part.[70]

Chamberlain's influence in this direction may be traced in a Memorandum of Conversation between Mr. Lloyd George and certain Unionist ex-ministers of 7 December 1916.[71] Lloyd George himself stressed in his memoirs the need for the Cabinet to be in session almost continuously. In his view, ministers who were charged with the day-to-day control of a department lacked the time and the detachment to form careful and objective judgments on general policy.[72] Hankey has suggested that the War Cabinet was a natural culmination of the development of the War Council, Dardanelles Committee, and War Committee—all of which originated in the desire to place the direction of war policy in the hands of a small and efficient body of ministers, and all of which had proved in turn that the co-existence of such a body and the Cabinet could never be enduring, satisfactory, or peaceful.[73] It is likely that personal factors had a more decisive influence on the War Cabinet's establishment. Lloyd George had argued that the Prime Minister of a normal Cabinet was too much burdened by his manifold tasks to be able to direct war policy on a day-to-day basis. But he was the last person to follow this precept after he became Prime Minister. Forming a small Cabinet and delegating most parliamentary business to Bonar Law, who was to act as Leader of the House of Commons, would free him of some important duties.[74] Bonar Law was agreeable to such an arrangement. Because prominent Liberals were not represented in the new Government and because the Conservative ministers co-operated willingly—the most ambitious among them, Curzon, was after

[69] *Life of Dawson,* p. 145; cf. Beaverbrook, 1917–18, p. 144 n.

[70] Chamberlain, *Down the Years,* pp. 128–29. These considerations do not explain, however, why a non-departmental Cabinet should be formed. A Conservative diehard, W. A. S. Hewins, proposed forming a War Cabinet, composed of the Prime Minister, the Foreign Secretary, the two Service ministers, and possibly the Chancellor of the Exchequer and the Colonial Secretary (cf. Hewins, *The Apologia of an Imperialist: Forty Years of Imperial Policy* [1929], II, 95–96.

[71] Beaverbrook, 1914–16, II, 322–23.

[72] Lloyd George, *Memoirs,* III, 1063–64.

[73] Hankey, *Diplomacy,* p. 56; Hankey, *Control,* pp. 32–41; Hankey, *Supreme Command,* pp. 439–44, 463–64; Hancock–Gowing, p. 36. In a letter to Beveridge in 1942, Hankey called himself "the architect of Lloyd George's system of the War Cabinet" (Beveridge, *Power and Influence,* p. 404). Cf. Lloyd George, *Memoirs,* II, 962–63. Against this, cf. Mackintosh, p. 272.

[74] Lloyd George, *Memoirs,* III, 1065.

all offered membership in the War Cabinet—the forming of such a small Cabinet was also politically possible, and perhaps, to mask the dearth of Liberal representation in the Government, even indicated. (Lloyd George himself later used this argument against eager candidates who pressed for membership in and hence enlargement of the Cabinet's select circle.)[75] By divorcing most ministers from the small War Cabinet, Lloyd George obtained the liberty he desired. As he frankly admitted, politically necessary but in themselves "weak ministerial appointments would not matter so much . . . if the Cabinet was really as predominant as he intended it to be."[76] Milner had declared at the outset that he was unwilling to take charge of an executive department.[77] For Henderson and the wing of the Labour Party that supported the Government, the fact that their Cabinet representative was to be one of five instead of one of twenty-three implied promotion. Labour representatives asked Lloyd George at the time whether such a small body would not in practice spell a dictatorship. Lloyd George retorted: "What is a government for, except to dictate? If it does not dictate, then it is not a government, and whether it is four or twenty-three, the only difference is that four would take less time than twenty-three."[78] The new War Cabinet heralded efficient action and conscious assumption of leadership where leadership had been lacking. The Press, waging war from the wings, almost universally applauded the Cabinet's ascent.

The Structure of the War Cabinet (1916–18)

The establishment of the War Cabinet had important consequences for the position of departmental ministers, the distribution of functions among departments, the relation between the Cabinet and the departments, and the decision-making process in the Cabinet.

The Position of Departmental Ministers

According to the Report of the War Cabinet for 1917:

The introduction of the War Cabinet system . . . has freed the various departmental ministers from the constant necessity which rested upon them under the old Cabinet system of considering those wider aspects of public policy which often had nothing to do with their departments, but for which they were collectively responsible. They are, therefore, now able to devote a far larger part of their time to those administrative duties, which have become more exacting as the national activities have expanded under the pressure of the war.[79]

The principle that the Cabinet was to be composed of the heads of the more important government departments was consciously abandoned. Except for Bonar Law, who was Chancellor of the Exchequer, the Cabinet mem-

---

[75] Life of Derby, p. 258.
[77] Life of Milner, p. 317.
[79] Cd. 9005 (1918), p. 4.

[76] Life of Dawson, p. 144.
[78] Lloyd George, Memoirs, III, 1060.

bers were "relieved of the day-to-day preoccupations of administrative work," and therefore their time was "entirely available for initiating policy and for the work of coordinating the great Departments of State."[80] The new developments undoubtedly lowered the status of the departmental ministers. Their work was coordinated from above. They had to execute decisions on which perhaps they were never consulted. They were invited to Cabinet meetings only when matters concerning their own department were discussed, and they had thus lost their right to share in the ultimate settlement of important political problems. They received the agenda of the War Cabinet, which indicated the hour that their particular business was likely to be discussed and were notified by telephone of changes in this schedule whenever possible. Once they arrived at 10, Downing Street, they had to wait in the antechamber until called in by the Secretary.[81] That final responsibility rested solely with the War Cabinet was clearly established.[82] The departmental ministers were nevertheless completely bound by the War Cabinet's decisions. They might have had no share in particular decisions and might even disagree with them. But as long as they stayed in the Government, they had to defend the War Cabinet's policies in Parliament. In this respect their status was little better than that of junior ministers, even though their resignation value was greater. This enabled them to exert some political pressure on the War Cabinet, which was threatened by many foes both inside and outside Parliament, notably by Asquith's Opposition, Press agitation, and the maneuvers of certain military leaders.[83]

The Distribution of Functions among Departments

The separation between Cabinet and departments had removed a strong barrier against an increase in the number of departments. Even under Asquith, the existing departmental divisions had proved inadequate to deal with many new government tasks. This had become apparent in the establishment of numerous interdepartmental committees to handle such important business as shipping, import control, the increase of food production in the British Isles, the determination of priorities between military and industrial mobilization, and the development of air power.[84] Since early 1916, Curzon had presided as Lord Privy Seal over various bodies that had some responsibility in these fields, including the Shipping

[80] *Ibid.*, p. 1.

[81] Hankey, *Supreme Command,* p. 583; Reconstruction Papers (Hankey), Folio 952; Curzon in 30 H. of L. Deb. (18 June 1918), vol. 269.

[82] The Memorandum of Conversation between Mr. Lloyd George and certain Unionist ex-Ministers, 7 December 1916, stated: "The new arrangement would relieve the Ministers not included in the small War Committee of Cabinet responsibility for the acts of Government. That responsibility would belong exclusively to the War Committee which . . . would be the Cabinet" (Beaverbrook, 1914–16, II, 323).

[83] Beaverbrook, 1917–18, *passim.*

[84] According to Hankey (*Supreme Command,* pp. 226–27), the number of committees registered in a special Directory of Committees was 20 in 1914, 38 in January 1915, 102 in December 1916, and 165 in 1918.

Control Committee and the Air Board.[85] During the summer of 1916 a Manpower Distribution Board had also been established. Such organs had done important work, but many ministers and departments suffered from a "readiness to assume that something resolved at a Committee was thereby an accomplished fact."[86] Lloyd George had long been of the opinion that committees could not effectively discharge executive duties.[87] Curzon agreed. Milner thought it an issue between "men and mandarins."[88]

Consequently, many new ministerial posts were established. There were precedents for such action. In 1915 the failure of a Munitions Committee of the Cabinet had led to the appointment of a Minister of Munitions. In the nineteenth century, too, many new ministerial posts had developed from a feeling that interdepartmental organs could show too little strength against existing departments and interests unless they were placed under responsible ministers of their own. Sometimes these new ministers had unorthodox titles, e.g., Shipping Controller and Food Controller. Sometimes their positions were somewhat uncertain, as in the cases of the Director of National Service and the President of the Air Board, a predecessor of the Secretary of State for Air. Lloyd George had "an incurable ambition for the improvisation of some spectacular expedient," one of his political lieutenants commented.[89] Beatrice Webb wrote in her diary at this time: "The Prime Minister intervenes suddenly, when matters become critical, peremptorily reorganizes some department or starts a new one in a few hours, and leaves the new organization to find its own level in a hostile world of old-established Government offices."[90]

For new posts Lloyd George often also attracted new men who for a time did not sit in Parliament. He appointed a puritanical shipping-owner, Maclay, as Shipping Controller; the manager of a wholesale firm, Devonport, as Food Controller; the Mayor of Birmingham, Neville Chamberlain, as (a rather unsuccessful) Director of National Services; and a lawyer-businessman, Robert Horne, as Director of Materials and Priority. A railway manager who had originally organized military transport behind the front lines in France, Eric Geddes, became Controller of Shipbuilding and later First Lord of the Admiralty. (He became an honorary general as well as an honorary admiral.) Important tasks were also given to newspaper owners. Lord Northcliffe became Chairman of the British War Mission in the United States and later Director of Propaganda in Enemy Countries. His brother, Lord Rothermere, was Secretary of State for Air for a short time. Beaverbrook became Minister for Information. With these appointments Lloyd George killed two birds with one stone: he obtained

---

[85] Cf. *Life of Curzon*, III, 142; Cd. 9005 (1918), p. 57 and *passim*.
[86] Lloyd George, *Memoirs*, III, 1250.
[87] *Ibid.*, p. 1218; Hankey, *Supreme Command*, p. 548ff.
[88] *Life of Carson*, p. 412.   [89] Addison, *Politics from Within*, II, 186.
[90] Beatrice Webb's *Diaries* (15 May 1917), p. 89; for resistance to the Ministry of Information, see Beaverbrook, *1917–18*, p. 288ff; to the Ministry of Shipping, Lloyd George, *Memoirs*, III, 1217–18; to the Ministry of Health, Addison, *Politics from Within*, II, 221ff.

the support both of self-appointed representatives of "public opinion" and of seasoned managers.

Eleven new departments had thus been instituted by the end of the war: the ministries of Labor, Shipping, Food, Air, National Service, Pensions, Information, Health, Reconstruction, Munitions, and Blockade. A number of them were to disappear fairly soon. But the precedent had been set. Public opinion would thereafter quickly demand the establishment of new departments whenever particularly serious problems arose. The solution to a bad distribution of existing government tasks among departments came to be sought not in the reform of the intra- or inter-departmental structure but in further division of tasks among new departments.

The Relation between the Cabinet and the Departments

Until 1916 each important department had direct access to the Cabinet through its minister. The minister represented in council the views he and his leading civil servants had threshed out. No civil servants were admitted to Cabinet sessions. Each minister was personally responsible for seeing that his department implemented Cabinet decisions. To remember these decisions, a minister could rely only on his memory, because only the Prime Minister, who had to submit a report of the Cabinet discussions to the King, could take notes at Cabinet meetings.[91]

The War Cabinet made basic changes in this procedure. Although each departmental minister received the Cabinet agenda and a list of persons invited and of outstanding issues to be discussed, and although he could request an invitation to a meeting that might touch directly on his department, to attend Cabinet meetings was now a privilege rather than a right. A network of committees intervened between the Cabinet and the departments. The authority and longevity of these committees differed widely. Some were charged only with investigating or settling a particular issue. Others received mandates to decide issues in a particular field independently. The only link between the Cabinet and these committees might be that a member of the War Cabinet presided over them.

Another important change was that the War Cabinet began to deal directly with officials, in certain cases over the heads of their nominal ministerial chiefs. This was true, above all, of the Service Chiefs. But Lloyd George insisted, more generally, that the War Cabinet had the right to summon any civil servant or expert to its meetings, and he eagerly did so.[92] No less than 248 outsiders attended War Cabinet sessions in 1917.[93] Lloyd George often harassed ministers with their own subordinates' views, which he collected in the most curious ways. This went so far that Carson as First Lord of the Admiralty found it necessary to issue a formal order forbidding his staff to gossip about departmental affairs even in the

[91] Asquith, *Fifty Years in Parliament*, II, 197; Hankey, *Diplomacy*, p. 75.
[92] Lloyd George, *Memoirs*, III, 1064, 1171; Curzon in 30 H. of L. Deb. (19 June 1918), col. 270.
[93] Cd. 9005 (1918), p. 2.

basement canteen, where some of Lloyd George's secretaries used to pick up tidbits of information.[94]

The Establishment of the Cabinet Secretariat

The Cabinet Secretariat developed from the Secretariat of the C.I.D. The Secretary of the C.I.D., Hankey, had served successively (and successfully) as Secretary of the War Council, the Dardanelles Committee, and the War Committee. But Asquith had continued to resist having a Secretary at actual Cabinet sessions. He considered this in conflict with "established constitutional doctrine and practice."[95] Such niceties meant little to a man like Lloyd George, who, according to Churchill, was, "the greatest master of getting things done and putting things through that I ever knew."[96] They also meant little to a businessman like Bonar Law or to proconsuls like Curzon and Milner, who had been accustomed to efficiently organized, self-contained colonial administrations.[97]

Under Hankey's guidance, the former Secretariat of the C.I.D. was therefore reconstructed in December 1916 into the Secretariat of the War Cabinet.[98] The staff, which had until then been recruited mainly from liaison officers of the Admiralty, War Office, India Office, and Colonial Office, was expanded by including ten Assistant Secretaries, each of whom was charged with maintaining close liaison with a particular group of departments.[99] Each Cabinet or Cabinet committee meeting was thereafter attended by at least two Secretaries, who were to record deliberations and decisions and index decisions systematically so they could be referred to on a moment's notice. Amery wrote, "The one injunction Hankey burned upon our souls was that a minute must always end with a definite decision. This was not easy after some particularly woolly discussions. But my experience was that if one invented the best decision one could think of, it was rarely queried by those concerned."[100] The complete

---

[94] Life of Carson, pp. 420–21; Laski, Reflections, pp. 124–25; Jennings, Cabinet Government, pp. 122–23. About a month after Lloyd George's arrival in 10, Downing Street Beveridge wrote: "For the moment not only the last Government but the whole civil service is out of office, and much of the subordinate government of the country is in the hands of amateurs" (Power and Influence, p. 142).

[95] Chamberlain, Down the Years, p. 111.

[96] Churchill, Thoughts and Adventures, pp. 59–60; cf. Churchill, World Crisis, III, 256–57.

[97] Life of Curzon, III, 126–27, 148–49; Curzon in 30 H. of L. Deb. (19 June 1918), cols. 262–82. For Curzon's views in 1904, see Esher Papers, II, 59. For those of Milner, see Beaverbrook, 1917–18, p. xxi.

[98] Hankey, Supreme Command, pp. 582–91.   [99] Cd. 9005 (1918), p. 3.

[100] Amery, My Political Life, II, 94. Clemenceau allegedly said at the end of a particularly stormy meeting at Versailles in 1919 that the matter might now safely be left to Hankey, who would undoubtedly know what had been decided (Hollis, One Marine's Tale, pp. 71–72). Cf. Sylvester, Lloyd George, pp. 30–31, and Hankey, Supreme Command, p. 790. During World War II, there circulated in the War Cabinet Secretariat a little rhyme that read:

> And so while the great ones depart to their dinner
> The Secretary stays, growing thinner and thinner
> Racking his brain to record and report
> What he thinks that they think that they ought to have thought.
>   (Alanbrooke, p. 320).

minutes were circulated, after revisions if necessary, to "the Secretaries of State and to the *more important* offices intimately concerned with the conduct of the war,"[101] and "in addition, copies of the War Cabinet minutes *affecting them* [were] sent to all other departments."[102] "Attention was regularly called in circulating the minutes to any decisions requiring action by a particular department, and to decisions which, while not calling for action, appeared to concern the department in any way."[103] Foreign Office and War Cabinet telegrams were circulated in similar fashion. At the same time, the Secretariat circulated to all departments weekly reports drafted in the Secretariat or in certain departments for the benefit of the War Cabinet.[104] Lloyd George wrote:

I also thought it not only desirable, but imperative, having regard to the number of decisions taken in the past which had not been carried out, to charge the Secretary with the duty of keeping in touch with further developments and of reporting to me from time to time what action had been taken in the various departments on these Cabinet orders.[105]

The Secretariat also commented on certain departmental proposals. It kept a constantly changing list containing the War Cabinet agenda for a given day; the matters that had been referred to individual War Cabinet members for settlement or report; and the matters that were not yet suitable for submission to the War Cabinet, but would be submitted in due course.[106]

Alongside the Cabinet Secretariat developed the Prime Minister's Secretariat, which functioned as Lloyd George's personal intelligence staff. With some prescience, Hankey had thought that difficulties might arise from such a staff. After a conversation with his new deputy, Tom Jones, on 12 December 1916, he "caught on to a scheme of organization of the office into two groups—machinery and ideas—which may fit with these people."[107] The Prime Minister's Secretariat was not housed, like the Cabinet Secretariat, in Whitehall Gardens, but in special quarters in the garden of 10, Downing Street, soon nicknamed the Garden Suburb. Its staff, headed by Professor W. G. S. Adams, was generally recruited from younger persons who had not risen through normal civil service channels. They soon provoked friction in Whitehall. "Of secretaries, Lloyd George never could have enough," Jones wrote.[108] Others have spoken, somewhat less kindly, of "his working through friends and sub-

101 Reconstruction Papers (Hankey), Folio 951. Italics mine.
102 Cd. 9005 (1918), p. 3. Italics mine.
103 Reconstruction Papers (Hankey), Folio 951.
104 Cd. 9005 (1918), p. 3.
105 Lloyd George, *Memoirs,* III, 1080–81 ; but cf. Mackenzie–Grove, p. 342.
106 Reconstruction Papers (Hankey), Folio 953.
107 Hankey, *Supreme Command,* pp. 589–90.
108 Jones, *Lloyd George,* p. 94. According to Milner, Lloyd George "scattered his ideas all around him like diamonds, but he had acquired a retinue to follow him to pick them up" *(Life of Milner,* p. 320).

ordinates who could not commit him."[109] Again and again it was emphasized that neither the Cabinet Secretariat nor the Prime Minister's Secretariat had any right to occupy themselves with business that properly
came under the legal jurisdiction of individual departments.[110] Jones
explained to the Haldane Committee:

The members of the Secretariat do not consider it to be within the scope of
their duties to initiate or carry out administrative action. Their instructions
are to deal directly with the ministers in charge of departments, and it rests
with the minister concerned to decide whether to transact particular pieces of
business personally or through his officers with members of the War Cabinet
Secretariat.[111]

But earlier Sir Hubert Llewellyn Smith had declared that

he was impressed with the danger of unduly increasing this personal staff [of
the Prime Minister] in size or influence, for the reason that the Prime Minister
and other ministers might tend to rely upon members of such a staff for advice
upon questions which should properly be referred to the administrative department whose duty it was to deal with them.[112]

A bitter quip soon circulated in Whitehall to the effect that the country
was governed by two persons, Lloyd George and the man with whom
Lloyd George had last spoken.[113] And Lloyd George spoke more often
with secretaries than with ministers.

The War Cabinet Appraised

There was widespread feeling that the introduction of the War Cabinet
system had greatly improved the decisiveness of the direction of the war.
After the War Cabinet's first session, Carson said that "more was done in
a few hours than used to be done in a year."[114] The Cabinet Secretariat
introduced a lasting improvement in preparing and executing Cabinet
business. The War Cabinet met almost daily: in 474 working days, it met
525 times, not counting interallied conferences.[115] Complicated or contentious issues were often delegated to individual War Cabinet members
for further investigation, a practice that at least cleared the agenda, and,
as Hankey caustically wrote, kept Lloyd George's colleagues "busy and
happy."[116] Curzon, for instance, specialized in matters relating to the
Middle East and shipping. Henderson, and after him G. H. Barnes,

---

[109] In a review of Jones' *Lloyd George* in *The Listener,* 11 October 1951.
[110] Reconstruction Papers (Hankey), Folio 954.
[111] Reconstruction Papers (Jones), Folios 966–67.
[112] Reconstruction Papers (Llewellyn Smith), Folio 778.
[113] Amery, *My Political Life,* II, 94–95; Amery, *War Leaders,* p. 70; Hankey,
Supreme Command, pp. 575–77. For Lloyd George's preference for oral briefs, cf.
Sylvester, *Lloyd George,* p. 252.
[114] *Life of Lloyd George,* p. 352.
[115] Curzon, 30 H. of L. Deb. (19 June 1918), col. 267.
[116] Hankey, *Supreme Command,* pp. 668, 789.

occupied themselves with labor problems. General Smuts, who became a member of the War Cabinet in 1917, presided over a War Priorities Committee that sought to allocate scarce resources.[117] The entire system remained flexible, however. Milner above all—"the hub of the machine"[118] and "the perfect chairman of a contentious committee"—managed, with Hankey, to reduce to order the numerous administrative problems that occurred at the top of the hierarchy.[119] Milner once described his own role as that of "the synoptic member of the Cabinet."[120] But he too grumbled: "I sometimes sigh for the old South African days of reconstruction, when there was only one directing brain. It made many mistakes, but it did make something."[121]

Machinery, in other words, could not solve the basic complexities of war at the top. Hankey, the staunchest defender of what efficiency there was in the 1916–18 Cabinet, has revealed that by May 1917 a "general exhaustion of the nation's principal organ of decision" was threatening.[122] He was forced to submit to Lloyd George a memorandum requesting that the first half hour of every Cabinet meeting be reserved for settling outstanding administrative issues. But as so often happens, conditions were perfect only until the next complaint. In June 1918, for instance, Addison protested in a letter to Lloyd George that the immediate problems of the war monopolized the attention of War Cabinet members to such an extent that important domestic issues did not receive due consideration. He wrote:

You are our Chief Minister, and as such hold responsibility for the proceedings and policy of the Government, whether at home or abroad. . . . The difficulties arising out of the war unfortunately are not confined to the field of battle. They exist in great numbers at home and require to be dealt with. If the members of the War Cabinet have their time and mind so occupied that they cannot attend to vital matters at home, it does not in any way detract from the importance of these matters, but it does indicate that as a Government our machinery is inadequate.[123]

This protest caused a change in the committee structure. A Committee of Economic Defence and Development and a Committee on Home Affairs were established. They succeeded in bringing a semblance of order.[124] But most departments continued to resist the non-departmental Cabinet system, and ministers who were not admitted to Cabinet membership protested frequently. One of them was Churchill, whom Lloyd George had brought back into the Government as Minister of Muni-

[117] Reconstruction Papers (Hankey), Folio 950.
[118] Amery, My Political Life, II, 98; Addison, Politics from Within, II, 33–34; cf. Attlee, As It Happened, p. 128; Life of Milner, pp. 316ff., 333–36.
[119] Jones, Lloyd George, p. 97.   [120] Life of Milner, p. 333.
[121] Markham, Return Passage, p. 153.
[122] Hankey, Supreme Command, p. 666ff.
[123] Life of Addison, pp. 164–65; Addison, Politics from Within, II, 226–27.
[124] Ibid., II, 253–55.

tions against great opposition. Churchill regarded as basically defective a system in which he himself "and also the Service ministers were excluded from the Cabinet . . . precluded from exercising any influence on the general policy of the War Cabinet and therefore on the government as a whole."[125]

In practice, moreover, the War Cabinet seldom met alone. "On the average there would be half a dozen others present, and when a highly controversial issue was at stake, an extra twenty might attend."[126] To quote Cecil, "The atmosphere was physically and morally overcrowded."[127] Some characterized the meetings as those of a "beargarden."[128] Yet the fundamental distinction between those who belonged to the Cabinet and those who did not remained intact. The attendance of many outsiders, Beveridge wrote during the Second World War, "no more made the War Cabinet itself into a large body than the presence of counsel, solicitors, and others in the Court of Appeal makes the Court anything but a small body."[129] The Cabinet members *could* meet alone at any time, even though they might have to do so by forming such a body as the War Policy Committee of June 1917 in which they thrashed out their views and differences on the long-run developments of the war in special sessions, uninterrupted by administrative details or urgent political or military decisions.[130]

The War Cabinet system has been severely criticized.[131] In the opinion of Herman Finer, it bore the title of Cabinet only "from habit."[132] Others have defended it with equal conviction, notably Hankey and Amery, in whose opinion "it deserved the title of Cabinet as fully as any Cabinet that I ever attended."[133] Personal factors must influence any definite appraisal. It could not be otherwise, because any judgment is above all dependent on a subjective opinion about the singular personality of Lloyd George, a man so versatile that an unfriendly critic like Keynes could say of him, "Lloyd George is rooted in nothing; he is void and without content; he lives and feeds on his immediate surroundings; . . . he is a prism, as I have heard him described, which collects light and distorts it and is most brilliant if the light comes from many quarters at once; a vampire and a medium in one."[134]

---

[125] Beaverbrook, 1917–18, pp. 126–27.
[126] Jones, *Lloyd George*, p. 96; cf. Hankey, *Supreme Command*, p. 583.
[127] Cecil, p. 16; Chamberlain, *Down the Years*, p. 132.
[128] Hancock–Gowing, p. 91.   [129] *The Times*, 14 February 1942.
[130] Hankey, *Supreme Command*, p. 672ff.
[131] See, e.g., Laski, *Government in Wartime*, pp. 9–10; Jennings, *Cabinet Government*, pp. 69–70, 281; Keith-Gibbs, pp. 110, 134–36. See also 30 H. of L. Deb. (19 June 1918), col. 239ff.
[132] Finer, *Theory and Practice*, p. 582.
[133] Hankey, *Control*, pp. 49–50; Amery, *My Political Life*, II, 107.
[134] Keynes, *Essays in Biography*, p. 37, cf. pp. 15, 36; Amery, *War Leaders*, pp. 71–72; and Hankey, *Supreme Command*, pp. 869–70.

FOUR

THE CABINET BETWEEN THE WARS, 1918–1939

Lloyd George's Coalition Government (1918–22)

Six days before the Armistice of 1918, King George V reluctantly agreed to Lloyd George's demand for a sudden dissolution of Parliament.[1] Elections were held before the end of the year. The coalition of Lloyd George and Bonar Law obtained, with 52 per cent of the votes, more than 80 per cent of the seats. Even Asquith was defeated in the constituency of East Fife, which he had represented for 32 years. Bonar Law said of Lloyd George, "He can be Prime Minister for life if he likes."[2]

Before the elections many ministers—Churchill among them—had pressed for an immediate restoration of the normal Cabinet.[3] The War Cabinet had disintegrated more and more as the year 1918 progressed.[4] Carson had resigned early in that year. Milner had formally left the War Cabinet in April, when he was appointed Secretary of State for War; in December he had even informed Lloyd George that he was no longer interested in a ministerial appointment after the elections, in view of the brusque way the Prime Minister treated him.[5] Curzon had complained in October 1918 about "the lack of frequency of Cabinet meetings."[6] Henderson's successor as Labour's representative in the War Cabinet, G. H. Barnes, who had never been very influential, lost whatever authority he had when he stayed on as a War Cabinet member in spite of the Labour Party's decision in November 1918 to withdraw from the Coalition.[7] Next to the duumvirate of Lloyd George and Bonar Law, Austen Chamberlain was probably the most influential Cabinet member. He had met Lloyd George outside a War Cabinet meeting only once since joining the Cabinet in April 1918.[8]

Between the day the election results were announced and the day he departed for the Paris Conference, Lloyd George had only a few days in which to form his Government. It soon became evident that he had no clear-cut ideas about how it should best be formed. "He had some ideas

---

[1] *Life of King George V*, pp. 328–30.   [2] Beaverbrook, 1917–18, p. 325.
[3] Churchill, *World Crisis*, V, 52; *Life of Lloyd George*, p. 495.
[4] Hankey, *Supreme Command*, pp. 789, 816–17, 843–44.
[5] Beaverbrook, 1917–18, pp. 329–30.   [6] *Life of Curzon*, III, 259–60.
[7] McKenzie, pp. 403–4; Snowden, *Autobiography*, I, 493–96.
[8] Chamberlain, *Down the Years*, p. 137.

about an Imperial Cabinet and a Home Cabinet," wrote Austen Chamberlain, who had suddenly been appointed Chancellor of the Exchequer.

He believed that Milner had communicated some similar plan to Bonar Law, but he had not had time to see it or work out his own ideas. If he brought me into the Cabinet, he would have to bring in others—Long, Churchill, other Secretaries of State, etc. . . . He asked, how could there be a Cabinet at home, when the Prime Minister, Bonar Law, and the Foreign Secretary were all in Paris. They must, to a large extent, be plenipotentiaries—they could not be constantly referring to a Cabinet at home for instructions. His idea had been not to appoint any Cabinet. I then inquired who would be responsible in his absence—who would be in a position to summon a meeting of Ministers if one was required—or to take decisions? "Ah there!" he said, "that is what the King asked. He is very gravely disturbed. I told him that I was prepared to support any decision which Bonar Law took."

Bonar Law, however, insisted that he too had to go to Paris, for a brief period, at any rate. He intended, he said, "to conduct the business by personal conference with individual ministers or groups of ministers." Chamberlain refused to accept the post of Chancellor of the Exchequer without a formal guarantee that he would belong to the Cabinet. "The Prime Minister repeated that he could not do this without including others, and again went through his list; to which Bonar Law retorted, 'that means a Cabinet of fifteen—and that is impossible.' "[9]

This discussion well illustrates the confusion into which the Cabinet system had been plunged as a result of war, the ensuing disturbances in traditional political alignments, and the new international political situation. Eventually, a compromise was reached. Lloyd George, Bonar Law, Curzon, Chamberlain, and Barnes would continue to form the Cabinet for the time being, on the explicit understanding that Chamberlain would join as a person and not ex officio, as Chancellor of the Exchequer. This situation was rather anomalous. In 1919 several ministers, Lloyd George above all, stayed in Versailles nearly all the time. Other ministers traveled to the French capital for *ad hoc* consultations with the Prime Minister. Lloyd George told some of them to remain in Paris.[10] Others, such as Lord Chancellor Birkenhead, he refused to see and ordered to return to London.[11] But such domestic problems as demobilization, financial and economic policy, and unemployment kept pressing. No longer was politics

[9] This paragraph is based exclusively on Austen Chamberlain's report in *Down the Years,* pp. 132–43. In his *Life of Austen Chamberlain* (II, 132–37), Petrie published some fragments of Chamberlain's contemporaneous notes, which contained no fresh information. Chamberlain's report has been accepted as reliable by Robert Blake in his *Life of Bonar Law* (pp. 397–98). Beaverbrook wrote of Chamberlain: "He was trusted and respected and he always told the truth, rare gifts for a man born to public affairs." Birkenhead said of him: "Austen always played the game, and he always lost it" (Beaverbrook, 1917–18, p. xiii).

[10] For an example, see Broad, *Winston Churchill,* p. 172.

[11] Beaverbrook, 1917–18, pp. 330–31.

concentrated on one goal : winning the war at any price. Instead, legitimate differences of opinion arose about the future conduct of affairs. Political ambition became stronger. No longer were the more important departments and departmental ministers content simply to obey directives from the top, nor were they satisfied with the opportunities that *ad hoc* consultations afforded. In practice the departmental ministers came to attend most Cabinet meetings, even though they were not yet among its official members.[12]

In November 1919, it was formally decided to return to the system of the ordinary Cabinet, composed of the more important departmental ministers. Initially, it had twenty members. The Ministers of Munitions, Food, Shipping, Pensions, National Service, and Reconstruction, the First Commissioner of Works, the Chancellor of the Duchy of Lancaster, the Postmaster-General, the Paymaster-General, and the Attorney-General were not included.[13] But the majority of the newer departments soon disappeared under strong parliamentary pressure.[14] The Ministry of Information had been dissolved in November 1918. The Ministry of National Service disappeared in March 1919 and the Ministry of Reconstruction in June. In 1921 the Ministries of Munitions, Shipping, and Food were dissolved. The Ministries of Transport and Pensions survived. But these departments did not obtain the status of the older departments, and usually their ministers were not admitted to the Cabinet, nor were the First Commissioner of Works and other ministers who had rarely crossed the Cabinet threshold even before 1914. The new Air Ministry was a bone of contention. In 1919 it was combined in a personal union with the War Office. Later a separate Secretary of State for Air was again appointed, but at first he too was not given Cabinet membership.[15]

At first, Cabinet committees were used more frequently than before 1914. According to Austen Chamberlain, the Home Affairs Committee was, for a time, "almost a Cabinet within a Cabinet."[16] But usually the task of Cabinet committees was restricted; they dealt with special problems rather than with a segment of Government policy. As time went by, the use of committees decreased. The number of Cabinet committees notwithstanding, the Cabinet itself had to meet more frequently : the average number of sessions per year increased from forty before 1914 to sixty in the interwar period.[17] The wartime practice of charging ministers with special assignments or specific coordinating tasks was maintained. But the House of Commons became increasingly suspicious of ministers without portfolio, whom it regarded as useless accretions. One of its victims was

---

[12] Chamberlain, *Down the Years*, p. 142.
[13] 120 H. of C. Deb. (27 October 1919), cols. 271–72.
[14] Hankey spoke of "mushroom departments" (*Control*, p. 52). An extensive survey of changes in the interdepartmental structure between 1914 and 1956 is given in Chester–Willson (Appendix C, pp. 385–420). For the period since 1956, see Willson, *Supplement*.
[15] Templewood, *Empire of the Air*, pp. 48–49, 94.
[16] Mackintosh, p. 361.   [17] Hancock–Gowing, p. 41.

Addison, who had, in fact, disliked accepting his appointment as Minister without Portfolio as he had readily learned to appreciate the drawbacks of a non-executive department when he served as Minister of Reconstruction during the latter part of the war.[18]

Meanwhile, irritation about the prevailing atmosphere in public life became more widespread. Many shared the opinion of a later chairman of the Conservative Party Organization who wrote to the King that the 1918 Parliament seemed full of "modern and . . . unscrupulous characters."[19] Numerous personal supporters of Lloyd George received knighthoods or peerages. More than a few people saw a connection between this selective shower of honors and the steadily increasing personal election fund that Lloyd George garnered. Many people became equally disturbed about the Prime Minister's publicity-ridden activities at endless international conferences. Within the Government, too, there grew strong resentment about his high-handed actions.[20] Through his direct contacts with foreign heads of Government, the Press, numerous social groups, and a few personal favorites, Lloyd George seemed to take action over the heads of both the Cabinet and the House of Commons. "Cabinet responsibility," complained a minister who was forced to resign, "was a joke."[21]

In particular, the Foreign Secretary, Curzon, was embittered at the way the conduct of foreign policy was largely taken out of his hands. In a letter to Lloyd George (which was never dispatched), Curzon voiced his dissatisfaction as follows:

There has grown up a system under which there are in reality two Foreign Offices: the one for which I am for the time being responsible, and the other at Number 10—with the essential difference between them that, whereas I report not only to you but to all my colleagues everything that I say or do, every telegram that I receive or send, every communication of importance that reaches me, it is often only by accident that I hear what is being done by the other Foreign Office; and even when I am informed officially of what has passed there, it has nevertheless been done, in many cases, without the Foreign Office for which I am responsible knowing that the communication was going to be made or the interview take place.

. . .

I have for long felt that such a situation should not be permitted to continue, and that, if it were not checked, you ought to have a Secretary who will more easily than I conform to this novel conception of Foreign Office duties. Indeed, I should find no pleasure in continuing now, were I not to receive a definite assurance from you that the constitutional relations between the two departments should be re-established and the Foreign Office shall resume its proper function in the State.[22]

---

[18] Jennings, *Cabinet Government*, pp. 73–76; *Life of Addison*, p. 173ff.

[19] *Life of King George V*, p. 333. The King wrote in the margin of this letter: "A great pity. G.R.I." Cf. *Life of Austen Chamberlain*, II, 139.

[20] Beaverbrook, 1917–18, pp. 324–46.

[21] E. S. Montagu, at Cambridge, 11 March 1922 (*Life of Asquith*, II, 337).

[22] *Life of Curzon*, III, 316–17. Curzon's letter was dated, in draft, 2 October 1922. It was never dispatched, presumably because the Coalition was already break-

The anxiety about Lloyd George's methods was also reflected in an attack on the Cabinet Secretariat, which, together with the Prime Minister's Secretariat, was thought to be symbolic of Lloyd George's supposed hankering after a personal, almost presidential, regime. The Secretariat, it was argued in a debate in the House of Commons on 13 June 1922, was unconstitutional.[23] It was prejudicial to the principle of free and secret Cabinet discussions among ministers who were political equals. It interfered with the constitutional responsibilities of the departments and was in fact an instrument the Prime Minister used to dominate his colleagues. The core of the problem, however, was in Lloyd George's highhanded conduct and unorthodox methods rather than in the existence of the Cabinet Secretariat itself. The Cabinet Secretariat, in other words, gained influence because of Lloyd George, more than Lloyd George because of the Cabinet Secretariat. Since 1916 the Secretariat had been saddled with a number of incongruous duties, mainly because Lloyd George had learned to appreciate its nearness and efficiency, and its master, Hankey. For this reason, it had been charged with handling all League of Nations correspondence.[24] For the same reason, Lloyd George used to take Hankey instead of the usual Foreign Office officials to international conferences.[25] If the Cabinet Secretariat thus invaded the professional sphere of other departments, Lloyd George was as much to blame as Hankey. There is some evidence that at various moments Lloyd George considered appointing Hankey to such diverse posts as Secretary of State for War, First Lord of the Admiralty, Chief of the Imperial General Staff, and Permanent Secretary to the Foreign Office. Hankey may at times have been more tempted by such offers than he has publicly suggested.[26] There is no doubt, however, that in the last analysis the Cabinet Secretariat was an auxiliary rather than an agent of power.

Meanwhile, conflicts within the Government and the Conservative Party became more acute daily. They led to a crisis in the autumn of 1922, when Lloyd George's pro-Greek policies threatened to lead to a war with

ing up. For previous indications, see *ibid.*, p. 315; Beaverbrook, 1917–18, pp. 332–34, 396–400; Churchill, *Great Contemporaries*, p. 280, and *Life of Derby*, pp. 428, 432–34. Curzon had himself intended to combine the Prime Ministership and the Foreign Secretaryship if he became Prime Minister of a Conservative Government (*Life of Curzon*, III, 366–67). See also *Life of King George V*, p. 367; Jennings, pp. 219–23; Keith–Gibbs, pp. 59–60, 71–73; Laski, *Reflections*, p. 104; and Carter, pp. 202–5. For a discussion of Curzon's personality and his relation to Lloyd George, see Beaverbrook, 1917–18, pp. 304–23, 334ff, 397ff.

[23] 155 H. of C. Deb. (13 June 1922), cols. 213–75. For a critical analysis of the objections against the Cabinet Secretariat, see Hankey, *Diplomacy* (pp. 61–82), which was written in 1922 but not published until 1946. In addition, see Smellie, pp. 236–37, 284; Carter, pp. 202–5; and Johnson, pp. 183–90.

[24] Chester–Willson, pp. 290–91. For the Commonwealth Prime Ministers' demand in 1918 that the Cabinet Office rather than the Colonial Office should handle business with the self-governing Dominions, see Hankey, *Supreme Command*, pp. 832–34.

[25] Sylvester, *Lloyd George*, pp. 27–28.

[26] Cf. Beaverbrook, 1917–18, p. 328; Hankey, *Supreme Command*, pp. 329, 594, 756, 794; and Johnson, p. 280.

Turkey. At the same time, the Lloyd George Liberals and the Conservatives began to discuss whether the Coalition should be maintained for the forthcoming elections. This issue was of vital importance to Lloyd George in view of the break-up of the Liberal Party, which he himself had engineered. He had long realized this, especially in 1921, when Bonar Law had been forced to resign his office because of ill health. At that time, Lloyd George had discussed the matter with the King's Secretary, who informed George V of the Prime Minister's quandary. The King had replied to his Private Secretary in a rather curious letter:

I am sorry the Prime Minister is low on account of B.L.'s resignation: but he must not be despondent as I firmly believe *he* is now more necessary to this country than he ever was & that the vast majority of the people are behind him. . . . I should agree to anything that would help him most. If the Cabinet resigned & there was a "general post" & he dropped out Illingworth, Addison or any others: or if he formed (as has been advocated) a National Party: but the latter I agree would take time, as it is a big change. . . . You can tell the P.M. that I have complete confidence in him & will do everything in my power to help him. . . . I am very strong in maintaining a Coalition Government. I am sure it is the best plan at the present moment & until these many very difficult questions have been settled. Anyhow I am against a general election which would upset everything. There really ought to be two P.M.'s! No man can do the work he, L.G., has to do now. I quite understand his feeling lonely & almost lost without B.L., who did so much for him.[27]

Lloyd George then stayed on for another year as an apparently unassailable Prime Minister.[28] He succeeded in enlisting the support of Churchill and the most important leaders of the Conservative Party—the new Leader, Austen Chamberlain; Balfour; Birkenhead; and the then Chancellor of the Exchequer, Sir Robert Horne—for entering the elections as a Coalition. But a few ministers—the President of the Board of Trade, Stanley Baldwin (regarded by Birkenhead and his friends as "the Idiot Boy of the Cabinet"),[29] Curzon (somewhat hesitantly) and a considerable number of Conservative undersecretaries—opposed the plan. Conservatives in the country had opposed the Coalition for a long time.[30] On 19 October 1922, a meeting of Conservative M.P.'s was held at the Carlton Club. Baldwin and Bonar Law, who had recovered his health and resumed active participation in politics, inspired the assembly to abandon the Coalition. Lloyd George at once resigned and never again served as a minister. Balfour, Birkenhead, Austen Chamberlain, and Horne followed him for some time into the political wilderness. Churchill heard the news in hospital and was soon to remark ruefully that within a few weeks he had lost his appendix, his seat in the Cabinet, and his seat in Parliament. The split

[27] Beaverbrook, 1917–18, p. 337.
[28] See, however, his letter to Austen Chamberlain in *Life of Austen Chamberlain*, II, 174–78.
[29] *Life of Derby*, p. 459.
[30] For an extensive analysis, see McKenzie, pp. 83–109.

between the "brains," between the "inner Cabinet" and the House of Commons, was complete.[31]

The Conservative Government of Bonar Law and Baldwin
(1922–24)

Bonar Law's Conservative Cabinet—according to Birkenhead's later secretary "a politically parvenu Cabinet"—won the elections of 1922.[32] Jones commented, "Baldwin and Bonar Law embodied the prevailing mood of negation perfectly: the widespread desire for stability in place of sensation, sobriety for fireworks, an end to personal government and inflated secretariats."[33]

During the election campaign Bonar Law had promised to abolish the Cabinet Secretariat. As often happens, campaign promises far exceeded government practice. The Garden Suburb was pulled down. All correspondence concerning League of Nations affairs was transferred back to the Foreign Office.[34] The number of persons working in the Cabinet Secretariat was cut from 144 in 1922 to 38 in 1923.[35] The limelight was definitely taken off the Cabinet Secretariat. Yet its role as a link between the Cabinet and the departments was fully preserved. Soon Hankey was to accompany Bonar Law, as he had accompanied Lloyd George, to a conference with the French Cabinet. Many Prime Ministers have since followed Lloyd George's example and used the Secretariat as their personal staff "to assist them in dealing with problems from a national as distinct from a departmental point of view."[36] Sir Warren Fisher, the Permanent Secretary to the Treasury, tried to bring the Secretary of the Cabinet under the Treasury but failed.[37] Hankey's personal position was strengthened by his appointment in 1923 to the venerable post of Clerk of the Privy Council.

Under Bonar Law the Cabinet resumed its traditional role as a meeting of the most important departmental ministers. The procedure was businesslike, the agenda strict. Debate was curtailed, if necessary, by referring contentious issues to special committees.[38] The Cabinet minutes were reduced to a short account of discussions and decisions. Names of individual ministers were no longer mentioned when divergent opinions were noted.[39] Ministers received letters of reminder containing the conclusions

---

[31] But see Bassett, pp. 11–12.

[32] Bechofer Roberts, *Stanley Baldwin: Man or Miracle?* (1936), p. 118.

[33] In his anonymously published "Lord Baldwin—A Memoir," issued as a pamphlet by *The Times* (1947), p. 6.

[34] Chester–Willson, p. 295.   [35] Carter, p. 202, n. 4.

[36] Hankey, *Diplomacy*, p. 80.   [37] Chester–Willson, p. 291.

[38] Amery, *My Political Life,* II, 246; Jones, *Diary,* p. xxviii.

[39] Jones, *Diary,* p. xix; Hankey, *Supreme Command,* p. 587. The point was thought important because the naming of persons in the minutes might create opportunities for members of the Cabinet "to hansardize one another." Salisbury, in particular, had resisted note-taking in Cabinet for this reason (Hankey, *Diplomacy,* p. 75). Apparently, an earlier decision had been made under Lloyd George to restrict

reached on their particular items of business instead of the full minutes.[40] The pace of politics slackened considerably. Asquith's daughter, Violet Bonham Carter, was to describe the the the difference between Lloyd George and Bonar Law as the difference between "one man suffering from St. Vitus' Dance and another from Sleeping Sickness."[41]

Originally, the Cabinet had only sixteen members, but it soon grew to nineteen under Baldwin, who replaced the dying Bonar Law in 1923. Baldwin's appointment over Curzon's head was a great surprise. Baldwin's rise to power was without much precedent. He had been a junior whip only six years earlier and a Cabinet minister for only two years; few had thought him likely to reach any heights, much less the Prime Ministership.[42] Yet he was to outlast in power most of his rivals, only to be vilified after he retired by public opinion, readily fed by his erstwhile rivals and political enemies, as well as by profound disillusionment with once generally shared pacifist inclinations.

From the structural point of view, little about the Baldwin Cabinet in 1923 was interesting. For a time Baldwin combined the Prime Ministership with the Chancellorship of the Exchequer.[43] Proposals to place the three Service ministers under one Minister of Defence were not accepted. In the autumn of 1923, Baldwin unexpectedly dissolved Parliament on the argument that an effective fight against the prevailing unemployment was possible only if the Conservative Government received a mandate to introduce a measure of protection for British industry. Baldwin's decision turned out to be, in the words of Snowden, "suicide during a fit of temporary insanity."[44] The Conservative Party polled almost as many votes as it had in 1922. But it lost about ninety seats to Labour and the Asquith and Lloyd George Liberals, who had reunited under the old banner of free trade. Although the Conservatives continued to be the strongest party in the House of Commons, the Government lost its work-

---

the Cabinet minutes to conclusions only (*ibid.*, p. 76; Amery, *My Political Life*, II, 92; Johnson, p. 187; Mackintosh, p. 366). According to Sidney Webb, Hankey still made the minutes too full in 1924, "putting in more than the bare conclusions come to; and not completely realizing the danger of their coming to light in politically hostile hands" (*Webb Memorandum*, p. 18). It has been argued that the naming of ministers in recording differences of opinion in Cabinet meetings conflicts with the principle of collective responsibility; since the King receives the Cabinet minutes, he would be informed unnecessarily and unconstitutionally of divergencies of opinion within the Cabinet (see Amery, *Constitution*, pp. 74–75; Jennings, *Cabinet Government*, pp. 330–38; and Morrison, pp. 12–14). When Eden resigned as Foreign Secretary in 1938, however, the King protested that he had not been informed in time about the pending disagreement. It was decided that the Cabinet minutes should henceforth be sent in draft to the King at the same moment that they were submitted to the Prime Minister for approval (*Life of King George VI*, pp. 334–36).

[40] Mackintosh, p. 366.   [41] Churchill, *Great Contemporaries*, p. 139.

[42] Heasman, p. 470.

[43] Baldwin had first offered the Exchequer to a former Liberal Chancellor, McKenna. McKenna was prepared to accept only if he received one of the two City of London seats. An attempt to achieve this failed. During the period when Baldwin himself took charge of the Treasury, the Financial Secretary, Sir William Joynson-Hicks, was made a Cabinet member (cf. Grigg, *Prejudice and Judgment*, pp. 117–18).

[44] Lyman, p. 18.

ing majority. Since neither the Labour Party with 191 seats nor the Liberals with 159 could claim a majority, Baldwin decided, at the King's insistence, not to resign at once but to meet Parliament.[45] On 21 January 1924, his Government was defeated by the combined votes of the Socialists and the great majority of the Liberals.

The First Labour Government of MacDonald (1924)

A period of complex intrigues had preceded Baldwin's dismissal.[46] The idea that as Leader of the Opposition the Socialist MacDonald might be charged to form a Government was frightening to many, and there were countless schemes to avoid it. There was agitation for a Conservative Cabinet with Liberal support or a Liberal Cabinet with Conservative support. There were pleadings for a non-political interim Cabinet or a temporary national coalition of all parties. New party alignments under different leaders were canvassed. Both the Conservative Leader, Baldwin, and the Liberal Leader, Asquith, opposed such anti-Socialist maneuvers, however. What MacDonald called "an insane miracle" happened.[47] For the first time in British history, the King appointed a Socialist Prime Minister.

Of the Socialist leaders, only a few—e.g., Henderson and Clynes, who had served under Lloyd George during the war—had had previous ministerial experience. Even the new Prime Minister had had none. To avoid internal squabbles and the undoubted inconveniences of direct election by the Parliamentary Party, MacDonald was given a free hand in choosing his Cabinet.[48] He was fortified by a memorandum from the ever-ready Clerk of Labour, Sidney Webb, who drew attention to various technical difficulties in such matters as representation in the House of Lords, the appointment of Household officers and Undersecretaries, "the possibility of strengthening weak ministers by putting their subjects under Cabinet committees," and the need for close social contacts with the Parliamentary Party.[49] But to find out what posts were to be filled, MacDonald consulted *Whitaker's Almanack*.[50]

Unprecedented problems arose.[51] In spite of the King's affable attitude in such matters as court etiquette and official dress, relations with the Court were not free of difficulties.[52] Lansbury, the left-wing Editor of

---

[45] *Life of King George V*, p. 382.
[46] *Life of King George V*, p. 383; Lyman, pp. 83–84.
[47] Bassett, p. 17.   [48] *Webb Memorandum*, pp. 8–9.
[49] *Ibid.*, pp. 9–10.
[50] Thomas, *My Story*, p. 75; Snowden, *Autobiography*, II, 596–98; *Webb Memorandum*, p. 8. For MacDonald's views on the place of the Prime Minister in the British political system, see his *Socialism and Government* (1909), II, 28ff.
[51] Cf. *Webb Memorandum*, p. 8ff, and Lyman, pp. 96–107.
[52] *Life of King George V*, pp. 391–92. But when King George was asked how he got on with his first Labour Government, he allegedly replied, "Very well. My grandmother would have hated it; my father would have tolerated it; but I move with the times" (cf. Mackintosh, p. 515).

the *Daily Herald,* was *persona non grata* in Buckingham Palace because of his professed republican sympathies. MacDonald offered him the Ministry of Transport without a seat in the Cabinet. He refused.[53] It was difficult to find persons in Socialist circles who were considered fit for the Household Offices. Acting on a suggestion of Webb, MacDonald proposed that the King do away with these appointments in the future.[54] But the suggestion was opposed by Balfour, who preferred to keep these traditional "sops wherewith to reward those supporters who were not qualified for ministerial office."[55]

More substantial difficulties arose with regard to the Government's representation in the House of Lords, in which the Labour Party had hardly any members. One was Lord (Bertrand) Russell, "but apparently his matrimonial history was an absolute bar to any appointment under the Crown."[56] The possibility of appointing new peers clashed with Socialist ethics, which rejected hereditary titles.[57] MacDonald sought the support of a few peers who had hitherto hardly been thought to belong to the Socialist fold. The ex-Liberal Haldane became Lord Chancellor. Lord Parmoor, "once a Conservative M.P. and a devout Anglican lawyer," became Lord President of the Council.[58] A former Indian Viceroy, Lord Chelmsford, was appointed First Lord of the Admiralty. He was introduced to the new Cabinet by Webb, "as he had met none of them before, except Haldane (and perhaps, Parmoor)."[59] The supervision of the Air Ministry was entrusted to a former officer, C. B. (soon Lord) Thompson. Such appointments offered a solution for filling offices for which Labour politicians were considered poorly qualified. They improved the Government's prestige in non-Socialist circles. "No one could pretend that a Cabinet containing Haldane, Parmoor, and Chelmsford was either contemptible or likely to ruin the Empire."[60] In Socialist circles, however, such appointments were often less well received.

There were also difficulties regarding the Law Officers. Haldane made his participation in the Government conditional on his becoming Lord Chancellor and being charged with directing the C.I.D. His Conservative predecessor, Lord Cave, was prepared to continue performing a number

---

[53] *Life of King George V*, pp. 384–85; *Webb Memorandum*, pp. 13–14; *Life of Lansbury,* p. 225; *Life of Cripps,* pp. 162–63. Under the second Labour Government, Herbert Morrison was admitted to the Cabinet as Minister of Transport. Rather ironically, Lansbury stated in 1934 (when he was Leader of the Labour Party) that "invariably, Cabinets have been too big. Everyone who had a big pull wanted to be in the Cabinet and every minister of importance needed a seat in it. The result was the Cabinet would not work" (*My England,* p. 128).

[54] *Webb Memorandum,* p. 9.

[55] *Life of King George V,* p. 390; cf. Anson, II, Part I, 157–58. Finally, some Household Offices were permanently taken out of politics.

[56] *Webb Memorandum,* p. 15.

[57] For a time Labour sought to compromise between ethics and expediency by raising only childless commoners to the peerage. When Sidney Webb became Lord Passfield, Beatrice Webb refused to use her new official title.

[58] Lyman, p. 99.   [59] *Webb Memorandum,* p. 13.

[60] *Ibid.,* p. 13.

of the Lord Chancellor's judicial duties in Haldane's place.[61] The office of Solicitor-General was given to a Socialist politician, who simultaneously became King's Counsel and a Member of Parliament. A Conservative Scottish lawyer became Lord Advocate of Scotland since no suitable Labour candidate was available.[62] The Cabinet counted a few more ex-Liberals among its members. This left less room for Trade Union representatives and the radical Clydesiders than each group thought it deserved. In many instances, these groups were deliberately passed over, as they were for the office of First Lord of the Admiralty. The Admiralty was "a most difficult post to fill," according to Webb; "the Sea Lords with Beatty at their head might have resigned in disgust if a Trade Unionist had been First Lord; and might have been sullen and obstructive if a mere 'socialist agitator' had been put there."[63] Contrary to his initial intention to confine the Cabinet to fourteen members, MacDonald had to increase its size to twenty, "various important persons having refused to take office unless in Cabinet."[64]

There was evident satisfaction among Socialists that the Labour Party had been invited to form the Government. But at the same time there was a good deal of uncertainty about whether it was tactically right to accept Government responsibility with less than a third of the seats in the House of Commons. One reason for accepting office was that otherwise the Liberals might have formed the Government and the Conservatives might have replaced Labour as the official Opposition, with Labour members occupying the invidious place below the gangway on the Government side of the House.[65] Since the Government was dependent on Liberal support, its program inevitably had to be very moderate. The position of the Cabinet, accused by its own more ardent followers of betraying the cause of socialism and treated patronizingly by the other two big parties, was far from easy. During its short life, it came face to face with the realities of government for the first time. As MacDonald said in the House of Commons:

Until you have been in office, until you have seen those files warning Cabinet ministers of the dangers of legislation, or that sort of thing, you have not had the experience of trying to carry out what seems to be a simple thing, but which becomes a complex, an exceedingly difficult, and a laborious and almost heart-breaking thing when you come to be a member of a Cabinet in a responsible Government.[66]

---

[61] Haldane, *Autobiography*, pp. 319–25; *Life of Haldane*, II, 145–47.
[62] Lyman, p. 103; *Webb Memorandum*, p. 9.
[63] *Webb Memorandum*, p. 12.
[64] *Webb Memorandum*, pp. 15–16, and Beatrice Webb's *Diaries, 1912–24*, p. 263. A remarkable incident occurred when MacDonald intended to exclude the only Socialist with Cabinet experience, Arthur Henderson, and charge him (as Labour Party Secretary) with maintaining liaison between the Government and the Party. Henderson refused the appointment and remained equally adamant when offered the Duchy. He finally forced MacDonald to appoint him Home Secretary (cf. Lyman, p. 102, and *Webb Memorandum*, p. 14).
[65] *Webb Memorandum*, p. 8.   [66] Lyman, p. 138.

Haldane thought MacDonald's Cabinet was "certainly the most businesslike Cabinet I have sat in."[67] "It is a great advantage," he wrote in April 1924, "having a Cabinet Secretariat with an agenda and minutes, and Hankey does his job to perfection. MacDonald is a better chairman than Asquith was, which may be due to the new system. He keeps us to the point and gets his decisions."[68] New rules were established for the timely circulation of Cabinet papers, before matters could come up for discussion in Cabinet.[69] The atmosphere in the Cabinet became less formal than before. The traditional ban on smoking was lifted, never to be reintroduced by later Cabinets.[70]

MacDonald's leadership was nevertheless subject to an objection that became increasingly serious as time passed. Against the express advice of the King, MacDonald had decided to combine the offices of Prime Minister and Foreign Secretary.[71] George V had warned that even Salisbury, in spite of all his experience, had been unable to do justice to his function as Foreign Secretary except at the expense of his qualities as Prime Minister, even though he combined the offices during a period (1895–1900) when business was far less pressing. MacDonald "worked all day, every day, and often far into the night."[72] But as the King's official biographer has written:

Mr. MacDonald's achievements as Foreign Secretary were quick, startling and beneficial. . . . But for these achievements he paid a formidable price. The effort of those nine months was so gigantic that it damaged his health; his powers of assimilation, memory, and concentration were seriously overstrained. The pressure of external affairs prevented him, moreover, from devoting to internal politics the close attention that they merited; mistakes were made. Above all, the cloud of overwork that hid the Prime Minister from his colleagues and supporters produced an impression of misty and even conceited aloofness—an impression which, as it hardened into a grievance, created an ever-widening rift between Mr. MacDonald and the rank and file of his own party.[73]

Baldwin's Second Conservative Government (1924–29)

MacDonald's first Cabinet lasted only ten months. After new elections (in which the Liberals lost 75 per cent of their seats), it was succeeded by a new Conservative Cabinet under Baldwin. The rift between the Liberals and the Conservative Coalitionists was ended: Austen Chamberlain became Foreign Secretary, Balfour soon afterwards became Lord

---

[67] Haldane, *Autobiography*, pp. 327–28; *Webb Memorandum*, pp. 19–20.
[68] *Life of Haldane*, II, 151, 160.
[69] Jennings, *Cabinet Government*, p. 246.
[70] Snowden, *Autobiography*, II, 705–6; *Webb Memorandum*, p. 19.
[71] *Life of King George V*, p. 385; cf. *Esher Papers*, I, 270.
[72] Petrie, p. 144.
[73] *Life of King George V*, p. 388; cf. *Life of Haldane*, II, 180–81; *Holmes-Laski Correspondence*, p. 628; H. R. G. Greaves, "Complacency or Challenge," *Political Quarterly*, XXXI (1961), 58–60.

President of the Council, and Birkenhead became Secretary of State for India.[74] Surprising even to Churchill, who had fought recent elections as an Independent Conservative, was his appointment as Chancellor of the Exchequer. Some slight alterations were made in the Government's structure. Once more, the Attorney-General became a member of the Cabinet, which had 20 members.[75] At the insistence of the Colonial Secretary, Amery, the Colonial Office was split into two departments, a Dominions Office, which dealt with the self-governing parts of the Commonwealth, and the Colonial Office, which continued to rule the dependencies. Although the number of departments was increased by this split, it as yet had little effect at Cabinet level, since Amery himself continued to act as Secretary of State for both the Dominions and the Colonies.[76] Decisions were not always easily made, and Baldwin "had a poor hand at keeping order."[77] But with the exception of the General Strike of 1926, the politics of the period was rather uneventful. The tranquillity of political life was reflected in the absence of drastic reforms in the Cabinet's structure. The pace of politics slackened again. "I am almost the only minister who is in London, and I am making it a three or four days a week affair," Birkenhead wrote in September 1928.[78] A Conservative member of the House of Commons sighed, "The snores of the Government resound throughout the country."[79] The average age of the Cabinet was high. To quote Birkenhead once more:

It seems certain that Baldwin, if returned to power at the next General Election, will find himself confronted by a depletion of old and experienced ministers, due either to ill-health or other causes, the like of which has not confronted a Prime Minister—not even Bonar Law—in my political memory. I am entirely in favor of giving a chance to the young men. Nor do I believe in too many new arrivals without departmental experience in the Cabinet at the same time.[80]

But the electorate freed Baldwin from this dilemma. In 1929 the Conservative Party was badly defeated. Once again MacDonald returned to office at the head of a Labour minority Government.

MacDonald's Second Labour Government (1929–31)

At first glance, political circumstances in 1929 seemed more favorable for a Labour Government than they had been in 1924. Britain had

[74] Sir Robert Horne, who had been Chancellor of the Exchequer in 1921 and 1922, was offered the Ministry of Labour. He refused, never to return to high office afterwards. For the low status of the Ministry of Labour, see also Beatrice Webb's *Diaries, 1912–24*, pp. 258, 264; and Snowden, *Autobiography*, II, 610.

[75] Grigg, *Prejudice and Judgment*, p. 147.

[76] Chester–Willson, p. 189. Sidney Webb also combined both posts in 1929, but the need to accommodate Thomas in a senior post in 1930 led to the latter's appointment as a separate Secretary of State for the Dominions. Under the National Government in 1931, Thomas again combined both posts.

[77] Vansittart, *The Mist Procession*, p. 354.

[78] *Life of Birkenhead*, II, 295.   [79] Brabazon, p. 162.

[80] *Life of Birkenhead*, II, 295.

learned that a Socialist Cabinet would not necessarily resort to a revolution nor hand over the country to the dogmatic experiments of inexperienced dilettantes. Labour was now stronger: it had almost a hundred more seats in the House of Commons than it had had in 1924. This seemed to give the party a better opportunity to follow its own policies. Within the party, too, the arrival of a new minority Government met with less resistance. The Trade Union leader, Ernest Bevin, had failed to persuade the Party Conference of 1925 to pledge the party against taking office with only a minority of seats in Commons.[81] Since then the failure of the General Strike of 1926 had further discredited the idea of direct industrial action. Hence, the advocates of moderate parliamentary action were securely in control by 1929.

The actual process of forming the Cabinet, however, was accompanied by considerable difficulties. MacDonald was given less freedom to choose his colleagues than he had enjoyed in 1924. A good deal of personal discord appeared among the "Big Five" in the Labour party: MacDonald, Snowden, Henderson, Thomas, and Clynes.[82] If he could not again combine the Foreign Office with the Prime Ministership, MacDonald wished to appoint his most trusted political lieutenant, Thomas, Foreign Secretary. Henderson, however, also claimed this post. MacDonald's offer to forgo the Prime Ministership and take office as Foreign Secretary found no support. Henderson succeeded in asserting his will. Thomas was charged as Lord Privy Seal with coordinating efforts to combat unemployment. Snowden again became Chancellor of the Exchequer.[83]

The greatest difficulties the Cabinet encountered in the two years of its existence were not so much in foreign policy as in domestic economic policy. Admittedly, a good deal of friction on foreign policy persisted between Henderson and MacDonald, who continued to play an active part, particularly in Anglo-American relations.[84] Some ministers were vexed at the obstinate attitude Snowden showed as Chancellor of the Exchequer in settling the problem of war reparations.[85] But such problems were eclipsed by the serious domestic economic and social dislocations of the depression era.

As Lord Privy Seal and Minister for Employment, Thomas bore the principal responsibility for devising measures to combat the depression

---

[81] *Life of Bevin*, pp. 258–60; McKenzie, p. 427; Bassett, p. 313.

[82] Bassett, pp. 27–28; *Life of King George V*, pp. 435–36; Dalton, *Memoirs*, I, 210ff; Jennings, *Cabinet Government*, p. 68.

[83] As in 1924, it was also difficult in 1929 to find suitable candidates for the Law Offices. The office of Attorney-General went to a Liberal, Sir William Jowitt, who then joined the Labour Party. A son of Lord Parmoor, Sir Stafford Cripps, became Solicitor-General although he did not find a seat in Parliament until long after his appointment. A Liberal lawyer who stood as Labour candidate for election later in 1929 became Lord Advocate. A non-political jurist who never became a member of the House of Commons became Solicitor-General for Scotland (see Bassett, p. 27).

[84] Vansittart, *The Mist Procession*, pp. 392–93; *Life of King George V*, p. 435.

[85] Vansittart, *The Mist Procession*, pp. 377–79; *Life of King George V*, pp. 440–42.

and its consequences. Three ministers were to assist him: the First Commissioner of Works, Lansbury (who, unlike 1924, was now included in the Cabinet), the Chancellor of the Duchy of Lancaster, Sir Oswald Mosley, and the Undersecretary of State for Scotland, T. Johnston. A number of high officials under Sir Horace Wilson, Permanent Secretary to the Ministry of Labour (who was appointed Chief Industrial Adviser in 1930), assisted Thomas and his colleagues. The personal relations among these ministers were not cordial, and their position with respect to the Cabinet, and in particular to the powerful Chancellor of the Exchequer, Snowden, was not very strong.[86] Mosley, whom Thomas regarded as "brainy" but "not a team asset," resigned in 1930 in protest against the lack of imagination of the Government's proposals.[87] He soon became a focus for certain malcontents within the Labour Party.[88] Early in 1931 some members of Parliament—John Strachey and Aneurin Bevan among them—published a pamphlet entitled *A National Policy: An Account of the Emergency Programme Advocated by Sir Oswald Mosley*. They also pointed their guns at the existing government machinery, which they deemed "antiquated and cumbersome."[89] They advocated establishing a "small inner Cabinet committee, consisting of five or six men . . . ministers without portfolio . . . free from the burden of running a great Department of State, so that their whole energies may be devoted to formulating and implementing the general policy of the Government."[90] This Committee should meet frequently with the Prime Minister in the chair, and its decisions should be binding on the departmental ministers, who were to meet from time to time in plenary Cabinet sessions. The scheme met with strong resistance, particularly from Beatrice Webb and from Harold Laski, who found that, if anything, the plan resembled the French *Directoire* of 1795.[91] The pamphlet's authors had denied such allegations. It was by no means their intention to introduce dictatorial methods, so they argued:

There is nothing either more or less democratic about entrusting the ultimate responsibility for the decisions of the Government to a Cabinet of five men, who are free from all men who are too busy to give real consideration to their most vitally important decisions. The only difference is that one system will work while the other does not.[92]

Such thoughts were representative of a feeling of despondency. They were also symptomatic of an attempt to solve problems of policy by tinkering with administrative structures. Almost simultaneously, some politicians who were about to establish a study group called Political and Economic

[86] Cf. Thomas, *My Story*, pp. 167–74; *Life of Lansbury*, pp. 252–59; Snowden, *Autobiography*, II, 874ff.

[87] Thomas, *My Story*, p. 167.   [88] *Life of King George V*, pp. 445–46.

[89] *Mosley Program*, p. 45; Strachey–Joad, p. 329ff.

[90] *Mosley Program*, p. 47.

[91] Beatrice Webb's *Diaries, 1924–1932*, p. 268, and *Life of Laski*, pp. 78–79.

[92] *Mosley Program*, p. 48; Strachey–Joad, pp. 335–36.

Planning (P.E.P.) published *A National Plan for Great Britain.* This contained a proposal to reduce the Cabinet to ten ministers, including a Minister of Defence and a new Minister for Economic Development, who, as chief of a National Planning Commission, would have to reorganize British industry.[93]

Within the Cabinet, too, ministers became increasingly concerned. No matter what measures the Government took and what alterations Mac-Donald made in the government's machinery, the financial and economic situation deteriorated.[94] The international financial crisis led to an alarming run on the British gold reserves. At the same time, government finance became unbalanced, as rising state expenditures faced decreasing tax revenue. Remedial measures were necessary but the various experts disagreed on the diagnosis, and held different opinions as to the nature, the dose, or even the necessity of the remedies. An influential committee under the leadership of Sir George May investigated the possibilities of retrenchment. The Bank of England received short-term loans from France and the United States, but the money was soon exhausted. It was intimated that the prospect of new loans from private bankers in the United States was dependent on whether the Cabinet would indeed introduce further economies in government expenditures. Certain measures were prepared and discussed in a Cabinet Economy Committee composed of Mac-Donald, Henderson, Snowden, Thomas, and the President of the Board of Trade, W. Graham. Simultaneously some discussions were held with the Opposition leaders. Being a minority Government, the Cabinet knew it was dependent on Opposition support, and hoped to find a national solution to a national emergency. But strong disagreement about the exact measures to be taken arose in the Cabinet Economy Committee and in the Cabinet itself. Conflict became particularly acute on the question of whether unemployment benefits might be cut to balance the budget. At the critical moment a small majority in the Cabinet was prepared to accept a cut. But at the same time almost half of the members of the Cabinet refused to go along. MacDonald was forced to tender the Cabinet's resignation.

The National Emergency Government (1931–32)

MacDonald's resignation on 23 August 1931 brought about a complicated political and constitutional situation. A minority Cabinet succumbed to internal discord at a moment when England was facing a very serious

[93] *Planning* (P.E.P.), XVI, No. 300 (11 July 1949), 24–25. One of the initial activities of P.E.P. was to establish a Machinery of Government Committee. It met frequently but produced few concrete results. But see *Planning*, No. 173 (15 July 1941), and *Planning* No. 214 (16 November 1943), proposing a Civilian General Staff. See also *Life of Cripps*, p. 153; Sir Stafford Cripps, ed., *Problems of a Socialist Government* (1933), pp. 60–62; and the report of a speech by Cripps in Manchester, *The Times*, 21 January 1935.

[94] See especially Bassett, *passim,* and *Life of King George V*, pp. 446–69.

financial crisis. Urgent decisions had to be made on short notice. Both the Conservatives and the Liberals had urged the necessity of the economies that a large part of the Labour Cabinet had refused to accept. Separately neither the Conservatives nor the Liberals had a sufficient majority in the House of Commons. Although both parties were prepared to accept the responsibility for unpopular decisions if necessary, they naturally preferred that Labour (or at least part of Labour) should share it. They especially feared the explosive political effect of the proposed reduction of unemployment benefits.[95]

Even before MacDonald resigned, the King had had certain contacts with the Opposition leaders.[96] In particular, the acting Liberal Leader, Sir Herbert Samuel, had pleaded for a National Cabinet composed of members of all three parties. If possible, this National Government should be headed by MacDonald. Baldwin (although willing to form a Government himself) was prepared to cooperate. The King himself was much in favor of a nonpartisan solution. When MacDonald tendered his Cabinet's resignation, the King, according to his Private Secretary's official account, "impressed on the Prime Minister that he was the only man to lead the country through this crisis and hoped he would reconsider the situation."[97] On 25 August 1931, the King conferred with MacDonald, Samuel, and Baldwin at Buckingham Palace. He again rejected MacDonald's resignation. "The King assured the Prime Minister that, remaining at his post, his position and reputation would be much more enhanced than if he surrendered the Government of the country at such a crisis." According to the same official report:

Baldwin and Samuel said that they were willing to serve under the Prime Minister, and render all help possible to carry on the Government as a National Emergency Government until an emergency bill or bills had been passed by Parliament, which would restore once more British credit and the confidence of foreigners. After that they would expect His Majesty to grant a dissolution.[98]

After this conference, the three politicians met by themselves. In principle, agreement was reached to form "a small Cabinet of twelve,"[99] or, to use the words Samuel wrote during the meeting, "The Cabinet shall be reduced to a minimum." The new Cabinet was not to be a coalition of parties but "a cooperation of individuals." When the crisis was over, each party was to reassume its individuality and enter the elections independently.[100]

The new Cabinet was quickly formed. It was composed of ten members. Four members stayed from the Labour Cabinet: MacDonald as Prime Minister, Snowden as Chancellor of the Exchequer, Thomas as

---

95 Cf. Bassett, pp. 126, 129–31.
96. *Life of King George V*, pp. 461–62; *Life of Samuel*, pp. 270–72.
97 *Life of King George V*, p. 464.   98 *Ibid.*, p. 466.
99 *Ibid.*, p. 466   100 *Life of Samuel*, p. 273.

Secretary of State for the Dominions and the Colonies, and Lord Sankey as Lord Chancellor. Four were Conservatives: Baldwin as Lord President of the Council, Sir Samuel Hoare as Secretary of State for India, Neville Chamberlain as Minister of Health, and P. Cunliffe-Lister as President of the Board of Trade. Finally, two were Liberals: Samuel as Home Secretary and Lord Reading as Foreign Secretary. The Cabinet received the support of practically all Conservatives and Liberals. Very few Socialists followed MacDonald.

Soon enough, it was evident that the institution of a "National Emergency Government" composed of men without party ties, who were at the same time the most important party leaders, was not devoid of difficulties.[101] Financial panic continued. Within a few weeks Britain was forced off the gold standard. A return to the "original party positions" did not seem desirable in these circumstances. For the erstwhile Socialist ministers, this possibility was ruled out by their expulsion from the Labour Party. For the other ministers, party considerations soon reasserted themselves. Many Conservatives pressed for immediate elections, since they expected heavy gains for their party. For this very reason, the Liberals offered strong resistance. Two special problems arose: should the Cabinet enter the eventual elections, and, if so, what kind of program should it offer? The Conservatives wanted to introduce protectionist measures, a plan the Liberals violently opposed. After a complicated process of negotiations, it was decided to ask the electorate for a "doctor's mandate" to remedy existing ills. Its result surpassed the wildest expectations. All former Socialist Cabinet members except Lansbury and those who had followed MacDonald were defeated in their constituencies. The Labour Party lost more than 200 seats and was reduced to 52 members. The Conservatives won an unprecedented majority over the Opposition and all other parties.

The election result had far-reaching consequences. Socialists were bitter. Many came to argue that the real cause of events had been sabotage, or even deliberate conspiracy on the part of bankers and reactionary civil servants to overthrow Labour.[102] If Labour wanted to have another chance to carry through its program effectively, the party would have to seize full power as soon as new elections were won. "Unless some adequate democratic machinery can be devised," Sir Stafford Cripps held, "Socialists will be left with but two alternatives: either to seize a dictatorship or else to abandon power and hand it back to the capitalists."[103] Even parliamentary business posed great difficulties for the Labour Party. It had lost nearly all its spokesmen and had to rely on the activities of only a few people: the new Leader, Lansbury, the Deputy Leader, Attlee, and

[101] See Bassett, pp. 264–83; *Life of King George V*, pp. 491–93; Samuel, *Memoirs*, pp. 207–12.

[102] For symptoms of similar attitudes already prevalent in 1931, cf. Bassett, pp. 173–76, and *passim*.

[103] Sir Stafford Cripps, ed., *Problems of a Socialist Government* (1933), p. 15; cf. Lansbury, *My England*, p. 138; *Life of Lansbury*, pp. 279–80, 295–96.

Cripps (who had only recently joined Parliament).[104] The absence of a numerically significant Opposition had indirect consequences for relations within the Conservative Party. When the King had urged Baldwin to take charge of the Treasury in the new Cabinet, Baldwin had preferred to become Lord President of the Council. He had assured the King that "there would be plenty for him to do, as the Prime Minister knew nothing of his new Party, especially the Conservatives—many of them young, impetuous and ambitious men—who had no chance of making reputations with no Opposition to speak against."[105]

The Liberal Party, too, suffered considerable difficulties. For years the party had been riddled by internal conflict, on which new disagreements were now superimposed. Liberals differed on the advisability of forming the National Government, on the expediency of the 1931 elections, and on the desirability of continued cooperation in a Government that now rested in fact on Conservative votes. Personal dissatisfactions could be somewhat relieved after the elections because the return to the normal Cabinet made it possible to offer more sops to the disgruntled. But this did not solve the problem of disagreement about policy. Discord about protection was particularly serious. It displeased the King, who had always thought a "combination of all decent-minded politicians" necessary and demanded that "party differences should be sunk."[106] Free Traders like Samuel and Snowden threatened to leave the Government. MacDonald informed the King that if they did, he would have no choice but to resign as Prime Minister of a National Government. Once again an expedient was found in the so-called "agreement to differ."[107] It was decided that the members of the Cabinet who could not accept the principle of protection might publicly express their views in debate and division, while the bill passed through Parliament. This unusual deviation from the principle of collective ministerial responsibility did little but defer difficulties. In the summer of 1932, a year after the National Emergency Government was formed, Snowden and the Samuelites left the Government. Thereafter it became increasingly difficult to distinguish the so-called National Governments of the 1930's from purely Conservative ones.

The National Governments of MacDonald, Baldwin, and Chamberlain (1932–39)

As elsewhere in Europe, the 1930's in England were a period of anxiety and uncertainty. Japan's increasing aggressiveness, the braggadocio of the Duce, the rise of Hitler's Germany, and the bloody Spanish Civil War posed heavy responsibilities on government and revealed bitter discord about the conducting of foreign policy. Many mortgaged their hopes to

---

[104] Attlee, *As it Happened*, pp. 77–78; *Life of Cripps*, pp. 143–47; *Life of Lansbury*, pp. 278–305.
[105] *Life of King George V*, p. 494.　　　　[106] *Ibid.*, p. 492.
[107] *Ibid.*, pp. 497–98; Samuel, *Memoirs*, pp. 217–18; Bassett, p. 354; Snowden, *Autobiography*, II, 1010–17; Winterton, *Orders of the Day*, pp. 181–82.

such vague conceptions as "disarmament," "the League," or "collective security." Others pleaded for a conscious re-orientation of foreign policy: some wished close cooperation with Italy against Germany, others sought for appeasement of Hitler, and still others hoped for a new anti-Fascist alliance with the Soviet Union. Many consoled themselves with the opinion that in any event Europe was far away.

Uncertainty also dominated domestic politics. The depression poisoned social relations. Some clung to the purity of laissez faire. Others saw possibilities in Fascism. Still others pointed to Roosevelt's New Deal, or to the results the U.S.S.R. seemed to attain with "planning." Politics was short-tempered and full of personal rancor.[108] Later judgments about Government policies in the era have been harsh. This inevitably had a substantial influence on the historical image of the Cabinets of this period and colored the reputation of the ministers who bore chief political responsibility during these years: MacDonald, Baldwin, Simon, Hoare, and Halifax.[109]

State interference increased strongly between 1931 and 1939 through detailed regulations about trade and production and through provision of social benefits, particularly for the numerous unemployed. Often new organs were created for such new government functions, which were sometimes deliberately insulated from the existing departmental organizations and direct parliamentary criticism. Of much greater importance for the organization of the Cabinet, however, were developments in organizing foreign policy and defense.

The activities of the Foreign Office had increased greatly since 1914 as a result of such developments as the increased number of sovereign states, the closer control of states over international trade, the establishment of the League of Nations and other new international organizations, and constant political conflict with France, and later with Italy and Germany.[110] The Foreign Secretary's burden had always been heavy, and the Undersecretary of State for Foreign Affairs had therefore often played a fairly important role. After 1918, however, more senior ministers were "seconded" to the Foreign Office. Thus in 1918, Lord Robert Cecil had been appointed Assistant Secretary of State for Foreign Affairs to act as deputy to the Foreign Secretary, Balfour, when the latter was away from London for allied conferences. In 1919 Curzon had done the same as Lord President of the Council. In 1922 Cecil was appointed Lord Privy Seal, and in 1924 he became Chancellor of the Duchy of Lancaster,

---

[108] Dalton, for instance, spoke at the Labour Party Congress in 1936 of "the sly evasions of Sir John Simon, the prim sentences of Sir Samuel Hoare, the feeble amiability of Mr. Eden, the lazy lack of leadership of Mr. Baldwin, the senile vanity of Mr. MacDonald" (Dalton, *Memoirs*, II, 102).

[109] For attempts to restore their reputations, see, in addition to *Life of Neville Chamberlain*, Simon, *Retrospect*, and Templewood, *Nine Troubled Years*; A. W. Baldwin, *My Father: The True Story* (1955); Bassett, p. 338ff, and R. Bassett, "Telling the Truth to the People: The Myth of the Baldwin Confession," *Cambridge Journal*, II (1948), 84–95.

[110] Strang, *Foreign Office*, pp. 30–47.

especially charged with League of Nations affairs. He resigned in 1927 because of a dispute with the Cabinet on disarmament.[111]

After 1931, Anthony Eden ranked high as Undersecretary of State for Foreign Affairs under Sir John Simon, who then was Foreign Secretary. Not all Conservatives were equally pleased with this situation. Amery, for instance, spoke caustically of Simon's "good-looking and eloquent young understudy. . . . who cheerfully voiced all the popular catchwords, and, being voted a success, tended largely to displace his official chief."[112] Eden was promoted in December 1933 to Lord Privy Seal, as yet outside the Cabinet, since MacDonald felt that to have two Foreign Secretaries in the Cabinet would not work.[113] By May 1935, Eden was clearly dissatisfied with this situation; when Baldwin was due to form his new Government, Eden asked him either to be appointed to another office, or to be left out of the Government altogether.[114] Baldwin still preferred Hoare to Eden for Foreign Secretary, but he offered Eden a Cabinet seat and a new title, Minister for League of Nations Affairs. Eden was not happy. As he was to write later:

The international situation was tangled and menacing; decisions would have to be taken quickly. Was I to know of each one of them before the Secretary of State acted? If so, that would mean a fifth wheel on the coach and, perhaps, dangerous delay. If not, I would have no choice but to acquiesce after the event and share responsibility.[115]

Eden nevertheless accepted the position. The Government then faced Churchill's blistering attack on the "new plan of having two equal Foreign Secretaries." Churchill had recently fought Hoare over the Government of India Bill. He now thought it "in the nature of poetic justice that the Foreign Secretary should, on leaving the India Office, have the personal experience of dyarchy in its direct and homely aspect."[116] The new experiment did not last long, however; in December 1935, Eden stepped into Hoare's place. Eden, in turn, was assisted by Lord Halifax, who was Lord Privy Seal from 1935–37 and Lord President of the Council from 1937–38. With some satisfaction, Eden noted in his memoirs that Halifax "did not have a room, nor a Private Secretary, or any official position, but he eased some of my burden, especially on my brief spells of leave."[117]

There is evidence, however, that the position of Halifax was in reality somewhat more than this. The threatening world situation, increasing disagreement about ways to deal with it, and the penchant of the new European dictators to deal directly with heads of Government all eroded the

---

[111] Clement Jones, "Viscount Cecil of Chelwood," *International Affairs*, XXXV (1959), 282, 283. During World War I Cecil was Minister of Blockade and a member of the War Cabinet (Hankey, *Supreme Command*, p. 547).
[112] Amery, *My Political Life*, III, 154; R. Churchill, *Eden*, pp. 72–75.
[113] Eden, *Facing the Dictators*, p. 51.   [114] *Ibid.*, pp. 216–17.
[115] *Ibid.*, p. 218.   [116] R. Churchill, *Eden*, p. 88.
[117] Eden, *Facing the Dictators*, p. 319.

Foreign Secretary's somewhat independent position. Traditionally, the Prime Minister could always exercise supervision over the Foreign Secretary, if he so wished. This might lead to tension, as had indeed existed between MacDonald and Henderson, and had arisen again between MacDonald and Simon.[118] Baldwin acted rather differently. He allowed his Foreign Secretary, as all other ministers, practically a free hand. This had the advantage of making it easier for him, and for the Cabinet, to drop Hoare in 1935, when public opinion denounced the Hoare-Laval pact. It also blocked some attempts to persuade Baldwin to enter into direct contact with Hitler, outside regular Foreign Office channels.[119] As Eden wrote after a conversation with Baldwin in 1941, "He did not understand the storms that raged without, nor did he make Neville's mistake of believing that he did."[120] As soon as Neville Chamberlain became Prime Minister, he made clear that to a considerable extent he intended to be his own Foreign Secretary.[121] Chamberlain and Eden disagreed profoundly on how to deal with the dictators.[122] Chamberlain did not wish to dispense with the services of Eden, who enjoyed considerable personal popularity. But Eden's influence could be lessened in many ways. One was through the Cabinet, where Eden's position was affected by the presence of a number of ex-Foreign Secretaries, as well as of his coadjutor, Halifax. To ensure even closer control, a Foreign Affairs Committee of the Cabinet was organized, where Eden tended to be in a minority during crucial discussions.[123]

Attempts at interfering with the Foreign Office were also made at the official level. In 1935, when Baldwin replaced MacDonald as Prime Minister, Sir Horace Wilson, then Chief Industrial Adviser, was seconded to the Treasury for service with the Prime Minister. It was felt that an aging Baldwin "should have someone on whom to lean who, not being a politician, would not arouse the jealousy of his colleagues."[124] Wilson's influence increased apace. Together with the Permanent Secretary to the Treasury, Sir Warren Fisher, Wilson sought to influence diplomatic appointments and other foreign policy matters.[125] Fisher and Wilson tried to persuade Eden's new Parliamentary Private Secretary, J. P. L. Thomas (later Viscount Cilcennin), to help them "to build a bridge between 10, Downing Street and the Foreign Office."[126] A chief obstacle was the then Permanent Secretary to the Foreign Office, Vansittart, who, far from being a conventional official, was, in Eden's words, "a sincere, almost

---

[118] Simon, *Retrospect,* pp. 177–78.   [119] Jones, *Diary,* pp. 179–81, 194ff, 218.
[120] Eden, *Facing the Dictators,* p. 446.
[121] Jones, *Diary,* p. 350; Eden, *Facing the Dictators,* p. 445.
[122] Eden's memoirs and Feiling's *Life of Neville Chamberlain* supplement each other on this point.
[123] Eden, *Facing the Dictators,* p. 560ff.   [124] Petrie, p. 158.
[125] *Ibid.,* pp. 183–85; Eden, *Facing the Dictators,* p. 319; H. Legge-Bourke's pamphlet *Master of the Offices* (1950); Beloff, pp. 23–24.
[126] Eden, *Facing the Dictators,* pp. 447–48.

fanatical crusader" on the dangers arising from Nazi Germany. Eden agreed to replace Vansittart with a more malleable Permanent Secretary, and when Vansittart refused the Paris Embassy, he was "promoted" to the specially created post of Chief Diplomatic Adviser.[127]

The Prime Minister himself took an increasingly direct part in day-to-day foreign policy. Finally, in the winter of 1937–38, he made secret contacts with Italian representatives, and with Mussolini himself, through the intermediary of his sister-in-law, Lady (Austen) Chamberlain, generally without Eden's agreement, and sometimes even without Eden's knowledge.[128] Matters finally came to a head, partly because Roosevelt took the initiative of calling for new standards in international relations, a move Eden applauded and Chamberlain felt might anger Hitler and Mussolini. Both Chamberlain and Eden agreed that cooperation between them was no longer possible.[129] Hints that Eden might wish to resign for health reasons were not taken. The passions raised between the Prime Minister and the Foreign Secretary come to life in the record of a conversation between Thomas (Eden's Parliamentary Private Secretary) and Horace Wilson a few weeks before the final break came. Thomas argued that if Eden resigned, "the country would then know that the P.M. preferred to turn down the help of a democracy in order that he might pursue his flirtations with the dictators untrammeled." Wilson, who was "in a towering rage," warned in turn that "he would use the full power of the Government machine in an attack upon A.E.'s past record with regard to the dictators and the shameful obstruction by the F.O. of the P.M.'s attempts to save the peace of the world."[130]

Halifax, who succeeded Eden as Foreign Secretary, cooperated cordially with Chamberlain, finding Wilson "extremely helpful, when the pressure of work was heavy, in ensuring that I was fully acquainted with the thought of the Prime Minister, and vice versa, and that neither was consciously drifting into any misunderstanding of the other's mind."[131] But then, Halifax' tenure at the Foreign Office was such that he was satisfied to let Chamberlain make decisions and settle the fate of the world at Godesberg, Berchtesgaden, and Munich without having either the Foreign Secretary or the Permanent Secretary to the Foreign Office present at the most crucial meetings.

Foreign policy was intimately related to defense questions (or weaknesses). As the awareness of Nazi Germany's military strength grew stronger, defense problems demanded increasing attention. More and more debates were held in Parliament. There was considerable pressure to choose Service ministers from the Commons rather than the Lords.[132]

---

[127] *Ibid.*, pp. 242–43, 521. Vansittart's name does not appear in the index of Feiling's *Life of Neville Chamberlain.*
[128] Eden, *Facing the Dictators*, Appendix D, p. 619ff.
[129] *Ibid.*, p. 592.   [130] *Ibid.*, p. 563.
[131] Halifax, *Fullness of Days*, pp. 231–32.
[132] *Life of King George VI*, pp. 339–40; Winterton, *Orders of the Day*, pp. 233–36.

Numerous opponents and some supporters of the Government demanded the appointment of a separate Minister of Defence. The Cabinet was not yet ready to comply fully. In an attempt to find a middle path between the existing situation and the new demand, Baldwin appointed a Minister *for the Coordination* of Defence. But the innovation proved hardly successful. Until 1939 the Cabinet also resisted pressure for a Ministry of Supply. But in 1938, Sir John Anderson was appointed Lord Privy Seal to organize civil defense.

As always, the working of the Cabinets between 1931 and 1939 was strongly affected by the personalities of their Prime Ministers. MacDonald's political position between 1931 and 1935 became increasingly artificial, hated as he was by the Labour Opposition, barely tolerated by the Conservative majority, and ridiculed by Churchill and other oppositional Conservatives. His health, and especially his eyesight, deteriorated.[133] In a memorandum of 1932, MacDonald insisted on reducing the number of Cabinet papers, adding that no document should be circulated before he had seen it. He sent a minute to this effect to the Secretary of the Cabinet, Hankey, "who told him, politely, that it was nonsense."[134] Even Baldwin admitted eventually that MacDonald had better resign, and in 1935 he and MacDonald changed places. In the ensuing elections MacDonald was defeated in his constituency, and great pains were taken to find him a university seat. He still gave a few rambling speeches for the Government in the House of Commons until one day a Scottish socialist shouted at him from the other side of the House, "Sit down man, sit down man, you're a ghastly tragedy."[135] His successor, Baldwin, proved not too effective as Prime Minister between 1935 and 1937. By temperament alone he was hardly suited for businesslike management, and his health also became an obstacle. As in MacDonald's case, long periods of leave brought Baldwin only temporary relief. His deafness became "a serious handicap in Cabinet."[136]

The structure of the central government organization was again subject to complaints in this period. "The Foreign Office," according to Jones's diary at the time, "has no organization and is as much under-machined as the Cabinet office is over-machined. . . . The latter breeds committees like rabbits. What tires the P.M. is largely compulsory attendance in the H. of C. hour after hour. But this crop is only proof of feebleness in reaching decisions in Cabinet."[137] Cecil and others made proposals for Cabinet reform as early as 1932.[138] The idea of "a smallish Cabinet" had also found some favor with Baldwin.[139] The Leader of the Labour Opposition, Attlee, argued in 1937 that "the Cabinet, as now constituted, sins against the first principle of good administration in that it does not distinguish between the function of planning broad strategy and

---

[133] Cf. Jones, *Diary*, pp. 69, 121–22, 128.
[135] Dalton, *Memoirs*, II, 86.
[136] Cf. Jones, *Diary*, pp. 69, 175, 188, 230.
[138] Cecil, *passim*.

[134] *Ibid.*, p. 69.

[137] *Ibid.*, p. 176.
[139] Jones, *Diary*, p. 142; cf. p. 228.

making decisions as to the detailed execution of plans."[140] At the same time, Amery persisted in campaigning against what he called "the nineteenth-century Cabinet," which he thought "incapable of handling the complex and urgent problems of the twentieth century," a system "of mutual friction and delay, with at best some partial measure of mutual adjustment between unrelated policies."[141] As Minister without Portfolio, Lord Eustace Percy was in 1935 specially charged to study problems of long-term policy. He soon was dubbed "Minister of Thought" and quickly resigned because of the futility of his office.[142]

The arrival of Neville Chamberlain brought great improvement in the Cabinet's efficiency. According to Hoare:

His personal influence was due to his mastery of facts, his clear head and his inherited gift of incisive speech. Being a remarkably quick worker, he was able to keep in touch with every important question, domestic as well as foreign, that concerned the Government. Ministers constantly visited Downing Street to discuss their affairs with him.[143]

Chamberlain's opponents gave a somewhat less friendly interpretation to this. "What was obvious," Amery wrote, "was that he did not think it mattered much what office he assigned to any particular colleague; the civil servants would keep him straight on ordinary administration; major policy he meant to conduct himself."[144] The uncertain political situation made the country demand more than businesslike proceedings alone. Munich for a time raised Chamberlain's prestige to such a pitch that both his supporters and his opponents expected him him to score a sensational victory, if he should decide to dissolve Parliament.[145] But even then Hoare could write to Chamberlain:

I believe that the country demands new blood. The difficulty is how to find it. . . . Is it not also worth considering whether you should not adopt for peace purposes the conception of the small War Cabinet. I believe that the country wants a change of this kind. People think our present machinery is slow and obsolescent.[146]

Others were more concerned with personnel. Proposals were canvassed to incorporate forceful personalities like Churchill, Lloyd George, or even Bevin in the Cabinet.[147] It was hopefully predicted that the administrative strength of the government might be enhanced by including

---

[140] Attlee, *Labour Party*, p. 173.   [141] Amery, *Forward View*, p. 443ff.
[142] Winterton, *Orders of the Day*, p. 203.
[143] Templewood, *Nine Troubled Years*, p. 375; cf. Jennings, *Cabinet Government*, pp. 191–95.
[144] Amery, *My Political Life*, III, 226. Lloyd George, lifelong antagonist of Neville Chamberlain, said: "Neville . . . has a retail mind in a wholesale business" (Jones, *Diary*, p. 422).
[145] *Life of King George VI*, p. 357; *Life of Neville Chamberlain*, p. 377ff; Churchill, I, 258–59; Halifax, *Fullness of Days*, pp. 199–200.
[146] Templewood, *Nine Troubled Years*, p. 386.
[147] Jones, *Diary*, p. 123.

an ex-civil servant like Anderson, or an ex-admiral like Lord Chatfield.[148]
Meanwhile, the Cabinet's size continued to increase, until in 1939 it had
twenty-three members. Only the Minister of Pensions, the Paymaster-
General, the Postmaster-General, the First Commissioner of Works, and
the Law Officers remained outside it. The Cabinet's influence on the
conduct of affairs did not become any greater for all its growth in size.

[148] *Ibid.,* p. 413.

FIVE

THE CABINET DURING THE SECOND WORLD WAR

The War Cabinet of Neville Chamberlain

After the end of the First World War, the C.I.D. had studied the problems of organizing the government in wartime. Four possibilities had been considered: first, retaining the normal Cabinet; second, continuing the normal Cabinet, which would delegate certain limited powers to a special War Committee; third, continuing the normal Cabinet, which would delegate most of its powers to a War Committee; and fourth, establishing a War Cabinet proper. The C.I.D. had concluded that only the fourth possibility would be adequate for an extensive war.[1]

When on 1 September 1939, German troops crossed the Polish frontier, the Secretaries of the Cabinet and the C.I.D., Sir Edward Bridges and Sir Hastings Ismay, submitted a memorandum along these lines to the Prime Minister.[2] Neville Chamberlain immediately decided to form a War Cabinet of ministers without portfolio. Originally he wished to include five members besides himself: Simon, who had been Chancellor of the Exchequer; Halifax, who had until then been Foreign Secretary; Chatfield, who had recently become Minister for the Coordination of Defence; and, as newcomers, Churchill, and Hankey who had until 1938 been Secretary of both the Cabinet and the C.I.D.[3] But on 2 September 1939, one day after he had been invited to join the War Cabinet, Churchill wrote two successive letters making certain objections to Chamberlain's intentions. Churchill thought the average age of the Cabinet members was too high and desired including Eden and the Liberal Leader, Sinclair, in the Cabinet. (Sinclair, however, refused to join.) Furthermore, Churchill advocated a change in "the composition and scope of the War Cabinet" as such.[4]

In his memoirs Churchill has not further elaborated on this. Chamberlain's biographer indicates that Churchill wanted to become First Lord of the Admiralty.[5] This supposition is plausible. The most bitter experience of Churchill's career had been his removal from the Admiralty in 1915. He had stayed on in the Cabinet as Chancellor of the Duchy of Lancaster. "In this position I knew everything and could do nothing," Churchill

---

[1] Hancock–Gowing, p. 46. According to Amery (*My Political Life,* III, 327), this decision was taken in 1923. But see Ismay, p. 87, and Johnson, p. 268.

[2] Ismay, p. 87.   [3] *Life of Dawson,* p. 397.

[4] Churchill, I, 317–19.   [5] *Life of Neville Chamberlain,* p. 421.

wrote in 1932. "The change from the intensive executive activities of the Admiralty to the narrowly measured duties of a counselor left me gasping. . . . At a moment when every fiber of my being was inflamed to action, I was forced to remain a spectator of the tragedy, placed cruelly in a front seat."[6] Lloyd George had again offered Churchill the Duchy of Lancaster in 1917, "with elaborated uses and functions." Churchill had refused. He had indicated in reply that he was prepared either to assist the Prime Minister in council in the War Cabinet or to take control of any war department as long as he had powers to assist actively in the defeat of the enemy.[7] In his memoirs, which appeared after the publication of Chamberlain's biography, Churchill confirms that he would have preferred the executive post of First Lord of the Admiralty to mere membership in the War Cabinet. At the same time, however, Churchill suggests that he did not himself raise this point.[8] This is an implicit denial of the thesis of Feiling and others that it was Churchill's preference for an executive department that led to the partial abandoning of the plan to form a War Cabinet composed entirely of ministers without portfolio.

However this may be, on 3 September 1939, it was announced that Chamberlain's War Cabinet would be composed of nine people. Besides the Prime Minister, it included three non-departmental ministers, Hoare, Lord Privy Seal; Chatfield, Minister for the Coordination of Defence; and Hankey, Minister without Portfolio. Also included were Halifax, Foreign Secretary; Simon, Chancellor of the Exchequer; and the three Service ministers, Churchill, First Lord of the Admiralty; L. Hore-Belisha, Secretary of State for War; and Sir Kingsley Wood, Secretary of State for Air. At first the new War Cabinet met almost daily. In addition to its actual members, certain other persons usually attended the meetings, notably the Secretary of State for the Dominions, Eden; the Home Secretary and Minister for Home Security, Anderson; the principal military advisers; and Chamberlain's man Friday, Horace Wilson, now Permanent Secretary to the Treasury.[9]

In September 1939 a number of new departments were introduced according to the instructions of the War Book and in accordance with the experiences of the First World War. In addition to the new Ministry of Supply, the Ministries of Economic Warfare, Food, Information (which was soon to be sharply criticized), Shipping, and Home Security were established. Shortly afterwards a number of Cabinet committees were

---

[6] Churchill, *Thoughts and Adventures*, p. 307. It was during this period, he wrote, in the "long hours of utterly unwonted leisure in which to contemplate the frightful unfolding of the war," that "the Muse of Painting came to my rescue" for the first time.

[7] Beaverbrook, 1917–18, p. 358; cf. *Life of Lloyd George*, p. 414ff.

[8] Churchill, I, 320; cf. p. 317.

[9] Hancock-Gowing, pp. 90–91; Churchill, I, 328. Churchill suggested at this time that the War Cabinet should meet more often alone, without either Secretary or other outsiders (*ibid.*, pp. 355–56, 361).

formed.[10] These included a Home Security Committee for civil defense matters and a Home Affairs or Home Policy Committee, which was to deal with all domestic problems, but which in practice showed little development. Also established were a Ministerial Priority Committee, which was to supervise the allocation of scarce resources, working through what Churchill called a "fearsome array of subcommittees," and a Food Committee.[11] After a certain amount of parliamentary pressure, an Economic Policy Committee was formed and met under the Chancellor of the Exchequer. Lastly, a Military Coordination Committee composed of Chatfield as Chairman and the three Service ministers was formed. In addition, the Lord Privy Seal, Hoare, was to act as "a kind of general purpose minister, undertaking duties that were either not covered by the departmental chiefs or needed coordination between them."[12] As he himself said, the experiment was not a happy one. Although he insisted that his possible interventions "should be specific for definite purposes rather than continuous with any kind of overriding authority," he was nevertheless ensnared in a number of parliamentary debates concerning matters about which he knew little. Lloyd George in particular used him as a butt for his attacks on the Government.[13]

The entire structure of Chamberlain's War Cabinet, too, was soon criticized. Attlee, Leader of the Socialist Opposition, pleaded on 26 September 1939 for a smaller and more real "War Cabinet" composed only of ministers without portfolio.[14] Similar ideas were propagated by *The Times,* still edited by Dawson, who since 1916 had actively advocated a non-departmental Cabinet as a certain war-winning instrument.[15] Not without an element of special pleading, the paper reminded its readers, and the Government, that in 1916 Major Edward Wood (now Lord Halifax) had been a fervent advocate of a War Cabinet of ministers without portfolio.[16] *The Times* also gave prominent place to Sir William Beveridge's criticisms. A few weeks after the outbreak of the war, Beveridge argued that a total war required total planning and efficient, centralized leadership. To ensure this, he strongly recommended "an organ for intelligence, making continuous synoptic survey of all that is happening in the country, of manpower and resources, of every check or failure leading to waste or misdirected energy." This organ, a genuine Economic General Staff, was to work directly under "a body of people, perhaps not more than three or four, who have nothing to do except to decide." Beveridge conceded that "personalities are as important as structure," but said it was unthinkable

---

[10] Hancock–Gowing, p. 93.   [11] Scott–Hughes, p. 409.
[12] Templewood, *Nine Troubled Years,* pp. 395–96.
[13] *Ibid.,* pp. 396–97, 428; cf. Brabazon, p. 182.
[14] 351 H. of C. Deb. (26 September 1939), cols. 1247–48; similar criticism came from the Leader of the Liberals, Clement Davies (352 H. of C. Deb. [18 October 1939], cols. 946–50).
[15] *Life of Dawson,* pp. 402, 407, 410, 413–14; cf. Churchill, I, 327–28
[16] *The Times,* 4 April 1940.

that Chamberlain's War Cabinet could act as "a group of unencumbered minds in continuous session." He also expressed doubt about whether Chamberlain's Government was powerful enough, especially since reasonable efficiency seemed to be ensured at lower, departmental levels.[17]

Criticism in Parliament and the Press was further aimed at two particular points. In the first place, many people questioned the duties of a Minister for the Coordination of Defence, since there were three Service ministers in the Cabinet. In the second place, there was widespread doubt about whether the Chancellor of the Exchequer should continue to coordinate economic affairs. Several times the Opposition urged the appointment of a Minister for the Coordination of Economic Affairs, who, as a War Cabinet member, and possibly aided by a small staff, should coordinate the activities of all departments concerned with military and civil production and transport. Such a minister, it was emphatically stated, would also have to keep the Chancellor of the Exchequer under control.

This line of criticism also had some influence on ideas about the need for over-all Cabinet re-organization. Laski, for instance, proposed establishing a completely functional Cabinet of coordinating ministers. In addition to the Prime Minister, the Foreign Secretary, the Chancellor of the Exchequer, and a Minister for the Coordination of Economic Affairs (who should be at least the Chancellor's equal), such a Cabinet should have an effective Minister of Defence instead of the three Service ministers; a Dominions Secretary, who was to handle contacts with all dominions and colonies; and a Minister for the Coordination of Home Services, who was to supervise all departments involved in domestic matters not yet coordinated otherwise. Finally, someone like Hankey might be included as a minister without portfolio on the strength of his long-standing experience in administration and war.[18]

Others rejected the idea of such specialized super-ministers because they thought such ministers would derogate from existing departmental responsibilities. These critics therefore stuck the more firmly to the principle of what they called a non-functional Cabinet. In their view, all Cabinet members should be free from departmental tasks. Although each member should occupy himself with special tasks from time to time, none should be given specific coordinating authority. Since they would only collectively direct the departments, the individual responsibility of every minister towards Parliament would not be impaired.[19]

In the final analysis, however, all these discussions had other roots. They were strongly influenced, for instance, by the feeling that Chamberlain was not a War Minister, by a long-held Socialist aversion toward Simon and Hoare, and by uncertainty about the position and influence of Churchill. Most arguments were therefore colored by strong personal emotions. They had little effect during the period of the Phony War,

---

[17] The Times, 3 October 1939.   [18] Laski, Government in Wartime, pp. 11–17.
[19] Beveridge in The Times, 6 February 1940.

when the political position of Chamberlain and his lieutenants was still firmly established, in spite of half-subdued feelings of irritation. Uneasiness was widespread in the winter of 1939–40.[20] Many felt that government authority and organization were unduly inflated. The number of Cabinet sessions soon decreased to five per week. A system of rotation among the leading ministers was introduced for Saturdays and Sundays.[21] The English week-end remained sacrosanct. If we are to believe Attlee, Chamberlain still managed at Chequers with a single telephone, located in the butler's pantry. Nor did Chamberlain strongly feel that a secretary need always be available.[22] Thus the entire organization could remain chiefly a system of quiet coordination; neither the want of leadership nor possible organizational gaps became clearly evident.

Chamberlain made a few alterations in his Cabinet in April 1940. The Minister for the Coordination of Defence, Chatfield, resigned. As senior Service minister, Churchill was put in charge of the Military Coordination Committee. Only a few days later, the Germans attacked Norway. Military disasters followed. In an embittered and emotional debate, many in the House of Commons turned against Chamberlain. Amery gave his famous speech denouncing Chamberlain in Cromwell's words: " 'You have sat here too long for any good you have been doing. Depart, I say, and let us have done with you. In the name of God, go!' "[23] Chamberlain lost his authority even though he still obtained a tenuous majority during a vote of confidence. The Labour Party again refused to join a National Government under Chamberlain's leadership, but declared itself willing to do so under a different Prime Minister. Chamberlain was forced to resign. For a short time there was uncertainty about who was to succeed him. King George VI, Chamberlain himself, many Conservatives, and a few Socialists preferred Halifax. Halifax, however, hinted that as a member of the House of Lords he would be unable to give the country the guidance it would need in the coming days of trial.[24] Churchill now became Prime Minister.

[20] Cf. Templewood, *Nine Troubled Years,* p. 419. During a stay at Cliveden, Thomas Jones wrote on 11 February 1940: "We are always making and unmaking Governments, canvassing the names of candidates for this post and that. No one is satisfied that Neville C. is directing the war with the necessary energy and imagination. He deals with the problem in front of him but he has no prevision nor circumvision. Halifax is timid and hesitant and can be got around by turning a problem into a moral issue . . . Winston has bursts of output but is far from being the Winston of 1914–1918. Simon is a Rolls-Royce brain but cannot steer. Chatfield is awed in the presence of the politicians. Hankey is old" (*Diary,* pp. 454–55).
[21] Hancock–Gowing, p. 91; Halifax, *Fullness of Days,* pp. 214–15; Templewood, *Nine Troubled Years,* p. 424.
[22] Attlee, *As It Happened,* p. 159.
[23] For Amery's own report, see *My Political Life,* III, 358–69.
[24] See, for instance, *Life of King George VI,* pp. 438–44; *Life of Neville Chamberlain,* p. 441; Halifax, *Fullness of Days,* pp. 219–20; Dalton, *Memoirs,* II, 306–7; Amery, *My Political Life,* III, 370–72. See also Churchill, I, 522–25.

The War Cabinet of Winston Churchill (1940–41)

Churchill brought many drastic changes to the Government. Originally his Cabinet was composed of five members: Churchill himself, as Prime Minister and Minister of Defence; Chamberlain, still leader of the Conservative Party, as Lord President of the Council; Halifax as Foreign Secretary; Attlee, Leader of the Labour Party, as Lord Privy Seal; and Greenwood, Deputy Leader of the Labour Party, as Minister without Portfolio. The Cabinet seemed in principle to satisfy the wishes of those who desired a War Cabinet modeled on that of Lloyd George. Only Halifax was in charge of a department. All other departmental ministers, including the Chancellor of the Exchequer, Wood, and the Service ministers —the Conservative Eden, Secretary of State for War; the Liberal Leader Sinclair, Secretary of State for Air; and the Socialist A. V. Alexander, First Lord of the Admiralty—remained outside the Cabinet.

The War Cabinet's formal structure was less important for the Cabinet's future development than were three other factors, however. First, as Prime Minister, Churchill—who said that the Prime Ministership does not bear comparison with offices two, three, or four—immediately assumed a dominant position and used it whenever he thought fit.[25] Second, the broadening of the Government's base to include Socialists and Liberals as well as Conservatives and some who did not belong to any party had certain consequences for the relations within the Government itself, as well as for the relation between the Government and Parliament. Third, Churchill appointed two ministers who at once deeply impressed their personalities on the nation, not without consequences for the internal life of the Cabinet. They were Beaverbrook, who took the newly created post of Minister of Aircraft Production, and Bevin, who became Minister of Labour and National Service.[26]

"I thought I knew a good deal about it all, and I was sure that I should not fail," Churchill wrote later.[27] He immediately and drastically asserted his will, especially in military affairs. The influence of the Service ministers and the War Cabinet itself on military policy soon declined. "Churchill is the Government in every sense of the word," Harry Hopkins reported to President Roosevelt in early 1941. "He controls the grand strategy and often the details."[28] The history of the Central Direction for War after 1940 was therefore in particular the history of the relations between Churchill and the Service Chiefs, and only to a lesser extent the history of the War Cabinet. Churchill exerted an equally considerable

---

[25] Churchill, II, 14.

[26] Bevin's nearest colleagues in the Trade Union Movement felt that he ought to have refused an office with such a low status. Bevin himself delighted in stating, however: "They say that Gladstone was at the British Treasury from 1860 to about 1930. They'll say that Bevin was at the Ministry of Labour from 1940 to 1990" (Evans, *Bevin*, pp. 176–77, 201, and Williams, *Bevin*, p. 217; *Life of Bevin*, pp. 652–54).

[27] Churchill, I, 527.   [28] Sherwood, I, 298; cf. 286, 314.

influence on war production. Here, too, he often relied directly on departmental experts, bypassing the responsible ministers. In the Defence Committee (Supply), Churchill had what the official historians have called a "steering wheel," a "personal instrument" that served to prepare an extensive war production program in a short time. This was to be a measure for future directives as well as a means for direct control over the execution of plans.[29]

Because of his immersion in military affairs, Churchill could exercise only incidental supervision in other spheres, the great number of directives to various ministers notwithstanding. Personal factors help to explain this difference of emphasis. When the Government was being formed, Amery had told Churchill that he might perhaps assist the Prime Minister "in dealing with the coordination of defense or of economic policy." "I soon realized," Amery wrote, "that he meant to keep defense entirely in his own hands and had no idea that economic policy mattered."[30]

Initially, Churchill's principal contribution to the organization on the domestic side was an order to curtail drastically the number of Cabinet committees—he thought Whitehall was in imminent danger of being overrun by committees, as the Australians were with the rabbits.[31] Attlee and Greenwood were chiefly responsible for implementing this order.[32] Greenwood became Chairman of an Economic Policy Committee and a Production Council, a place the Chancellor of the Exchequer had filled under Chamberlain. Attlee directed a Food Policy Committee and a Home Policy Committee.[33] But much more important than these committees became the Lord President's Committee, composed of the chairmen of the earlier Cabinet committees and the Chancellor of the Exchequer. It was charged to act as a steering committee for arranging the division of work among the other committees.

These first reforms did not last long, however. Soon the production of aircraft, under Beaverbrook's highly personal guidance, and the mobilization of manpower—military and civilian, women as well as men—under Bevin, outweighed all other aspects of the war effort. Beaverbrook entered the Cabinet in August 1940, Bevin in September. The War Cabinet began to lose its non-departmental character.

Difficulties in War Production and in Allocating Priorities (1941–42)

Originally, Churchill had wished to put Beaverbrook in charge of both the Ministry of Supply and the Ministry of Aircraft Production. Beaverbrook's asthma, however, made it impossible for him to accept this heavy

---

[29] Scott–Hughes, pp. 425–29. An outward sign of this development was that for a time certain supply secretariats were put under the Cabinet Office (Chester, *Cabinet*, p. 40; Robinson, p. 46ff).
[30] Amery, *My Political Life*, III, 373; but see Harrod, *The Prof*, pp. 197–99.
[31] Churchill, II, 560, and his minute of 4 January 1941.
[32] Attlee, *As It Happened*, p. 115.   [33] Hancock–Gowing, pp. 217–18.

combination of duties.[34] In the autumn of 1940, Churchill decided to abolish the Economic Policy Committee and the Production Council. In their place he created a Production Executive and an Import Executive. The Production Executive was composed of Bevin as chairman, the Ministers of Supply and Aircraft Production, and the First Lord of the Admiralty. The Import Executive had the Minister of Supply in the chair and the other supply ministers, the President of the Board of Trade, and the Minister of Food as members.[35] The idea behind these Executives, Bevin declared in Parliament, was that the responsibility for all war production and imports should rest with the ministers directly responsible. Supported by their departmental authority, these ministers could take the necessary decisions and ensure their execution without continuously relying on experts.[36] The difference between an Executive and a Committee was still not clear to everyone, however. Strong antagonism soon developed between Bevin and Beaverbrook. Beaverbrook, who had speeded up the production and repair of aircraft in 1940 in the most unorthodox ways, stuck firmly to the autonomy of his department. The conflict[37] reached such heights that Bevin threatened to bring legal action against Beaverbrook if the latter did not comply with the regulations of the Minister of Labour.[38]

At the same time, outsiders argued again and again that a committee composed of departmental ministers who were rivals in the matter of allocating scarce resources could at best reach uneasy compromises. Objective decisions, they maintained, could only be taken by a minister who stood above the contestants. Churchill long rejected this view. No single minister, he felt, unless he were at the same time Prime Minister, could ever have the necessary authority. Moreover, the antagonism between Bevin and Beaverbrook made the very idea of having one supervising minister highly unrealistic. It was impossible to think of either Bevin or Beaverbrook as chief of or subordinate to the other, but Churchill deemed both indispensable. He therefore increasingly relied on Neville Chamberlain's successor as Lord President of the Council, Anderson. As early as January 1941, Churchill had instructed Anderson "to take the lead prominently and vigorously" in the Lord President's Committee on all larger issues of economic policy.[39]

The Lord President's Committee increasingly dominated the entire field of economic and domestic policy. Anderson had great experience as a high-level civil servant. He himself was an extremely efficient ad-

---

[34] 377 H. of C. Deb. (14 February 1942), col. 1402.
[35] Hancock–Gowing, pp. 218–19.
[36] 368 H. of C. Deb. (21 January 1941), cols. 81–83; cf. Churchill, *ibid* (22 January 1941), cols. 256–65.
[37] Cf. Scott–Hughes, pp. 423–25.
[38] Williams, *Bevin*, p. 229. According to Morrison, Beaverbrook placarded his office with such slogans as "Committees are the Enemies of Action" and "Organization is the Foe of Results" (Morrison, *Autobiography*, p. 196; cf. pp. 180–81 and 196–99).
[39] Churchill, III, 102–3; *Life of Anderson*, p. 257ff.

ministrator. Because he had no pronounced political past, he was an acceptable chairman to ministers of widely different persuasion.[40] "Don't let Churchill send Anderson away," Smuts once said to Attlee. "Every War Cabinet needs a man to run the machine. Milner did it in the last war, and Anderson does it in this."[41] Churchill himself called the Lord President's Committee "almost a parallel Cabinet on home affairs."[42] In addition, Anderson personally performed many important tasks in the course of the war, notably by pinpointing, "for decision of the War Cabinet, issues of general policy which concerned several departments—for example, the allocation of manpower, the heavy bomber program, or plans for the military occupation of Persia."[43] He also acted as Churchill's representative for "tube alloys," the atom-bomb project, which was not entirely known even to Attlee.[44]

The Production Executive and the Import Executive succumbed to internal discord in 1941 and 1942, respectively. At the same time, conflicts between the supply departments became more serious when Beaverbrook, after a short interlude as Minister of State, became Minister of Supply in June 1941. He proved unable to let his old Department of Aircraft Production alone.[45] When Churchill visited the United States in December 1941, he learned that the entire U.S. war production effort was under the direction of one man, Donald Nelson.[46] Churchill then decided to appoint one Minister of Production in Britain as well. He had intended to appoint Beaverbrook to this new post, and thus give him a position above instead of on a level with the other Supply ministers.[47] Labor problems, however—Bevin's domain—would remain outside the new minister's realm. Hence the work of the Production Executive was in practice divided between Beaverbrook and Bevin. Due to poor health, Beaverbrook remained in office only a few weeks.[48] He was succeeded by Oliver Lyttelton, who was to encounter many difficulties. Until 1945, however, he remained, as Minister of Production, a leading member of the War Cabinet.

The Malaise of 1942; Cripps and the Cabinet

The appointment of a Minister of Production in February 1942 came at a moment when Churchill and his Government were being widely criticized. Criticism was fostered by the traumatic loss of the *Prince of Wales* and the *Repulse* near Malaya, the fall of Singapore, and the loss of Cyrenaica and Western Egypt. Many shared Shinwell's feeling that a

---

[40] Chester, *Machinery*, pp. 10–11; Hancock–Gowing, pp. 220–23.
[41] Attlee, *As It Happened*, p. 128.
[42] 378 H. of C. Deb. (24 February 1942), col. 38.
[43] Hancock–Gowing, p. 221; *Life of Anderson*, pp. 258–323.
[44] Attlee, *As It Happened*, p. 135; cf. p. 161; *Life of Anderson*, pp. 287, 324–25.
[45] Churchill, IV, 54–55; Brabazon, pp. 201–3.
[46] Scott–Hughes, pp. 430–31, 451–52; and 378 H. of C. Deb. (12 March 1942), col. 1205.
[47] Churchill, IV, 54–55.   [48] Churchill, IV, 65–69, 74–75.

vote supporting Churchill but censuring his Government was necessary.[49] Beveridge once again criticized the Government. He reproached Churchill for having abandoned the Lloyd George War Cabinet model and thus having made the central command "congested . . . lumbering . . . lacking in speed and decision." In addition, he complained that Churchill's choice of colleagues was too much influenced by personal and political motives, that he allowed a bad distribution of tasks between the departments to continue, that he was wrong in combining the two heaviest Government functions, the Prime Ministership and the Ministry of Defence, in one person.[50] Many insisted, with Beveridge, that a War Cabinet modeled on Lloyd George's with perhaps some modification was necessary. In January 1941, the Liberal Leader Clement Davies had advocated a War Cabinet of only three ministers without departments, who were to be supported by five super-ministers, each coordinating a certain group of departments in areas of finance, domestic affairs, external affairs, defense, and production, respectively.[51] Beaverbrook, too, urged Churchill to form a War Cabinet of only a few ministers—he was thinking of Bevin, "the strongest man in the present Cabinet," Eden, "the most popular member," and Attlee, Leader of the Socialist Party—each of whom would preside over groups of departments. He dissuaded Churchill from yielding to the clamor for a separate Minister of Defence, however, because no one could ever satisfy both the public and Churchill at the same time.[52] Churchill completely agreed with this. He wrote later about this period:

More difficulty and toil are often incurred in overcoming opposition and adjusting divergent and conflicting views than by having the right to give decisions oneself. It is most important that at the summit there should be one mind playing over the whole field, faithfully aided and corrected, but not divided in its integrity. I should not of course have remained Prime Minister for an hour if I had been deprived of the office of Minister of Defence.[53]

During this period of serious malaise, Cripps returned to England from his ambassadorship to the Kremlin. He reported on Russian war efforts on the B.B.C. His talks deeply impressed the public. It looked as if he were becoming the focus for a possible new opposition. Churchill therefore thought it desirable to take Cripps into the Government.[54] In January 1942 he offered him the post of Minister of Supply. But Cripps refused to work under a Minister of Production unless he had direct control over the allocation of raw materials and was a member of the War Cabinet. Cripps's demands were incompatible with Churchill's intention to appoint a Minister of Production, and the matter thus rested for a time.[55] However, when the news from the fronts became even worse, Churchill

[49] Shinwell, *Conflict without Malice*, p. 146.
[50] *The Times*, 26 January 1942.
[51] 368 H. of C. Deb. (21 January 1941), cols. 224–25.
[52] Churchill, IV, 73–74.   [53] *Ibid.*, p. 80.
[54] *Ibid.*, p. 56.
[55] *Life of Cripps*, pp. 273–77; Churchill, IV, 63–64.

looked for what he himself called "a new expedient."[56] In February 1942, with Attlee's consent, Churchill offered Cripps Attlee's office of Lord Privy Seal together with one of Attlee's actual duties, the Leadership of the House of Commons. Attlee himself was given the unofficial title of Deputy Prime Minister as well the office of Secretary of State for the Dominions—a post of considerable weight at this particular moment, since the Japanese advance caused Australia and New Zealand to demand a greater influence in the War Cabinet's deliberations.[57] Greenwood was left out of the Government, and the Chancellor of the Exchequer was once again excluded from the Cabinet. After this reconstruction the Cabinet consisted of seven members: Churchill, Attlee, Eden, Anderson, Bevin, Cripps, and Lyttelton. Besides Churchill, at least four people had charge of important departments. In addition, Anderson had a very special task of his own. The same was partly true of Cripps. "In direct contrariety to a strong current of opinion," Churchill wrote, "I had now given full effect to my view that War Cabinet members should also be the holders of responsible offices and not mere advisers at large with nothing to do but to think and talk and take decisions by compromise or majority."[58]

Churchill's views were soon contested within the new Cabinet, however. In the late summer of 1942, Cripps had a number of long discussions with Churchill. Cripps ultimately indicated that in view of his strong objections against the existing Cabinet organization and the handling of military affairs, he could not continue in office.[59] When he had joined the Cabinet, so Cripps recapitulated his views in a letter to Churchill on 21 September 1942, he had insisted on the need for a "War Cabinet of non-departmental ministers which could act as a central 'thinking and planning machine' in connection with the whole conduct of the war, strategically, domestically, and internationally." Now, after actual experience in the Cabinet, he was more than ever convinced of the necessity of this:

Problems of strategy are conceived by the War Cabinet hurriedly, without sufficient information and often in isolation. This has tended to a dispersal rather than a concentration of force. Internal problems are not kept under constant review and are hardly considered at all except when some major difficulty arises, and then a hasty solution has to be sought to the particular problem. A War Cabinet which sometimes meets only once a week and then with ten to fifteen other people present cannot really be said to be "conducting" the war, especially when three of its seven members are not on the Defence Committee and have no knowledge of the discussions and decisions in that Committee. Under such conditions it is not right, in my view, that the War Cabinet

---

[56] *Ibid.*, p. 70.
[57] *Ibid.*, pp. 4–17; *Life of King George VI*, pp. 679–83.
[58] Churchill, IV, 75. This preference did not prevent Churchill from inviting Lloyd George on various occasions to become a member of the War Cabinet. For Lloyd George's ambivalent attitude toward Churchill, see Sylvester, *Lloyd George, passim.*
[59] *Life of Cripps*, p. 300; Churchill, IV, 497–502.

should appear to carry responsibility for the conduct of war, since it is not in a position to discharge that responsibility.

To this letter Cripps added the following appendix:

1. The War Cabinet should consist of no more than seven members, all without departmental responsibilities.
2. They should work together in the same building and should meet every day to review the whole situation and to receive progress reports. Each one of them should see every document of importance that issues from or is received by the War Cabinet or Prime Minister's Office.
3. The Defence Committee should be abolished and its important work transferred to the War Cabinet. Its less important work should be discharged by the Defence Minister in association with the Service ministries.
4. Each War Cabinet minister should have the supervision of a section of Government departments and should sit as the Chairman of a sub-Cabinet consisting of the ministers of those departments. Such sub-Cabinet should have the power of decision in all matters except those that the Chairman decides should be referred to the War Cabinet.
5. The Dominion and Indian representatives should attend an Imperial Cabinet once a week and otherwise when especially summoned by the Prime Minister.[60]

Cripps furthermore objected to the system whereby the operational Chiefs of Staff were responsible for drawing up military plans. He proposed forming an independent War Planning Directorate with three members, who would take over strategic planning from the Chiefs of Staff under the Minister of Defence. Churchill strongly resisted the proposal. "This was in truth a planner's dream," he wrote later. "The guiding principle of war direction is, in my opinion, that war plans should be formulated by those who have the power and the responsibility for executing them." Cripps's plan, Churchill went on,

would have created two rival bodies, one responsible and one irresponsible, yet both nominally of equal status. . . . It would have led at once to immediate and violent friction. . . . Any clever person can make plans for winning a war if he has no responsibility for carrying them out. . . . I was not . . . prepared to invite a disembodied Brains Trust to browse among our secrets and add to the already immense volume of committees and reports.[61]

Shortly after Cripps's *démarche,* the Chief of the General Staff, Sir Alan Brooke, also implicitly condemned Cripps's propositions. A short time before the conquest of Tripoli, on 21 January 1943, Brooke wrote in his diary:

When an operation has finally been completed, it all looks so easy, but so few people ever realize the infinite difficulties of maintaining an object or a plan and refusing to be driven off it by other people for thousands of good reasons. A good plan pressed through is better than many ideal ones which are continually

---

[60] *Life of Cripps,* pp. 298–99.
[61] Churchill, IV, 498–99; *Life of Cripps,* pp. 299–300.

changing. Advice without responsibility is easy to give. This is the most exhausting job, trying to keep the ship of war on a straight course in spite of all the contrary winds that blow.[62]

Shortly thereafter Cripps accepted the offer of the Ministry of Aircraft Production, and proved to be an efficient minister. Churchill has called Cripps's attitude during the summer of 1942 one of the best illustrations of his thesis that a non-departmental minister may become a dangerous element in the ministerial hierarchy for lack of concrete work. Churchill wrote, "For a man of his keen intellect, as yet untempered by administrative experience, his exalted ideas, and his skill in theoretical exposition, this form of activity [an exalted brooding over the work of others] held a strong though dangerous appeal. His great intellectual energy needed to be harnessed to a more practical task."[63] Cripps's biographer, Colin Cooke, has essentially accepted this judgment.[64]

The War Cabinet after 1942

Eden succeeded Cripps as Leader of the House of Commons in November 1942. At the same time, Herbert Morrison, Home Secretary and Minister for Home Security, became a member of the War Cabinet. Thereafter its composition changed only slightly. In September 1943, after the death of Wood, Anderson became Chancellor of the Exchequer, which once again ensured the Treasury of direct representation in the Cabinet. Attlee succeeded Anderson as Lord President of the Council. Finally, in November 1943, Lord Woolton was taken into the War Cabinet as Minister of Reconstruction.[65] On 11 February 1944, a debate about Woolton's position was held in the House of Commons.[66] It became evident that there was uneasiness about the relation of the new minister to the existing departmental ministers. It was asked whether Woolton was authorized to give actual instructions to the departments and, if so, whether this did not impair the constitutional responsibility of the departments to Parliament. Conversely, if the new minister did not have such powers, could he really perform his duties? *The Times* declared *ex cathedra* on 12 February 1944 that the new minister's responsibility apparently lay somewhere between the responsibility of each individual Minister to both the Cabinet and Parliament, and the collective responsibility of the Government as a whole. Then *The Times* continued wistfully: "Parliament will no doubt use the experience, which it has already acquired during

---

[62] Alanbrooke, p. 537.   [63] Churchill, IV, 503.

[64] *Life of Cripps*, pp. 300, 302; cf. Williams, *Triple Challenge*, p. 80.

[65] For a time, reconstruction matters had been the responsibility of Greenwood, who had worked in the same field during the First World War (cf. Addison, *Politics from Within*, II, 264–65). After Greenwood's departure, Sir William Jowitt had been in charge, first as Paymaster-General, then as Minister without Portfolio.

[66] 396 H. of C. Deb. (11 February 1944), cols. 2049–85; cf. Woolton, *Memoirs*, pp. 261–65, 297, and Morrison's comments, *Autobiography*, p. 196.

the war, in determining the distribution of responsibility between Lord Woolton and his departmental colleagues for their respective contributions to the total result."

The Prime Minister, the War Cabinet, and the Ministers outside the Cabinet

From Churchill's first day as Prime Minister, military problems predominated in the Cabinet. War Policy was largely decided by Churchill himself, in constant consultation with the Chiefs of Staff and a few others who enjoyed his personal confidence. Only they knew all military plans, including the dates and details of operations. Immediately after this inner circle came the members of the Defence Committee (Operations) of the War Cabinet, which, in addition to Churchill, Attlee, and the Chiefs of Staff, consisted of the Service ministers, the Foreign Secretary, Eden and the Minister of Production, Lyttelton. But the importance of the Defence Committee declined considerably after 1941.[67]

The members of the Defence Committee and other members of the War Cabinet had access to the most important memoranda and telegrams and were consulted about future strategic decisions in a general way. The meetings of the War Cabinet were also often attended by certain other ministers, the so-called "constant attenders."[68] But in practice the War Cabinet's influence on war policy declined just as much as the Defence Committee's.[69] The War Cabinet generally met once or twice a week unless unexpected events necessitated a special meeting.[70] In addition, there was a weekly "Monday Cabinet Parade."[71] In addition to the members of the War Cabinet, the Service ministers, the Home Secretary, the Chancellor of the Exchequer, the Secretaries of State for India and the Dominions (and frequently, in later years, the Dominion representatives themselves), the Minister of Information, and the Permanent Secretary to the Foreign Office attended these Monday sessions. At these meetings, the Chiefs of Staff and the Foreign Secretary gave a general survey of military and political developments of the week. When Churchill found, as he wrote in a minute in 1940, that "our colleagues not in the War Cabinet but above the 'line' are depressed at not knowing more of what is going forward in the military sphere," he instructed the Service ministers to inform these ministers each week in rotation. "Nothing must ever be said to anybody about future operations: these must always be kept in the most narrow circles," Churchill wrote at that time.[72]

The War Cabinet retained most of its powers on matters outside the immediate military sphere. After 1942, the details of supply policy rested with the Minister of Production and the principal Supply Ministers.

[67] Ehrman, *Strategy*, p. 325.   [68] Churchill, IV, 77–78.
[69] Ehrman, *Strategy*, p. 324.   [70] Morrison, p. 10.
[71] Churchill, II, 18 and IV, 78.
[72] Minute of 5 July 1940, Churchill, II, 566–67.

Churchill himself and the War Cabinet, however, exercised ultimate control over the allocation of manpower and scarce resources among the immediate requirements of the Front, military production for future use, and the needs of the civilian population. Most domestic problems were settled by the Lord President's Committee, virtually a meeting of the War Cabinet without Churchill and Eden.[73]

The number of departments continued to increase during the period. In addition to those that had been established in 1939, the following new departments were founded during the course of the war: the Ministry of Aircraft Production (1940), the Ministry of War Transport (resulting from an amalgamation of the Ministries of Transport and Shipping in 1941), the Ministry of Production (1942), the Ministry of Fuel and Power (1942), the Ministry of Town and Country Planning (1943), the Ministry of Reconstruction (1943), the Ministry of National Insurance (1944), and the Ministry of Civil Aviation (1944). The ministers outside the Cabinet were drawn into the activities of the War Cabinet by numerous Cabinet committees of varying tasks and composition. They also received *ad hoc* invitations to special War Cabinet meetings. War Cabinet members took on special tasks of coordination and supervision. Their influence as such was based not only on their higher status as members of the War Cabinet, but also on their chairmanship of certain committees, on the strength of their personalities, and especially on their relationship to Churchill, who delegated special tasks to them or who might see them through possible conflicts with other ministers.

Unlike their predecessors in the Lloyd George War Cabinet, these Cabinet members were often in charge of certain departments whose importance had increased greatly because of the war. If not, they were at least charged with specific duties, as was the case with Cripps, who was Leader of the House of Commons, and with Anderson and Attlee, who, as Lords President of the Council, in fact, acted from 1940 to 1943 and from 1943 to 1945, respectively, as Prime Ministers of a sub-Cabinet. "I did not like having unharnessed ministers around me," Churchill wrote later. "I preferred to deal with chiefs of organizations rather than counselors. Everyone should do a good day's work and be accountable for some definite task, and then they do not make trouble for trouble's sake or to cut a figure."[74] Yet it was on this exact point that Churchill was criticized again and again. When the first Minister of Production was appointed in 1942, Beveridge wrote that such an explicit grouping of departments

has two grave disadvantages; first that the super-minister in charge of a group of departments is almost bound to interfere with the sense of responsibility and speed of action of his subordinates; second, that he is almost bound to become absorbed in executive details, leaving him no time to think, to read, to discuss, to plan ahead. The tradition that a minister of a named department is re-

---

[73] See especially Chester, *Machinery*, pp. 8–14; also Hancock–Gowing, pp. 220–23.

[74] Churchill, I, 419.

sponsible for everything done by that department, and therefore must be prepared to know about everything, if asked, is strong and not easily shaken in
this country.[75]

Ten years later, Churchill was to face similar criticism when he again
appointed special coordinating ministers, this time during peacetime.

Finally, some very special ministerial appointments were made because
of the war. Again and again, the War Cabinet was confronted with knotty
problems abroad that it could not grapple with well or quickly enough
from London, but that nevertheless touched important political nerves.
Among them were cooperation with the Americans and the Free French,
political developments in the Middle East and the Far East, and military
operations in the Mediterranean. In a number of such cases, Churchill
appointed ministers who could act as War Cabinet spokesmen on the spot.
As early as the winter of 1940, he requested Halifax, then Foreign Secretary, to go to Washington as Ambassador, while retaining his War Cabinet
seat.[76] In July 1941, Churchill appointed Lyttelton Minister of State
Resident in the Middle East, and both Lyttelton and his successor in 1942,
the Australian R. G. Casey, became members of the War Cabinet.[77] Other
appointments on this pattern followed in the course of the war. Among
them were Duff Cooper's appointment as Minister of State for Far Eastern
Affairs in 1941 and Harold Macmillan's as Minister Resident at Allied
Force Headquarters, Mediterranean Command in December 1942.[78] Similarly, a Minister Resident for Supply was appointed in Washington. During part of the war, there was also a Minister Resident in West Africa.

The number of ministerial portfolios greatly increased as a result of
these and other ministerial creations. The number of ministers of Cabinet
rank—which, including the Law Officers, had been 30 in 1939—had by
1945 increased to 47. Churchill could certainly not be critized for a reluctance to innovate.

Churchill as Leader of the Cabinet

Many have sought to compare Lloyd George and Churchill as war leaders. "The main difference," wrote Hankey to Beveridge, "is that Lloyd
George's method was devised to secure delegation of administration without impairing ministerial or department responsibility. The present
system is in theory and practice a 'one-man show.' "[79] This argument
could be buttressed by considerable evidence. Sure of his grip on the
country, Churchill was the unchallenged master of the entire government
apparatus between 1940 and 1945. The Government therefore partook

---

[75] *The Times,* 14 February 1942.
[76] Cf. Halifax, *Fullness of Days,* p. 236; Eden, *Full Circle,* p. 266.
[77] Churchill, III, 312–14.
[78] *Ibid.,* pp. 379, 543–44, and IV, 600–601.
[79] Beveridge, *Power and Influence,* p. 404; cf. Hankey, *Control,* pp. 64–66;
Kennedy, *Business of War,* p. 317; Amery, *War Leaders,* pp. 55–73; Petrie, pp.
163–64.

of both his strength and his weaknesses. His astounding capacity for work, his intelligence, and his fertile imagination found expression particularly in a steady flow of minutes directed to countless ministers, committees, and civil servants, and often labeled "Action this Day." Because such minutes frequently began with the word "pray," Whitehall soon dubbed them "prayers."[80]

Many have felt that these minutes had considerable use in activating the government apparatus.[81] But this did not gainsay the widespread feeling that the departments could have done with fewer of them.[82] Churchill's orders were not always to the point. They were far from being a substitute for regular coordination and control. A considerable number of Churchill's minutes originated with his intellectual alter ego, Professor Lindemann (soon to become Lord Cherwell), who was not too well liked by the ordinary civil servant in Whitehall.[83] But an infinite number of ideas also sprang from what Baldwin once called Churchill's hundred horsepower mind.[84] "There's Winston," Lloyd George once said to Attlee. "He has half a dozen solutions to it and one of them is right, but the trouble is he does not know which it is." "This," wrote Attlee, "is putting the matter extremely, but I think that Churchill does need men around him, who, while ready to support a good idea, however novel, are prepared on occasion to take an emphatic line against a bad one."[85] The biography of Brooke, Chief of the Imperial General Staff after 1941, supports this view. A hostess who saw Churchill and his new military adviser together for the first time wondered how the new Chief of the Imperial General Staff would manage "to get on with Winston. . . . He spent all the afternoon sitting on the sofa and seemed all the time to be saying: 'No, no, Sir, you can't.' "[86]

The personal element of Churchill's war leadership was also strongly apparent in the choice of his ministers and private advisers. Without him, presumably neither Beaverbrook nor Lyttelton nor Woolton would have risen to such important positions. At lower levels, personal factors also had considerable influence. Examples include Cherwell's appointment to Paymaster-General in 1942; Lord Leathers' promotion to Minister of War Transport in 1941, combining the former portfolios of Transport and Shipping under him; the unprecedented elevation of Churchill's former Private Secretary, Sir James Grigg, from Permanent Secretary at the War Office to Secretary of State for War in 1942; and the appointment

---

[80] Grigg, *Prejudice and Judgment*, pp. 391–92.

[81] Dalton, *Memoirs*, II, 416 n.

[82] Grigg, *Prejudice and Judgment*, p. 392; Alanbrooke, I, 26; Kennedy, *Business of War*, pp. 60–61, 114–15, 123, 178; Woolton, *Memoirs*, p. 378. The General Staff spoke of "banderillas" and "bludgeon strokes" (Kennedy, *op. cit.*, p. 204).

[83] Cf. Churchill, I, 368.   [84] *Life of Baldwin*, p. 106.

[85] Attlee, *As It Happened*, p. 140; cf. Lloyd George, *Memoirs*, III, 1067; *Life of Addison*, p. 154. One of Churchill's closest friends and admirers was Lord Birkenhead. He too said, "But when he is wrong—my God!!" (Vansittart, *The Mist Procession*, p. 386).

[86] Alanbrooke, I, 22–23, and *passim*.

of his political supporter Brendan Bracken to Minister of Information in 1941. Hopkins, Roosevelt's personal agent, who in 1941 considered it his duty to become "a catalytic agent between two prima donnas," wrote, "I want to try to get an understanding of Churchill and of the men he sees after midnight."[87] These were chiefly Bracken, Cherwell, Beaverbrook, and Lyttelton. Churchill's physical strength and his preference for transacting business or testing ideas in the middle of the night became somewhat of a problem for a number of ministers, high military officials, and civil servants.[88] "Mrs. Bevin took a firm line with the Prime Minister about [Bevin's] attendance at Cabinet discussions after midnight," wrote one of Bevin's biographers.[89] But not every minister had a Mrs. Bevin.

Nevertheless, Churchill retained a sharp eye for political exigencies. His first Cabinet was little more than a committee of the five most important party leaders in 1940. Cripps's inclusion in the Government in 1942 was clearly a political act. In lower-ranking ministerial appointments, too, Churchill rarely lost sight of political factors. Although he sometimes did appoint outsiders, he generally confined himself in his ministerial selections, much more than Lloyd George had done, to the traditional political circles of the House of Lords and House of Commons. However great his personal authority, Churchill did not rule over the heads of the War Cabinet. Again and again, the records show that he consulted Attlee and the War Cabinet when abroad before entering into definite commitments.[90]

Churchill's Caretaker Government (1945)

The surrender of the Third Reich broke up the National Coalition in Great Britain. The 1935 Parliament had long exceeded its constitutional term. More and more disagreement about steps to be taken arose among the Coalition partners. Churchill would have preferred to continue the National Coalition until the eventual defeat of Japan. Most Labour leaders, however, were not prepared to postpone a new election any later than the autumn of 1945. In that case, the Conservatives much preferred a snap election.[91] On 23 May 1945, Churchill submitted the resignation of the National Government. The King commissioned him to form a new Government. Churchill's Caretaker Cabinet was composed of 16 members, all entrusted with portfolios that pre-dated 1939. The non-Socialist mem-

[87] Sherwood, I, 289–90.
[88] Alanbrooke, *passim;* Morrison, p. 63. According to Hankey, Lloyd George thought caring for the physical fitness of ministers was one of the most important principles of good government (see *Supreme Command,* p. 165, and *Control,* p. 42). But then, Lloyd George liked going to bed early. For a weak defense of Churchill's nocturnal habits, see Ismay, pp. 175–76.
[89] Williams, *Bevin,* p. 232.
[90] See, for instance, Sherwood, I, 438–39, for differences between Roosevelt and Churchill in this respect; cf. Mackintosh, pp. 425–29.
[91] Churchill, VI, 508–17, and Attlee, *As It Happened,* pp. 134–38.

bers of the 1940–45 War Cabinet formed its core: Churchill, Eden (Foreign Secretary), Anderson (Chancellor of the Exchequer), Woolton (Lord President of the Council), Beaverbrook (Lord Privy Seal), and Lyttelton (President of the Board of Trade and Minister of Production). The three Service ministers, as well as the Secretaries of State for Scotland, Dominions, Colonies, India, and Burma, and the Minister of Agriculture, were also in the Cabinet, to which R. A. Butler and Macmillan were promoted for the first time, as Minister of Labour and Secretary of State for Air, respectively.

The Lord Chancellor, the Ministers of Education, Health, (War) Transport, Works, and Pensions, the Postmaster-General, and the Paymaster-General, all Law Officers, and all ministers who headed departments formed after 1938 remained outside the Cabinet. Even apart from the Law Officers and the still-remaining Ministers Overseas, the number of ministers of Cabinet rank outside the Cabinet was greater than the number inside. All non-party ministers who had come into office under Churchill during the war remained members of the new Caretaker Government together with the Conservatives and the National-Liberals. At the elections of July 1945, they acted together as National candidates. Few were successful in their electoral bids. Only some who held university seats, as did Anderson and Sir Arthur Salter, returned to Westminster in 1945.

SIX

THE LABOUR GOVERNMENT, 1945–1951

Attlee and the Formation of the Cabinet in 1945

When Attlee was definitely chosen Leader of the Labour Party after the elections of 1935, Hugh Dalton wrote in his diary: "A wretched, disheartening result . . . a little mouse shall lead them."[1] Attlee's selection as Leader was a result of special circumstance. As one of the few former Socialist ministers who had kept their seats in the House of Commons in the anti-Labour landslide of 1931, he had been elected Deputy Leader under Lansbury. When Lansbury resigned from the Leadership in 1935 because of his pacifist convictions, Attlee temporarily succeeded him. But in the 1935 elections a large number of former Labour leaders were again returned to the House of Commons. A new decision had to be made about the party Leadership. Dalton worked to elect Morrison, others Greenwood. Attlee was elected on the second ballot only because Greenwood's supporters preferred him to Morrison.[2]

Since that time, Attlee's prestige had risen. But even in 1945, some prominent party members felt that a Labour Cabinet could be led more advantageously by someone else. Both Laski, who was Chairman of the Labour Party in 1945, and Morrison sought to dissuade Attlee from accepting immediately appointment to the Prime Ministership by the King. The new Parliamentary Party ought first to decide definitely on its Leader, Laski argued in a letter to Attlee. Only then would the latter have the right to accept the office of Prime Minister in the name of the Labour Party. Attlee apparently replied to Laski in a letter of fourteen words: "Dear Laski, I thank you for your letter, contents of which have been noted."[3]

When the elections of 1945 secured Labour a great majority in the House of Commons, Attlee accepted his appointment as Prime Minister without further consultation. And as soon as he began forming his Cabinet, he made his influence strongly felt. He decided to appoint Bevin, who preferred the post of Chancellor of the Exchequer, as Foreign Secretary,

---

[1] Dalton, *Memoirs,* II, 82.
[2] *Ibid.,* p. 79ff; Attlee, *As It Happened,* pp. 80–81; Morrison, *Autobiography,* pp. 163–64.
[3] See Dalton, *Memoirs,* II, 467ff; Williams, *Bevin,* pp. 238–39; Attlee, *As It Happened,* pp. 145, 156; McKenzie, pp. 328–33; and Morrison's denial that he conspired against Attlee (*Autobiography,* p. 164; cf. pp. 236, 245–47, 260).

and Dalton, who preferred the office of Foreign Secretary, as Chancellor
of the Exchequer.[4] Morrison (who, according to Dalton's rather partisan
information, had demanded the post of Foreign Secretary), became Lord
President of the Council, Deputy Prime Minister, and Leader of the House
of Commons.[5] At least one of Attlee's reasons for this rather abrupt
switching of Bevin and Dalton was that he did not want to bring Morrison
and Bevin together in a single field, domestic policy. Both men were
strong antagonists, and only a short while earlier Bevin had resisted any
attempt to unseat Attlee.[6]

Since 1931, Attlee had gained quite varied parliamentary experience.
First he served as Deputy Leader of the very few members of the Parliamentary Labour Party of 1931–35, which was "virtually a tea party,"
according to Morrison.[7] Since 1935 he had been Leader of His Majesty's
Opposition.[8] Between 1940 and 1945, he had presided over numerous
War Cabinet meetings as Deputy Prime Minister whenever Churchill was
ill or was absent from London. No greater difference between two chairmen could be imagined. Under Attlee, Cabinet meetings were shorter,
and the chairman was less inspiring and more to the point.[9] Between 1945
and 1951, Attlee proved to be a Prime Minister who asserted himself in
all fields and did not hesitate to rid himself of colleagues—even of old
friends such as Greenwood—who did not satisfy the demands he made
upon them.[10]

Attlee's Views on Cabinet Organization

Before 1940, Attlee had pleaded as Leader of the Opposition for drastic
reforms in the organization of the Cabinet. The existing Cabinet, he had
argued in 1937, was too much concerned with particular items of unequal
importance and urgency. This system might work well when the content
of government was small, and the main lines of policy were merely the
acceptance of the status quo. But it would be inadequate as an instrument

[4] Dalton, *Memoirs*, II, 469, and III, 8–14; *Life of King George VI*, pp. 636–39;
Williams, *Bevin*, p. 237ff; Evans, *Bevin*, pp. 204, 210–11. King George, too, advised
Attlee to appoint Bevin rather than Dalton to the Foreign Office, possibly on the
advice of Churchill. It is clear, however, that Attlee was also moved by a number of
other circumstances. Morrison claims that he suggested appointing Bevin to the
Foreign Office because Dalton had a temper, which was bad for diplomatic work
(*Autobiography*, pp. 246–48).
[5] Dalton, *Memoirs*, II, 474.
[6] Williams, *Bevin*, pp. 230–31, 237–40; Attlee's review of Wheeler-Bennett's
Life of King George VI in *The Observer*, 23 August 1959; and Dalton, *Memoirs*,
II, 469, 473, and III, 237.
[7] Morrison, *Autobiography*, p. 164.
[8] Attlee, *As It Happened*, pp. 75–78; *Life of Cripps*, p. 146.
[9] See, for instance, Alanbrooke, I, 285; Morrison, p. 39; Morrison, *Autobiography*, p. 209.
[10] *The Times*, 8 December 1955; Williams, *Triple Challenge*, pp. 48–64; cf.
Attlee, *As It Happened*, p. 155. Retrospective admiration has made Attlee seem a
more powerful "butcher," however, than he actually was (or could have been). Cf.
Heasman, pp. 321–24.

for a plan of reconstruction of society. Attlee had then developed his own ideas about Cabinet reform:

It is, in my view, essential to make a distinction of function between ministers who are responsible for detailed administration and those to whom is entrusted the work of dealing with the broader issues. There are a number of ministerial posts which have no very heavy departmental duties, but as a rule these are assigned to persons whose inclusion is desired either on account of their representative capacity or as an acknowledgment of past services and distrust of their administrative abilities. Frequently these persons are mere passengers in the boat.

These posts should be filled by ministers who have the faculty of directing broad issues of policy. They should be in charge of functions, not departments. Each should, in his own sphere, be, so to speak, the representative of the Prime Minister in relation to a particular group of services, and should preside over a committee of the ministers charged with administration. Thus the general coordination of the social services would fall to one minister. Defense would be the care of another, economic policy of a third, and external relations of a fourth. There should be a continuous contact between these ministers. The Prime Minister is necessarily the responsible head of the Ministry, but he needs to be assisted by a small group of members of the Cabinet whose specific function is coordinating policy and giving general direction. This does not mean the supersession of the Cabinet by a small *Junta* and the relegation of departmental ministers to an inferior status. On the contrary, the ministers who are charged with coordination will be in constant and close contact with the ministers in their respective groups, who will, through them, be able to make their views felt more effectively.[11]

It is not altogether clear from this passage whether Attlee wanted a Cabinet composed exclusively of coordinating ministers. As we saw, that idea had found favor with some Labour politicians in the 1930's. Cripps, for instance, had pleaded for it both at that time and during the war. Attlee had gained practical experience during the war in a Cabinet in which "senior ministers were given a general oversight over a range of functions," and from which the great majority of departmental ministers had been excluded. "I had myself been attracted by this idea," Attlee wrote, "though I was well aware that considerations—both political and personal—would make it difficult to adopt it in its entirety."[12]

The Cabinet Attlee formed in 1945 differed substantially from his own ideal model. It had twenty members: all the ministers who had been included in Churchill's Caretaker Cabinet, plus the Lord Chancellor, the Minister of Education, the Minister of Health (Aneurin Bevan), and the Minister of Fuel and Power (Emanuel Shinwell). The inclusion of Bevan and Shinwell was at least as much due to their personal status as to the political importance their departments would acquire through the changes the Labour Government intended to bring about in the areas of national

---

[11] Attlee, *Labour Party,* pp. 173–75; cf. Attlee in 356 H. of C. Deb. (1 February 1940), col. 1416.
[12] Attlee, *As It Happened,* p. 152.

health and fuel and power. Like Churchill, Attlee assumed the title of Minister of Defence. The Service ministers, too, were included in the Cabinet while the war against Japan continued.

Attlee later wrote that the Cabinet was rather larger than was desirable.[13] Its increase in size was partly due to the assertion of claims by individual politicians and political groups on the Government benches. In addition, a Machinery of Government Committee of the Coalition Cabinet during the war and, in 1945, the most senior members of the Cabinet Office —the Secretary of the Cabinet, Sir Edward Bridges, and Sir Norman Brook—had urgently advised against excluding the main departmental ministers.

In later years, Attlee tried to reduce the size of the Cabinet. By excluding the Service ministers in 1946 and abolishing the position of Secretary of State for India and for Burma in 1947, he succeeded temporarily in cutting the membership to sixteen. But personal factors soon made the number rise again to eighteen.[14] After 1946, the composition of the Cabinet did not change fundamentally until the end of Labour's rule. More important were alterations in its internal organization.

The Organization of the Labour Government (1945–51)

The structure of the Labour Government differed in at least three respects from the type of organization that had prevailed between the two world wars. First, the number of important government departments had greatly increased. Since the size of the Cabinet was simultaneously decreased, a considerable number of ministers remained excluded from the Cabinet, even in peacetime. Second, in order to get through the considerably increased amount of Cabinet business and to improve the coordination between Cabinet and non-Cabinet ministers, an extensive system of fixed and *ad hoc* Cabinet committees developed. Third, on the strength of undisclosed orders from the Prime Minister, senior ministers acted as coordinators for various fields of government administration.

The Cabinet and the Ministers outside the Cabinet

The exclusion of a number of important departmental ministers from the Cabinet caused the same problems that had arisen during both world wars. Exclusion implied that certain ministers were only indirectly involved in making the most important Government decisions. In spite of a *pro forma* equalization of salaries, rank, and precedence, they were reduced to ministers of the second order. Morrison mentions that Attlee tried to draw these ministers into the activities of the Cabinet as much as

---

[13] *Ibid.*, p. 154.

[14] After he resigned as Chancellor of the Exchequer in 1947, Dalton returned to the Cabinet in 1948 as Chancellor of the Duchy of Lancaster. Similarly, after 1950, A. V. Alexander (raised to the peerage as Viscount Alexander of Hillsborough) remained a member of the Cabinet in the same post, while Dalton became Minister of Town and Country Planning.

possible. They received the Cabinet agenda and minutes and a great number of (though not all) Cabinet papers. Attlee often arranged the composition of Cabinet committees in such a way that a number of members who had no immediate interest in the subject under discussion were always included. According to Morrison, this had "the value of bringing into the consultations the voices of ministers above the battle," and gave ministers outside the Cabinet "an important share in collective discussions and the reaching of decisions." Moreover, the ministers outside the Cabinet could formally ask to be invited to particular Cabinet meetings and, in addition, they could always informally submit their views to leading Cabinet members.[15]

Morrison's picture is undoubtedly somewhat rosy. There is clear evidence that the exclusion of many ministers from the Cabinet caused considerable frustration. John Strachey, Minister of Food, frequently attended Cabinet sessions on matters outside his special province. Some senior ministers took exception to this, and Attlee had to give Strachey a special hint not to do so any longer. Strachey was so indignant that he contemplated resigning.[16] Another minister excluded until 1950, Patrick Gordon Walker (whom Attlee then promoted to the Cabinet as Secretary of State for Commonwealth Relations), has given the following, far from gay, picture of the relations of non-Cabinet ministers to the Cabinet:

Non-Cabinet ministers are called to the Cabinet for questions that touch their departmental competence. This can be a testing ordeal. You are invited to attend at a stated hour when your business is expected to be reached—your appearance is nearly always premature; though occasionally, if the Cabinet goes unexpectedly fast, you may have to rush over from your office on a sudden summons. Usually you have to wait outside the Cabinet room, alone in the antechamber, which is the only place I know bleaker than a dentist's waiting-room. When the Secretary calls you in, you enter a Cabinet in full swing; find an empty chair where you can; hurriedly open your papers; and, at the Prime Minister's invitation, embark on an exposition of your case. When the point is settled, you rise and leave the Cabinet to get on with its remaining business.[17]

Undoubtedly, civil servants also considered the exclusion of "their" departments as a sign of deliberate underestimation of their work.[18]

The Creation of Permanent Cabinet Committees

The disturbances resulting from the war, together with the drastic legislative program Labour wished to carry through Parliament, made the pressure of government business increase strongly. The Cabinet met twice weekly, but there was a limit to the time busy departmental ministers could spend on Cabinet affairs. Also, care had to be taken to main-

[15] Morrison, p. 31; cf. pp. 23–25, 55.   [16] Dalton, *Memoirs*, III, 270–71.
[17] Gordon Walker, p. 21; K. C. Wheare in *The Listener*, 25 November 1954, p. 902.
[18] Cf. Attlee, *As It Happened*, p. 153.

tain adequate liaison with non-Cabinet ministers. A far-reaching delegation of tasks to standing Cabinet committees became inevitable.[19] In
doing so, ministers and senior officials built on experiences gained during
the war.[20] Morrison, as Lord President of the Council, once more presided over a committee that he later described as a "sub-Cabinet" or
general purposes committee.[21] Other permanent committees were also
founded. Among them were a committee for defense, various committees
on economic policy, and committees on manpower, social legislation, foreign policy, and Commonwealth affairs. Of great importance, too, was
the so-called Legislation Committee, which judged the degree of urgency
of bills to be introduced in Parliament.[22] Numerous other committees
were charged with more narrowly defined problems such as the independence of India and Burma, the introduction of the new health scheme,
and housing. As a rule, neither the existence nor the composition of these
committees was officially disclosed while Attlee's Cabinet was in office. Referring explicitly to the view of Anderson, who now sat on the Opposition
benches, Morrison and others argued that publicity about internal government organization and procedure would harm free deliberation in the
Cabinet.[23] Such publicity might impair the authority of ministers whose
activities were in a wider context coordinated by certain committees.
Moreover, it might lead to the undesirable situation in which certain
chairmen of coordinating committees would be held publicly responsible
for matters that were essentially controlled by the departmental ministers
normally responsible to Parliament. Both collective and individual ministerial responsibility would therefore suffer.

The Coordinating Ministers

Attlee appointed as chairmen of the most important committees those
members of his Cabinet who perhaps best fitted into the plan he had
outlined in 1937—that such chairmen should be "ministers who have the
faculty of directing broad issues of policy."[24] Attlee immediately took it
upon himself to supervise the defense sector. In addition, he acted, until
1947, as chairman of a committee on the independence of India and in
that year was chairman of a committee on overseas economic policy. Morrison performed coordinating duties in domestic affairs, including, until
1947, domestic economic policy. As Leader of the House of Commons, he
furthermore greatly influenced political strategy. Bevin ruled supreme
in foreign policy, which he conducted in intimate and continuous contact
with Attlee but in such a personal fashion that an official of the Foreign
Office could exclaim: "Up to now, Secretary of State, we have not been
the Foreign Office for years. We have been merely a Post Office for No.

---

[19] Morrison, p. 18; Chester, *Cabinet,* pp. 41–55; Chester, *Planning, passim.*
[20] Attlee, *As It Happened,* p. 154.   [21] Morrison, p. 20.
[22] *Ibid.,* pp. 222–24; cf. pp. 239–41.
[23] 419 H. of C. Deb. (28 February 1946), cols. 2128–32; Anderson, *Machinery,*
pp. 17–18.
[24] Morrison, p. 37ff; cf. pp. 18–23; Attlee, *As It Happened,* p. 164.

10, Downing Street."[25] But Bevin also dealt with domestic politics. Until 1947, for instance, he was chairman of the Committee on Manpower. Greenwood acted as coordinator of the social services and the legislative program until 1947. His personal life made him just as unsuccessful in this function as he had been during the first years of the war, however. Attlee dismissed him in 1947.

Initially, Attlee allowed most departmental ministers considerable freedom in matters concerning their own departments, but this policy was somewhat changed after 1946. After the fuel crisis of the winter of 1946–47, Attlee took over from the minister hitherto in charge by forming a special committee of ministers and high officials under his own chairmanship. He took similar steps when a food shortage threatened.[26] In August 1947, he decided to make a drastic change in the responsibilities for economic policy. Thereafter he himself presided over a new high-level committee for economic policy. Cripps was charged with the direct supervision of the conduct of economic affairs. Morrison lost a considerable part of his duties through these changes, but found some compensation in taking over tasks that had hitherto been under Greenwood's control.[27] As early as the fall of 1946, Attlee had delegated as much direct control of defense matters as possible to A. V. Alexander, who held the new post of Minister of Defence. The aged Addison, Labour Leader of the House of Lords, who as a Liberal had performed coordinating functions even under Lloyd George, acted as coordinator for various sectors.[28]

The Formal and Informal Structure of the Labour Government

Lord Francis Williams, who was Attlee's public relations officer during the first years of the Labour Government, and who later wrote a biography of Bevin and published the book *A Prime Minister Remembers* (1961), based on often somewhat unreliable taped conversations with Attlee, gave in 1948 the following picture of the structure of the Labour Cabinet:

For a Cabinet of equal departmental ministers under a Prime Minister who is himself the "first among equals" there has been substituted a pyramidical pattern of government designed to secure greater rapidity in action and a tighter centralized control of general political strategy. . . . At the apex of this pyramid sits the Prime Minister. Directly underneath him come a group of three senior "functional" ministers, Ernest Bevin, Foreign Secretary, Stafford Cripps, Chancellor of the Exchequer, Herbert Morrison, Lord President of the Council. Directly under these three again come a group of five ministers with coordinating functions of an important but less major character: A. V. Alexander, Minister of Defence, Viscount Addison, Lord Privy Seal, Viscount Jowitt, Lord Chancellor, Chuter Ede, Home Secretary, Hugh Dalton, Chancel-

[25] Evans, *Bevin*, p. 215.
[26] Williams, *Triple Challenge*, pp. 43–44.
[27] Morrison, p. 21, and Williams, *Triple Challenge*, pp. 84–85.
[28] Cf. Attlee, *As It Happened*, pp. 69–70, and *Life of Addison, passim*.

lor of the Duchy of Lancaster. Below this group are the eight senior departmental ministers who are also members of the Cabinet and who therefore have the right to take part in Cabinet discussions not merely on their own departmental affairs but on any aspect of policy: the Secretaries of State for the Colonies, for Commonwealth Relations, and for Scotland, the Ministers of Labour, Health, Agriculture, and Education, and the President of the Board of Trade. In this group two ministers stand out somewhat from the others, Aneurin Bevan for personal reasons, and George Isaacs, Minister of Labour, because manpower problems affect all departmental programs.

Below the departmental Cabinet ministers come twelve Heads of Departments who, although formally of Cabinet status and paid the same salary as Cabinet ministers, are not members of the Cabinet itself and only attend when specifically invited by the Prime Minister to deal with matters concerning their departments. John Strachey, Minister of Food, is included among this group, but he attends Cabinets more frequently than most of the others because of the key position of food policy. Finally, forming the base of the pyramid are those, such as the two Ministers of State and the Paymaster-General, who are not heads of departments of their own, the Law Officers, and in a lower status the parliamentary secretaries.[29]

According to Williams, the Cabinet remained the "final arbitrator of policy," with the right "to approve all major decisions and . . . reject or alter what comes before it. But the important preliminary planning of policy and the general direction of strategy now lies outside it."[30] The picture Williams drew shows a deliberate matter-of-factness and a formal hierarchic structure that cannot be accepted offhand. Whatever its formal organization, in the last analysis the Cabinet was based on very special personal relationships and qualities. In 1947, *The Times* spoke of "the balance of personal forces, of which Mr. Attlee has been the expression and embodiment ever since he took over the leadership of the party.[31] Williams said the same in somewhat friendlier words: "Bevin, Cripps, Morrison, each of these has dominating talents; each overtops Attlee in some single respect; but none of them possesses the balance of qualities that he does."[32] In fact, bitter rivalry between such men as Bevin, Morrison, Dalton, Cripps, and Bevan introduced considerable disharmony at the top. This alone allowed Attlee to exercise influence on the direction in which the various coordinators carried out their activities.[33] What made other ministers seek or accept the support of these men was not so much their formal position as coordinating ministers, however, as their personal influence and prestige in the party, the country, or the Cabinet. For the very same reasons, Attlee was at times compelled *nolens volens* to accept their authority. In the circumstances, it was not of great importance which posts they held. Until 1951, Morrison did not hold an administrative post

[29] Williams, *Triple Challenge,* pp. 43–45.
[30] *Ibid.,* pp. 47, 43.   [31] *The Times,* 8 October 1947.
[32] Williams, *Triple Challenge,* p. 63; cf. Mackintosh, pp. 430–31.
[33] In addition to Leslie Hunter's rather unpleasant *Road to Brighton Pier* (1959), the best available source to date is Dalton's partisan *High Tide and After* (1962).

of great weight; yet he was pre-eminently a leading coordinator. Bevin controlled a large department and was also a leading coordinator. Dalton was Chancellor of the Exchequer until 1947, but until then the question was whether the Treasury could be coordinated in the general context of economic policy, rather than whether the Chancellor should be a leading coordinating minister. Cripps, on the other hand, was charged with coordinating economic policies, first as Minister for Economic Affairs (in September 1947), and shortly after as Chancellor of the Exchequer. If personal factors are not taken into account, these differences cannot be understood.

Great changes were also necessary in the committee structure, both in 1947, when Morrison fell ill and when Cripps was appointed first Minister for Economic Affairs and then Chancellor of the Exchequer, and in 1951, when Morrison left the Lord Presidency of the Council for the post of Foreign Secretary. Addison's position, too, was largely due to personal qualities.

Rising Tension in the Labour Cabinet (1950–51)

The influence of personal factors is also apparent in the developments after 1950. In the elections of February of that year, Labour obtained an absolute majority of only six seats over the Opposition parties. This made the Government dependent on every vote it could mobilize in the House of Commons. During part of this period, the Conservative Opposition endeavored to bring down the Government by forcing night sessions in the House of Commons, which physically exhausted the Labour ministers. At the same time, the Cabinet lost its backbone as ill health compelled Cripps and Bevin to give up their posts in 1950 and 1951, respectively. Internal relations in the Cabinet became more embittered as personal rivalries were less checked by superior power in the upper layers. The seemingly ready acceptance of a hierarchic Cabinet structure, as posthumously described in the public writings of senior ministers in the 1950's, was visibly cracking toward the end of the Labour Cabinet. Conflicts at last ran so high that Bevan, only recently appointed Minister of Labour, and the young President of the Board of Trade, Harold Wilson, resigned from their posts. Such physical and political strains made Attlee decide to call for an election.[34] Labour again received a majority of votes, but the Conservatives captured a majority of seats.

[34] *Life of King George VI*, pp. 791–96, and Attlee in *The Observer*, 23 August 1959.

SEVEN

CHURCHILL AND THE OVERLORDS, 1951–1955

The Formation of Churchill's First Peacetime Cabinet

In the fall of 1951, Churchill became Prime Minister of a peacetime Government for the first time. For more than six years the Conservatives had been in Opposition, a position they had not occupied for any length of time since 1915. This situation was not without effect. Not all Conservatives had found it easy to accept Churchill as party Leader in 1940. Memories of the period before the First World War, when Churchill had abandoned the party of his father, Lord Randolph Churchill, to become one of its fiercest opponents, still rankled. Churchill had returned to the fold in 1924. But many Conservative M.P.'s still had not forgotten the strong stand Churchill had taken against Baldwin and Chamberlain in the 1930's. For his part, Churchill had, in 1945, only reluctantly relinquished his high position as National Leader to become Leader of the Conservative Party.[1]

But since that time the old animosities had slowly faded. After 1945, the Conservative Party machine underwent a drastic overhaul at the hands of Woolton.[2] Under the influence of Butler, the moving spirit of the Conservative Political Centre, the official party line was brought more closely into agreement with the realities of the Welfare State.[3] Not all Conservatives viewed this development with equal approval. Right-wing Conservatives spoke of Socialist contamination, and Labour taunted the Conservatives with the scornful American label "me-too-ism." It was widely felt that Churchill himself was far from enthusiastic about the new program. Butler's Modern Conservatism seemed to accord ill with Churchill's temperament, notwithstanding his liking for a Tory Democracy (which he had inherited from his father) and the radical ideas of his Liberal years. Had he not once declared that he found it easier to deal with the working classes and with aristocrats than with the middle classes?[4] But

---

[1] Churchill, VI, 512. He had even thought it possible that the party might be persuaded to select Anderson, who had not formally joined the party, as its Leader, in case something happened to himself and Eden at the time of the Yalta Conference (*Life of King George VI,* p. 797).

[2] Cf. Woolton's own report in his *Memoirs,* p. 331ff.

[3] See *The Industrial Charter: A Statement of Conservative Industrial Policy* (Conservative and Unionist Central Office [1947]).

[4] Grigg, *Prejudice and Judgment,* p. 210; cf. Amery, *My Political Life,* II, 510.

his position as Leader of the party and his personal prestige blunted any possible criticism from the Conservative rank and file. Whatever criticism was made was restricted to private conversations or at least clothed in words of praise or even love for the war leader's inspiring genius.

The Cabinet formed by Churchill after the elections of 1951 again had sixteen members.[5] The Ministers of Education and of Agriculture and Fisheries were excluded. The new Chancellor of the Duchy of Lancaster, Lord Swinton, was also left out, although he had gained considerable Cabinet experience before 1945. But the total number of non-Cabinet ministers (13) was no greater than it had been under Attlee. Anticipating his intention to amalgamate certain departments, Churchill appointed one Minister for Transport and Civil Aviation and one for Pensions and National Insurance. Cherwell was reappointed Paymaster-General and now became a Cabinet member, replacing the Chancellor of the Duchy of Lancaster. It was announced that Cherwell would also be entrusted with supervising atomic-energy projects and nuclear research. It was further stated that Cherwell would occupy the official residence of the Chancellor of the Exchequer at 11, Downing Street; the new Chancellor, Butler, would continue to live at his private address, although he would work from No. 11.

Many other members of Churchill's war team also obtained Cabinet seats. His personal staff officer, Ismay, was appointed Secretary of State for Commonwealth Relations. Lyttelton became Secretary for Colonial Affairs, Eden again was Foreign Secretary, and Woolton once again became Lord President of the Council. It was officially announced that Woolton would take upon himself the coordination of the Agriculture and Food departments, which remained outside the Cabinet. A new office of Secretary of State for the Coordination of Transport, Fuel, and Power was also established. To head it Churchill appointed his constant companion at Allied conference between 1940 and 1945, the former Minister of War Transport, Leathers.

It was reported that Churchill had asked Eden to act as Leader of the House of Commons, as he had done from 1942 to 1945. After a few days, Eden asked to be excused from this assignment, in view of the very heavy burden of the Foreign Office. The function was hence entrusted to the Minister of Health, Captain H. F. C. Crookshank, who was given a Cabinet seat. It was further understood that Churchill had invited his old friend Bracken to accept a Cabinet post, but Bracken had refused because of poor health. Churchill also offered a peerage to Anderson and asked him to return to the Cabinet as Chancellor of the Duchy of Lancaster, and to supervise in this capacity the Treasury, the Board of Trade, and the Ministry of Supply. Anderson declined the offer, since he thought the construction wrong in principle and the Duchy unattractive for one

[5] Unless otherwise indicated, the following pages are based on press accounts and information obtained by interview.

who had previously held the offices of Home Secretary, Lord President, and Chancellor of the Exchequer.[6]

On the official level, also, Churchill preferred familiar faces. The retirement of Bridges, the former Secretary of the War Cabinet, now Permanent Secretary to the Treasury, was postponed. It was also reported that Brook, then Secretary of the Cabinet, whose appointment as Chief Planning Officer and Deputy Permanent Secretary to the Treasury had already been announced, had agreed to stay in his old post for the time being.[7] The number of new faces in the Cabinet was small. Butler, the Chancellor of the Exchequer, and Macmillan, Minister of Housing and Local Government, had been leading party members for a considerable time, and had been members of Churchill's Caretaker Government. Sir Walter Monckton, Minister of Labour, and Sir David Maxwell Fyfe, the Home Secretary, who had been Attorney-General in 1945, were well known. The sole representative of a younger generation was Peter Thorneycroft, the President of the Board of Trade. Other younger Conservatives found places outside the Cabinet, sometimes as heads of one of the lesser departments, more often as junior ministers.

The Overlords Controversy

The Labour Opposition soon voiced sharp criticism of the Cabinet's composition, thus starting the debate about the so-called Overlords. This controversy caused a great stir at the time and has continued to have a strong influence on ideas about the most desirable Cabinet structure. The debate of 1951–53 on this issue will therefore be discussed at some length.[8]

About a week after Churchill formed his Government, Attlee criticized the appointment of so many peers to the Cabinet, which he called a return to nineteenth-century or even eighteenth-century practice. He rejected the combining of the offices of Prime Minister and Minister of Defence in peacetime, on the ground that neither office would receive the proper attention. Furthermore, Attlee wanted to know who would answer questions raised in the Commons about major policy decisions on food, agriculture, transport, and fuel and power, now that ministers in the Lords had the power of decision and departmental ministers were responsible merely for the administration of their own departments. Attlee argued that Churchill seemed to have devoted little attention to the importance of ministers dealing with economic affairs. Who was to be the main coordinator in this field—the Chancellor of the Exchequer or someone else —was not clear to him. Neither was the exact relationship between the Chancellor and the other supervising ministers. Attlee continued:

---

[6] *Life of Anderson*, pp. 352–53.   [7] Cf. Chester, *Treasury*, pp. 19, 21.

[8] There is still not very much literature on this controversy, but see R. S. Milne, "The Experiment with 'Coordinating Ministers' in the British Cabinet, 1951–1953," *The Canadian Journal of Economics and Political Science*, XXI (1955), 365–69; and Morrison, Chap. 3. The following pages are mainly a précis of the discussion carried on in Parliament and the editorial columns. For critical comment, see Part III of this volume.

I do not believe very much in the system of supervising ministers. I think that duty is better done by coordination within a Government rather than by professed coordinating ministers, because one is apt to take away responsibility from the departmental ministers. I should like to know just how the machinery is to work.[9]

Churchill argued in reply that the exact relationship between supervising and departmental ministers was sufficiently known to Attlee from the war years. He stated:

The rights and responsibilities of the Members of Parliament are in no way affected by the fact that . . . problems are studied in the larger bracket from a position of some detachment from the departments which are grouped together. I believe very much in the policy of grouping departments where it is possible, and that really is the designing principle upon which the Government was constructed.

He had taken charge of the Ministry of Defence himself in order to master the situation in this sphere. Churchill evaded the criticism about the great number of ministers in the House of Lords by comparing the number of peers in the entire Government, not just in the Cabinet, with the number in the previous Labour Government. The latter had counted three peers in the Cabinet but sixteen in the Government, as compared with six in the Conservative Cabinet and eighteen in the Conservative Government.[10]

A week later, on 13 November 1951, Morrison said in the House of Commons that his campaign prediction about Churchill's intentions had come true: he had formed "a Government of himself and his hangers-on."[11] During the war and the Labour Government, Morrison argued, there had been Cabinet committees and chairmen of Cabinet committees, but the Government had not revealed their nature or composition.[12] In contrast, the coordinating ministers now had specific responsibilities that had been publicly announced, thus taking responsibilities away from the departmental ministers. Parliament had a right to know who would answer questions in the House of Commons on behalf of the coordinating peers. The departmental ministers could not possibly fulfill this task since they were no longer responsible.[13] A week later, Churchill announced that, if necessary, he would answer such questions himself.[14]

In the meantime, the Press also paid attention to the problems of the coordinating ministers, soon nicknamed "Overlords." On 3 November 1951, *The Economist* argued that the success of the experiment depended on the ability of the subordinate ministers to work effectively with the

[9] 493 H. of C. Deb. (6 November 1951), cols. 66–67.
[10] *Ibid.*, cols. 74–75.
[11] 493 H. of C. Deb. (13 November 1951), col. 833.
[12] This statement is true only to a very limited extent. Attlee gave extensive information about the composition of Cabinet committees in the House of Commons in 1940 (361 H. of C. Deb. [4 June 1940], cols. 769–70). Churchill did the same in 1941 (368 H. of C. Deb. [22 January 1941], cols. 261–64).
[13] 493 H. of C. Deb. (13 November 1951), cols. 834–35.
[14] 494 H. of C. Deb. (20 November 1951), cols. 229–31.

coordinator. It was necessary, the paper held, for the coordinating minister and the departmental ministers concerned to form a committee that was collectively responsible not only to the Cabinet but also to the House of Commons. For this reason, it was a pity that the burden of coordination rested so heavily on ministers in the House of Lords.

The *Sunday Times* of 11 November 1951 was also rather skeptical. Responsibility of all ministers for their departments was one of the fundamental principles of the British Constitution, the paper argued. It was as difficult to see how ministers could be relieved of this responsibility as to see how they could really bear the responsibility whenever the policy of a coordinating minister did not fully correspond with their own views. The only solution, according to the paper, would be for every "Overlord" and his "subsidiary ministers" (*The Economist* and the Labour Opposition preferred the term "subordinate ministers") to form a sectional, minor Cabinet, which would collectively be responsible to Parliament. Only thus might the disadvantages of divorcing general policy from daily departmental administration be avoided. The Overlords ought to work in daily contact with the leading officials. Logically, the system would in the end lead to the establishment of a number of comprehensive "super-ministries," of which the existing departments would form only subsections. The *Sunday Times* concluded:

Clearly, the system by itself does not affect any administrative economy. Wrongly developed, it would, indeed, relieve the Cabinet merely at the expense of adding below it a fresh storey of administration to the departmental edifices. Rightly developed, on the other hand, it could eventually reduce the scale and weight of the top-level administrative machinery in the subsidiary departments, and even reduce their number.

On 21 November 1951, controversy again flared in a Commons debate on a supplementary estimate for the salaries of some of the new ministers. The Chancellor of the Exchequer, Butler, argued that in addition to the existing instruments of coordination—to wit, the Government's natural unity of purpose and outlook and the activities of the Prime Minister and the Cabinet, assisted by a series of Cabinet committees—the task of coordinating some fields might well be left to one person. Unlike a committee, all of whose members had other things to do, a special coordinator could devote himself full time to this task. The coordinating ministers, Butler declared, would have no special staff aside from a small private office, and the departmental ministers would remain directly responsible to Parliament for all powers imposed on them by statute.[15]

When Butler finished, Gaitskell gave a rather bitter speech on behalf of the Opposition. This provoked Churchill into making a number of interruptions, one of which was, "I hate the word 'coordination.' "[16]

15 494 H. of C. Deb. (21 November 1951), cols. 427–34.
16 *Ibid.*, col. 434.

Several times, Gaitskell argued, the Chancellor had evaded the question of whether he himself still maintained the responsibility for economic coordination. Gaitskell asked if Cherwell's undefined duties would not interfere with the work of the Statistical Office and the Economic Section of the Cabinet Office. He also asked if it were really desirable to put another minister between the Prime Minister and the Chancellor, who ought to be the Prime Minister's chief economic adviser. Interrupting Gaitskell, Churchill declared that Cherwell's tasks were not economic but statistical. Without Cherwell's support, he said, he could not have taken a great many of the detailed measures he took with advantage during the war. He therefore felt all the more entitled to Cherwell's assistance, now that the scene was far more confused and complicated, since it lacked the simplicities the war introduced. With an obvious reference to the rather strained relations between Churchill and Butler, and the known antipathy to Cherwell in Whitehall, Gaitskell replied that he hoped good personal relationships would smooth out a bad settlement.

Continuing his argument, Gaitskell declared that the area to be coordinated was much wider than the area covered by the coordinating ministers. Their appointment betrayed a lack of confidence in the ability of departmental ministers to manage their own affairs. Did the Overlords have access to departmental officials without going through the ministers concerned, Gaitskell asked. Were the departmental ministers present in the Cabinet when their affairs were being discussed? If so, their case for being represented in the Cabinet through coordinators disappeared entirely. If not, it was disgraceful, since their exclusion completely undermined their position in the Government. For a proper organization of the Government, Gaitskell held, there should be no blurring of responsibilities. Needless delay in reaching decisions ought to be avoided. And proper coordination was necessary to ensure that the implications of one minister's decisions for other ministers were fully understood. In his view, this could be achieved far more effectively through a system of Cabinet committees.

Gaitskell concluded his speech by stating that given the uncertainty about the Chancellor of the Exchequer's position in the matter of economic coordination, confusion was likely. He advised the Prime Minister to consider carefully whether he could not achieve his desire to take counsel from his old friends in a way involving less danger of administrative confusion and personal misunderstandings.[17]

The debate was soon carried over to the columns of *The Times*. On 23 November 1951, the paper held that having so many coordinating ministers with seats in the House of Lords was not really an awkward problem. As long as some minister was answerable to the House of Commons, and the House knew which minister to question, it could perform its task. There was no evidence that the balance between Lords and Com-

[17] *Ibid.*, cols. 434–48.

mons had been seriously upset. Every Cabinet reflected the personality of its Prime Minister. Therefore the structure the Labour Cabinet had found useful did not establish a norm. The fact had to be faced that in recent years, even with the existence of Cabinet committees, the role of non-Cabinet ministers in deciding important issues of policy affecting their own departments had progressively diminished. It was possible, the paper suggested, that the non-Cabinet ministers could in fact exert a stronger influence on the making of general policy through their coordinating ministers under Churchill's system than under Attlee's, which suffered from the weakness that some ministers were not directly represented in the Cabinet at all.

Gaitskell replied to this article in a Letter to the Editor, published in *The Times* of 28 November. He fully agreed that every administration must reflect the personality of the Prime Minister to some extent and also must be adapted to circumstances as they arose. Labour had never contended that there existed some "artificial absolute standard" that ought to determine the structure of all Governments. But this was no reason to go to the opposite extreme and suggest that there were no general principles that could serve as a guide in these matters. During the Labour Cabinet, economic ministers outside the Cabinet were always present when the Cabinet discussed general economic policy. The initiative on policy always rested with the departmental ministers. But before they could take final decisions on important matters, they were required to discuss them with other ministers whose departments might be affected. Gaitskell felt from personal experience that this requirement in no way undermined their sense of responsibility. The system of having a Secretary of State to "coordinate" two ministers was a very different matter. There simply was not enough pure "coordinating" work to be done in such a narrow field. It seemed clear that the two "Overlords" were really expected to "supervise" each of the departments under them. "Our objection," Gaitskell wrote, "is that these appointments blur the administrative responsibility at ministerial level and yet do almost nothing to solve the problems of economic coordination." The main problem of economic coordination lay in reconciling the views and interests of all four departments to be coordinated plus several others, especially the Treasury, Labour, and Supply departments.

At the end of January 1952, Churchill decided to transfer the Ministry of Defence to Viscount Alexander. The number of Overlords thus increased. Not all Socialist newspapers were equally indignant about this. The *New Statesman and Nation* of 23 February 1952 did, it is true, regret that the Inner Cabinet leaned so heavily on the House of Lords. But the paper also argued that an Inner Cabinet of non-departmental Overseers could have certain advantages over the structure of the Labour Cabinet, in which Bevin and Cripps had worked themselves to death, while several policy blunders had to be attributed to "inadequate thought by an overworked Cabinet."

Meanwhile, criticism in the House of Commons continued, often in the form of scornful questions suggesting that the Overlords were unnecessary accretions to the ministerial structure or irresponsible wielders of immense power. The agitation reached new heights in April and May 1952. On 30 April 1952, during a Lords debate on agriculture, the Opposition complained that the Minister of Agriculture had no seat in the Cabinet. Some peers wondered what the results of Woolton's coordinating activities were. In reply, Woolton declared that in his view the work of the coordinators was not "a responsibility to Parliament" but "a responsibility to the Cabinet."[18] This declaration caused a stir. Questions were put in the House of Lords the next day. The Leader of the House of Lords, Salisbury, replied, "What my noble friend had in mind was that the coordination of the work of departments is a function within the Government, an allocation of duties by the Prime Minister for purposes of administrative convenience."[19] This did not affect the direct responsibility of departmental ministers to Parliament nor the long-established principle of collective ministerial responsibility to Crown and Parliament. Salisbury tried to evade further questions: "I am both too cautious and too conscious of my own limitations to pontificate on these extremely difficult points on the very short notice which I have received," he declared.[20] The former Socialist minister Lord Stansgate delivered a strong attack on what he called "a new class of ministers . . . who are not responsible to Parliament." "Supposing they give an order," he said. "How can the departmental minister be held to be responsible to Parliament when he himself has received an order from a minister who himself declares that he is not responsible to Parliament?"[21] Salisbury promised an early statement. The Labour Opposition kept harping on the subject, both in the Lords and in the Commons.

On 6 May 1952, Churchill gave a detailed explanation in the Commons. Salisbury read it in the Lords at the same time.[22] It was a rather formal statement, carefully formulated but of little moment. A fundamental principle of the British system of Parliamentary democracy was that every departmental minister was responsible to Parliament for the policy and administration of his department, so the statement ran. But it was an equally respectable and necessary principle that ministers as a body were collectively responsible for Government policy as a whole, which meant that a minister's personal responsibility for departmental policy must be exercised in harmony with the views of his ministerial colleagues. The work of the so-called "coordinating ministers" was an aspect of collective responsibility. For many years, the Prime Minister had from time to time entrusted a senior colleague with the duty of overseeing, on behalf

18 176 H. of L. Deb. (30 April 1952), col. 475.
19 176 H. of L. Deb. (1 May 1952), col. 523.
20 *Ibid.*, cols. 523–24.　　　　　　　　21 *Ibid.*, cols. 524–27.
22 500 H. of C. Deb. (6 May 1952), cols. 190–93, and 176 H. of L. Deb. (6 May 1952), cols. 627–30.

of the Cabinet, matters of special importance that did not fall within the jurisdiction of a single department of State. Such tasks had usually been assigned to holders of one of the old sinecure offices. An example was Thomas, who was given the special responsibility of coordinating measures for handling unemployment when he was Lord Privy Seal in 1929.

The growing complexity of Government business, the increasing extent to which policies had to be administered jointly by two or more departments, and the establishment of many new departments that were not directly represented in the Cabinet had made it increasingly convenient to ask senior ministers to act in coordinating roles. Usually, they did so as chairmen of Cabinet committees. The appointment of Woolton and Leathers carried this development a stage further in one respect, and in one respect only—namely, that the specific area of coordination assigned to each was publicly announced on his appointment. Leathers' coordinating function did not differ, in the constitutional sense, from Woolton's. The coordinating ministers had no statutory powers. In particular, they had no power to give orders or directives to a departmental minister who always had access to the Cabinet. When a departmental minister found that he could not win the support of his ministerial colleagues, he should accept their decision. Of course, no departmental minister could be expected to remain in a Government and carry out policies with which he disagreed. Thus the existence and activities of these coordinating ministers did not impair or diminish the responsibility to Parliament of the departmental ministers whose policies they coordinated. Those ministers were fully accountable to Parliament for any act of policy or administration within their jurisdiction. It did not follow that the coordinating ministers were "non-responsible." Having no statutory powers as coordinating ministers, they performed in that capacity no formal acts. But they shared in the collective responsibility of the Government as a whole, and, as Ministers of the Crown, they were accountable to Parliament. Unlike the other coordinating ministers, the Minister of Defence had statutory functions of his own for which he was directly accountable to Parliament, like every other departmental minister.[23]

When Churchill had read this statement, Attlee suggested that the difficulty had really arisen in the naming of certain ministers as coordinators. When Churchill asked Attlee if he thought all these difficulties would have been smoothed away if, for instance, Leathers had been appointed Minister without Portfolio, Attlee said yes. He called this attempt at over-precision a source of the difficulty.[24] It was now known that Leathers had certain powers, but no one could question him or find out what he did. Churchill retorted, "If the gravamen of the charge against me is that

---

[23] The statement threw no light on the relation between the Overlords and the officials in the departments under their hegemony. It also evaded the question of whether the ministers concerned were automatically invited to attend the Cabinet to discuss items that directly or indirectly touched their departmental responsibilities.
[24] 500 H. of C. Deb. (6 May 1952), cols. 193–94.

I have not succeeded in hashing it all up as well as the right honorable gentleman did, I can bear that with composure." He had thought that a public announcement would give greater prominence in the public mind to the importance of some of the greatest problems of modern government. In that case, the Opposition again argued (through Henderson), the duties of the publicly announced coordinating ministers would have to be specified, and (said Morrison) ministers would also have to accept responsibility for their immediate duties towards Parliament.[25]

In the House of Lords, on the same day, Stansgate and others also persisted in their criticism. Salisbury had produced the argument, Stansgate held, that the Overlords were, in reality, merely a Cabinet committee of one, which in his view was surely the most convenient Cabinet committee. It was now clearly established that whereas the Overlords were undoubtedly discharging heavy and responsible duties, they had no responsibility save the collective responsibility of Cabinet membership, and even this responsibility was impaired by the fact that some of these ministers were practically permanent absentees from the House of Lords.[26]

Salisbury replied that a difficulty of the public anouncement was that the public might form the opinion that the Overlords had more power than they actually did. The departmental ministers had to agree as before to anything the Cabinet decided. They also had the same duty of initiation, but they had someone to help them initiate; and when a decision was ultimately taken, they had to agree with it themselves. If they did not agree, the proper course was for them to resign. Salisbury concluded by saying that the Opposition was really making a mountain out of a molehill, since every Lord on the Opposition Front Bench had known that all this had been going on, and the responsibility had been apportioned for years exactly as it was now.[27]

In the days that followed, Labour M.P.'s continued to ask questions about the division of responsibilities between "Overlord" and "Underling." Their barrage of questions included the problem of the relationship between Cherwell and the Minister of Supply with regard to atomic energy.[28] No really new views were expressed. Churchill was willing to grant that the departmental ministers had a lower status in the ministerial hierarchy. But he did not think it possible to make hard and fast rules about the working relationship between ministers: "They settle it among themselves," he declared, "and Parliament is the judge of the result."[29] Churchill accused Morrison of confusing counsel by suggesting that this was the first time in British history that ministers were subordinated to other ministers. Morrison knew better from the war years, Churchill stated. The suprem-

25 *Ibid.*, cols. 194, 195.
26 176 H. of L. Deb. (6 May 1952), col. 632.
27 *Ibid.*, cols. 633–35.
28 Cf. 500 H. of C. Deb. (12 May 1952), cols. 862–63; 500 H. of C. Deb. (13 May 1952), cols. 1110–12; 500 H. of C. Deb. (14 May 1952), col. 1434.
29 500 H. of C. Deb. (13 May 1952), col. 1111.

acy of the Cabinet was in no way affected, and the departmental ministers had access to it at all times.

In 1952, Woolton fell ill. In November Salisbury replaced him as Lord President of the Council. From a reply Churchill made to a question in the House of Commons on 24 March 1953, it became clear that Woolton's coordinating tasks were not being fulfilled by another minister. Churchill was not willing to say that the Overlord system had been entirely abandoned and continued to insist that the practice of assigning coordinating functions to ministers without departmental duties had been found, in peace as in war, a valuable aid to the efficient conduct of government business. But in a reply to a question by Morrison, Churchill publicly stated, "I think it may be admitted that the need which I found so very important in time of war has not presented itself in the same precise form now that we are at peace."[30]

It was soon rumored that Leathers had also been relieved of his coordinating tasks. For the time being, Members of the House of Commons amused themselves with such remarks as: "Can nothing be done to relieve Lord Leathers of the boredom associated with his post?"[31] In August 1953, Leathers submitted his resignation. In a farewell letter, Churchill wrote: "Your contribution in this office has been essentially a personal one, and the justification for this special post will disappear when your services are no longer available. Now that we are in smoother water we can rely on the normal methods of Cabinet procedure to secure coordination between the departments which have been under your general charge."[32]

The Times was quick to praise the new developments. "It is good news, too," it declared on 4 September 1953, "that the opportunity has been taken to discard the otiose system of ministerial 'Overlords' and to revert formally to the coordination of policy by Cabinet committees." Not so *The Economist*. On 10 May 1952, it had argued that "super-ministers would be exceedingly hard to fit into the British Constitution." It had hoped that the Overlords would in fact be no more than committee chairmen. But on 12 September 1953, the paper changed its tune. Churchill's experiment, it declared, had failed chiefly because of personal factors and because of the great number of peers charged with coordinating tasks. "Simply to abandon the Overlords is to give the impression that the experiment has failed, when in truth it has not really been tried." A hierarchical committee structure, *The Economist* proclaimed, could not efficiently tackle such important problems as food and agriculture, fuel and energy. "An important additional part might be played by a few senior ministers without day-to-day departmental duties of their own, but each of whom specializes in a group of subjects, acts as a chairman of Cabinet committees and as a spokesman for the Government, and is able to give

[30] 513 H. of C. Deb. (24 March 1953), cols. 650–51; cf. Churchill's answer to Attlee in 520 H. of C. Deb. (3 November 1953), col. 20.

[31] 518 H. of C. Deb. (18 July 1953), cols. 1089–90.

[32] *The Times,* 4 September 1953.

the thought to long-term policy for which a departmental minister rarely has time."[33]

The Background of the Overlords Controversy

In 1953, the Overlords system was not only abandoned but publicly discredited. Various arguments told against the system. It was not very popular in official circles. The Labour Opposition had readily used the issue to weaken the prestige of the Conservative Government. This could be done the more successfully because the internal relationships of the Labour Cabinet were as yet insufficiently known, and were in fact strongly idealized. It was therefore possible to compare the theory of the Labour Cabinet with the reality of the new Government, visibly the result of Churchill's attempt to recreate his war team in drastically changed circumstances. From the outset, therefore, the discussion about Churchill's Cabinet structure was colored by personal factors. The difference was not primarily in the extent of secrecy observed (by no means so absolute under Labour as Morrison and others suggested). If the internal structure of the Labour Government escaped much of the criticism leveled against Churchill's Government, it was because the leading personalities in the Labour Cabinet and party were one. Unlike the Overlords, who owed their position mainly to Churchill himself, Labour's coordinators had undisputed authority. "I had no experience of being Prime Minister in time of peace," Churchill declared on 3 November 1953, "and I attached . . . importance to the grouping of departments so that the responsible head of the Government would be able to deal with a comparatively smaller number of heads than actually exists in peacetime."[34]

This admission explains why the same Churchill who in his memoirs not long before had pronounced against "that exalted brooding over the work done by others which may well be the lot of a minister, however influential, who has no department," now himself appointed some ministers who, in practice, came to be in much the same position.[35] It was evidently Churchill's intention that Woolton, Leathers, Alexander, Cherwell, and others would indeed have the actual direction over their specific spheres of action, on the strength of his *plenitudo potestatis* and in full responsibility to himself. This intention was defeated, on the one hand, because Churchill could not regain the almost dictatorial position he had held during the war, let alone delegate full powers to his personal friends. The scheme was defeated, on the other hand, because the departments held on to their customary right to fight out differences of opinion, if necessary, before the supreme tribunal of the Cabinet itself. Peacetime differed from wartime, and during the six years of Attlee's leadership the departments had regained much of their traditional status.

[33] Cf. Mackenzie–Grove, p. 346: "There is no evidence that the Overlords worked badly as an administrative device." A judicious reader of this work in manuscript added that there is also no evidence that they worked well or at all.

[34] 520 H. of C. Deb. (3 November 1953), col. 20.

[35] Churchill, I, 320; cf. IV, p. 560.

It is likely, moreover, that several younger Conservatives who had been put in charge of departments bore a grudge against the system because they did not really accept the authority of the Overlords.[36] Churchill "rarely sent for ministers of Cabinet rank who were not in . . . the Inner Cabinet for a general conversation about what they were doing.[37] Future historians will probably interpret the development of the Churchill and Eden Governments in the light of the gradual supersession of Churchill's circle and older Conservative leaders by a new political generation. Ismay, Alexander, Leathers, Cherwell, and Woolton all stepped down within a few years. Only five members of the Cabinet Churchill formed in the fall of 1951 still had seats in Macmillan's first Cabinet in January 1957.[38] Of the eighteen members of Eden's 1955 Cabinet, only six were still in office by the end of 1962. Churchill evidently was not able to prevail against the Chancellor of the Exchequer, Butler, even in matters of military expenditure, let alone in other fields.[39] The Treasury soon regained its authority in economic policy, which had momentarily been threatened by the Overlords and even more so by Churchill's abortive attempt to persuade Anderson to return to office. In the spring of 1953, both Churchill and Eden were seriously ill. Salisbury and Butler acted for them in foreign affairs and home affairs, respectively. Churchill recovered, but he never regained the unparalleled authority of 1940, or even 1951.[40]

Toward the end, Churchill's Prime Ministership was apparently becoming somewhat of a hindrance for the efficient dispatch of day-to-day Cabinet business. Again the old anecdote began to circulate that, whereas Labour ministers, on leaving the Cabinet, used to congratulate themselves on the great amount of work they had gotten through, Conservative ministers commented on how great a man their leader was.[41] Unfinished business accumulated. Ministers and Service Chiefs spent long hours waiting in the hall of 10, Downing Street because the parts of the agenda for which they had been summoned were never reached. The speedy revival of an extensive system of Cabinet committees—against Churchill's initial resistance—was apparently due in large part to the need of getting decisions not easily obtainable in Cabinet.[42] Outwardly, not much changed in the structure of the Cabinet when Eden became Prime Minister in 1955, but the transaction of business at Cabinet level did improve considerably.

---

[36] Between 1939 and 1955, no more than twenty regular Conservative Members of Parliament were admitted to the Cabinet. They had spent an average of sixteen years in the House of Commons before being admitted. The twelve new ministers who were admitted to the Cabinet between 1951 and 1955 had spent, on the average, six years in subordinate office (Willson, *Routes of Entry*, p. 229). The impression Woolton (*Memoirs*, pp. 363–64) seeks to create about the formation of the Government in 1951 is misleading.

[37] Woolton, *Memoirs*, p. 377.　　　　　[38] Dogan–Campbell, pp. 332–33.
[39] McCloughry, pp. 211, 240.　　　　　[40] Eden, *Full Circle*, p. 52.
[41] *The Economist*, 10 July 1954. For the same anecdote during the war years, see Kennedy, *Business of War*, p. 191; *Life of Laski*, p. 158; and Roy Jenkins, *Mr. Attlee: An Interim Biography*, London (1948), pp. 229–30.
[42] *The Economist*, 10 July 1954; Woolton, *Memoirs*, pp. 376–77, cf. p. 419; Beloff, pp. 26–27.

EIGHT

THE CONSERVATIVE GOVERNMENTS AFTER 1955

Eden and His Cabinet

From the outset Eden had the great disadvantage of following a living legend. Since he had been the recognized "crown prince" for almost fifteen years, his arrival in office lacked the luster of unexpectedness.[1] The Cabinet he inherited was to a very large extent his predecessor's *équipe,* rather than his own choice or the natural produce of his party. In addition, Eden had had an unusually narrow preparation for the top post. Except for some eight months at the Dominions Office in 1939–40, and an even shorter period as Secretary of State for War in 1940, his only ministerial experience had been in the Foreign Office. Eden was not a Churchill. Both physically and mentally, he lacked the relaxed robustness the latter had so amply displayed. He frankly confessed to a dislike of parliamentary speeches.[2] Elections he "endured."[3] Yet expectations of Eden were high, and his ambition to make good as Prime Minister was considerable. He immediately set out to be Prime Minister in fact as well as in name. He sent a wide variety of memoranda to his colleagues. He sought to improve the administrative efficiency of Cabinet meetings and to lessen the pressure on the Cabinet by having frequent preparatory talks with his colleagues.[4] His views on home politics tended to be somewhat cliché and uncertain, however. His tenure was short, and his Prime Ministership ended ignominiously in the political confusion of the Suez affair. With the certainty of hindsight, many have stated that this anticlimax to Eden's glamorous career was inevitable.[5] They have pointed to certain signs that Eden's political position was fairly weak, even before the fatal autumn of 1956.[6] As long as no more sources are available, such views are too speculative to merit discussion. It should always be realized, however, that nothing fails like failure.

Under Eden three men occupied key political positions from 1955 to 1957 : Butler, Macmillan, and Salisbury. Butler seemed very much the number two man in the Cabinet. By the end of 1955, however, personal distress and exhaustion caused him to give up the Chancellorship of the

---

[1] Eden himself spoke of "the long era as crown prince . . . a position not necessarily enviable" (*Full Circle,* p. 266).
[2] *Ibid.,* p. 271. [3] *Ibid.,* p. 278.
[4] *Ibid.,* pp. 269–70 ; cf. Mackintosh, p. 435.
[5] Cf. R. Churchill, *Eden, passim.* [6] *Ibid.,* pp. 207–8.

Exchequer and to take on instead the office of Lord Privy Seal and the Leadership of the House of Commons. As Undersecretary of State, Salisbury (then Lord Cranborne) had resigned from the Foreign Office with Eden in 1938. Because of his family background, experience, and personality, Salisbury enjoyed massive prestige. In 1955 Eden deemed Salisbury his natural successor as Foreign Secretary. But he thought it politically impossible to appoint a peer to head the Foreign Office, as he explained in his memoirs:

The House of Commons would never take an important statement on foreign affairs from a junior minister. A member of the Cabinet would therefore have to be the spokesman of the Foreign Office in the House of Commons on all major issues. This could only be the Prime Minister. . . . I would have had to be principal Foreign Office spokesman in the House of Commons myself, a heavy additional load upon any Prime Minister. . . . I was sure that there was a danger of misunderstanding if foreign policy statements, or an important part of them, were made in the Upper House, and if the main debates were held there. On the other hand, neither the Foreign Secretary nor I would find it tolerable if the more important speeches on foreign affairs were made by the Prime Minister in a House to which the Foreign Secretary did not belong. The conclusion was inescapable. I felt it impossible to ask a member of the House of Lords to be Foreign Secretary.[7]

Eden decided to appoint Macmillan instead. But when Butler resigned the Chancellorship in December 1955, Eden transferred Macmillan to the Treasury, feeling that only one of the most senior ministers had sufficient weight for such a key portfolio. Since December 1954, therefore, Macmillan had filled the offices of Minister of Defence (five and a half months), Foreign Secretary (eight and a half months), and Chancellor of the Exchequer (a year and a half). He thus established a somewhat fortuitous reputation for varied ministerial experience, which facilitated his appointment as Prime Minister over Butler's head in 1957.

Butler's position as coordinating minister from 1955 to 1957, under a Prime Minister who very much wished to be a supreme coordinator himself, and alongside a powerful Chancellor of the Exchequer with a strong mind of his own, turned out to be weaker than Butler himself may have expected.[8] A further consequence of the reshuffle of December 1955 was the appointment of Selwyn Lloyd as Foreign Secretary. This was proof to many, if proof was still required, that Eden indeed intended to be his own Foreign Secretary, much as (to Eden's distaste) Chamberlain had wanted to be in the 1930's. Contrary to initial expectations, Eden's downfall also came over foreign policy, rather than through internal disagreement in the Cabinet about economic questions.

The Suez affair is still veiled in secrecy. From the few accounts that are as yet available, the following picture emerges.[9] Eden himself was the

---

[7] Eden, *Full Circle*, pp. 273–74.   [8] Cf. *The Economist*, 19 January 1957.
[9] See Eden's own story in *Full Circle* and R. Churchill's treatise *The Rise and Fall of Sir Anthony Eden*. For an interesting review of the latter by Attlee, see *The Observer*, 21 June 1959.

unmistakable formulator of policy. He consulted with an informal group of ministers ("the Suez Group"), which seems to have included Butler, Macmillan, Salisbury, Lloyd, and Antony Head. (Head was Secretary of State for War until October 1956, when he replaced his theoretical superior, Monckton, as Minister of Defence, only shortly before hostilities broke out.)[10] The remainder of the Cabinet seems to have been generally faced with accomplished decisions or accomplished facts. When some protested, Eden allegedly replied: "A lot of my present colleagues never served in a War Cabinet."[11] Practically all members of the Cabinet and of the Conservative Party in Parliament agreed to the Suez policy, however, and in most cases probably heartily approved it. One of the few who publicly took a stand against it was Anthony Nutting, Minister of State at the Foreign Office, who resigned.

Throughout the period, leadership was very uncertain. At least four factors seem to have been responsible for this: Eden's own hesitations, deriving from inner tension and compounded by overwork and poor health; attacks of unexpected and unprecedented violence by the Labour Opposition in Parliament; a series of highly intricate diplomatic, military, and economic considerations that kept changing very quickly; and the peculiar climate in which decisions had to be taken. It is worthwhile in this connection to quote Eden's own description in full:

The pace was faster and the strain more intense upon the principal members of the Government during these days and nights than at any time during the Second World War. It is true that we had held debates then of the first importance, the results of which were sometimes critical, but these had not been frequent. Now they were continuous. They took place virtually every day during the decisive period and lasted throughout the session. This always made it difficult, and often made it impossible, to deal with even the most urgent work while the House was sitting, which was at least from 2:30 P.M. to 10 P.M. and sometimes later. Added to this was the problem of the difference in time. During the war there was hardly any communication by telephone across the Atlantic. For one thing it was not safe; the Germans might listen in, and did. Now all this was changed. It was after midnight, our time, that the United Nations and Washington became most active, both by telegram and telephone. I had always to be available and so had the Foreign Secretary. . . .

My day ran something like this. While I was shaving, bathing, or dressing, Mr. Allan [Eden's Parliamentary Private Secretary] would report to me and raise any points he wished. Sometimes one of the private secretaries would break in with an immediate telegram, or the Chief Whip, Mr. Edward Heath, with whom lay the responsibility for guiding and marshaling our forces in the House of Commons, would arrive with some suggestion or point for decision. . . . The morning was the only time we ever had for the urgent affairs of the nation. Into this period had to be crammed Cabinet sessions, special meetings to deal with the military, financial, economic, or diplomatic aspects of the crisis, messages to and from Commonwealth Prime Ministers, consultation with individual colleagues, and a chance to think.[12]

[10] R. Churchill, *Eden*, pp. 277–78; Mackintosh, p. 432.
[11] R. Churchill, *Eden*, pp. 277–78.   [12] Eden, *Full Circle*, p. 549.

Eden's health finally broke down, shortly after American resistance and a run on the pound had compelled the Government to halt the Suez action half-way. Soon afterwards Eden was to bow to doctor's orders rather than political defeat; Gallup-poll evidence was actually pointing to increasing domestic support for Eden's actions. His resignation was timely, however; self-righteous opposition was proved right, and accomplices seemed suddenly innocent.

The Conservative Government under Macmillan

Contrary to Press expectation, the Queen did not summon the unofficial Deputy Prime Minister, Butler, to the palace. For a time no summons came at all, except to two statesmen who were obviously not candidates for the Prime Ministership, Churchill and Salisbury. Government whips were busily sounding the Parliamentary Party. Two Cabinet members, Salisbury and the Lord Chancellor, Kilmuir, meanwhile apparently took a straw poll in the Cabinet. It is reported that only the Minister of Works expressed a definite preference for Butler.[13] The selection of Macmillan as Prime Minister caused some constitutional comment. The Labour Party even issued a formal motion insisting that if a Labour Prime Minister should resign or die in office, no new Prime Minister should be appointed by the Crown until the Parliamentary Party had been allowed a free vote on its next Leader.[14] The Conservatives offered no objections; all traditional forces of loyalty and expediency went out to the new Prime Minister, including those of his disappointed rival, who saw but meager compensation in being awarded the Home Office, which he held until 1960 in conjunction with the Privy Seal and the Leadership of the House of Commons.

Macmillan's first major task was to mend fences, both abroad and at home. He first visited Eisenhower, whom he had known well since December 1942, when he had acted as Minister Resident at Allied Force Headquarters, Mediterranean Command, and later carefully nurtured the idea of a summit meeting in an effort to re-establish the reputation of British world statesmanship. Slowly, the Government began to move closer to Europe. Much more relaxed than his predecessor, Macmillan proved an astute party manager at home. Behind an insouciant façade that appealed to traditional Conservatives, he sheltered a definite readiness to go back on imperial commitments that were politically and economically unbearable to the world at large, but not yet so in the eyes of his right-wing supporters. Within a few months of taking office he could even afford to lose the support of Salisbury, who had been so influential in his own selection, over Cyprus.

The importance of party management also came out in a number of

---

[13] *Life of Derby,* p. 505n; Mackintosh, p. 523.
[14] Cf. critical comment in *The Economist,* 19 January 1957.

other provisions in Macmillan's Cabinet. The Chief Whip, Heath, who since the Suez crisis had successfully kept the Conservative forces in the House of Commons together and in reasonable spirits, became Macmillan's close companion and a constant attender of the Cabinet (to which he was formally admitted without other ministerial experience in October 1959 as Minister of Labour). Senior Cabinet ministers (Lord Hailsham from September 1957 to October 1959, Butler from October 1959 to October 1961, and thereafter Iain Macleod) were charged with the Chairmanship of the Conservative Party Organization, which Butler and Macleod combined with the Leadership of the House of Commons. Failure of public relations led to a concentration of information services under the erstwhile Radio Doctor of the B.B.C., Dr. Charles Hill, who became Postmaster-General in December 1956 and Chancellor of the Duchy of Lancaster, with a Cabinet seat, in January 1957.[15] In addition, Macmillan greatly refashioned his ministerial team, thus honoring Gladstone's counsel to be a good "butcher." He did not hesitate to cut off the very colleagues who had preferred him to Butler. As soon as he became Prime Minister in 1957, he replaced five ministers. Two other senior ministers, Salisbury and Thorneycroft, resigned in 1957 and 1958, respectively. In major reshuffles—in October 1959, July 1960, and October 1961—more ministers left the Cabinet. Finally, in July 1962, no less than seven Cabinet members were replaced, thus leaving unaffected only a third of the ministers who had begun with Macmillan in 1957.

Many political commentators have attempted to find some principle in these rather wholesale changes. Perhaps they were motivated by somewhat frantic attempts to give the Government an electoral face lifting? But some who were left out were popular with the party and enjoyed national prestige. Perhaps then reasons of administrative efficiency, or longterm party management? More than Churchill and Eden, Macmillan gave brilliant younger men of the postwar political generation a chance to hold ministerial office, thus holding out promise of future quality in the party leadership. Some observers have particularly stressed that Macmillan may have played a careful game to enhance his own status and to cut short any premature Prime Ministerial ambitions. The uncertainty among ministers resulting from frequent changes and dismissals consolidated his power. Otherwise unanswerable criticism of his Government could be deflected by careful adjustments of ministerial personnel, which simultaneously tended to raise the Prime Minister himself above reproach. The problem of the eventual succession remained studiously unsettled. Butler remained number two, but a little as a potential Prime Minister manqué. After Thorneycroft resigned, both the Foreign Office (with Lloyd and Lord Home) and the Chancellorship of the Exchequer (with Heathcoat Amory and Lloyd) went to men who at the time seemed unlikely to be either

[15] 563 H. of C. Deb. (24 January 1957), cols. 397–99; *The Economist*, 2 February 1957.

Macmillan's rivals or his potential successor: useful lieutenants, with a helpful standing in the party, valuable counterweights to the various younger men who seemed of Prime Ministerial timber, but not just yet. Internal disagreement about policy, heightened by a worsening of political prospects, also affected the rate of turnover of ministers, as appeared in the resignation of Thorneycroft in 1958 and the dismissal of Lloyd in 1962, the latter forced, so it seems, by an ultimatum from some of his colleagues.

Whatever the explanation for the frequent ministerial changes, skillful management did not achieve all. In 1957 and 1958, the Conservatives succeeded in recovering from a very low point in their political fortunes and gained an unprecedented third victory in 1959 using the slogan: "You never had it so good." But after 1960, the party's political fortunes were on the downgrade since many of its erstwhile supporters voted a Liberal protest ticket. Slow economic growth and a further decline in Britain's international position beclouded the horizon at the end of 1962. Whereas in 1960, political prophets tended to forecast a lifetime of Conservative Government, few were willing to put their money on a fourth term for the party two years later.

Changes in Ministerial Organization since 1955

Throughout the period, various political, administrative, and personal pressures caused a number of changes in the ministerial structure.[16]

The Heavy Ministerial Burden

The Suez crisis and Eden's breakdown made many wonder whether ministers were not too heavily burdened for sensible government. Labour members in the House of Commons and correspondents in *The Times* urged Macmillan to agree to a Select Committee to investigate the situation and to recommend ways to relieve it. Instead, Macmillan invited an informal committee of experienced Privy Councillors under Attlee to do so. Its members were Crookshank, Clement, Davies, Chuter Ede, and J. Stuart. The Committee reported in the autumn of 1957, but its views were not made public. Apparently, the Committee saw no easy solution; its main recommendation was that the Commons should be more willing in the future to deal with subordinate ministers.[17] To the extent that this proved politically possible, the status of these subordinate ministers increased somewhat; and, at any rate, a further increase in their number seemed more readily justifiable.

The Appointment of a First Secretary of State

From 1957 to 1962, Butler retained his number two position from the Home Office. As will be treated more fully later, the title Deputy Prime

[16] An excellent factual survey is given in Willson, *Supplement*.
[17] 568 H. of C. Deb. (11 April 1957), cols. 1296–87; 570 H. of C. Deb. (21 May 1957), cols. 1039–41; *The Economist*, 27 April and 16 November 1957.

Minister had been informally used since 1942; but this position was not officially recognized because of constitutional objections by the Crown. In October 1961, it was officially intimated that Butler was assisting the Prime Minister over a wide area, especially in relation to the Common Market negotiations. In July 1962, Macmillan secured the Queen's approval for making Butler First Secretary of State, in practice an office without departmental duties, but one of sufficiently high standing—the First Secretary took precedence over all other Secretaries of State—to accommodate someone with such special duties and seniority.

Changes in the Administration of Foreign Affairs

Pressure to the contrary notwithstanding, Lloyd had served as Foreign Secretary for three and a half years after the Suez crisis. But in July 1960, Macmillan decided to shift Lloyd to the Treasury to replace Amory, who had resigned. According to Macmillan, Lloyd came to his new department "as a somewhat reluctant debutant." But Macmillan insisted that he should be freed "from the cruel and grueling position at the Foreign Office," as he did not wish to see "the decay of one man after another under the frightful pressure of this particular task."[18] Instead, Macmillan now made the Secretary of State for Commonwealth Relations, Lord Home, Foreign Secretary. At the same time he appointed Heath Lord Privy Seal, to act as "Deputy Foreign Secretary . . . with the full status of a Cabinet minister," and charged to give special attention "within the department to European questions."[19]

Gaitskell criticized the appointment of a peer to the Foreign Office in 1960 as "unnecessary and unwise . . . constitutionally objectionable and [not] good for the conduct of our affairs in the world."[20] He quoted Eden's views in evidence. The Liberal Leader, Davies, likewise judged the innovation "a retrograde step."[21] Macmillan rejected the Opposition's arguments that "the great offices of power and responsibility within the State" should never be given to a member of the House of Lords.[22] Had anyone objected to the Commonwealth Secretary's being a peer? Had not Labour itself had the Secretary of State for India in the Lords in the crucial period from 1945 to 1947? He felt "that it would be a very bad precedent to set to say that this or that ministry should be forever debarred from being given to a Member of the House of Lords, with a fixed pattern of which posts are to be allocated to either House."[23] Given that the Prime Minister's prominent role in foreign policy was now not "a matter of choice" but "a matter of fact," Macmillan's personal confidence in Home must be accepted as sufficient reason for the appointment.[24]

The whole Government was, of course, answerable to the House of

[18] 627 H. of C. Deb. (28 July 1960), cols. 1993–94.
[19] Cf. *ibid.*, cols. 1997, 1998.
[20] *Ibid.*, col. 1983.   [21] *Ibid.*, col. 1986.
[22] As suggested by Gaitskell, *ibid.*, col. 1973.
[23] *Ibid.*, cols. 1995–96.   [24] *Ibid.*, col. 2000.

Commons in every Department of State. Through the Prime Minister and the Lord Privy Seal, the House of Commons had as much opportunity as it wished to question the Government; in many ways, the opportunity was better than it had been previously. Foreign commitments now caused the Foreign Secretary to be absent from the United Kingdom for considerable periods. In 1959, Lloyd had been out of the country for 125 days, 75 of them while Parliament was sitting. He was able to answer questions in Parliament on only 5 out of 24 Foreign Office days. In practice, therefore, the Ministers of State or undersecretaries had to answer; but however excellent their work, they did not have "the status at home or abroad, to give them the full authority." The solution was an additional Cabinet minister who would be "second in command of the Foreign Office over the whole field."[25] Gaitskell had also pointed out the danger of "treble control" by the Prime Minister, the Foreign Secretary, and the Lord Privy Seal over the Foreign Office.[26] Macmillan retorted that personalities and teamwork would obviate any difficulties.

Since 1960, the issue does not seem to have caused major complications, possibly because of Home's unassuming role, Heath's practical concentration on the Common Market negotiations, and Macmillan's dominant position. Heath's position remained a very special one, however. As a Cabinet member, a close friend of the Prime Minister, and chief negotiator for the Government, Heath had a strong personal influence. But Common Market questions were of such political and departmental importance to a great number of ministers and interest groups in Britain that considerable coordination and harmonization was necessary within the British Government. A special Cabinet committee was set up under Butler to supervise the negotiations. In practice, therefore, Heath was both a member of the team and a subordinate in some respects to at least three senior colleagues: Macmillan, Butler, and Home. At the same time, a considerable number of other ministers had a vested interest in his actions. As this book went to press, observers in Brussels as well as in London were watching Heath's tightrope act with great interest and appreciation. If his labors were eventually to fail, it was not for want of intelligent efforts.

Commonwealth and Colonial Affairs; the Secretary for Technical Cooperation

With the rapid emancipation of a large number of colonies, the main task of the Colonial Secretary became to work himself out of a job. Before this was achieved, numerous intricate political questions had to be faced and a difficult balancing act performed to reconcile the forces of new nationalism in the colonies and old nationalism in the Conservative Party. The Colonial Office became a key Government post (and ministerial testing ground) in very different ways from previous years. As colo-

---

[25] *Ibid.*, cols. 1996–97, 1998.   [26] *Ibid.*, col. 1982.

nies became independent, relations with them were transferred either to the Commonwealth Relations Office or to the Foreign Office, depending on whether or not they elected to join the Commonwealth.[27] Relations between the Colonial Office and the Commonwealth Relations Office were not always easy, since they sometimes showed a rather different appreciation of the emancipation process in certain areas of the world, particularly in the case of the Central African Federation. Sandys, as Secretary of State for Commonwealth Relations, became identified with the interests of the Federation and an autonomous Southern Rhodesia. Maudling, as Colonial Secretary, felt responsible for the possibly secessionist interests in Northern Rhodesia and Nyasaland. Conflicts rose to such heights that Macmillan decided to establish a separate Central African Office. According to the official announcement:

While responsibility was divided between the Commonwealth Secretary and the Colonial Secretary, the two ministers were apt to be regarded in some quarters as identified with conflicting sectional interests in the Federation; and for this reason it would not be practicable to secure the desired unification of ministerial responsibility by transferring the functions of either to the other.

Therefore with the full agreement of the two Secretaries of State concerned . . . I have invited the Home Secretary [Butler] to take this responsibility.[28]

In other areas of the world, too, difficulties arose, notably in relation to the plan for a Malaysian Federation. In July 1962, Macmillan decided to appoint Sandys as Secretary of State to both the Colonial Office and the Commonwealth Relations Office. Each department retained its separate existence and its own subordinate ministers, but one man was now fully in charge of both the increased Commonwealth Relations Office and the greatly decreased Colonial Office. The Central African Office, however, remained under the direction supervision of Butler.

The rise of many new nations to independence caused complex administrative problems in the field of technical aid. New forms of aid as well as an increasing number of requests made coordination particularly difficult. Depending on the legal status of the country demanding aid, such requests had hitherto been channeled through the Colonial Office, the Commonwealth Relations Office, or the Foreign Office. In 1961, it was decided to concentrate such duties in a new Department of Technical Cooperation. This was given a rather special status, as Macmillan explained in the House of Commons:

The new department will be in charge of a minister. His rank will be equivalent to that of a Minister of State. The Foreign Secretary, the Commonwealth Secretary, and the Colonial Secretary will continue to be responsible for matters of general policy, but within these general limits the new department will take over responsibility for the provision of technical assistance—other than capital projects—which is at present undertaken by the three overseas departments.[29]

[27] Willson, *Supplement*, pp. 175–77.   [28] *The Times*, 16 March 1962.
[29] *The Times*, 22 March 1961.

The Times hesitated in placing the new minister in the political hierarchy. It pontificated that since his department was run on a separate vote, "the minister is more than a junior coordinator, if less than a senior overlord."[30] The new department was given special statutory existence and duties. According to a statement by Lord Mills in the House of Lords: "It would always be open to the minister to initiate consideration of policy on technical assistance . . . the new minister would of course have access to the Prime Minister." Some peers were not satisfied, however. One called the new department "something of a Cinderella."[31]

Defense Organization

After Macmillan became Prime Minister, defense policy was also subject to considerable experimentation. As will be related more fully in Chapter 12, the appointment of Sandys as Minister of Defence in January 1957 seemed for a time to augur the abolition of the Service ministries. But the attempt to abolish them was unsuccessful at the time. By the end of 1962 uncertainty about the long-range prospects of defense policies and defense organization touched a new nadir. Considerable changes also took place in supply organization. The Ministry of Supply had been shorn of a number of its powers after 1951. It occupied a declining position in the ministerial hierarchy and was abolished in 1959. Most of its functions were reassigned to the Air Ministry and the War Office, but at the same time a new Ministry of Aviation, first under Sandys and then under Thorneycroft, was established to take charge of missile development and to reunite military and civil aviation problems in one department. For a brief period the post had some political appeal, since its minister had a Cabinet seat. Much of its life went out of the new ministry, however, with the cancellation of the Blue Streak missile program (announced 13 April 1960), and in 1962 the department was again excluded from the inner circle.

Economics and Finance

After 1955, the Chancellorship of the Exchequer came under increasing pressure, both in a political sense and in an administrative sense. Of the five Chancellors between 1951 and 1962, two resigned voluntarily (Butler in 1955 and Amory in 1962) because they no longer wished to carry the burden. Two others (Thorneycroft and Lloyd) went down in intra-Cabinet defeat, and only one (Macmillan himself) derived political benefit. As will be discussed in Chapter 15, ministerial and official personnel in the Treasury were strengthened. First informally, and later formally, a new Cabinet minister was added to assist the Chancellor in his burdensome tasks. A similar doubling-up tendency was appearing at the official level. New agencies were established to promote economic growth and restrain wage inflation. International factors made themselves increas-

---

[30] *Ibid.*   [31] Report in *The Times*, 2 June 1962.

ingly felt, leading to a greater concern with economic affairs in the Foreign Office, as well as concern with foreign affairs in the various economic departments.[32] Consequently, new forms of coordination were required, and at times a special minister was put in charge. In 1957, Maudling, the Paymaster-General, was designated to represent the Cabinet in the Free Trade Area negotiations. He was given a small office and was soon included in the Cabinet. As previously mentioned, in 1960 the Lord Privy Seal, Heath, was given a similar task, though of greater political moment, in connection with the Common Market negotiations.

The Minister of Power

In 1957, Macmillan appointed a non-politician, Sir Percy Mills, to a new Cabinet post as Minister of Power, raising him to a peerage at the same time. To the new minister were entrusted the existing functions of the Ministry of Fuel and Power with respect to coal, gas, electricity, and oil. He was further charged with extending the use of atomic energy as a source of industrial power, and in addition took over from the President of the Board of Trade responsibilities for iron and steel.[33] Macmillan appointed Mills, an industrialist with wartime government experience, mainly because of the strong personal bond between them. Mills was Minister of Power until October 1959. His successor was excluded from the Cabinet, but Mills stayed on, first as Paymaster-General until October 1961, and later as Minister without Portfolio until July 1962. He was one of the seven ministers dismissed from the Cabinet that summer, which made it easier for the political correspondent of *The Times* to greet the dismissals with the headline: "Oldest and Closest Not Spared."[34]

The Minister for Science

In 1951, the return of Cherwell had led to a reordering of government responsibilities for scientific research. In particular, responsibilities for atomic energy had since then drifted through the government organization, from the Minister of Supply to Cherwell in 1951, to the Lord President of the Council in 1953, and after Salisbury's resignation, in April 1957, to the Prime Minister personally, who was thus, for a short while, given a departmental statutory task.[35] In October 1959, Macmillan honored an election promise in appointing Hailsham Lord Privy Seal and Minister for Science. As such, Hailsham took over the Prime Minister's responsibilities for atomic energy, as well as the Lord President's existing powers in matters of scientific research and the supervision of space research. Until then the Lord President had been "much less a departmental minister than a combination of figurehead, general overseer, advocate, parliamentary defender, and ministerial adviser on scientific policy."[36] Immediately after his appointment, Hailsham went out of his way to

[32] Beloff, *passim.* Cf. Strang, *Foreign Office*, p. 39.
[33] *The Times*, 14 January 1957.   [34] *The Times*, 14 July 1962.
[35] Cf. Chester–Willson, pp. 261, 267–69; Willson, *Supplement*, pp. 183–88.
[36] Willson, *Supplement*, p. 185.

stress that he did not intend to change very much in his new role. In an official statement, he said:

The last thing I would want to do is to put this forward as a great new empire. It is a job which will show its results only over a long period. It will require a great deal of thought—of creative imagination—but will not call for tremendous skill because much of the work is being done by executive councils with responsibilities of their own. I shall not take away from them the duties Parliament has given them. I am their friend at court, not their master.[37]

The new minister, it was stressed, was not Minister *of* Science, but Minister *for* Science. In November 1960, a Parliamentary Secretary was appointed to represent Hailsham in the Commons.[38] Since 1957, the Minister for Science has been in the Cabinet, but only because the post was combined with the office of Lord Privy Seal or of Lord President of the Council. Both offices were held by Hailsham, who must have appreciated the value of old titles for ministerial standing.

The Minister of Public Buildings and Works

Concern about inefficiencies in the building industry and the growing imbalance between home- and office-building led Macmillan to extend the task of the Ministry of Works, and to signal this by conferring a new title, which was reminiscent of a somewhat similar title used from 1942 to 1944, when factory building had been a crucial bottleneck in the war effort. The new minister remained, as previously, outside the Cabinet.

The Minister for Welsh Affairs

Nationalist sensitivities in Wales led the Conservative Government to appoint a special Minister for Welsh Affairs. Little changed at Cabinet level, as the post was combined with that of Home Secretary from 1955 to 1957, and since 1957 has been combined with the Ministry of Housing and Local Government. But the appointment in 1958 of a Minister of State for Welsh Affairs, mainly residing in Wales, gave the position more than formal significance for those immediately concerned.

Ministers without Portfolio

Since 1954, successive Prime Ministers had again appointed ministers without portfolio. Until 1961, such posts had invariably been given to ministers in the House of Lords, who assisted there in debate and fulfilled special tasks. They were not in the Cabinet. Because of a dearth of sinecure offices in 1961, Macmillan could keep Mills in the Cabinet only by appointing him Minister without Portfolio. In July 1962 William Deedes, a well-known journalist (who had been columnist Peterborough of the *Daily Telegraph*), was appointed to the same post to take over the coordinating of home-information services from Dr. Charles Hill, who had been left out of the Cabinet in the reshuffle of that month.

[37] *The Times,* 15 October 1959.   [38] *The Times,* 3 November 1960.

The Cabinet and the Ministry

Like Attlee, Churchill, Eden, and Macmillan were under constant pressure to include certain politicians and departments in the Cabinet. They met this pressure partly by increasing the number of Cabinet ministers. Under Churchill the number rose from 16 in 1951 to 18 in 1955, under Eden from 17 in 1955 to 19 in December 1956, and under Macmillan from 17 after Salisbury's resignation in April 1957 to 21 in 1962 (see Table IV). The Churchill Cabinet in 1951 was the smallest of the postwar period. It had just 16 members (the inclusion of two Overlords, Leathers as Secretary of State for the Coordination of Fuel and Power and Cherwell as Paymaster-General, notwithstanding) only because Churchill himself took on the Ministry of Defence, and because he excluded the Ministers of Agriculture and Education, as well as the Chancellor of the Duchy of Lancaster. Since 1954, however, the Cabinet has again had a hard core of at least seventeen portfolios: the Prime Minister, the Lord Chancellor, twelve departmental ministers (the Home, Foreign, Colonial, and Commonwealth secretaries, the Secretary of State for Scotland, the Chancellor of the Exchequer, the President of the Board of Trade, and the Ministers of Defence, Education, Labour, Agriculture, and Housing and Local Government), and a minimum of three sinecure offices (the Lord President of the Council, the Privy Seal, and the Chancellor of the Duchy of Lancaster). Since 1957, the Minister of Transport has also been a permanent member of the Cabinet, making for a normal complement of eighteen. In addition, other offices have regularly or occasionally been included. The office of Paymaster-General was used to accommodate such diverse personages as Cherwell (1951–53), Monckton (after Head replaced him as Minister of Defence in October 1956), Maudling (as minister for Free Trade Area questions and assistant to the Chancellor of the Exchequer, 1957–59), and Mills (as Macmillan's confidential partner, 1959–61). Other offices were occasionally included in the Cabinet, generally for personal reasons. The Minister of Health was in the Cabinet from 1951 to 1952, when the post was combined under Crookshank with the Leadership of the House of Commons; in 1962 the department was readmitted under Enoch Powell. From 1954 to 1955, Churchill and Eden invited the Minister of Pensions and National Insurance, Osbert Peake, to join. Under Eden a former Chief Whip of the party, Patrick Buchan-Hepburn, was admitted as Minister of Works. As we saw, Mills was in the Cabinet as Minister of Power from 1957 to 1959. Also, from 1959 to 1962, the newly constituted Ministry of Aviation found representation when headed by Sandys and Thorneycroft. Only the Service ministers and the Postmaster-General were always out after 1946.

The only way to limit *both* the number of Cabinet ministers *and* the number of non-Cabinet ministers was to cut down the number of separate ministerial portfolios. Since 1951, Conservative Prime Ministers have attempted to achieve this through three separate expedients: by abolishing

TABLE IV

CABINET AND NON-CABINET MINISTERS, 1945–1962

(+ indicates Cabinet minister, − indicates non-Cabinet minister)

Office	Government							
	Churchill June 1945	Attlee Dec. 1946	Attlee March 1950	Churchill Nov. 1951	Churchill Jan. 1955	Eden Jan. 1956	Macmillan Jan. 1957	Macmillan July 1962
Lord Chancellor	−	+	+	+	+	+	+	+
Lord President of the Council (and Minister for Science)	+	+	+	+	+	+	+	+
Lord Privy Seal	+	+	+	+	+[6]	+[10]	+[10]	+
Chancellor of the Exchequer	+	+	+	+	+	+	+	+
Secretary of State:								
for the Home Department	+	+	+	+	+	+	+	+
for Foreign Affairs	+	+	+	+	+	+	+[10]	+
for Scotland	+	+	+	+	+	+	+	+
for the Dominions (Commonwealth Relations)	+	+	+	+	+	+	+	+[17]
for the Colonies	+	+	+	+	+	+	+	+[17]
for India and Burma	+	+						
for the Coordination of Transport, Fuel, and Power				+				
for War	+	−	−	−	−	−	−	−
for Air	+	−	−	−	−	−	−	−
First Lord of the Admiralty	+	−	−	−	−	−	−	−
Minister of Defence	= P. M.	+	+[2]	= P. M.	+	+	+	+
President of the Board of Trade (and Minister of Production)	+	+	+	+	+	+	+	+
Minister of Labour (and National Service)	+	+	+	+	+	+	+	+

134

Minister of Agriculture and Fisheries (and Food)	+	+	+	+	+	+	+	+
Minister of Food	−	−	−	−				
Minister of Education	−	+	+	+	−	−	−	+
Minister of Health	−	+[1]	+[1]	+[1]	−	−	−	+
Minister of Town and Country Planning (Housing and Local Government)	−	−	−	+[4]	+	+	+	+
Minister of (War) Transport (and Civil Aviation)	−	−	−	−	−	−	−	+
Minister of (Civil) Aviation	−	−	−	−	−	−	−	+
Minister of Supply (and Aircraft Production)	−	−	−	−	−	−	−	−
Minister of Aircraft Production	−							
Minister of (Fuel and) Power	+[2]	−	−	−	−	−	+[14]	+
Minister of Pensions (and National Insurance)	−	−	−	−	−	+[8]	−	−
Minister of National Insurance	−	−	−	−	−			
Minister of (Public Buildings and) Works	−	−	−	−	−	+[11]	−	−
Postmaster-General	−	−	−	−	+[6]	−	−	−
Paymaster-General (and Chief Secretary to the Treasury)	+[3]	−	−	+[5]	+[7]	−[13]	−[15]	+
Chancellor of the Duchy of Lancaster	−	−	−	−	+[9]	+[13]	+[16]	+[18]
Minister without Portfolio	−	−	−	−	−	−	−	+[19]
Minister of Information	−							
Minister Resident in Middle East	−							
Minister Resident in West Africa	−							
CABINET MINISTERS	16	18	18	16	18	18	18 (19)[15]	21
NON-CABINET MINISTERS	19	13	13	14	11	10 (11)[12]	10 (9)[15]	8

[1] Aneurin Bevan
[2] Emanuel Shinwell
[3] The Lord Privy Seal, Arthur Greenwood
[4] Hugh Dalton
[5] Lord Alexander of Hillsborough
[6] H. F. C. Crookshank, Leader of the House of Commons
[7] Lord Cherwell
[8] Osbert Peake
[9] Lord Woolton
[10] R. A. Butler, Leader of the House of Commons
[11] P. Buchan-Hepburn, ex-Chief Whip of the Conservative Party
[12] The office of Paymaster-General was not filled from December 1955 to October 1956
[13] Lord Selkirk
[14] Lord Mills
[15] Reginald Maudling was included in the Cabinet in September 1957
[16] Dr. Charles Hill
[17] Duncan Sandys
[18] Iain Macleod, Leader of the House of Commons
[19] William Deedes

or amalgamating certain departments, by having one minister occupy more than one post at a time, and by putting a particular post in temporary abeyance. Thus after 1951, the Ministries of Civil Aviation, National Insurance, and Food were abolished and joined with the Ministries of Transport, Pensions, and Agriculture, respectively. The Ministry of Supply was disbanded in 1959, but was succeeded at the same time by the Ministry of Aviation. Joint tenures have occurred particularly when a senior minister combined a sinecure office with a departmental office. Thus both Salisbury and Home held the Lord Presidency of the Council at various times concurrently with the Commonwealth Relations Office. Butler was both Home Secretary and Lord Privy Seal between 1957 and 1960. The new posts of Minister for Welsh Affairs and Minister for Science have so far invariably been held by Cabinet ministers with other portfolios, and since 1962 Sandys has headed both the Commonwealth Relations Office and the Colonial Office. Occasionally, the office of Paymaster-General has not been filled. Thus at one time the total number of ministers in the Government (excluding the Law Officers and the Ministers of State) was reduced to 27; at the same time the number of ministers outside the Cabinet declined from 14 in 1951 to 8 in 1962 as a result of both a decrease in the number of ministerial personnel and an increase in the Cabinet.

The ratio between Cabinet and non-Cabinet ministers was most "favorable"—i.e., the smallest Cabinet with the smallest number of ministers outside it—under Eden and Macmillan between 1955 and September 1957. Since then, new Cabinet posts have been created, forcing a further increase in the size of the Cabinet. Three new Cabinet posts were created after 1961: the First Secretary of State, the Chief Secretary to the Treasury, and a minister without portfolio.[39] Some of these appointments were motivated by personal factors, of course, but they also resulted from simultaneously increasing political and administrative pressures. These have been so diverse that the existing number of sinecure offices proved inadequate to handle them. At least one, and generally two sinecure offices have had to be reserved to give adequate freedom or at least sufficient standing to the Leaders of the House of Lords and the House of Commons. In addition, the system of double-banking the Foreign Office and the Treasury has monopolized—and in the case of the Chief Secretary and Paymaster-General actually frozen—two more sinecures. To retain flexibility, Macmillan therefore had to create two new Cabinet posts in 1962, to accommodate the Deputy Prime Minister (specifically charged with coordinating the Common Market negotiations and the Central African Office) and to retain at least one minister without departmental duties, available for special assignments. Thus the deliberate cut in the number

---

[39] The net increase in the size of the Cabinet was only two, because the Chief Secretary to the Treasury also took the office of Paymaster-General; the number of ministers increased only by one (the First Secretary of State), or by two if the Secretary for Technical Cooperation is regarded as a minister, rather than a Minister of State.

of ministerial portfolios through joint tenures, etc., proved largely self-defeating. What was gained with one hand was lost with the other.

By the end of 1962, therefore, the Government again showed its traditional ragged character in full measure. There were two formal co-ordinators over the whole field, the Prime Minister and the Deputy Prime Minister; two Cabinet ministers at both the Foreign Office and the Treasury; a minister without portfolio; and a Lord President, who also carried the appealing title of Minister for Science and led the House of Lords. The Cabinet also included the Chancellor of the Duchy of Lancaster, who led the Commons and the Party Organization; a Minister of Housing and Local Government, who was also adorned with the title of Minister for Welsh Affairs; and a Secretary of State for Scotland. Also included were one minister in charge of both the Commonwealth Relations Office and the Colonial Office; a somewhat ambiguously placed coordinating Minister of Defence; and such "regular" ministers as those for Trade, Agriculture and Fisheries, Labour, Transport, Education, and Health. All in all, there were 21 Cabinet members.

The ministers of Power and Aviation were again outside the Cabinet, as they had been before 1957 and 1959, respectively. A new Minister of Public Buildings and Works, the Postmaster-General, and a Minister of Pensions and National Insurance were also sadly outside the Cabinet. Finally, three Service ministers lived a life of their own as somewhat nostalgic remnants of the past, as yet strongly supported by corporate service loyalties, but clearly on the way to oblivion.

In addition to the four Law Officers, the Government counted the Secretary for Technical Cooperation, who was a low-grade technical co-ordinating minister under senior guidance; six Ministers of State; two fairly high-placed junior ministers at the Treasury; and an ever-growing number of parliamentary secretaries, whips, assistant whips and parliamentary private secretaries. From the top, the Government presumably offered an interesting panorama of political humanity; from the bottom it certainly offered a hazardous climb. In December 1961, it was decided to hold weekly meetings during which a Cabinet member would explain policy to non-Cabinet and junior ministers, and offer to answer questions. It was hoped that in this way the non-Cabinet and junior ministers might "eventually come to play a larger part in the formulation of policy outside their own departments."[40]

[40] *The Times,* 11 December 1961; cf. Heasman, p. 482, n. 29.

PART TWO

THE CENTRAL ORGANIZATION FOR DEFENSE
AND ECONOMIC POLICY

NINE

THE DEFENSE ORGANIZATION BEFORE 1914

Until the turn of the century, the military position of Britain had given little cause for alarm. Except for the Crimean War, the country had not been directly involved in any continental war for almost a hundred years. Britannia ruled the waves. The Navy made the country secure from invasion, guaranteed the lifelines of the Empire, and formed a mobile police unit, which defended the British flag and British interests the world over. Compared with the armies of other European powers, the British Army played a rather minor role. Occasionally, a war scare had aroused fear in some circles that the country might suffer a sudden invasion. Advocates of this "bolt from the blue" doctrine had pleaded for a strong national army, and at times fortifications had been erected at certain strategic places along the British coast. But on the whole, the "blue-water school," which held that an invasion of the British Isles was impossible as long as the British Navy maintained its dominant position, had prevailed. The British Army was small. It consisted of standing professional units, which served in England and the colonial garrisons, and of a complicated reserve of "militia," "yeomanry," and "volunteers," which might be called on in time of war. The Indian Army was relatively the most substantial force in the Empire.

The rather special military position of the British Empire had far-reaching consequences for the command structure of each Service, as well as for their relation to one another.

The Position of the Services in the Nineteenth Century

Through the centuries the Navy, "the Silent Service," had developed into an almost mystical institution. Its special political and social position gave it a natural claim on national pride and national resources. The Board of Admiralty was securely in control of strategy and command, shipbuilding and armor, victualling and training. The Board formed an effectively functioning body: each member had a specialized task, but at all times the Board was collectively responsible for the state and preparedness of the fleet. The First Lord, who was chairman of the Board, represented the element of political control. In the final analysis, he could prevail even against his own Board. But in practice its professional members and particularly the First Sea Lord had an almost decisive voice. "The Lords of the Admiralty," Churchill has written, "hold quasi-ministerial appointments."[1] The First Lord of the Admiralty, consequently, had a slightly lower position in the ministerial hierarchy than his opposite number, the Secretary of State for War.[2]

The position of the Army was more complicated. Throughout the nineteenth century, the monarch had continued to exercise a strong personal voice in Army affairs. The highest Army officer, the Commander in Chief, was directly responsible to the Crown, and contacts between the Crown and the military were frequent and intimate. Since the seventeenth century, the Army had been an object of political controversy between the Crown and Parliament. Parliament had sought to wrest control, and insisted on economies and drastic military reforms. But it had not been fully successful. Until well into the nineteenth century, important responsibilities had rested with various semi-independent boards. More than one minister had been in charge of Army matters. Political responsibilities were therefore ill-defined, which provoked more criticism and stimulated the demand for further reforms.[3] Not until 1863 were all Army matters concentrated under one Secretary of State for War. But even then, his relation to the Crown and the Commander in Chief was far from clear. The office of Secretary of State carried high status in the ministerial hierarchy. But the Secretary's powers were limited and his difficulties great. Between 1860 and 1880 no less than seventeen Royal Commissions, eighteen Select Committees, nineteen departmental committees within the War Office, and thirty-five committees of professional officers reported about problems of Army organization.[4] In 1905, the position of the War Office had become so invidious that, in the opinion of Campbell-Bannerman, "Nobody [would] touch it with a pole."[5]

Until 1900, there was little organized cooperation between the two Services. Army and Navy each had its own tasks. Such coordination as there was was provided *ad hoc,* usually through a decision of the Cabinet. Detailed military preparations were not required, since a great war was only a distant possibility. Armament, not military planning, dominated strategic thinking, and neither the Navy nor the Army had a well-developed staff organization. Only two sides exerted pressure for more regular modes of coordination. The Colonial Office was concerned about the defense of certain strategic points for which it knew close cooperation of the Navy and the Army to be vital. Others saw a possibility for re-

---

[1] Churchill, *World Crisis,* I, 82; cf. *Esher Papers,* I, 269: "The Navy is a constitutional force. . . . The Army is a royal force, and while the Queen never interferes with the Navy, she interferes very much with the Army."

[2] *Esher Papers,* II, 93.

[3] Cf. Anson, II, Part II, 222–43; Ehrman, *Cabinet, passim*; Gibbs, *passim.*

[4] Ehrman, *Cabinet,* pp. 6–7.

[5] Haldane, *Autobiography,* p. 173. Grey regarded the "War Office" as one of the "most beastly things" (*ibid.,* p. 180). Balfour spoke of "the Cinderella of Departments" (*Life of Balfour,* p. 275), and Lansdowne called it a "thankless post" (*Life of Lansdowne,* p. 130).

trenchment if the Army and Navy were made to cooperate more closely. The influence of the first factor became apparent in the establishment, in 1885, of a Colonial Defence Committee. This Committee was composed of official representatives of the Colonial Office, the War Office, and the Admiralty. It attempted to keep the specific defense problems of each overseas territory under continuous surveillance.[6] The drive for economy was mainly responsible for the creation, in 1887, of the Hartington Commission, which was charged "to enquire into the civil and professional administration of the naval and military departments and the relation of those departments to each other and to the Treasury."[7]

The Report of the Hartington Commission (published in 1890) rejected a proposal to appoint a Minister of Defence.[8] The Commission felt that the absence of individual representatives of each of the Services from the Cabinet would be detrimental to their interests. Since the complexities of a Service department were so great that even now ministers found it difficult to master its details, no minister in charge of both departments could adequately do so. Moreover, there was a danger that the influence of the Army in a jointly administered department might be so great that the interests of the Navy would suffer. The Commission rejected, at the same time, a proposal of Lord Randolph Churchill, who had resigned in 1886 from the office of Chancellor of the Exchequer, when he had found insufficient Cabinet support for his desire to economize on military expenditure.[9]

Lord Randolph proposed abolishing the existing functions of the Secretary of State for War and the Board of the Admiralty. In their place should be appointed a Lord High Admiral of the Navy and a Captain-General of the Army, each of whom should exercise, subject to the Government, supreme control over and responsibility for the administration of his respective service. They were to be professional officers and would serve as ministers for a period of five years. To allow the Cabinet to gain military and naval advice at first hand, they should be created Privy Councillors and summoned to all Cabinet councils when military and naval questions were under consideration. But to preserve and ensure financial control by Parliament and Government, and to supply the much-needed link between the two Services, there should be created, in addition, the office of Secretary of State and Treasurer for the Sea and Land Forces of the Crown. This minister would settle with the responsible heads of the Services the amount of annual expenditure to be submitted to the Cabinet, and he would defend the agreed estimates in Parliament. Furthermore, he would be charged with controlling, managing, and taking responsibility for the Ordnance departments, and with making all great contracts for the Army and the Navy. The Secretary of State would not interfere

[6] Gibbs, pp. 9–13; Yu, pp. 272–78; Mackintosh, p. 261.
[7] Cmd. 5979 (1890).
[8] *Ibid.,* para. 15.   [9] *Ibid.,* pp. vii, xv–xvii.

nor necessarily be held responsible for the administration of the Services, except in matters of supply and expenditure. For the rest, he should function as an "authoritative and acceptable arbitrator," with the Cabinet deciding only if the ministers of the Army and Navy disagreed, either singly or jointly, with the Secretary of State.

The Hartington Commission did not think this proposal acceptable. To quote from its report:

> The minister who would be in direct contact with the House of Commons would be the civilian minister responsible for proposing the annual expenditure on the two Services, and we believe that there would be a constant and inevitable tendency to hold him responsible as well for the administration of the Services as for the supplies which he would demand from Parliament.

In practice, therefore, the position of such a minister would gradually become more powerful than intended, and ultimately it would approach closely that of the Minister of Defence, which the Commission had earlier rejected.[10] As an alternative, the Commission suggested establishing a Naval and Military Council composed of the Prime Minister, the two Service ministers, and their main professional advisers. The Commission urged that the proceedings and discussions of the new Council be duly recorded, "instances having occurred in which Cabinet decisions have been differently understood by the two departments and have become practically a dead letter."[11]

For a while, the Report of the Hartington Commission remained itself a dead letter. Its only result was the establishment of a rather unimportant Joint Naval and Military Committee, which occupied itself mainly with issues of coastal defense. Criticism therefore persisted.[12] In 1895, the new Salisbury Cabinet formed a Defence Committee of the Cabinet, largely at the instigation of the Leader of the House of Commons, Balfour.[13] Hartington (now Duke of Devonshire) was appointed to preside over the new committee. But it gained little practical importance. The Service ministers resisted what Goschen termed "the beginnings of a Court of Revision, a surveillance by other Cabinet ministers."[14] There was no provision for regular consultation with the Service Chiefs. Nor were the proceedings of the Defence Committee recorded. It consequently lapsed into an ineffective body that dealt mainly with financial disputes between the Services.[15]

---

[10] One often encounters in the literature (e.g., Hancock–Gowing, p. 32) the suggestion that Lord Randoph proposed the appointment of a Minister of Defence. But in his minority report to the Report of the Hartington Commission, he only rejected paragraphs 16 and 17, which criticized his own proposals, not paragraph 15, which dismissed the case for a Minister of Defence (*ibid.*, p. xii).

[11] *Ibid.*, p. viii.   [12] Johnson, pp. 31–32.

[13] *Ibid.*, pp. 32–35.   [14] Mackintosh, p. 264.

[15] Gibbs, pp. 16–17; Balfour in 118 H. of C. Deb. (5 March 1903), col. 1579; *Life of Balfour*, I, 274–75; cf. *Esher Papers*, I, 376–77; Smellie, pp. 158–59; Johnson, pp. 34–35.

The Consequences of the Boer War; the C.I.D. and the War Office
(Reconstitution) Committee (1902–1904)

By the end of the nineteenth century, the military position of Great Britain began to change. Colonial rivalry led to renewed diplomatic conflicts with the European powers. The growing military and economic strength of a unified Germany affected the balance of power on the European continent, and at the same time the German naval program began to threaten Britain's position at sea. Splendid Isolation was coming to an end, as British foreign policy moved slowly in the direction of new alliances. This required a thorough revision of time-honored premises of foreign and defense policies. At the same time, the Boer War exposed considerable shortcomings in Britain's military organization. Military reform again became a burning issue : after 1900, there was constant pressure to reform the War Office, form a General Staff, and modernize the fleet. The central government machinery for defense was also viewed in a new and critical light.

In November 1902, only shortly after the end of the Boer War, the Secretary of State for War, St. John Brodrick, and the First Lord of the Admiralty, Selborne, presented Balfour with an urgent memorandum. Threatening to resign if no action was taken, they demanded a drastic reform of the Defence Committee. They argued that at the present time, there was not enough opportunity to investigate problems "which are neither purely naval nor purely military, nor purely naval and military combined, but which may be described as naval, military, and political."[16] Balfour readily agreed. In December 1902 he established a reorganized Defence Committee, which was soon called the Committee of Imperial Defence. This Committee was instructed

to make it its duty to survey as a whole the strategical military needs of the Empire, to deal with the complicated questions which are all essential elements in that general problem, and to revise from time to time their own previous decisions, so that the Cabinet shall always be informed and always have at its disposal information upon these important points.[17]

The Committee was to act on its own initiative. It should seek advice from outside experts and keep records that would also be available to future Governments in order to ensure the continuity of British defense policy.

Besides the Prime Minister, the following were ex officio members of the Committee : the Lord President of the Council, the two Service ministers, the First Sea Lord, the Commander in Chief, and the Directors of Intelligence of both Service departments. For the time being, the Duke of Devonshire continued to be President of the Committee, but from the outset, Balfour himself attended all its meetings. After a Cabinet crisis

---

[16] *Life of Balfour*, I, 275–76, and 118 H. of C. Deb. (5 March 1903), cols. 1578–86 ; cf. Esher, *C.I.D.*, p. 16ff ; Johnson, p. 52ff.
[17] 118 H. of C. Deb. (5 March 1903), col. 1579.

in 1903, he went further. He took the chair of the Committee himself. He decreed that the Prime Minister was to be its only official member. All other participants in the Committee's business were to be invited *ad hoc*, depending on the business under consideration. Balfour's main reason for the latter reform was his wish to preserve as much flexibility as possible so that both British and Dominion representatives, politicians as well as military professionals could be invited freely to take part in the meetings of the Committee, and to do so as equals, regardless of their official positions.[18]

In the autumn of 1903, a War Office (Reconstitution) Committee had been set up to investigate the organization of the War Office. The War Office had come under particularly heavy fire from a number of committees that had been enquiring into various aspects of the Boer War. Members of the Committee were Lord Esher, *éminence grise* of Edwardian politics, Admiral Sir John Fisher, who was soon to be appointed First Sea Lord, and Sir George Clarke, one-time Secretary to the Colonial Defence Committee and the Hartington Commission. Esher was the driving force behind the Committee.[19] But its report also reflected the thoughts of its Secretary, Colonel (later General) Gerald Ellison. "In him," Amery wrote, "I discovered the most 'German' British soldier I had ever met, not only in squareness of head but in what that head contained in the way of an intimate knowledge of German army organization and of a clear understanding of the principles on which it had been evolved."[20]

The Esher Committee introduced three important reforms in War Office organization.[21] First, the office of Commander in Chief was abolished, and the control over the Army put under a new collective body, the Army Council. Modeled on the Board of Admiralty, the Army Council had four military and three civilian members, who met under the chairmanship of the Secretary of State for War. Second, the Esher Committee forced through the establishment of a General Staff in the War Office, which, to give it sufficient authority, would report directly to the Secretary of State for War.[22] The Chief of the General Staff (renamed Chief of the Imperial General Staff in 1907) was soon to become, like the First Sea Lord in the Board of Admiralty, the most important professional member of the Army Council. The Committee moreover wished to free those who were charged with thinking out long-term policy from routine work; they also urged the divorce of administration from executive command, and the decentralization of the latter.

Third, the Esher Committee pointed to the absence of adequate pro-

18 139 H. of C. Deb. (2 August 1904), cols. 617–22; Gibbs, pp. 20–22; *Life of Balfour*, p. 275ff.
19 Cf. *Esher Papers*, II, 14–23; Falls, p. 247; Johnson, p. 60ff.
20 Amery, *My Political Life*, I, 193–94.
21 Cd. 1932 (1904) ; cf. *Life of Roberts*, p. 392ff.; *Life of Henry Wilson*, I, 55–64.
22 Part of the credit for this reform belongs to the then Commander in Chief, Lord Roberts. See G. F. Ellison, "Lord Roberts and the General Staff," *Nineteenth Century*, CXII (1932), 722–32; *Life of Roberts*, pp. 404–8; and Amery, Preface to *Life of Roberts*, p. x.

vision for "the scientific study of Imperial resources, the coordination of the ever-varying facts upon which Imperial rule rests, the calculation of forces required, and the broad plans necessary to sustain the burden of Empire."[23] Although they acknowledged the valuable work of the C.I.D., they feared that "the guarantees for, first, the permanent and continuous labors of the Committee, and, second, their adequate discharge" were not at present secured.[24] Like the Hartington Commission before them, they pointed to the advantages of the German General Staff. But they thought such a system not fit for reproduction in Britain, "where the responsibility for efficiency and sufficiency of preparations for war rests upon Parliament and, in a special sense, upon the Prime Minister."[25] Instead, they proposed establishing a permanent staff for the C.I.D. composed of a Permanent Secretary and six officers of not-too-high rank, two each seconded by the War Office, the Admiralty, and the India Office, for a period of two years. This Secretariat would have the duty of making a continuous study of defense issues, "of exercising due foresight in regard to the changing conditions produced by external developments, and of drawing from the several departments of State, and arranging in convenient form for the use of the Cabinet such information as may at any moment be required."[26] The Secretariat's duties would be only advisory, not executive. But it would provide the Cabinet and the Prime Minister with the documentation necessary to make effective judgments on defense problems. At the same time, it would ensure consistency and continuity of thought on matters of defense policy.

After some hesitation, Balfour accepted the suggestion, and established a permanent Secretariat for the C.I.D. in a Treasury Minute of May 1904. Clarke, a member of the Esher Committee, was appointed its first Secretary. He was to be assisted by two Assistant Secretaries, one nominated by the Secretary of State for War, the other by the First Lord of the Admiralty.[27] In August 1904, Balfour defended the new machinery in the House of Commons. For those who might feel uneasy with the Esher Committee's description of the C.I.D. as "the coordinating head of all the departments concerned in the conduct of, and in the preparation for war,"[28] Balfour stressed again that the C.I.D.

has no executive authority at all. It has no power to give an order to the humblest soldier in His Majesty's Army or the most powerless sloop under the control of the Admiralty. . . . We cannot interfere with administration in any way either at home or abroad. It is only by thus strictly limiting our functions that we can have that authority which I hope we shall more and more gain in the general scheme of Imperial Defence, and that our opinions will carry that weight which will be all the more effective because there is behind them no power of coercive authority.[29]

[23] Letter from the Esher Committee to Balfour, Cd. 1932.
[24] *Ibid.*   [25] Cd. 1932, pp. 3–4.
[26] *Ibid.*, p. 3.   [27] Johnson, p. 92.
[28] Letter from the Esher Committee to Balfour, Cd. 1932.
[29] 139 H. of C. Deb. (2 August 1904), cols. 618–19.

The Role of the C.I.D. before 1914

The establishment of the C.I.D. had important consequences. For the first time, politicians and professional military officers were brought together for regular discussion of important defense problems. No less than eighty-two Committee meetings were held before Balfour went out of office in December 1905. This number declined to fifteen under Campbell-Bannerman between 1905 and 1908, and thirty-one under Asquith between 1908 and 1914.[30] But at the same time, much more work came to be performed by subcommittees, which drew from an ever-widening circle of experts and departments. The Secretariat ensured continuity and concentration. Since the Committee was intended to have advisory functions only, representatives of the Dominions could and did take part in its proceedings without constitutional difficulty. But the Committee encountered many more problems than *laudatores temporis acti* have made us believe.[31] These concerned, in particular, the relation between the C.I.D. and the Cabinet, between its secretariat and the departments, and between the C.I.D., the War Office, and the Admiralty.

The C.I.D. and the Cabinet

Technically, the C.I.D. was not a committee of the Cabinet; it was an advisory committee to the Prime Minister only. At least one practical advantage of this was that the Committee was not bound by constitutional precedent. It could freely record its discussions in official minutes and establish whatever subcommittees it wished without reference to the full Cabinet. Theoretically, the Committee's deliberations were merely speculative. It discussed measures that *might* be taken in case of war, but it did not take decisions that were directly binding upon the departments.

In practice, however, this distinction between an advisory C.I.D. and a responsible Cabinet was not so easy to maintain. The presence of leading ministers in the C.I.D. could not but give it a certain power. It was difficult to distinguish clearly between *preparations* for a certain eventuality, and possible *commitments* when such an eventuality might actually arise. Since December 1905 there had been secret consultations between the French and British General Staffs about measures the two countries might take in case of a German invasion of French territory. Technically, these discussions did not fall under the C.I.D.'s jurisdiction, and its Secretariat did not know of these talks until a fairly late date.[32] But the ministers who had authorized the talks were the same ministers who dominated the work of the C.I.D., and the full importance of these talks was initially brought to light during a famous meeting of the C.I.D., on 23

---

[30] Mackintosh, p. 267.

[31] Cf. Hancock–Gowing, pp. 31–35; Hankey, *Control, passim*; Hankey, *Diplomacy*, pp. 83–104; Smellie, pp. 282–83; and, in particular, Mackintosh's critical evaluation, pp. 265–73.

[32] Hankey, *Supreme Command*, pp. 62–64.

August 1911, at the time of the Agadir crisis. Even then the Cabinet was not taken into full confidence, but the facts soon became known in a wider circle. There were angry scenes in the Cabinet in November 1911, and again in 1912, when ministers not on the C.I.D. accused the Committee of withholding essential information and of committing the country to measures that had not been given Cabinet approval.[33] It was formally set down that only the Cabinet could sanction any further commitments. The Foreign Secretary, Grey, was charged to stipulate this in an official communication to the French Government.[34]

One consequence of the Cabinet's increased suspicion of the C.I.D. was that its membership increased. Whereas until 1911 only some four ministers used to take part regularly in the work of the Committee, some nine to eleven now participated.[35] Its professional membership also grew, as many retired soldiers continued to sit with the Committee. Finally, the Committee was practically as large as the Cabinet, and more and more of its work was in practice delegated to subcommittees.[36] In 1912, the Cabinet itself authorized the Admiralty to enter into certain agreements with the French naval authorities about the disposition of the French and British fleets in case of war. Again there was conflict, in 1914, about the extent to which such dispositions were binding upon the British government if war should break out. Under whatever auspices—whether of individual ministers, the C.I.D., or even the Cabinet—these exploratory conversations were carried on, they tended to create commitments that it proved difficult not to honor.[37] To this extent, the free choice of the Cabinet was undoubtedly impaired.

The Secretariat of the C.I.D. and the Departments

It had been Esher's original intention that the members of the C.I.D. Secretariat would be little more than "orderlies," charged with collecting the necessary data, on which the Prime Minister and the C.I.D. could base their deliberations.[38] But at the same time, Esher had thought it essential that the Secretary of the Committee should have considerable authority. He was angry to find that instead of being given a seat at the Council table, Clarke had been assigned a separate table in the Council room. "I have written to Clarke on the subject," wrote Esher to Fisher, "and told him that he *must* sit on the left hand of the President of the Committee and *assert* himself."[39] And again when the joint support of Esher and Fisher had led to the appointment of Hankey as Secretary of the C.I.D., Esher feared that Hankey would have insufficient authority with the highest military leaders. "He must wear a tall hat and a black coat," wrote Esher. "If he were ten years older he might disregard these

---

[33] See especially Mackintosh, pp. 316–24.
[34] *Ibid.*, p. 320.   [35] *Ibid.*, p. 321.
[36] Hankey, *Supreme Command*, p. 178.
[37] Cf. Chamberlain, *Down the Years*, pp. 95–96.
[38] *Esher Papers*, II, 38.   [39] *Fisher Correspondence*, I, 367, n. 72.

things." Esher agreed with Fisher that Hankey had Napoleonic qualities, but, so he replied, "I am not yet sure that he will carry the necessary weight. You know how personality counts in this world. He doesn't *look* Napoleonic."[40] To compensate for this defect, Esher attempted to get Hankey a knighthood.

The Secretariat of the C.I.D. was, as we saw, charged with documenting all defense problems from a non-departmental angle. By registering the decisions of the Committee and its many subcommittees, and by constant personal liaison with the departments, it was to ensure that at all times the Prime Minister and the Cabinet could be presented with adequate information for any decision that might have to be taken. In practice, however, the relation between the C.I.D. and the departments showed many variations. With some departments contacts were constant and intimate; with others they were not. The fact that some departmental representatives might have taken part in meetings of the C.I.D. or one of its subcommittees did not imply that ministers in charge of these departments were always in agreement with any conclusion arrived at or indeed thought themselves bound by any decision. Even so, the Committee went on formalizing its conclusions. In 1909, Esher spoke of "the settled plans of the executive Government based upon the Committee of Imperial Defence Reports."[41] According to one authority, at least 95 per cent of the business of the C.I.D. was transacted directly with the ministers and the executive departments without passing through the Cabinet.[42] From 1911 onwards, a complete War Book was prepared. This War Book summed up a number of measures the departments would have to take in case the Cabinet should decide to introduce the so-called Precautionary Stage. As Hankey was to record later:

Several members of the Cabinet misunderstood what was involved in the decision to enforce what was called the Precautionary Stage of the War Book. The situation was saved from chaos, however, by a provision which had been inserted in the War Book in anticipation of the possibility of some such misunderstanding in the Cabinet, and which threw on the War Office the responsibility for notifying the decision to all the departments concerned.[43]

For the first time, departments were charged to perform certain tasks without an explicit order of the responsible ministers. As Hankey wrote proudly: "From the King to the printer, everyone knew what he had to do."[44]

[40] *Ibid.*, pp. 434, 441, n. 1 ; cf. Hankey, *Supreme Command,* p. 54.
[41] *Esher Papers,* II, 428 ; cf. p. 430.
[42] Johnson, pp. 130–31.
[43] Hankey, *Diplomacy,* p. 31, and Hankey, *Supreme Command,* pp. 155–56. For a similar role of the War Book in 1939, when it was introduced in stages under the supervision of a Committee chaired by the Secretary of the Cabinet, see Ismay, p. 98 ; cf. Johnson, pp. 268–71.
[44] Hankey, *Supreme Command,* p. 139.

The C.I.D., the War Office, and the Admiralty

The weakness of the C.I.D. as a coordinating agency became clearest in its checkered relations with the two Service departments. Since 1904, the Admiralty under Fisher had been engaged in a thorough modernization of the British Navy. Fisher, a brilliant, colorful, but obstinate figure, did not wish the C.I.D. to come between him and the fleet, and he rejected the idea of a Naval Staff, which he regarded as at most "a very excellent organization for cutting out and arranging foreign newspaper clippings."[45] Fisher had some reason to be angry when the C.I.D. Secretariat intervened in matters that were properly the responsibility of the Admiralty, as when Clarke sought to block his Dreadnought plan. Clarke was dismissed for that reason, and replaced by a Fisher man, Captain Charles L. Ottley.[46] But even then, Fisher remained uncooperative. Esher reproached him at various moments for taking an "Achillean attitude in regard to the Defence Committee," and asked him to bury the hatchet.[47] But Fisher remained unresponsive, and wrote to Esher on 7 October 1907:

I don't care what you say, my unalterable conviction is that the Committee of Imperial Defence is tending rapidly to become a sort of Aulic Council, and the men who talk glibly and write Clarke-ly and argue Haldane-ly . . . will usurp the functions of the *two* men who *must* be the "Masters of the War"—the First Sea Lord and the Chief of the General Staff.[48]

The relation between the War Office and the C.I.D. was altogether different in this period. The reforms in the War Office in 1904 had been carried through in close conjunction with changes in the structure and functions of the C.I.D. Balfour and Esher had watched over both in 1904 and 1905. The new Secretary of State for War in the Liberal Cabinet, Haldane, was a staunch supporter of the idea of a General Staff as well as of the C.I.D. Haldane had made some study of the German General Staff,[49] and he found a congenial adviser in the Secretary of the Esher Committee, Ellison, whom he appointed as his private military secretary on Esher's advice.[50] While the Admiralty continued to boycott much of the work of the C.I.D., the War Office embraced it eagerly. Esher even expressed the fear that the General Staff was likely to develop into a Frankenstein that would devour most functions of the C.I.D.[51]

Haldane concentrated his efforts on creating an adequate Expeditionary Force. Since Campbell-Bannerman was not greatly interested in the C.I.D., Haldane often directed its activities. This could not but fan the Admiralty's suspicions of the C.I.D. Fisher privately regarded the very

[45] Fisher, *Memories*, p. 102ff.
[46] Hankey, *Supreme Command*, pp. 51–52; Johnson, p. 74.
[47] Cf. *Esher Papers*, II, 182, 219–20, 247–48, 251–52.
[48] *Fisher Correspondence*, II, 144.
[49] Haldane, *Autobiography*, pp. 206–7; cf. pp. 199–200.
[50] *Esher Papers*, II, 126–27.   [51] *Ibid.*, pp. 144–45; cf. p. 412.

idea of shipping an Expeditionary Force to France as an "act of suicidal idiocy."[52] But in council, the Admiralty generally responded by silence. It consistently refused to divulge its own war plans to the C.I.D., until at one time certain papers were explicitly demanded by the Prime Minister.[53] In ministerial circles, serious concern and irritation arose. Haldane, in particular, demanded reforms. He advocated establishing a Naval Staff, which would work out the details for the necessary combined military actions in cooperation with the General Staff in the War Office.[54] Fisher rejected the idea, because guns, armor, and a correct instantaneous maneuvering of ships by well-trained naval officers would decide a naval battle, not any a priori planning.[55] Haldane gained the support of some admirals like Lord Beresford who were Fisher's personal enemies.[56] Rumors that Haldane desired to become Minister of Defence began to circulate among Fisher's friends. Fisher dubbed him Napoleon B[onaparte].[57]

The smoldering conflict finally erupted in August 1911. During the session of the C.I.D. mentioned earlier, the War Office, through Sir Henry Wilson, put forward a thoroughly prepared plan for deploying the Expeditionary Force in France. The Admiralty followed with a rambling, ill-considered exposé by Fisher's successor as First Sea Lord, Sir Arthur Wilson, who rejected the Army scheme and proposed instead to tie down enemy troops in Germany itself by pinpoint landings on the German Baltic coast.[58]

This evidence for the first time fully revealed to ministers that, seven years of C.I.D. work notwithstanding, no real cooperation had been achieved between the two Service departments, each having gone its own way in planning and preparations. Haldane was aghast and threatened to resign unless a drastic change took place immediately at the Admiralty. He asked Asquith to allow him to take over the Admiralty, to put its house in order. Asquith was at the same time subject to pressure from Churchill, who also coveted the office of First Lord. Asquith did not wish to snub the Admiralty so openly as to put its erstwhile enemy in charge, and, in addition, he thought it necessary for the First Lord to sit in the Commons.[59] Haldane and Churchill worked out a compromise whereby the latter declared himself willing to work closely with Haldane, and to establish a Naval Staff.[60] A "high-level bridge" composed of the First Lord, First Sea Lord, the Secretary of State for War, the Chief of

---

[52] *Fisher Correspondence,* II, 218.   [53] Johnson, p. 86.
[54] *Life of Haldane,* I, 243–47; *Life of Haig,* I, 115–16.
[55] Fisher, *Memories,* p. 102ff.; *Fisher Correspondence,* II, 214; *Life of Haldane,* I, 247, 276–77; *Esher Papers,* III, 70–71.
[56] *Fisher Correspondence,* II, 206–93, especially p. 210ff.
[57] *Fisher Correspondence,* II, 309–10, 375–76; cf. *Esher Papers,* II, 408.
[58] Haldane, *Autobiography,* pp. 223–32; *Life of Haldane,* I, 280ff.; Churchill, *World Crisis,* I, 55–69; *Life of Henry Wilson,* I, 99–101; Hankey, *Supreme Command,* p. 78ff.; Johnson, p. 114ff.
[59] *Life of Haldane,* I, 284–87; Sommer, *Haldane,* pp. 245–49.
[60] Churchill, *World Crisis,* I, 90–93.

the Imperial General Staff, and a few other officers from both departments was instituted to elaborate joint plans. To ensure coordination with the C.I.D., Hankey was made its Secretary.[61] Some improvement resulted, but the reforms came too late to ensure the effective *rapprochement* that was essential for real joint planning.

Later claims notwithstanding, therefore, the C.I.D., cannot be said to have been effectively in charge of strategic planning before 1914. Even Hankey, who can hardly be accused of lack of parental appreciation for the C.I.D., has admitted that "there was not that close and minute joint scrutiny of plans which a more perfect system should ensure."[62] The C.I.D. did not control or even succeed in clearing business between the two Service departments in major fields of war preparation. It engaged in interesting discussions that did not definitely commit anyone. It collected important documentation. It prepared extensive instructions for action to be taken at the outbreak of war. But neither long-term strategy nor the effects of war on civilian life was adequately studied or foreseen. Stated differently, the C.I.D. formed a useful piece of machinery. But it did not prevail against the concentrated power of the individual Service departments. Nor did it really transcend the limitations that a century of almost unbroken peace had fixed in the minds of British politicians and public alike.[63]

---

[61] Hankey, *Supreme Command*, pp. 78, 140.
[62] *Ibid.*, p. 140.   [63] Cf. Mackintosh, pp. 266–72.

TEN

THE DEFENSE ORGANIZATION, 1914–1932

From the military point of view, Britain seemed fairly well prepared at the outbreak of World War I. The Expeditionary Force was small, but well trained and ready for action. The British Navy stood at the peak of its strength. Relations with the French Allies were cordial. Few expected that the war would last long.

Initial optimism soon wore off, however. By the end of 1914, and especially after the failure of the Dardanelles expedition in 1915, it became evident to all that England had to prepare for a long war. As soldiers began to dig themselves into their trenches, men and materials were demanded in ever-increasing quantities. Submarine warfare became a deadly peril, threatening not only the war effort but also the living conditions of the British population itself. Zeppelin raids brought the war to homes of ordinary citizens.

These developments presented both the political and the military leadership with increasingly complicated problems. Serious conflict arose over whether Britain could or should suffer a "war of attrition." Politicians and military leaders did not have a high regard for each other's qualities, and hardly saw eye to eye on where military expertness began and political interference should stop. Amateur schemes became all the more popular as military successes eluded the nation on the Western Front. There was serious disagreement about the structure of the Army command and about the ways in which the individual efforts of the Allies might best be coordinated. In 1917, the withdrawal of Russia from active combat and the entry of the United States into the war created further problems. Uncertainty and distrust were widespread.

The influence of these new forces on the structure of the Cabinet was traced in detail in Chapter 3. In this chapter, we will be concerned with developments within the War Office and the Admiralty, complications arising from the development of a third Service, and, finally, the issue of supply organization.

Developments in the War Office, 1914–18[1]

During the first two years of the war, the developments in the War Office centered around the personality of the Secretary of State, Kitchener.

---

[1] This section is based particularly on the biographies of King George V, Asquith, Kitchener, Lloyd George, Grey, and Bonar Law; on the autobiographies of Asquith, Lloyd George, Samuel, Esher, and Robertson; and on Churchill's *World Crisis;* Beaverbrook, 1914–16 and 1916–18; Hankey, *Supreme Command;* and Maurice, pp. 118–71.

Kitchener's appointment was practically unprecedented. The first serving soldier to be admitted to the Cabinet since 1660, he was nominated not because of his politics or political skill, but because of his professional standing and his place in public esteem.[2] His appointment was popular with the great masses of the people. His colleagues in the Cabinet, too, were for a time well satisfied to leave the direction of war in what they thought were his competent hands. Some military leaders had initially greeted the appointment with more suspicion. They feared that Kitchener was to be used by the politicians as an instrument to interfere with pre-arranged military plans.[3] There was also friction with the Commander in Chief in France, Sir John French, who chafed because he had less senior military rank than his Secretary of State.

In 1914, Kitchener's military fame and political control made him practically the dictator of military strategy. This situation was not without problems. For one thing, Kitchener had little interest in staff work. He allowed the General Staff in the War Office to shrivel; many of its leading members joined the Expeditionary Force, and the remaining ones were practically never consulted.[4] For another thing, he was busy with many tasks. His foremost role in 1914 and 1915 was the recruiting of massive armies. Unlike most, Kitchener was convinced that the war would last for years, and he recruited accordingly. He had "unparalleled thoroughness, and an unparalleled drive."[5] But he found it difficult to delegate tasks or to profit from teamwork. This was bound to create friction in those matters in which he himself was not greatly interested.

As the war continued, both military men and politicians became more and more distrustful of his secretiveness, which they denounced as "oriental."[6] Military reverses, and erratic decisions by Kitchener, increasingly affected his status within the inner circle. But Asquith's unwavering support and the powerful influence of Kitchener's name on the public stultified any attempts at reform for at least the first year of the war. Only after protracted failure at the Dardanelles did the Cabinet decide to force the establishment of a competent General Staff. Not until November 1915 were actual measures taken. While Kitchener was temporarily at the Dardanelles, Asquith himself took charge of the War Office. Both the Commander in Chief of the British Expeditionary Force and the rather weak Chief of the Imperial General Staff were relieved of their posts.

Kitchener's own powers were now drastically curtailed. Sir William Robertson, nominated to the post of Chief of the Imperial General Staff, took care to outline his views on the role of the Chief of the Imperial General Staff in a formal memorandum to the Prime Minister and Kitchener. In draft, the main clauses of this memorandum read:

---

[2] *Life of Kitchener*, p. 278.   [3] *Ibid.*, p. 278.
[4] *Ibid.*, p. 318.   [5] *Ibid.*, p. 380.
[6] *Esher Papers*, III, 276.

In order that the War Council may be able to reach timely decisions . . . it is is essential that it should receive *all* advice on matters concerning military operations through one authoritative channel only. With us that channel must be the Chief of the Imperial General Staff. . . .

All orders for the military operations required to put into execution the approved policy should be signed and issued by the Chief of the Imperial General Staff, under the authority of the War Council, and *not* under that of the Army Council. Similarly, all communications from General Officers Commanding regarding military operations should be addressed to the Chief of the Imperial General Staff. . . .

The Secretary of State for War is responsible for the raising, maintenance, and equipment of the forces which the policy of the War Council makes necessary. This is of itself a task of great magnitude in the circumstances in which we are placed, and the Secretary of State for War can therefore be connected with actual military operations only on the same footing as any other member of the War Council.[7]

On receipt of this memorandum, Kitchener advised Asquith to accept Robertson's conditions, but he also submitted his own resignation. Asquith prevailed on Kitchener to stay in office, after some changes were made in Robertson's memorandum. The hurtful last paragraph was deleted. To meet Kitchener's constitutional objection that under the new arrangement the Secretary of State would no longer be responsible to Parliament, the Chief of the Imperial General Staff was to issue commands under the authority of the Secretary of State for War, not of the War Council. But in substance, Kitchener lost control over strategy, as he had previously lost control over war production when a separate Ministry of Munitions was established.

For a time, good personal relations between Kitchener and Robertson smoothed out most theoretical difficulties of the new arrangement. But when Kitchener was lost at sea in June 1916 at the start of a mission to Russia, Lloyd George became Secretary of State for War. He had taken an active part in curtailing Kitchener's powers. But he himself was not a man who agreed easily to a position of diminished stature, nor did he have so much faith in any one expert that he was satisfied to let Robertson be the sole professional adviser to the Cabinet. As soon as he took office as Secretary of State, Lloyd George explicitly stated that even though the Chief of the Imperial General Staff had direct access to the Cabinet, the Secretary of State would remain ultimately responsible to the Prime Minister, Parliament, and the country. Hence, he insisted, the Secretary of State should be informed of everything. The Chief of the Imperial General Staff should at all time explain to and discuss with the Secretary of State the lines on which he was framing his advice to the Cabinet. And it was

[7] *Life of Kitchener,* p. 370. Cf. p. 367ff; Robertson, *From Private to Field-Marshal,* pp. 239–41; and *Esher Papers,* III, 294–96. Robertson argued at the same time that the War Committee should have full executive responsibility to prevent the Cabinet from reopening discussion on military affairs, once these had been decided in the War Committee (*op. cit.,* pp. 239–40).

up to the Secretary of State to advise the King and the Cabinet about military appointments.[8] Even so, Lloyd George chafed under the restrictions imposed on him. They were one reason why he desired a total change in the central direction of war; many thought his proposal to establish a practically dictatorial War Committee in November 1916 was primarily motivated by his desire to control or even oust Robertson.[9]

The extent to which personalities rather than formal functions predominated was readily illustrated in December 1916. Once he became Prime Minister, Lloyd George was no longer greatly interested in the specific authority of the Secretary of State. What had begun as an attempt to strengthen the position of the Secretary of State ended in further lowering it vis-à-vis the Chief of the Imperial General Staff. No longer was the Secretary of State to be a member of the Cabinet.[10] In a Memorandum of Conversation between Lloyd George and Unionist ex-ministers, it was even explicitly stated that Robertson should participate in all War Cabinet meetings "as the occasion required."[11] Not the Secretary of State but the Chief of Staff, not the minister but his professional military adviser was to represent the War Office in the highest councils of war.

Subsequent developments were no longer concerned with the delimitation of duties. They were chiefly a confused conflict stemming from mutual distrust between the War Cabinet members and their professional advisers, in which the Secretary of State for War, Lord Derby, sided mainly but not very effectively with the military.[12] The main point at issue was what sacrifices the nation should make for further offensive action against the strong German front in France.[13] The politicians hesitated to meet fully the manpower demands of the military, partly because they distrusted the strategic abilities of their professional advisers (Robertson as Chief of the Imperial General Staff and Sir Douglas Haig as Commander in Chief), and partly because they were highly conscious of the importance of saving manpower for civilian tasks on the home front, notably for shipbuilding, farming, and producing munitions.

Lloyd George attempted various stratagems to sidestep his professional advisers, not daring to challenge them to their faces, because they enjoyed the powerful support of the Court, Asquith's Liberals, part of the Conservative Party, and the public generally. But he tried, in various ways, to secure independent military advice for the Cabinet. Partly for this reason, he invited General Smuts to join the War Cabinet. In June 1917, he organized a War Policy Committee in which the leading politicians met,

[8] *Life of Lloyd George,* p. 321.   [9] Beaverbrook, 1914–16, II, 133.
[10] See on this point the explicit correspondence between Lloyd George and Derby in *Life of Derby,* pp. 255–58.
[11] Beaverbrook, 1914–16, II, 323.
[12] Beaverbrook, 1917–18, Chap. 6; *Life of King George V,* pp. 302–22; Jennings, *Cabinet Government,* pp. 121, 129–30; Robertson, *From Private to Field-Marshal,* pp. 253–55, 319–20; Carter, pp. 319–23; Hankey, *Supreme Command,* pp. 693ff, 711ff, 775ff. Cf. Lloyd George, *Memoirs,* VI, 3407–26; *Life of Derby,* p. 242ff.
[13] Cf. Lloyd George, *Memoirs,* IV, Chap. 63, pp. 2110–2251.

without their military advisers, to debate the main problems of the war.[14] In October 1917, he proposed establishing a Council of War to which, in addition to the Chief of the Imperial General Staff, French and Sir Henry Wilson were to be invited. The plan failed because Robertson, supported by some Conservative ministers, threatened to resign.[15]

But shortly afterwards, Lloyd George forced the setting up of a Supreme War Council, in which the heads of the Allied Powers would meet for joint discussions on the war. They were to be advised by a Committee of Permanent Military Representatives, meeting in Versailles, which would *not* come under the immediate authority of the respective Chiefs of Staff. Early in 1918, these Permanent Representatives were given executive command of the inter-Allied Reserve. Robertson was offered a choice between becoming British representative at Versailles and remaining Chief of the Imperial General Staff, without direct control over the former. He resigned because he found such a division of responsibilities unacceptable.[16] He was succeeded by a far more political General, Sir Henry Wilson, but Wilson was not given the same full powers Robertson had enjoyed. Derby was soon forced to be satisfied with the Paris embassy. In April 1918, Milner, long an antagonist of the Robertson-Haig school, was appointed Derby's successor as Secretary of State for War. But the politicians did not triumph completely. Partly through his influence with the Court and public opinion, partly by his skillful maneuvering, and partly by luck, obstinacy, and mettle, Haig succeeding in retaining his post until the end of the war.

Developments in the Admiralty, 1914–18[17]

In the Admiralty, too, personal factors were of paramount influence. Soon after the outbreak of war, the First Lord, Churchill, had insisted— against the wishes of many, including the King—that Fisher be recalled from retirement to become First Sea Lord.[18] In the beginning, relations between Churchill and Fisher were cordial. But Churchill had a burning interest in strategy. Had he not declared in the autumn of 1914, in an emotional outburst to Asquith, that "a political career was nothing to him in comparison to military glory"?[19] Soon Fisher was to complain that Churchill out-argued him on questions of strategy.[20]

Disagreement became serious when Fisher failed to share Churchill's confident hope of a successful expedition to the Dardanelles. Fisher held that, as an official, he had to abide by the decisions taken by the respon-

---

[14] Hankey, *Supreme Command,* pp. 672–73, 682–89.
[15] *Ibid.,* p. 712ff.
[16] Lloyd George, *Memoirs,* V, pp. 2784–2833; Robertson, *From Private to Field-Marshal,* pp. 328–38; Hankey, *Supreme Command,* p. 775ff.
[17] See the studies mentioned in n. 1 to this chapter and, in addition, Fisher, *Memories* and *Records; Life of Carson;* and *Report of the Dardanelles Commission,* Cd. 8490 (1917).
[18] *Life of King George V,* pp. 251–52.   [19] Asquith, *Memories,* II, 46.
[20] *Ibid.,* p. 57; Hankey, *Supreme Command,* pp. 269, 300.

sible ministers, and hence remained "sullen and silent" in Council.[21] But in May 1915, he suddenly resigned his office. His exit spelled the end of the Liberal Cabinet. The new Conservative partners in the Coalition Government refused to have Churchill remain at the Admiralty. Fisher was asked to return, but he made himself impossible by a touch of megalomania. In an ultimatum to Asquith, he stipulated at least six conditions for his return. These conditions were to be publicly announced, and included the following points:

That Mr. Winston Churchill is not in the Cabinet to be always circumventing me, nor will I serve under Mr. Balfour.

That there shall be an entire new Board of the Admiralty, as regards the Sea Lords and the Financial Secretary. . . .

That I shall have complete professional control of the war at sea, together with the absolute sole disposition of the fleet, and the appointments of all officers of all rank whatsoever, and absolutely untrammeled sole command of all the sea forces whatsoever.

That the First Lord of the Admiralty should be absolutely restricted to policy and parliamentary procedure. . . .[22]

The situation with Balfour as First Lord of the Admiralty between 1915 and 1916 was less difficult, mainly because Balfour had no great executive drive, and Fisher's successor as First Sea Lord little stature. Issues were also less controversial after the withdrawal from the Dardanelles by the end of 1915. Thereafter, the main task of the Navy was to check the German fleet in the North Sea. The Battle of Jutland in 1916 did not end very satisfactorily, and consequently the Admiralty leadership was criticized in both ministerial and naval circles. In December 1916, Lloyd George shifted Balfour from the Admiralty to the Foreign Office.

A more serious conflict occurred in the winter of 1916–17 over submarine warfare. For a long time, the Admiralty had refused to introduce convoys for merchant shipping, arguing that this would weaken the Navy without sufficiently strengthening the merchant fleet. The War Cabinet did not share these views and decided to intervene when unlimited submarine warfare began to threaten the entire war effort. In possession of counterintelligence provided by junior naval officers, and reinforced by a memorandum about the possibility of a convoy system drafted by that "sleuth hound of the politicians," Hankey, "who had a lawful foot in every camp—naval, military, professional, political," Lloyd George decided to intervene, over the explicit protests of the First Lord of the Admiralty, Carson.[23] To quote from Beaverbrook's description:

---

[21] Hankey, *Supreme Command*, p. 313; see also cd. 8490 (1917), p. 19; Fisher, *Memories*, pp. 57–59, 69–72; cf. Churchill, *World Crisis*, I, 240.

[22] Asquith, *Memories*, II, 93, and especially Hankey, *Supreme Command*, p. 316. For a more moderate but equally definite criticism of Churchill's habit of intervening actively in details of naval strategy, see a memorandum by the other Sea Lords of 16 May 1915, in Asquith, *Memories*, II, 91–92.

[23] Cf. Churchill, *Thoughts and Adventures*, pp. 130–34; Hankey, *Supreme Command*, pp. 641–51.

On 30 April 1917, the Prime Minister descended upon the Admiralty and seated himself in the First Lord's chair. This was possibly an unprecedented action. It was well within the powers and competence of the Prime Minister; yet there may be no parallel in our history.[24]

With Lloyd George in the chair, the Board of Admiralty changed front and agreed to introduce convoys. Lloyd George's intervention was a serious blow to the prestige of the Admiralty leadership. Before the end of 1917, both the First Lord and the First Sea Lord had been dismissed. Carson was given a sinecure office, with a seat in the War Cabinet. Sir Eric Geddes, organizer of railway transport in France, a man completely unknown in political circles before 1914, was put in charge of the proud Service.

The Development of the Air Service

Both the Army and the Navy had engaged in some experiments with aircraft before 1914. On the recommendation of the C.I.D., a Royal Flying Corps had been established in 1912. A consultative Air Committee composed of War Office and Admiralty representatives provided whatever coordination between the Services was thought necessary. Before 1914, Seely, as Secretary of State for War, was the main backer of the Royal Flying Corps in ministerial circles. But he had to resign over the Curragh incident during the spring of 1914. At the Admiralty, meanwhile, Churchill went his own way. In July 1914, the naval wing of the Royal Flying Corps was given separate status as the Royal Naval Air Service. When war broke out, a formal division of duties was decided on. The Royal Flying Corps was sent to France to carry out flights over German positions along the front. The Royal Naval Air Service was charged with naval reconnaissance and coastal defense. Soon the competition between the Admiralty and the War Office for the limited output of airplanes, aircraft, and engines, and the short supply of flyers, became, in Hankey's understatement, "almost a scandal."[25]

Some, like Curzon, advocated establishing a separate Air Ministry. First, other means of coordination were tried. From March 1916 to May 1916 a Joint War-Air Committee met under the then Undersecretary for War, Derby. Its members rarely agreed, and Derby resigned from his post after eight meetings.[26] In May 1916 a new Air Board was formed. It was composed of Curzon as Chairman, two representatives from both the Admiralty and the War Office, and two civilian members, Clarke (now Lord Sydenham), and the Board's spokesman in the House of Commons. In principle, all members were advisers to the chairman of the Air Board, who was given the right to appeal to the Cabinet whenever either the Admiralty or the War Office refused to abide by the Board's decisions. From the outset, Curzon had argued that the Board would work only if

[24] Beaverbrook, 1917–18, p. 155.   [25] Hankey, *Supreme Command*, p. 549.
[26] *Ibid.*, pp. 549–50.

the two Service ministries gave it their loyal cooperation. This proved to be both a pious wish and a realistic forecast.[27]

When Lloyd George formed his Government in December 1916, it was decided to give the Air Board the status of an independent government department. The Board would be responsible for producing aircraft and allocating it to the two Services.[28] The system had an unexpected result: soon more planes were produced than either Navy or Army required. At this time Zeppelins appeared above London, and the British Press urged that German cities be bombarded in retaliation. A Cabinet committee presided over by Smuts concluded that for purposeful action an entirely separate Air Service was required. Bitter resistance from the two Service departments notwithstanding, an Air Ministry was established in January 1918 under its own Secretary of State for Air and an Air Council, organized along the lines of the Army Council and the Board of Admiralty. The Royal Flying Corps and Royal Naval Air Service were amalgamated into one Royal Air Force. The Air Force was greatly increased. More than half the orders of the Ministry of Munitions still outstanding when the Armistice was signed in 1918 were for the Air Force alone.[29] But the first months of the new ministry were not happy. The First Secretary of State, Lord Rothermere, and the first Chief of the Air Staff, Sir Hugh Trenchard, came into strong disagreement, and both resigned.[30] Rothermore was replaced by an industrialist, W. D. Weir, who for some time had no seat in Parliament.[31]

The Organization for War Production, 1914–18

Until 1914, the Admiralty and the War Office each saw to its own supply organization.[32] Before 1860, there had been a few independent boards that handled arms production and other supplies; they had generally degenerated into nests of political jobbery and corruption.[33] The concentration of the supply organizations in the Service ministries, where they came under the direct responsibility of special members of the Board of Admiralty and the Army Council, had therefore been considered an improvement. A measure of practical cooperation had developed between the two departments for certain aspects of supply. Occasionally, further centralization of the supply organizations of both Service departments under a separate minister had been canvassed, notably by some who expected economies from such an organizational change. But on the whole, the reform movement was dominated by the view that questions of long-term planning were neglected precisely because too much attention was being paid to routine duties and to specific issues of supply. Rarely had

[27] *Life of Curzon*, III, 142–45; Cd. 9005 (1918), pp. 56–66; Lloyd George, *Memoirs*, IV, pp. 1844–80.
[28] Cf. Chester–Willson, p. 209ff.   [29] Ehrman, *Cabinet*, p. 103.
[30] Beaverbrook, 1917–18, Chap. 7.
[31] Templewood, *Empire of the Air*, p. 46.
[32] Chester–Willson, p. 215ff.   [33] Cf. Keir, pp. 501–2.

ministers paused to consider whether the two Service departments were suitable agencies for supply purposes in case of an extensive war. Haldane had feared that Britain might fall behind Germany in technological development. For this reason he had initiated such specialized organizations as a Chemical Research Department, an Aeronautical Navigation Committee, and a Royal Aeronautical Establishment in Farnborough, which sought to develop new weapons.[34] British naval power, on the other hand, seemed well secured.

But when the war broke out in 1914, serious deficiencies soon came to light. In particular, munitions production fell short of need. Certain ministers feared that the War Office under Kitchener was not adequately equipped for its task.[35] For this reason the Cabinet had established two munitions committees. One functioned to December 1914 and failed after six meetings because its Chairman, Kitchener, was too much occupied by other business to attend. The second was formed in April 1915, under Lloyd George. Serious friction developed between Lloyd George and Kitchener, who refused to delegate any tasks to the new Munitions Committee and even starved it of the necessary figures and other data.[36] Shortly afterwards, the Northcliffe Press, aided by private revelations from the Commander in Chief, French, and abetted by Lloyd George, started a campaign about an alleged shell shortage. This campaign was a subsidiary factor in the fall of the Liberal Cabinet. The new Coalition Cabinet established a separate Ministry of Munitions under Lloyd George and C. Addison. This new department was extremely active in mobilizing factories and manpower for armament production. But conflict with the War Office continued, especially on the question of what and how many weapons were to be produced. Over Kitchener's protests, the Ordnance Department of the War Office was transferred to the Ministry of Munitions in November 1915.[37]

The longer the war lasted, the more pressing the problems of manpower and raw materials became. It proved difficult to allocate the priorities fairly. Figures were often not available, and there was little precedent to go on. The armed forces and the armament factories competed for manpower. Steel was a source of constant conflict between the Ministry of Munitions and the Admiralty, which succeeded in retaining control over shipbuilding. Churchill, who became Minister of Munitions in 1917, found normal procedures inadequate to reach a settlement. He decided to allocate the Admiralty as much steel as could possibly be found. "We watched with unsleeping attention the accumulations which soon began of ship plates in every yard," Churchill wrote. "Not until the moment was ripe did we unmask the guilty fact. The effect was decisive. The proud

---

[34] Cf. Haldane, *Autobiography*, pp. 232–34; Brundrett, p. 248.
[35] Cf. Lloyd George, *Memoirs*, I, 125–236; Amery, *War Leaders*, pp. 59–60; Hankey, *Supreme Command*, pp. 308–12; Churchill, *World Crisis*, II, 309; Grey, II, 242–43; Chester–Wilson, pp. 218–23; *Life of Kitchener*, p. 331ff.
[36] *Life of Kitchener*, pp. 333–34.   [37] Lloyd George, *Memoirs*, II, 614–39.

department condescended to parley, and eventually the modest requirements of the tank program were satisfied."[38]

Great difficulties also occurred in other sectors. In particular, the
question of the control of aircraft production became one of the fiercest
controversies of the war, with protagonists of the Service departments,
the Air Board, and the Ministry of Munitions each demanding ultimate
control.[39] Only a semblance of a solution was reached by concentrating the
rival supply organizations of the various ministries in one building.[40]

All reorganizations notwithstanding, the discussion about the most
suitable organization for war supply did not subside. On the one side
were ranged those who advocated concentrating all authority for war production—for the Navy, the Air Force, and the Army—in one Ministry of
Supply. Against them was a powerful combination of vested interests
who regarded the Ministry of Munitions as an upstart department, the
product of peculiar and undesirable circumstances in the War Office and
one which should not be assigned a place in an effective military organization.[41]

The Influence of World War I on the Defense Organization

Important changes in defense organization resulted from the war.
Instead of the two Service departments of 1914, there were four in 1918:
the Admiralty, the War Office, the Air Ministry, and the Ministry of
Munitions. The war had penetrated deeply into civilian life, thus erasing
forever the traditional dividing line between the military and civilian
spheres. But even after numerous drastic reforms, many difficulties continued to exist in 1918. No real solution to the problem of supply organization had been found. There was still considerable rivalry among the
three Services, the older two agreeing on little but their dislike of the development of an independent Air Force. Each Service had developed an
independent staff organization, but there was as yet little organized cooperation between them. To quote Ismay: "There was no recognized machinery by which the War Cabinet could receive military advice, using the
word 'military' in its broadest sense to embrace all the Fighting Services;
nor was there any machinery for forward planning."[42]

Throughout the war, the relations between politicians and military
leaders, between "frogs" and "brass hats," had been tense. Ultimately,
the political leaders had retained control, even though the Court and a
considerable part of the Press had urged greater delegation of power to
the military leaders, apparently to remedy military defeats. A considerable
number of professional commanders and staff officers had been replaced.
The principle of a collective Board or Council in control of each of the
Services was preserved unimpaired, the political position of the Service

---

38 Churchill, *World Crisis,* IV, 312; cf. pp. 295–97.
39 Hankey, *Supreme Command,* p. 551.   40 Chester–Willson, p. 224.
41 *Ibid.,* pp. 224–27.   42 Ismay, p. 49.

minister guaranteeing that in the last analysis political considerations might prevail. It had proved practically impossible, however, to overrule the military in their own sphere of expertness. A subtle change in the relation between the military and the Cabinet was thus becoming apparent. Instead of being advisers to the Service ministers, the Chiefs of Staff were becoming advisers of the Cabinet. This initiated a slow but steady decline in the position of the Service ministers. At the very time that the independent *political* position of the military experts was declining, their *professional* role was becoming potentially stronger.

Retrenchment (1918–32)

The end of the war in 1918 greatly affected the defense organization. In the autumn of 1919, the War Cabinet was replaced by the normal Cabinet. Most ministers again concentrated on non-military affairs. The C.I.D. was resurrected, and Hankey combined the Secretaryship of the Cabinet with that of the C.I.D. The Secretary of State for War and the First Lord of the Admiralty returned to the Cabinet, and they regained for a time most of the authority they had lost during the war. Generals and admirals could do little but seek to temporize the drive for economies—and refight the military and political battles of the Great War in memoranda and memoirs.

Retrenchment assisted the agitation of those who sought to rationalize the machinery for defense. In 1919 the Cabinet decided in principle to concentrate all matters of war production in one Ministry of Supply. The scheme was not executed, however, because of the joint resistance of the three Services, each of which feared that such a reform would lead to inadequate attention to their specific demands. In 1921, the Ministry of Munitions was abolished; its duties were transferred back to the Service departments.[43]

The War Office and the Admiralty still demanded their own separate air forces. This made the situation of the independent Air Ministry precarious for a long time. In January 1919, Churchill had been appointed Secretary of State for War *and* Secretary of State for Air.[44] He was the last to underestimate the potential of the new air weapon. But in practice, War Office interests nevertheless tended to overshadow those of the Air Force. Seely, who as Undersecretary of State had been put in charge of day-to-day matters in the Air Ministry, resigned later in 1919 in protest against economies and against Churchill's appointment rather than his own as Chairman of the Air Council.[45] In 1921 a relative of Churchill, F. E. Guest, was appointed a separate Secretary of State for Air, but without a seat in the Cabinet.[46]

[43] Chester–Willson, pp. 225–27.
[44] Cf. the criticism of this in 112 H. of C. Deb. (12 February 1919), col. 219ff.
[45] Johnson, p. 173.
[46] Templewood, *Empire of the Air,* pp. 48–49.

In 1919, the Air Ministry had also been charged to stimulate civil aviation. The two older Service departments saw in this a ready argument to propose that the Air Ministry should concentrate on this task exclusively, while the War Office and the Admiralty would look after the development of military and naval air forces respectively.[47] In return, the Air Ministry argued that the air could be conquered only if both civil and military aviation remained concentrated in one hand. The advocates of an independent ministry developed their own—and for the time rather extremist—strategic doctrines. Aircraft, they suggested, would make battleships superfluous, while bombers could easily take over many of the traditional functions of the Army. Agreement was hard to find. "In 1922," Hankey wrote, "the situation was most embarrassing to the Committee of Imperial Defence, who, in many matters of policy and strategy, were constantly confronted with advice based on widely differing theories. It was necessary to find means to bring them into focus."[48]

Official proposals to appoint a Minister of Defence were made both in Parliament and by the (Geddes) Committee on National Expenditure. It was not always clear, however, what the proponents had in mind. Some wished a complete amalgamation of the three Services, operating under one Combined General Staff. Others proposed consolidating only those functions that were common to all three departments. Still others, Geddes among them, wished to preserve the separate identity of the Services, but to put each service under the control of a Parliamentary Secretary, who would be responsible to one Minister of Defence.[49]

In 1923 the problem was subjected to an exhaustive inquiry by the Salisbury Committee, a subcommittee of the C.I.D. charged to investigate the relations of the Navy and the Air Force, and the coordination of the defense forces as a whole. The Committee (of which Hankey was ex officio Secretary) heard a number of witnesses. Particularly influential was the testimony of Haldane.[50] He had now come to doubt the wisdom of establishing a Ministry of Defence. The special position of Britain as an island, and as center of the British Commonwealth, posited very special military and political requirements, which could much better be met by the flexible system of the C.I.D. than by any one minister. The Dominions were unlikely to be willing to put their vital interests under the control of a British minister who sat in Whitehall and who was not responsible to their Parliaments at all, while the British public was trained to look to the Cabinet rather than to a "one-man business." The advantage of the C.I.D. was that it brought professional experts and politicians together in a way that prevented the military from interfering with politics,

---

[47] Ibid., p. 55.
[48] Hankey, Control, p. 55; cf. Ehrman, Cabinet, pp. 103–4.
[49] Johnson, pp. 173–82; Chester–Willson, pp. 299–300; Hankey, Diplomacy, pp. 97–98; Maurice, p. 171.
[50] Life of Haldane, II, 77–87; cf. Smellie, p. 262. According to Johnson (pp. 178, 220, 263), Hankey, too, resisted the campaign for a Minister of Defence, both in 1922–23 and in 1936, possibly because he feared that this might threaten his own position.

and the politicians with military decisions. Haldane thought it desirable to counter a tendency toward undue preponderance of the civilian element over the technical advisers. It was necessary to ensure close cooperation and joint planning by the staffs of the three Services. Instead of forming one "semi-military higher General Staff," such cooperation could be much better achieved

if they come as grown intelligences, not dependent upon someone else, and put their minds together in a common pot and think out the objectives they have in common with the special knowledge which belongs to each . . . each bringing to bear the fully developed personality which can only arise from the sympathy and inspiration of their own Service, as the home in which they have been bred and as the place where they rise to pre-eminence.[51]

The Prime Minister should at all times retain supreme authority. But it would be useful if he were assisted by a deputy who could give all his time to the business of the C.I.D.

The Salisbury Committee advised that an independent Air Ministry be retained.[52] The remainder of its report followed Haldane's views.[53] It rejected the plan to subordinate the ministerial heads of the three Fighting Services to a separate Minister of Defence as well as the idea of amalgamating the three Service departments into a new super-ministry. Instead, it recommended continuing and consolidating the practice (which had already grown up incidentally) whereby under the Prime Minister one minister would be appointed chairman of the C.I.D. It would be the task of such a minister:

(i) To preside over the Committee of Imperial Defence in the absence of the Prime Minister;

(ii) To report to the Prime Minister (when he himself has not presided) and to the Cabinet the recommendations of the Committee of Imperial Defence;

(iii) In matters of detail, to interpret the decisions of the Prime Minister and the Cabinet thereupon to the departments concerned.

(iv) Assisted by the three Chiefs of Staff . . . to keep the defense situation as a whole constantly under review so as to ensure that defense preparations and plans and the expenditure thereupon are coordinated and framed to meet policy, that full information as to the changing naval, military and air situation may always be available to the Committee of Imperial Defence and that resolutions as to the requisite action thereupon may be submitted for its consideration.[54]

---

[51] *Life of Haldane*, II, 79–80.

[52] Templewood, *Empire of the Air*, pp. 60–66; cf. p. 94. When appointing him in 1922 as Secretary of State for Air, Bonar Law told Hoare that it had been decided, in principle, to abolish the independent Air Ministry (*ibid.*, p. 36). For the low status of the Air Ministry in Whitehall at the time, *ibid.*, pp. 48–52; Snowden, *Autobiography*, II, 598.

[53] Cmd. 2029 (1924); cf. Hankey, *Control*, pp. 55–56; Maurice, pp. 164–65; *Life of Haldane*, II, 81–83.

[54] Cmd. 2029 (1924), para. 7.

The Salisbury Committee also recommended joining the Chiefs of Staff in a permanent Committee and charging each of them with "an individual and collective responsibility for advising on defense policy as a whole, the three constituting, as it were, a Super-Chief of a War Staff in Commission." They would continue to advise their own Board or Council on questions of sea, land, and air policy.[55]

Haldane himself was to implement most of the proposals of the Salisbury Committee. As a prize for participating as Lord Chancellor in MacDonald's first Cabinet in 1924, he demanded the chairmanship of the C.I.D.[56] The Chiefs of Staff Committee was now formally established. Haldane also stimulated the establishment of some important subcommittees of the C.I.D. : the Principal Supply Officers Subcommittee, composed of the Directors of Supply of the three Service departments, who met under the President of the Board of Trade ; and a Manpower Subcommittee.

The principle of regular consultation among the three Services as well as the duty of each Chief of Staff to give professional advice directly to the Cabinet was now much more securely established than before 1914. In 1927, a Joint Planning Committee, composed of the Directors of Plans of the three Services, was organized on the same principle. In 1936, this Committee was further strengthened by a committee of deputies who were employed full time on joint planning work.[57] Parallel to it, a Joint Intelligence Staff was instituted in 1936, under the chairmanship of a high official of the Foreign Office, to coordinate the work of the three Directors of Intelligence of the three Services. The Imperial Defence College, where staff officers and officials of the three Service departments came for joint training, was introduced in 1927.

These new developments could not but influence the role of the C.I.D. and its Secretariat. The C.I.D. remained the most important forum for politicians and Service Chiefs, and it was through the C.I.D. that contacts were maintained between the military and the civilian departments. Hankey symbolized the organization: he was Secretary of the Cabinet and Clerk of the Privy Council, Secretary of the C.I.D. and of the Chiefs of Staff Committee. But the Secretariat of the C.I.D. was no longer the main channel of coordination between the Services below Cabinet level. Perhaps the Secretariat was still, as in Esher's time, "the cornerstone of the whole edifice. But the Chiefs of Staff Committee had become the power plant."[58]

[55] *Ibid.*, para. 8.
[56] Haldane, *Autobiography*, pp. 319–25 ; *Life of Haldane*, II, 176–77.
[57] Ismay, p. 76.
[58] Hankey, *Control*, p. 58; Johnson, p. 206. But Hankey's special position was threatened at this time by the proposal of Sir Warren Fisher, Permanent Secretary to the Treasury, to subordinate the Secretary of the Cabinet to the Treasury. Hankey immediately offered his resignation. He feared that he would lose the confidence of the Services if he were placed under the supervision of the adversary of the Service departments in the traditional struggle over the Service estimates (cf. Chester–Willson, p. 291).

The appointment of a separate chairman of the C.I.D. proved less enduring than the establishment of the various Joint Staffs. After the fall of MacDonald's Cabinet, Curzon acted as C.I.D. Chairman for a short period. But Baldwin soon decided to take the chair himself. He gave three reasons for his action in the House of Commons in 1928. First, the Prime Minister should have full knowledge of matters to be brought before the Cabinet; second, he ought to be aware of developments in case a war should break out; and third, he could effectively arbitrate in conflicts about the Estimates only if he were well acquainted with the problems of defense.[59]

The Report of a Study Group of the Royal Institute of Public Administration on the organization of British Central Government, 1914–1956, gave, in addition, the following reasons why the experiment was unsatisfactory. First, the presence of a non-military chairman inhibited the frank interchange of views and any genuine desire to compromise among the Chiefs of Staff. But at the same time they were not prepared to accept the arbitration of anyone except the Prime Minister on any major issue. Second, the chairman's lack of status weakened the position of the C.I.D.: in meetings over which he presided, the level of attendance tended to decline, and with it the authority of its recommendations. Third, the Prime Minister and his Deputy often disagreed about the handling of the C.I.D. or the Chiefs of Staff Committee, or both; this led to the Prime Minister's taking over himself, which in turn further lowered the Deputy's position. Finally, the new system threw an extra burden on the already overworked official machinery under Hankey.[60]

Compared with the situation before 1914, the central machinery of defense had potentially improved. For a time, however, this had little effect. The military situation seemed as yet without great problems. As the official historians have written: "The work of the Committee of Imperial Defence was a kind of leisurely essay-writing on the kind of action that would have to be taken in the event of a great war."[61] As Chancellor of the Exchequer between 1924 and 1929, Churchill enforced stringent economies on military expenditure. It was on his insistence that the so-called Ten Year Rule was adopted. According to this directive, the departments were charged to plan their work on the assumption that no great war was likely for the next ten years, this assumption automatically moving forward every year, unless the rule were explicitly rescinded.[62]

[59] A. W. Baldwin, *My Father: The True Story* (1955), p. 200; Jennings, *Cabinet Government*, p. 302; Keith–Gibbs, p. 114; cf. Hankey, *Supreme Command*, p. 142.
[60] Chester–Willson, pp. 302–3.
[61] Hancock–Gowing, p. 45; Ismay, p. 50ff.
[62] Cf. Templewood, *Nine Troubled Years*, pp. 112–13, 207.

ELEVEN

THE DEFENSE ORGANIZATION, 1932–1945

Rearmament and the Minister for the Coordination of Defence (1932–39)

In 1932, the Ten Year Rule was withdrawn. In November 1934, the C.I.D. directed its subcommittees to base their plans on the assumption of a possible war with Germany within five years.[1] At first, such decisions had little practical impact. Many might have a feeling of fear and disgust about the rise of Nazism. Some might doubt the value of the League of Nations and desire stronger British armaments. But even among ministers and parliamentarians there was little urgency or concern.

For a long time, therefore, defense planning took place in a political vacuum. Those most intimately concerned could not but feel frustrated.[2] Some high officers and officials formed active groups to expedite rearmament as much as they could. Between November 1933 and February 1934, for instance, Hankey presided over a Defence Requirements Committee, which was composed of such stalwart supporters of rearmament as Vansittart, Permanent Undersecretary of State for Foreign Affairs; Sir Warren Fisher, Permanent Secretary to the Treasury; and the three Service Chiefs. The report of this committee was whittled down considerably, however, by a special Cabinet committee and by the Cabinet itself.[3] Treasury control remained decisively negative.[4] Many new committees were established, sometimes with conflicting terms of reference. In 1935, for instance, a Defence Policy and Requirements Committee was appointed. It practically duplicated a somewhat unwieldy C.I.D., of which it was technically a subcommittee.[5] But no amount of committee work could prevail as long as the leading politicians in favor of rearmament were outside the Government.

When German rearmament proved to move more quickly than had been expected, urgency mounted a little. At about the same time, the weakness of Britain's military position became painfully clear when war with Italy over Abyssinia seemed possible. Attlee, who had succeeded the pacifist Lansbury as Leader of the Labour Party in 1935, established

---

[1] Ehrman, *Cabinet,* pp. 112–13.
[2] Cf. Lord Ismay in Preface to Hollis, *One Marine's Tale,* pp. 11–12.
[3] Johnson, pp. 225–26; Vansittart, *The Mist Procession,* p. 443; Grigg, *Prejudice and Judgment,* p. 53; Templewood, *Nine Troubled Years,* pp. 137–38.
[4] Cf. *Hore-Belisha Papers,* p. 170ff.   [5] Johnson, p. 229.

a special Defence Committee, which elaborated a scheme for a Ministry of Defence.[6] Similar proposals were advocated from the Conservative and Liberal benches. *The Times,* too, urged an end to "trinitarianism," and retired Service Chiefs added their voices to the chorus.[7] In 1935, Lord Trenchard, for instance, wrote to *The Times*:

[The Chiefs of Staff Committee] has done very little to explore, and still less to settle larger problems of defense policy. . . . Unanimity has been too often reached by tacit agreement to exclude vital differences of opinion, to avoid issues on which such differences might arise, and to restrict the scope of the Committee's reports to matters on which agreement can be reached by "give and take." What is wanted in the higher examination of defense policy is not that the Government should get unanimous reports, but that means should exist for the examination of defense requirements untrammeled by departmental compromises. We want to promote free discussion and not drive differences of opinion underground.[8]

The campaign reached high tide in February 1936, when both Attlee, as Leader of the Opposition, and Conservatives like Amery demanded the appointment of a Minister of Defence.[9] The Government was not yet ready, however, to do more than appoint a Minister for the Coordination of Defence. This new minister, the Government announced in the House of Commons, was to be charged with

the general day-to-day supervision and control on the Prime Minister's behalf of the whole organization of the Committee of Imperial Defence; the coordination of executive action and of monthly progress reports to the Cabinet, or of any committee appointed by them, on the execution of reconditioning plans; discernment of any points which either have not been taken up or are being pursued too slowly, and (in consultation with the Prime Minister or other ministers or committees as required) of appropriate measures for their rectification.[10]

Perhaps the intrinsic possibilities of these terms of reference were not so limited as most have argued with the advantage of hindsight. The Government had some pertinent objections, moreover, to appointing a Minister of Defence.[11] It feared that such a minister would be no match for the Chiefs of Staff. He might weaken the machinery of the C.I.D. and damage the extent to which the civil departments were drawn into defense deliberations. In addition, two very influential experts, Hankey and the Chairman of the Chiefs of Staff Committee, Chatfield, were personally op-

---

[6] Attlee, *As It Happened,* pp. 98–99; Dalton, *Memoirs,* II, 91, 127; cf. *Life of Laski,* p. 117, and *Mosley Program,* p. 60.

[7] Johnson, p. 228.

[8] *The Times,* 16 December 1935; Smellie, p. 261; and Montgomery, *Memoirs,* pp. 490–91. See also Ismay, p. 52; Johnson, pp. 201–3; and Attlee in 309 H. of C. Deb. (9 March 1936), col. 1849.

[9] 308 H. of C. Deb. (14 February 1936), cols. 1295–1378; cf. Attlee, *Labour Party,* p. 259.

[10] 309 H. of C. Deb. (27 February 1936), col. 655; Cmd. 5107 (1936).

[11] Johnson, pp. 233–34.

posed to appointing a Minister of Defence.[12] To prevent friction, the new minister was therefore not given a staff of his own, except for two secretaries and three women clerks.[13] He enjoyed no executive responsibilities or control over the allocation of finance between the Services. If he wished, he could meet with the Chiefs of Staff, but he did not have the right to give them instructions. All statutory responsibilities stayed with the Service ministers, who remained Cabinet members in their own right. Even in the official list the new minister ranked lower than the Service ministers.[14]

A powerful minister might have succeeded in overcoming these limitations. But Neville Chamberlain refused the post.[15] Hoare was willing, but to appoint him only a short while after his fall from office over the Hoare-Laval Pact of December 1935 was not thought opportune.[16] Both Churchill and Amery were anxious to serve, but Baldwin did not think their inclusion in the Government desirable, for reasons of domestic or foreign policy, or both.[17] Only two days after Hitler ordered his troops into the Rhineland, Sir Thomas Inskip, "an able lawyer,"[18] "free of all foreign associations,"[19] was appointed to the new post. Someone dubbed his elevation "the most remarkable appointment since Caligula had made his horse consul." Attlee was soon to criticize both the personality of the minister and the inadequate powers of the new office, repeating a statement Inskip himself had once made: "Responsibility divorced from authority is a sham."[20] Inskip's labors notwithstanding, Attlee's statement was justified. In January 1939, Inskip was replaced by Chatfield. But Chatfield also failed. He soon became convinced that the office was useless as long as the existing Service departments preserved their present positions.[21]

The Supply Organization before the Second World War[22]

Agitation for a Ministry of Supply revived at about the same time as that for a Ministry of Defence. After the Ministry of Munitions was abolished in 1921, administrative control of war production had rested with each of the Service departments, which coordinated as much of their

---

[12] *Ibid.*, p. 263.

[13] 326 H. of C. Deb. (27 July 1937), col. 2900.

[14] Heasman, p. 320.

[15] *Life of Neville Chamberlain*, pp. 277–78.

[16] Templewood, *Nine Troubled Years*, p. 200.

[17] Churchill, I, 156–57; Amery, *My Political Life*, III, 196. Cf. *Life of Neville Chamberlain*, p. 278.

[18] Churchill, I, 156.   [19] Jones, *Diary*, p. 186.

[20] 312 H. of C. Deb. (21 May 1936), col. 1426; cf. 356 H. of C. Deb. (1 February 1940), col. 1416. Further criticism of the Minister for the Coordination of Defence was expressed in 309 H. of C. Deb. (9 and 10 March 1936), cols. 1827ff, 1973ff.

[21] Chatfield, *It Might Happen Again* (1947), Chap. 23; cf. Hankey, *Control*, pp. 83–85.

[22] See especially Scott–Hughes, *passim*; M. M. Postan, *British War Production*, London (1952); Chester–Willson, pp. 227–31; Churchill, I, Appendix C, pp. 536–37; and Churchill in 312 H. of C. Deb. (21 May 1936), cols. 1443–48.

work as they wished through a "rabbit warren" of interdepartmental committees under the aegis of the C.I.D.[23] Official plans were aimed at retaining this organization in wartime, except that the controversial issue of allocating raw materials was to be delegated to a special Cabinet committee, acting through an independent Ministry of Materials.[24] Even in peacetime, however, difficulties arose. Under the auspices of the Principal Supply Officers Committee, a rather active interdepartmental body, the Supply Board, was in charge of day-to-day coordination. In 1935, it was proposed that a permanent chairman of this Board be appointed. And the suggestion was accepted, with a scholastic annotation by the Treasury that the purely consultative character of the Supply Board was apparently being abandoned.[25]

Another step in the same direction was the appointment of the Minister for the Coordination of Defence to the chairmanship of the Principal Supply Officers Committee. This appointment, in theory, provided a ministerial coordinator for strategy and war production. The minister again lacked any real power, however, and in practice Inskip restricted himself mainly to questions of a financial and purely administrative character. The weakness of the interdepartmental committee system came to light in 1938 when the three Service departments recalled their representatives from the Supply Board because they had more important work for them in their own individual rearmament programs.[26]

Parliamentary pressure to appoint a Minister of Supply could only be strengthened by such developments. But the Government continued to show considerable reluctance to yield to such pressures (except for the Secretary of State for War, Hore-Belisha, who was willing in March 1938 to see such a ministry established).[27] Many in the Service departments clung to the traditional argument that only the user could accurately judge the type, the quality, and the quantity of weapons needed. The Prime Minister, too, was a consistent antagonist of the proposal. Chamberlain feared that to establish a new department in the middle of the rearmament program would only lead to confusion and delay. In addition, he sensed in the agitation a lack of confidence in his appeasement policies.[28]

But in the winter of 1938–39, the climate of opinion changed. Hitler's annexation of what was left of Czechoslovakia in March 1939 made it clear to all that "peace in our time" was not to last very much longer. Britain made new commitments to Poland, and the rearmament program was further accelerated. Public clamor for a Ministry of Supply could no longer be profitably ignored. Administrative requirements were hence regarded in a new light.

The Service departments were often not very well equipped for

---

23 Ismay, p. 84.   24 Scott–Hughes, p. 69.
25 Ibid., p. 56.   26 Ibid., p. 56.
27 Hore-Belisha Papers, pp. 155–60, 170.
28 Life of Neville Chamberlain, pp. 384, 386; Templewood, Nine Troubled Years, pp. 377–78; cf. Grigg, Prejudice and Judgment, p. 333; Ironside, p. 169.

negotiating large orders with private industries, and this disadvantage became more apparent as orders became more frequent and more important. The new defense program also increased the burden on the Service departments in other ways. The introduction of conscription, in particular, brought so much new work to the War Office that it was glad to part with some of its responsibilities. The Admiralty, on the other hand, remained adamant in its wish to keep shipbuilding under its own control. The Air Ministry, too, feared that the establishment of a new department might hinder the rapid execution of its expansion program. Consequently, the Ministry of Supply (instituted in the summer of 1939) was charged mainly with producing War Office requirements. Thus it became the oldest and most prestigious of the supply departments, but not the coordinator of war production in general, which so many had advocated.

From Phony War to Total War (1939–40)

When war broke out Chamberlain immediately decided to introduce a War Cabinet. As we saw earlier, he did not realize his initial intention to form an entirely non-departmental War Cabinet; besides the Minister for the Coordination of Defence, the Service ministers also became members, thus retaining a direct influence on matters of war policy. Initially the Cabinet met daily. But ministers were for a time unable (and perhaps unwilling) to take the initiative. Discussions therefore tended to be theoretical and unsatisfactory. On 18 September, the Chief of the Imperial General Staff, Ironside, irritably wrote in his diary: "How are we to stop these stupid conferences of the Chiefs of Staff and the War Cabinet, discussing the little details of the nothings that have happened?"[29] By the end of October it was decided to appoint a Military Coordination Committee, which would predigest matters for later consideration by the War Cabinet.[30] It was composed of Chatfield as Chairman, the three Service ministers, and the three Chiefs of Staff, and charged "to keep under constant review on behalf of the War Cabinet the main factors in the strategical situation and the progress of operations, and to make recommendations from time to time to the War Cabinet as to the general conduct of the war."[31]

The Military Coordination Committee did not function very happily. Its deliberations tended to duplicate the meetings of the Chiefs of Staff Committee and the War Cabinet. This added to the burden of conferences, which rested on the shoulders of ministers and military men alike. At the same time, its composition did not lend itself easily to a discussion of the most important question in the twilight zone between peace and *Blitzkrieg*: rearmament and its priorities.[32] Its membership was also incongruous. Churchill could not be expected to work easily under someone like

---

[29] Ironside, p. 110.   [30] Ismay, p. 109.
[31] Ironside, p. 145.
[32] Ehrman, *Strategy,* p. 323; Ismay, p. 109; Ironside, pp. 144–45.

Chatfield. The Secretary of State for War, Hore-Belisha, seemed anxious to rival Churchill's prominence, without the latter's thorough preparation in matters of warfare; and the Air Minister, Sir Kingsley Wood, was considered very much one of the "guilty men" of the 1930's.[33] The relations between the Chiefs of Staff were also far from harmonious. During the first year of the war, each Service went very much its own way. As a somewhat partial observer wrote: "The Army in France was under French command and acted in accordance with French plans. The Air Force was directly under the War Cabinet, and the Navy followed a self-appointed course. Most of the planning carried out by the Chiefs of Staff was therefore for the Army."[34]

Relations between military men and politicians were often strained. The military commanders could not forgive men like Chamberlain, Simon, and Hoare for letting them fight a war with considerable shortages in armaments. Few War Cabinet ministers had any direct knowledge of warfare except Churchill, Chatfield, and Hankey, who were not the most influential. Distrust was widespread, notably of Hore-Belisha, whom Chamberlain sacrificed to military sensitivities in January 1940.[35] It looked for a time as if the strained relations that existed between ministers and military men from 1914 to 1918 were about to be revived in all their ugliness.

In April 1940, mounting dissatisfaction led to drastic changes. Early in April, Chatfield resigned as Minister for the Coordination of Defence. His post was not filled. Instead Churchill, as senior Service minister, was appointed to preside over the Military Coordination Committee.[36] Only shortly afterwards, Hitler invaded Norway. Immediately, the meetings of the Military Coordination Committee became, in Ismay's words, "at once more frequent, more controversial and . . . more acrimonious."[37] Churchill himself felt uneasy. As he was to write later:

I had . . . an exceptional measure of responsibility, but no power of effective direction. . . . I had to carry with me both the Service ministers and their professional chiefs. . . . There was a copious flow of polite conversation, at the end of which a tactful report was drawn up by the Secretary in attendance and checked by the three Service departments to make sure there were no discrepancies. Thus we had arrived at those broad, happy uplands where everything is settled for the greatest good of the greatest number by the common sense of most after the consultation of all. . . . Alas, I must write it: the actual conflict had to be more like one ruffian bashing the other on the snout, with a club, a hammer, or something better.[38]

After a week, Churchill asked Chamberlain to take the chair himself, so that at least decisions could be taken.[39] This did not prevent the Norwe-

[33] Cf. Ironside, pp. 105, 160ff, 192ff.   [34] Ibid., p. 100.
[35] Hore-Belisha Papers, pp. 234, 250ff; Ironside, p. 192ff; Life of King George VI, pp. 431–34.
[36] Churchill, I, 463–65, 505–7.   [37] Ismay, p. 111.
[38] Churchill, I, 464.
[39] Ibid., pp. 464–65, 505–7; Ismay, p. 111ff.

gian operations from degenerating into a major disaster, since both at the front and in London decisions were uncertain, and coordination between the Services practically nonexistent. Churchill became even more restless. According to Ironside, he declared on 26 April that he was not merely "going to attend a Coordination Committee and give his opinion, to be weighed with other opinions."[40] He demanded from Chamberlain the right to preside over the Chiefs of Staff Committee, and to guide and direct its work on behalf of the Military Coordination Committee, going, if necessary, straight to the Prime Minister to get his decisions.[41] Ismay was appointed his personal staff officer and made a member of (instead of the secretary to) the Chiefs of Staff Committee. In addition, Churchill wanted to form a private staff, in which trusted assistants like Lyttelton, Morton, and Lindemann would occupy key places.[42] The new experiment did not last long, however; Chamberlain fell as Prime Minister over the Norwegian disaster. Churchill was now given the opportunity to apply his ideas with the full authority of the Prime Ministership.

The Defense Organization under Churchill (1940–45)[43]

As soon as Churchill became Prime Minister, he also took on the title of Minister of Defence. The system of command was changed: military orders were no longer to be given under the authority of the Service ministers individually, but by the Chiefs of Staff jointly. Churchill established two new committees, the Defence Committee (Operations) and the Defence Committee (Supply), which were nominally in charge of strategy and supply under the ultimate authority of the War Cabinet. The Service ministers remained members of these Defence Committees. But their Chiefs of Staff effectively replaced them as representatives of the Services in the War Cabinet.

As the war proceeded, moreover, the importance of the Defence Committees declined; they met less frequently and occupied themselves with issues that lay at the periphery rather than the center of strategic policy. Not only the Service ministers but also the War Cabinet lost most of their influence on matters of strategy, as the settlement of war policy came to rest more and more with Churchill (in his dual function of Prime Minister and Minister of Defence) and the Chiefs of Staff. Other ministers were informed by Churchill and the Chiefs of Staff during the informal meetings Churchill chose to call his "staff conferences." But the Prime Minister and the Service Chiefs had almost full discretion in determining who was invited to such meetings, and what they were told.[44]

Various explanations could be advanced for these developments. Churchill had always been devoted to the study of war. Before 1939,

---

[40] Ironside, p. 284.   [41] *Ibid.*, pp. 289–90.
[42] Ismay, pp. 112–14.
[43] Churchill, II, 19–22. See especially Ehrman, *Strategy,* pp. 315–37; Ismay, pp. 159–78; Alanbrooke, pp. 20ff, 320–21; Smellie, pp. 292–93.
[44] Ehrman, *Strategy,* pp. 324–26.

he had warned with more conviction and insight than anyone else against the rising threat from Nazi Germany, and throughout the 1930's he had been a staunch advocate of rearmament. He knew, and had faith in, his own qualities; in writing on the First World War, he had given his own views on the importance of war leadership:

Things do not get better by being let alone. Unless they are adjusted, they explode with shattering detonation. Clear leadership, violent action, rigid decision one way or the other, form the only path not only of victory, but of safety, and even of mercy.[45]

Almost as soon as he took office, moreover, Churchill knew he was the voice of all Britain in its darkest hour; his authority therefore became, in a very short time, almost absolute. The growing influence of the Chiefs of Staff was a logical consequence of the war situation. But Churchill did not regard himself a dilettante in strategic matters. The vagaries of war made it impossible, moreover, to build up a coherent strategy during the first years; on the contrary, the rapid succession of events offered every opportunity for and necessitated personal intervention by the War Minister. Most military problems in the early 1940's had a strong political cast, as they were closely intertwined with diplomatic considerations. In addition, the continuous military defeats of the first two years were not likely to raise the prestige of the military leaders; the Chiefs of Staff knew they were fully dependent on all the backing Churchill could muster.

Both Lords and Commons were well aware of this almost indissoluble link between Churchill and the Chiefs of Staff. The series of military reversals in 1941 and 1942 led to strong criticism of this situation. In particular, retired officers and ex-ministers like Hore-Belisha argued that not even a Napoleon or a Caesar could have shouldered the task Churchill attempted. Criticism was not clearly focused, however. Some desired to substitute an integrated General Staff for the Chiefs of Staff Committee. Others sought a solution in the appointment of a separate Minister of Defence under Churchill. And still others pleaded for a rehabilitation of the Service ministers.[46] Churchill challenged his critics in the House of Commons by asking for a vote of confidence in the summer of 1942. He won easily.[47] The happier direction the war took after 1942 was sufficient to make the issue a purely theoretical question for the rest of Churchill's wartime tenure.

Nevertheless, developments after 1942 did have a definite influence on the relations between Churchill and the Chiefs of Staff. Paradoxically, his power vis-à-vis his professional advisers began to decline at the very

[45] Churchill, *World Crisis,* III, 239.
[46] Cf. 380 H. of C. Deb. (19 May 1942), col. 53ff, and (20 May 1942), col. 251ff. See also Ismay, pp. 163–67; Broad, *Winston Churchill,* p. 395ff; Alanbrooke, I, 306–7; Kennedy, pp. 114–15. For a time, Churchill considered conferring the title of Deputy Minister of Defence on Sir John Dill, who was the British representative at the Combined Chiefs of Staff in Washington (Alanbrooke, p. 285, n. 2).
[47] Churchill, IV, 57–63.

moment when his political and parliamentary power was growing to unprecedented strength. After the fall of Singapore, Churchill decided to appoint the Chief of the Imperial General Staff, Sir Alan Brooke, as Chairman of the Chiefs of Staff and as their spokesman in the War Cabinet, sidestepping the seniority principle that had generally prevailed.[48] Brooke's clarity of mind; his resolute insistence on his position as the highest military expert; his readiness to resist the Prime Minister (often by simply remaining silent), notwithstanding Churchill's brilliant gifts and occasional bad temper; and the confidence, finally, which, for all their clashes, Churchill came to have in Brooke, caused the Chiefs of Staff to become not only the executives but also, to a large degree, the makers of military policy.[49]

Churchill's massive influence was, at the same time, somewhat curtailed by the need to adjust British policy to that of the American ally. The close personal relationship between Churchill and Roosevelt was very important for the smooth working of Allied relations. But the establishment of the Combined Chiefs of Staff for the two Allied Powers in March 1942 increased the influence of professional military men on war policy. Roosevelt, unlike Churchill, was not inclined to intervene at all closely in matters of military strategy. In addition, the turn of the war after November 1942 and the increasing importance of long-term planning of strategy shifted matters of policy more and more to the execution of preconcerted plans. This left somewhat less opportunity for political intervention.[50] At all times, however, Churchill and the Chiefs of Staff worked in the closest possible proximity and intimacy. The Prime Minister had access to all facts and was fully conversant with all plans. The Chiefs of Staff, in turn, could at all times rely on Churchill's support in the War Cabinet and in Parliament. Irritation there might at times be, on both sides, but there was no recurrence of the great distrust that had prevailed in the First World War.[51]

Below Churchill and the Chiefs of Staff there operated a complex array of agencies. A key place was occupied by the War Cabinet Secretariat, alias the Office of the Minister of Defence.[52] In addition to the Secretary to the War Cabinet, Bridges, Ismay, formally Deputy Secretary (Military) of the War Cabinet, played a role whose importance is difficult to overestimate. Ismay, who had been Secretary to the C.I.D. from 1938 to 1939, became Churchill's personal staff officer, even before Chamberlain's fall from power. In this capacity he attended all meetings of the Chiefs of Staff Committee throughout the war but did not sign its reports or accept

---

[48] Cf. Alanbrooke, I, 315, 321, but cf. Ismay, pp. 166–67.

[49] Cf. Ehrman, *Strategy,* p. 327.

[50] Cf. *ibid.,* pp. 335–37.

[51] Mackintosh, p. 425ff.

[52] Ehrman, *Strategy,* pp. 333, 377 (note by Sir Edward Bridges); cf. Johnson, p. 289ff; Hollis, *One Marine's Tale,* pp. 66–71; Alanbrooke, I, *passim;* and Ismay, *passim.*

formal responsibility for its conclusions.[53] He became what the official historian was to call "the patient, levelheaded, and scrupulously honest intermediary between the political and professional interests."[54]

Ismay's two principal assistants, Major-Generals Sir Leslie Hollis and E. I. C. Jacob, acted as Secretaries to the Chiefs of Staff Committee and to the most important planning and supply committees. Below the Chiefs of Staff, a Vice-Chiefs of Staff Committee and an Assistant-Chiefs of Staff Committee sought to handle as much business as possible and to clarify the remaining issues for ultimate decision by the Chiefs of Staff Committee. The entire apparatus was assisted by a number of joint staffs, especially the Joint Planning Staff and the Joint Intelligence Staff, which in turn controlled an extensive network of specialized subcommittees composed of representatives of the three Service ministries and of other ministries whenever relevant. Members of the War Cabinet Secretariat were to assure the dispatch of business and to guard as much as possible against duplication of effort.[55]

Though the machinery was built on the three existing Services, Churchill succeeded to a considerable extent in welding it into one organization. Theoretically, there was a subtle difference in the ultimate responsibilities of the Chiefs of Staff, the Joint Planners, and the War Cabinet Secretariat. Each Chief of Staff, though sharing collectively in responsibility for military advice and command, first and foremost represented his own Service. The Joint Planners, though derived from each Service department, had the duty before everything else to represent an inter-Service point of view. To this end, they were placed directly under the Minister of Defence. The Secretariat, finally, had no direct link with any of the Services, knowing a loyalty only to the central organization.[56]

But the machinery did not always run smoothly. Conflicts arose between Churchill and the Chiefs of Staff about the ultimate responsibility of the Joint Planners and the Secretariat.[57] Difficulties occurred when Churchill established direct contacts with military commanders on the various fronts.[58] Churchill's highly personal support for Air Marshal Sir Arthur Harris, Chief of the Bomber Command ("Bomber Harris"), and his exclusive reliance on the scientific advice of Cherwell caused the Bomber Command to become largely independent of the Chief of the Air Staff, and thus to carry out a policy that was often in conflict with explicit desires of the Chiefs of Staff Committee.[59] Such factors created considerable problems, both in the determination of priorities in war production and in the formulation of military policy.

In addition, the Chiefs of Staff tended to be so much preoccupied with

[53] Ismay, p. 172. The same was true of Mountbatten, when he was made a member of the Chiefs of Staff Committee as Chief for Combined Operations, in 1942.
[54] Ehrman, *Strategy*, p. 333.
[55] *Ibid.*, pp. 328–29; Hollis, *One Marine's Tale*, p. 69; Alanbrooke, I, 387.
[56] McCloughry, pp. 213–16.
[57] See, e.g., Hollis, *One Marine's Tale*, pp. 131–32.
[58] Cf. Kennedy, *Business of War*, p. 115.
[59] *Ibid.*, pp. xv, 7, 97, 178, 237–38, 302, 323–25; Snow, pp. 47–51; and McCloughry, p. 121ff. Cf. Ironside, p. 139ff, for the appearance of this problem in 1939.

day-to-day tasks (among which their continuous contacts and conflicts with Churchill loomed large) that they had little time to concentrate on long-term problems. For this reason, the Joint Planning Staff not only reviewed initiatives from the Chiefs of Staff but also came to play a rather independent role in the making of long-term policy.[60] But even the Joint Planners found their work complicated by the need to report again and again on yet another of Churchill's strategic brainwaves. Churchill once called the Joint Planning Staff a "machinery of negation."[61]

Finally, the war did not bring convincing proof that a staff organization built on the free cooperation of three separate Services with potentially conflicting interests was the best instrument for working out a long-term strategy that was more than an uneasy compromise between contending views. This was as much true of the Combined Chiefs of Staff as of the British part of that organization. In May 1943, after a conference of the Combined Chiefs of Staff, Brooke jotted down the following note in his diary:

I still feel that we may write a lot on paper, but that it all has little influence on our basic outlooks, which might be classified as under:
a. King thinks the war can only be won by action in the Pacific at the expense of all other fronts.
b. Marshall considers that our solution lies in a cross-Channel operation with some 20 or 30 divisions, irrespective of the situation on the Russian front, with which he proposes to clear Europe and win the war.
c. Portal considers that success lies in accumulating the largest Air Forces possible in England and that then, and then only, success lies assured. . . .
d. Dudley Pound, on the other hand, is obsessed with the anti U-boat warfare and considers that success can only be secured by the defeat of this menace.
e. Alan Brooke considers that success can only be secured by pressing operations in the Mediterranean to force a dispersal of German forces, help Russia, and thus eventually produce a situation where cross-Channel operations are possible.
f. And Winston? Thinks one thing at one moment and another the next moment. At times the war may be won by bombing, and all must be sacrificed to it. At others it becomes necessary for us to bleed ourselves dry on the Continent, because Russia is doing the same. At others our main effort must be in the Mediterranean directed against Italy or the Balkans alternately, with sporadic desires to invade Norway and "roll up the map in the opposite direction Hitler did." But more often than all, he wants to carry out all operations simultaneously, irrespective of shortage of shipping.[62]

In the United States, too, coordination was difficult to achieve. This was one reason why Roosevelt decided to appoint, in 1942, an independent chairman of the American Chiefs of Staff Committee.[63] At the same time,

[60] Ehrman, *Strategy,* pp. 330–32.   [61] Ismay, p. 122.
[62] Alanbrooke, I, 625–26.
[63] See Walter Millis et al., *Arms and the State: Civil-Military Elements in National Policy* (1958), p. 105ff; Samuel P. Huntington, *The Soldier and the State: The Theory and Practice of Civil-Military Relations* (1957), p. 315ff; Johnson, p. 315ff.

the Americans pressed for the appointment of supreme commanders on the various fronts. Such ideas were unpopular with most Britons, who parted with the Joint Staff principle with little conviction at the front, and kept it intact to the last at the London end.[64] American ideas were yet to exercise some influence after the war.

Ultimately, one of the inner circle was to write:

> It is probably true to say that personalities are all-important at these top levels of command. . . . With the best will in the world, it is hardly ever possible at these rather stratospheric levels to have a nice tidy hierarchy. . . . The fact is (or so I have always found) that, provided the high-level commanders are sensible, friendly, efficient men, determined to get on with the war, almost any system can be made to work, however awful it looks on paper. If they are not—or even if one of them is not—no system will work smoothly, however nice and tidy it looks in a diagram.[65]

The Supply Organization, 1939–45; The Minister of Production

In Chapter 5, the predominant role played by matters of war production in the War Cabinet was discussed. As Chairman of the Defence Committee (Supply) and in close conjunction with the Chiefs of Staff, Churchill determined military requirements and priorities. The execution of the programs rested with the individual departments, in particular with the Ministry of Supply, the Ministry of Aircraft Production, and the Admiralty. We saw to what heights tempers rose between Bevin and Beaverbrook and among the supply ministers. Things were not made easier by the fact that the Ordnance Board and the Ministry of Supply were Cherwell's pet aversions.[66] Attempts to find a way out by means of various types of committees failed. We also saw that Churchill long hesitated to yield to the clamor for a Minister of Production, who, as his agent if not as his equal, should determine all matters of war production. Not until the United States entered the war, thus creating a need to adjust British plans to those of the Ally on the other side of the Atlantic, did he change his mind.

The office of Minister of Production was, however, a different thing to different people. Outside the circle of ministers intimately concerned, most wished the appointment of a super-minister who would have full authority over the whole field. The Cabinet Office spoke of the necessity to make the new minister "a strong and effective focus" on the ministerial level. He would have the same relation to the Defence Committee (Supply) as the Minister of Defence did to the Defence Committee (Operations), and would be aided by "a little ministry in petto." Macmillan, then Parliamentary Secretary to the Minister of Supply, devised a scheme by which

[64] Ehrman, *Strategy*, pp. 351–61; but see Johnson, pp. 284–85, for the pleas of a number of former Service Chiefs for a unified General Staff in 1942 and 1943.

[65] Sir John Slessor, in reviewing Ehrman, *Strategy*, in *The Listener*, 22 November 1956.

[66] Ismay, p. 174.

the Minister of Production would "allocate to subordinate ministers" all basic factors of production—raw materials, machine tools, and labor. He would be aided by a program staff drawn from the Ministry of Supply and the War Cabinet Secretariat. But people soon spoke of coordination instead of control, a private office instead of a super-department, a Joint Staff of the supply departments instead of a Production General Staff of the Minister of Production.[67]

Churchill's final decision was therefore something like a Solomon's judgment. The new minister became a member of the War Cabinet (unlike the other supply ministers). He was given responsibility for "the allocation of available resources of productive capacity and raw materials (including arrangements for their import), the settlement of priorities of production where necessary, and the supervision and guidance of the various departments and branches of departments concerned." But at the same time it was explicitly stated that "the responsibility to Parliament of the ministers in charge of departments concerned with production for the administration of their departments [remained] unaltered," and that "any ministerial head of a department [had] the right to appeal either to the Minister of Defence or to the War Cabinet."[68] The supply ministers generally had forceful personalities. The Minister of Production did not obtain the right to intervene directly in the execution of production programs. Bevin's position as Minister of Labour made it impossible to subordinate questions of manpower to the Minister of Production.

The first Minister of Production, Beaverbrook, stayed in office only a few weeks. It was left to his successor, Lyttelton, to bring the new post to life.[69] Lyttelton's two main reforms were to establish a Joint War Production Staff and a small department, the Ministry of Production. The Joint War Production Staff was composed of representatives from the Service ministries, the supply departments, and the Ministries of Labour and War Transport. The Minister of Production or his deputy, Sir Walter Layton, head of the War Planning Staff, took the chair at meetings of the Joint War Production Staff. It was the task of this new body to measure military requirements against the productive potential available at home and abroad, and thus to make the Services aware of the limitations that civilian production imposed on their planning. Conversely, it was to ensure that the supply departments would comply to the best of their ability with the production program approved by the Cabinet.[70] In addition, the Joint War Production Staff was to supply the Minister of Production with the data on which he could formulate instructions for his representatives on the various Combined Boards in Washington.

The Joint War Production Staff was served by a Joint War Production Planning Group.[71] The latter was composed of the Directors of Pro-

[67] Scott–Hughes, pp. 430–32.
[68] Cf. Cmd. 6337 (1942); cf. Churchill, IV, 68–69.
[69] Scott–Hughes, p. 435ff.   [70] Ibid., pp. 441–42.
[71] Ibid., p. 442.

grams of the departments concerned. Its chairman and secretary were both from the Ministry of Production. The entire organization was patterned after the Joint Staffs on the defence side. Its members worked together in one building, but to ensure constant liaison they also had desks in their own departments. The presence of an independent chairman and secretary, and a directive that all reports from the departments to the Joint War Production Staff should pass through the Planning Group, were meant to guarantee that all data and proposals would be scrutinized from all angles before they reached the top of the governmental pyramid. In this fashion it was tried to steer a middle course between the Scylla of overcentralization and the Charybdis of inadequate coordination. The one might lead to shipwreck because of insufficient assessment of the many complicated factors that entered into the priority problems. The other could run aground on interdepartmental conflicts in which considerations of prestige and accidental compromise rather than the national interest were likely to prevail.

Between these two extremes, however, there appeared to be still considerable room to maneuver. Over the years, the Ministry of Production gained in influence. But it always worked within strict limitations. Leading officials of Lyttelton's staff were anxious to extend the role of the Minister of Production to controlling the execution of war production programs. They advocated establishing—besides the Joint War Planning Staff—a Joint Industrial Staff composed of representatives of the supply departments and the Ministry of Production. This staff would inquire into all difficulties that might arise in the implementation of programs and devise suggestions for their solution.[72] The scheme broke down on resistance from the supply departments. The relations between the Ministry of Production and the Ministry of Labour remained unsettled. Lyttelton failed in an attempt to put the Board of Trade's production activities under his supervision.[73]

[72] *Ibid.*, pp. 458–60.   [73] *Ibid.*, pp. 499–501.

TWELVE

THE DEFENSE ORGANIZATION SINCE 1945

From War to Peace: The White Paper of 1946

The National Government came to an end before Japan surrendered. Churchill remained Minister of Defence in the Caretaker Government of 1945, but the Service ministers were readmitted to the Cabinet. Attlee followed this example when he formed his Government in July 1945, but under his direction the Defence Committee of the Cabinet increased somewhat in importance.[1]

When two atom bombs ended the Second World War, however, priorities changed. The main task of the Labour Government became the rebuilding of a worn-out Britain. Attlee shared the general view that the Prime Minister should at all times retain supreme responsibility for defense matters. But he was equally aware that in the changed circumstances a Prime Minister had to occupy himself with many other tasks.[2] In order to free manpower, increase civilian production and channel government expenditures in other, more desirable directions, the Government insisted on far-reaching defense economies and rapid demobilization. Uneconomical military commitments in India and elsewhere were abandoned. The Chiefs of Staff again became rivals for the very limited defense outlays, rather than colleagues jointly engaged in the prosecution of the war.[3] The ending of the war also had consequences in the personal sphere: Brooke, Ismay, Jacob, and many others left their jobs. Military commanders just back from the war assumed their places.[4]

The new situation rekindled discussion about the most desirable defense organization. The agitation to amalgamate the three Services in one Ministry of Defence revived, as it had after the First World War. Again it was argued that only by thus combining the Services could unity in defense policy, decisiveness, and economy in expenditure be ensured. At the same time, the idea of one Combined General Staff found new supporters.[5] Within the Government such conceptions met with strong objec-

---

[1] Ehrman, *Strategy,* p. 326.

[2] Cmd. 6923 (1946), paras. 8, 21–25; Carter, p. 231; Attlee, *As It Happened,* pp. 99, 164; and 493 H. of C. Deb. (6 November 1951), col. 66.

[3] Hollis, *One Marine's Tale,* pp. 151–52; Hollis, Preface to James Leasor, *War at the Top* (London, 1959); Montgomery, *Memoirs,* pp. 487–90.

[4] Montgomery, *Memoirs,* p. 487.

[5] Hollis, *One Marine's Tale,* pp. 147–50; cf. Cmd. 6923 (1946), para. 15.

tions, however. Ismay, in particular, was a strong antagonist of the latter proposal, which to him smacked of German heresies.[6] He strongly influenced The Defence White Paper of 1946, which read on this point:

Our own experience . . . and a close study of captured German archives showing the working of the German Oberkommando der Wehrmacht combine to demonstrate that this conception is not only inferior to our Joint Staff system, but it has defects which in practice proved disastrous. The German system failed because the Planning Staffs of the O.K.W. were not drawn from the headquarters of the three Services. The plans they produced had later to be handed to those headquarters for execution, and were often found to be unrealistic. The cleavage between planning and execution set up dangerous antagonisms, and entirely nullified any theoretical advantages of the German system.[7]

Traditionally, the German system had also been rejected with the argument that it introduced a most unrealistic and undesirable divorce between military and political centers of decision.[8] Attlee wanted a Minister of Defence apart from the Prime Minister, however. He had been a warm advocate of such a minister since 1936, and the appointment fitted in well with his general desire to construct the Cabinet as much as possible along lines of functional policy rather than immediate departmental representation. These various currents flowed together in a new defense organization that was largely a consolidation of the practices that had evolved in the Second World War. The new organization was publicly announced in the White Paper just mentioned, which set out the following arrangements:

The Prime Minister would retain supreme responsibility for defense. A Defence Committee, under the chairmanship of the Prime Minister, would take over the functions of the C.I.D. and would be responsible to the Cabinet both for reviewing current strategy and for coordinating departmental action in preparation for war. Unlike the C.I.D., the Defence Committee would have executive authority. To relieve the Prime Minister, a Minister of Defence would be appointed. He would be Deputy Chairman of the Defence Committee and would head his own department. Only the Minister of Defence, not the Service ministers, would belong to the Cabinet. Apart from his duties as Deputy Chairman of the Defence Committee, the Minister of Defence would be given statutory authority for the following functions:

(a) The apportionment, in broad outline, of available resources between the three Services in accordance with the strategic policy laid down by the

    [6] McCloughry, pp. 182–83.
    [7] Cmd. 6923 (1946), para. 16; cf. Johnson, p. 306.
    [8] See, e.g., Lloyd George, *Memoirs*, VI, 3411; Churchill, *World Crisis*, I, 242, IV, 405; Churchill, *Thoughts and Adventures*, pp. 149–62, and especially pp. 153, 157; Churchill, *Great Contemporaries*, pp. 111–21; Hankey, *Control*, pp. 15–17, 74–75; Hankey, *Supreme Command*, p. 543; Maurice, pp. 147–49; *Life of Asquith*, II, 194; Bridges, *Portrait*, pp. 17–20.

Defence Committee . . . includ[ing] the framing of general policy to govern research and development, and the correlation of production programs.

(b) The settlement of questions of general administration on which a common policy for the three Services is desirable.

(c) The administration of inter-Service organizations, such as Combined Operations Headquarters and the Joint Intelligence Bureau.[9]

The Chiefs of Staff Committee would remain responsible for preparing strategic appreciations and military plans, and for submitting them to the Defence Committee. It was essential, however, that the Cabinet and Defence Committee have direct and personal access to the Chiefs of Staff for advice on all technical questions of strategy and defense. Their advice to the Defence Committee or the Cabinet would therefore not be presented only through the Minister of Defence. But at the same time, the organization on which they relied in their collective capacity would be within the Ministry of Defence, and the Chiefs of Staff would meet under the chairmanship of the new minister whenever he or they might so desire. A Chief Staff Officer—Sir Leslie Hollis, after Ismay's departure—would moreover attend all meetings of the Chiefs of Staff Committee as the personal representative of the Minister of Defence. Like Ismay, this Staff Officer was simultaneously Deputy Secretary (Military) of the Cabinet, having direct access to the Prime Minister at all times and directing the military side of the Cabinet Office. Great importance was attached to thus maintaining direct liaison between the Cabinet Office and the Ministry of Defence, and hence between the civil and military sectors of the government.[10]

The Service ministers were again and now permanently excluded from the Cabinet; they continued to be responsible to Parliament for administering their Services in accordance with the general policy approved by the Cabinet and within the resources allotted to them. They were also members of the Defence Committee, and met with the Minister of Supply under the chairmanship of the Minister of Defence in a special Coordination Committee on matters of personnel, supply, etc.

The new organization still bore the stamp of compromise. It retained the supreme authority of the Prime Minister. It attempted to meet the the objections against a Minister for the Coordination of Defence by giving the new minister statutory responsibilities and a department of his own. The Service ministers were further reduced in rank and influence. But the Service ministries continued to exist. To allay sensitivities it was decided to restrict the new Ministry of Defence to a small nucleus of officials and military experts who would mainly perform coordinating and secretarial functions. The Chiefs of Staff kept the right and the duty to advise the Cabinet directly, and each chief remained in charge of his own Service. The joint staff principle was also fully respected on lower levels.

[9] Cmd. 6923 (1946).
[10] Hollis, *One Marine's Tale,* pp. 146–47 ; Chester–Willson, p. 321.

The Organization of 1946 in Practice

Even the scarce literature as yet available has revealed enough to show that the new organization was not free from serious strains.[11] After 1945, the Chiefs of Staff lived in an atmosphere of tension caused by personal rivalries and conflicting interests. The meetings provided a forum for a struggle between the Services, rather than an instrument for the joint planning of strategy. Collective responsibility forced them to make some joint reports, but they tended to reach weak compromises or to delegate even more unresolved problems to the Joint Planning Staff than they had during the war. Their joint reports notwithstanding, each Chief of Staff tended to plead a separate case via his Service minister, the Minister of Defence, or the Prime Minister.[12] The Minister of Defence could do little to prevent this. He lacked the support of a sufficiently strong apparatus to form his own independent judgments on strategic questions, and his political position (unlike that of a Prime Minister who was Minister of Defence) was not so strong that he could easily intervene in or arbitrate between the Service departments.

Personal factors also made their influence felt. The first Labour Minister of Defence, A. V. Alexander, developed relatively little strength in his office. The members of the Chiefs of Staff Committee, on the other hand, knew they were secure in their military fame. Montgomery, in particular, "made himself a nuisance in Whitehall" as Chief of the Imperial General Staff between 1946 and 1948. He did not hesitate to fight personal and military conflicts to the very end. In the process, he developed certain views about improving the defense organization. In an extensive memorandum of March 1948, he suggested that an organization in which each Chief of Staff was responsible for his own Service, but in which the Chiefs of Staff should jointly tender collectively approved strategic advice, could not produce any results. "They take refuge in not reporting at all, or in furnishing wishy-washy recommendations which lead nowhere," Montgomery wrote. He thought it would be better if the Chiefs of Staff were to put their conflicts openly before the Minister of Defence. But preferably, a separate Chief of Staff to the Minister of Defence who could act as an impartial chairman of the Chiefs of Staff Committee should be appointed. Initially, Montgomery found little support for his proposals. Soon he was engaged in a plot to confront Attlee with an ultimatum to dismiss either Alexander or the Chief of Staff.[13]

The Turning Point in Defense Policy (1948–56)

After the beginning of 1948, the international situation deteriorated quickly. The Communist seizure of Czechoslovakia the blockade of Berlin, the Korean War, and the explosion of the first Russian atom bomb

---

[11] See especially the writings of Hollis and Montgomery.
[12] McCloughry, pp. 247–48; cf. pp. 200–20.
[13] Montgomery, *Memoirs,* pp. 476–505.

destroyed the basis of Labour's thrifty defense policies. In 1950, the Cabinet decided on a drastic three-year rearmament program. Soon, defense was to absorb nearly 10 per cent of Britain's gross national product.[14]

These changes in policy (aided by changes in personnel) apparently caused an improvement in the workings of the Chiefs of Staff Committee. The Service Chiefs were again confronted with concrete tasks, while greater defense expenditures lessened the difficulty in agreeing on programs. Emanuel Shinwell replaced Alexander as Minister of Defence in 1950. Montgomery shifted his activities to the international scene. The establishment of NATO necessitated a greater amount of internal coordination, so that instructions to the various representatives at the NATO high command in Paris could be formulated. The Minister of Defence was charged with instructing these delegates through a complex committee system in which the Secretary of the Cabinet played a considerable role.[15]

Ministerial direction became a good deal stronger in 1951, when Churchill returned to power. Immediately the familiar series of minutes, directives, and queries again began to arrive. But Churchill did not regain the influence he had had during the war. The complex processes of rearmament and long-term planning offered less scope for personal intervention than day-to-day warfare. His interest in new military techniques notwithstanding, Churchill retained a somewhat traditionalist preference for the three Services, notably for the Admiralty. Neither did he succeed in prevailing against the Treasury.[16] The balance of payments, adverse movements in the economy, and electoral considerations posed substantial limitations on the defense programs. After the end of the Korean War, it was decided to slow down rearmament efforts: the conception of the long haul replaced that of a short and decisive rearmament spurt.

Churchill soon discovered that he was no more able than Attlee to combine the Prime Ministership with the Ministry of Defence. For a short while he tended to rely on the informal assistance of Ismay, whom he had appointed Secretary of State for Commonwealth Affairs.[17] But Ismay soon departed to become the first Secretary-General of NATO. At the beginning of 1952, Churchill appointed Field-Marshal Alexander of Tunis Minister of Defence. Attlee criticized the appointment of a professional officer to the new post.[18] But there was little to fear. The appointment tended to weaken rather than strengthen the position of the Ministry of Defence. Alexander was faithful to the traditions of inter-service cooperation, and limited himself mainly to formal chairmanship and mediation between the departments, rather than to directing defense policy.[19] At least one additional reason for the weak position of the Min-

---

[14] Cf. Britain's Defence Services, Central Office of Information, R. 3877, July 1958, pp. 3–4.

[15] Beloff, p. 54.   [16] McCloughry, pp. 211, 240.

[17] Ismay, pp. 452, 457.

[18] 479 H. of C. Deb. (5 March 1952), col. 538.

[19] Cf. McCloughry, p. 212.

ister of Defence was indicated by Eden: "Sir Winston, whatever his head ordained, never accepted in his heart the position of a Minister of Defence divorced from his own authority. In impatient moments he would sometimes murmur that the post did not exist."[20]

Alexander's potentially more influential successor, Macmillan, was therefore unhappy in his office. The centrifugal tendencies of the Service departments were further strengthened in that five Ministers of Defence (Alexander, Macmillan, Lloyd, Monckton, and Head) held office successively between 1952 and 1956, during a period when the Service ministeries were headed by less senior but active ministers who stayed in office for a considerable time.

Shortly after he became Prime Minister, Eden attempted to strengthen the position of the Minister of Defence.[21] On 25 October 1955, he announced the following reforms in the House of Commons:

The Minister of Defence's responsibility for the apportionment of available resources between the three Services extends to a responsibility for seeing that the composition and balance of forces *within* individual services meets the strategic policy of the Defence Commitee. [Italics mine.][22]

At the same time, the Chief of the Air Staff, Sir William Dickson, was replaced and became instead the Chairman of the Chiefs of Staff Committee. These reforms sought to strengthen the Minister of Defence in two respects. The first gave him the authority to intervene directly with the policy of each individual Service. And the appointment of an independent chairman made it possible, in theory, to force the deliberations of the Chiefs of Staff Committee out of the vicious circle of "coordination by mutual consent."[23]

In the beginning, these reforms did not realize their maximum potential. The rapid turnover of Ministers of Defence continued between 1955 and 1957. In practice, Dickson was little more than a formal chairman of the Chiefs of Staff meetings. At most, he was a faithful go-between who smoothed out (and perhaps evaded) difficulties instead of solving conflicts. He had no staff of his own. In the words of Sandys, he was a mouthpiece "more or less isolated with no actual authority and very little influence."[24]

The Reforms of 1957 and 1958

Since the early 1950's, dissatisfaction among the British public about defense policies had grown. Many who sympathized with rearmament in principle had started from the tacit supposition that after a first sharp

---

[20] Eden, *Full Circle,* p. 274.   [21] *Ibid.,* p. 374.
[22] 545 H. of C. Deb. (25 October 1955), col. 34; cf. 194 H. of L. Deb. (8 November 1955), col. 328ff; *The Times,* 27 October 1955.
[23] Cf. McCloughry, p. 212.
[24] 592 H. of C. Deb. (28 July 1958), vol. 955.

spurt would come a period of consolidation, which would automatically lead to a decline in defense expenditure. Such hopes were confounded by the rapid developments in arms techniques. Scientific research and technological development of new military inventions demanded considerable funds, all the greater because Britain knew it was even more dependent on quality arms than either the United States or the Soviet Union.[25] The fast pace at which both offensive and defensive weapons were being developed made existing weapons obsolete much sooner than had been foreseen. Britain no longer had economic resources comparable to those of either the United States or the Soviet Union. The voices of those who argued that Britain could not go it alone became louder. But until the end of the decade both parties continued to agree that Britain should have its own deterrent and its own means of delivery, first by aircraft, later by modern missiles. Both parties desired as well that the growing national income be spent not only on defense, but also on a rising standard of living for the British population at large.

Such subterranean rumblings erupted in force after the Suez crisis in 1956. A brief rise in nationalist fervor was soon followed by a feeling of anticlimax. It became clear that there had been no real meeting of minds between the Prime Minister and his military advisers. At times, the Chiefs of Staff had apparently been unable to get their views through to a Prime Minister whose mind seemed clouded by his own uncertain policies. It was hinted that the Chairman of the Chiefs of Staff Committee, Dickson, "infinitely pleasant to his superiors," prevented Eden from hearing unwelcome information.[26] Similar accusations were leveled against Head, a former combined planner turned politician, who as Secretary of State for War had taken an active part in planning the Suez action, and had replaced Monckton as Minister of Defence only a few weeks before the military action started.[27] From all reports, political leadership had been wavering, control divided, and planning divorced from execution. At the beginning of the crisis, military operations in the Canal area were begun somewhat reluctantly. Then, when victory was imminent, the operations were suddenly halted. Typically, financial considerations, more than diplomatic or military ones, had dictated the cancelling of the expedition.

The political *échec* led to much soul-searching. Even before he became Prime Minister, Macmillan strongly advocated reform. He himself had unhappy memories of his short term as Minister of Defence. As Chancellor of the Exchequer in the turbulent days of 1956, he was the focus of the serious conflicts between the demands of the Services, the other spending departments, and the economic situation as a whole. The immediate financial and economic dislocations that followed the failure of the Suez action were now superimposed upon these problems. At his insistence a Cabinet session to discuss the entire problem of defense priorities and

[25] Williams, *Science*, p. 264 ; Johnson, pp. 305–6.
[26] Cf. the political correspondent of *The Observer*, 4 January, 1959.
[27] R. Churchill, *Eden*, pp. 303–5.

the defense burden was scheduled. It did not take place, however, because Eden resigned.[28]

In forming his Government in January 1957, Macmillan replaced Head with Sandys. Sandys was explicitly charged with "the task of reshaping and reorganizing the Armed Forces in accordance with current needs and in the light of the economic capacity of the country."[29] In the House of Commons, Macmillan also announced a further extension in the powers of the new minister:

Subject as necessary to consultation with the Cabinet and Defence Committee, and with the Treasury on matters of finance, the minister will have authority to give decisions on all matters of policy affecting the size, shape, organization and disposition of the Armed Forces, their equipment and supply (including defense research and development) and their pay and conditions of service. He will similarly have power of decision on any matters of Service administration or appointments which, in his opinion, are of special importance.[30]

At the same time, Dickson was appointed personal Chief of Staff to the Minister of Defence, as well as Chairman of the Chiefs of Staff Committee, thus outwardly signaling Sandys' intention to take personal control. After only a minimum of consultation but with the full backing of Macmillan, Sandys personally drafted a new White Paper on Defence entitled *Outline of Future Policy* (1957). It announced a drastic reordering of defense priorities.[31] Britain would henceforth concentrate on the nuclear deterrent as its most important means of defense. For this deterrent to be effective, Britain should have its own means of delivery, initially bombers, but eventually ballistic missiles. Britain's disproportionately large commitments in land and air forces on the European Continent would be cut. To protect the interests of the Empire and honor Britain's commitments under such alliances as the Baghdad Pact, SEATO, and the ANZAM defense system, Britain would henceforth rely on reduced local forces and a strengthened, highly mobile Central Reserve of Land, Sea, and Air Forces, stationed in Britain itself. Such a scheme, according to the White Paper, would increase the effectiveness of Britain's defense, and at the same time help to relieve the strain upon the economy. As the new forces would require less, if better-trained manpower, conscription could end, and military recruitment revert to voluntary enlistment.

The new scheme involved, in the words of the White Paper, "the biggest change in military policy ever made in normal times."[32] Many existing weapons and units would be abolished. Many observers felt that the *raison d'être* of the individual Services would disappear with the new reforms. There were many suggestions—often of a semi-official char-

---

[28] Cf. the political correspondent of *The Observer*, 6 July 1958.
[29] Cmnd. 476 (1958), para. 1.
[30] 563 H. of C. Deb. (24 January 1957), col. 400; cf. *The Economist*, 2 February 1957.
[31] Cmnd. 124 (1957); cf. *The Economist*, 13 April 1957.
[32] Cmnd. 124 (1957), para. 67.

acter—that the individual Service ministers and the Minister of Supply were soon to vanish, or at least to be further demoted.[33] The new authority of the Minister of Defence to give decisions on matters of policy and to have a say in administration and appointments within the Service departments opened the way to drastic intervention. Sandys used his powers in a highhanded fashion, which created fear as well as disgust among the professional military.

After the first few months, however, a certain hesitation recurred. The doctrine of the nuclear deterrent, which was the linchpin of the new reforms, was contested by those who thought a war with conventional means not less but more likely as a result of a nuclear stalemate. It was argued that the new scheme was not based on a careful consideration of strategy and defense priorities, but on the wish of the Conservative Government to have an independent deterrent for an appealing price. The Service departments regained some of their lost composure. Both the Service ministers and the Service Chiefs used their right of direct access to the Prime Minister and to the Cabinet, which they had maintained under the new reforms. The Services did not hesitate, either, to fight through devious publicity campaigns.[34] They scored some success. On 23 July 1957, Macmillan publicly announced in the House of Commons:

The Government have no intention of merging the three Fighting Services into a single defense force. The development of new weapons and new techniques of warfare will call for even closer cooperation between the Services in training and in the field; and measures for more effective coordination are being studied both in the command structure and in the central administrative organization. But each of the three Services will continue to have its separate role and function and each will continue to maintain its separate identity and traditions.[35]

There followed in Whitehall a period of struggle that one M.P. was unkindly to characterize as "Kilkenny cat-fighting and feuding . . . behind closed doors."[36] It may readily be assumed that Sandys attempted to lower the Service ministers further to the rank of Ministers of State, and to deny the individual Service Chiefs the right to present their views directly to the Cabinet and its members.[37] Sandys could not overcome all resistance, however, and the only net result was a new White Paper, *Central Organization of Defence* (1958), which was little more than a painful compromise between Sandys' desires and the existing situation.

According to the new proposals, the Prime Minister would again, as in the days of the C.I.D., be the only official member of the Defence Committee. Other ministers were to attend only when invited for specific

---

[33]Sandys himself made such a suggestion during a television interview on 8 April 1957.
[34] Cf. *The Economist,* 10 May 1958: "The Air Force Shows Its Shopping List."
[35] 574 H. of C. Deb. (23 June 1957), col. 223.
[36] 592 H. of C. Deb. (28 July 1958), col. 1027; cf. cols. 970–71.
[37] Cf. *The Economist,* 19 July 1958: "No O.K.W. for Mr. Sandys."

business. Technically, this created the possibility of excluding the Service ministers from participating, but immediately afterwards it was stated that "full regard to the ministerial responsibilities involved" would be maintained at all times.[38] The Chiefs of Staff remained the professional advisers to the Defence Committee and the Cabinet, and it was explicitly reaffirmed that they always had access to the Minister of Defence, and if necessary to the Prime Minister. The Chairman of the Chiefs of Staff Committee was now appointed Chief of the Defence Staff. As such, it was his duty to advise the Minister of Defence, to inform him of possible differences of opinion between the Chiefs of Staff, and to add his own comments to their views. The Joint Planning Staff was put immediately under him, and it was clearly stated that he could call on the staffs of the individual Services at any time. Finally, it was decided that military orders were henceforth to be signed by the Chief of the Defence Staff instead of by the Chiefs of Staff Committee.[39]

On 28 July 1958, an extensive debate about the new organization was held in Parliament. Some felt that the reforms had been too drastic. They feared that vital differences of opinion would be driven underground. The appointment of a separate Chief of the Defence Staff, they repeated, might result in the fatal division between planning and execution that the British organization, unlike its German counterpart, had so happily avoided. Others, like the shadow Minister of Defence, George Brown, thought, on the contrary, that the reforms did not go far enough. They wished a separate staff for the Chief of the Defence Staff which might provide him with his own independent brief, and resisted what they called the "O.K.W. bogey." At the same time they pleaded for an integration of the Services, starting at first with the level of lieutenant-colonels and their equivalents upwards. Calling the new scheme "a half-way house" and "a half-baked scheme," the Labour Opposition demanded the appointment of a new Esher Committee.[40]

Sandys' position as Minister of Defence, at the head of an organization he had challenged but not conquered, was not a happy one. He had created so much conflict that he was becoming somewhat of a liability as Minister of Defence. In the words of the *Daily Telegraph,* written during the height of the fight on 25 April 1958, it had "come to the point where politicians, officers, and officials ask themselves whether they oppose integration of defense because Mr. Sandys is the minister, or whether they oppose Mr. Sandys because he believes in integration."

The strategic basis of the 1957 White Paper was being further eroded, when difficulties began to appear in the missile program. In October 1959, Sandys was transferred to a new Ministry of Aviation, charged with all aspects of developing missiles and aircraft. The Permanent Secretary at the Ministry of Defence, Sir Richard Powell, who had been closely identi-

---

[38] Cmnd. 476 (1958), para. 4.   [39] *Ibid.,* paras. 15–19.
[40] 592 H. of C. Deb. (28 June 1958), cols. 954–1075. For a critical analysis of the new organization, see Howard, *passim,* and Willson, *Supplement,* pp. 191–98.

fied with the Sandys policy, was shifted soon afterwards to the Board of Trade. The Minister of Transport, Harold Watkinson, was appointed Minister of Defence.

If this was regarded as promotion for Watkinson, it was equally considered a demotion of the Ministry of Defence. The Ministry of Defence threatened to become a graveyard for ministerial reputations, and hence to lead to a vicious circle: powerful ministers might seek to avoid the post, and only powerful ministers might increase its impact. Defense matters were of the utmost importance for Government policy as a whole, but this very fact could not but lessen the influence of the Minister of Defence bound to be uncomfortably poised between the Prime Minister, the Cabinet (which included a number of former Ministers of Defence now risen to more senior positions), the Chiefs of Staff Committee, and the Service ministers.

For a time, strategic developments also strengthened the vested interests of the Service departments. The cancellation of the Blue Streak project implied, for instance, the temporary return to favor and apparent promise of manned aircraft, strengthened in the future by the Skybolt missile. There is not much evidence that the Service ministers succeeded in staging a comeback. On the contrary, it was becoming a general assumption that ministers who did well in these offices were likely to move on. The actual conflict between individual Service views and forces for centralization has generally been fought more in the Chiefs of Staff Committee, and among the Service Chiefs, the Minister of Defence, and the Prime Minister, than on the more purely ministerial plane of the Service ministers and the Minister of Defence.

Relations in the Chiefs of Staff Committee were affected when Lord Mountbatten replaced Dickson as Chief of the Defence Staff in 1959. Mountbatten brought to the post all the glamour of his personality (if also somewhat of a political mortgage, since some Tories could not forgive him for his part in the emancipation of India, and some socialists would not forget his relationship to the Royal Family). Mountbatten had unrivaled experience and prestige, and he was a known manager of men. He soon developed a private office, staffed by officers from the various defense departments, who were seconded to service with the Chief of the Defence Staff (unlike the officers working in the Joint Planning Staff, who remained attached to their individual Services). The influence of the Chief of the Defence Staff was also furthered by the establishment of an ever-ready operational headquarters under his direction in the Ministry of Defence, which was reinforced after the Kuweit operation in 1961 had revealed certain deficiencies.

But Mountbatten, nevertheless, could not deprive the other Service Chiefs of their independent status and their secure backing by the Service departments and Service loyalties. He, too, apparently experienced the invidious side of being a non-departmental coordinator, rather than the head of a powerful administrative apparatus. In a speech of September

1961 to a group of officers and officials of some thirty developing countries, he issued a "warning not to allow strong separate establishments to develop in their own armed forces." Somewhat enviously, he added : "Young emergent countries have a unique chance to train their cadres at a single defense college. When you start from scratch, it is easy to have one defense ministry and one minister with a combined staff."[41]

In July 1962, Watkinson was replaced as Minister of Defence by Thorneycroft, still remembered as the "Iron Chancellor," who had resigned over an expenditure of £50,000,000 in 1958. Defense seemed on the way to further retrenchment. By the end of 1962, a feeling of profound malaise had settled over the question of defence organization, as the scrapping of the Skybolt missile program by the United States once more destroyed the slender basis of current strategic planning as well as the hope for a continued independent existence of a strategic bomber command. Soul-searching about effective responsibility for past error mingled with anger about the unwillingness of the Americans to foot the bill, while a continued desire to preserve Britain's independence and greatness on a moderate defense budget battled with the view that Britain should finally face the facts of present-day power politics. The voices of those who hoped to solve such dilemmas by merging the three Services in one Ministry of Defence, under one Combined General Staff, again became louder.

Supply Organization since 1945

The problem of supply organization had been solved no better in the Second World War than in the First. In 1945, the War Office and Air Ministry pleaded that effective control over technical stores be restored to them. With equal conviction, others advocated a centralized Supply Ministry (either for general stores or for developing and producing all weapons and other military requirements). Still others sought a solution in separating the responsibility for developing weapons (which should be retransferred to the individual Service departments) from the responsibility for producing them (which might profitably fall under a somewhat curtailed Ministry of Supply).[42]

The National Government had discussed the matter in 1944 without agreeing on a solution. But the advocates of a Ministry of Supply had a civilian friend at court. When Attlee took office, he decided to merge the Ministry of Aircraft Production with the Ministry of Supply, and to make the new department the sponsor of the engineering and heavy metal industries, irrespective of whether these industries were engaged in civilian or military production.[43] Arms development, too, was entrusted to the Ministry of Supply. So for a time was responsibility for nuclear matters. The Admiralty kept control over providing most of its own military requirements. The office of Minister of Production lapsed, but in 1946 the

[41] *Manchester Guardian,* 22 September 1961.
[42] Chester–Willson, pp. 236–39.   [43] *Ibid.,* p. 237.

new Minister of Defence was charged with "the framing of general policy to govern research and development, and the correlation of production programs."

Within the new Ministry of Defence was instituted a Defence Research Policy Committee composed of "those responsible, both from the operational and scientific angle, for research and development in the Service Departments and the Ministry of Supply."[44] The new committee was chaired by the Scientific Adviser of the Ministry of Defence, the first one being Sir Henry Tizard.[45] As the importance of weapons technology increased, this adviser tended to gain in influence. When Sir Frederick Brundrett occupied the post, he even regularly attended the Chiefs of Staff Committee meetings. In order to provide coordination between the Service departments and the Ministry of Supply, a system was developed whereby officers of the three Service departments were regularly seconded for service with the Ministry of Supply.[46]

The position of the Ministry of Supply weakened over the years, however. After the Korean crisis, the department lost control over raw materials to a special Ministry of Materials (1951–54). When the latter was disbanded, the remnants of its powers did not revert to the Ministry of Supply but were transferred to the Board of Trade. Due to the dismantling of physical controls and the denationalization of iron and steel, the Ministry of Supply lost its responsibility for heavy industry to the Board of Trade. The development of atomic energy, too, was taken from it in 1951, when Churchill put Cherwell in charge (but it retained authority over the actual production of atomic weapons). The Ministry of Supply was thus reduced to a more definitely military department.[47]

The more important weapons technology became, for both defense policies and defense expenditures, the greater its political importance became. In the new strategic doctrines elaborated by Sandys, missiles became of predominant interest. Consequently, the immediate influence of the Ministry of Defence in this field increased. At the same time, the Ministry of Supply was strongly criticized by the aircraft industry and by the Air Ministry, which wanted both government sponsorship and private ownership to become more concentrated so that future projects could be undertaken successfully. In October 1959, a drastic reform was instituted to meet the wishes of both Sandys and the aircraft industry. The Ministry of Supply was abolished. Sandys was put in charge of a new Ministry for Aviation, which was made responsible for missile and aircraft developments in both the military and the civilian spheres. Ordnance questions reverted again to the War Office. At the same time, the Admiralty transferred its powers over civilian shipbuilding to the Ministry of Transport.

[44] Cmd. 6923 (1946), para. 9.
[45] Cf. Tizard, pp. 14–15; McCloughry, p. 21; Brundrett, p. 248ff; William, *Science*, pp. 254–62.
[46] Chester–Willson, p. 239.　　　　　　[47] *Ibid.*, p. 239.

Except in the aircraft industry, a sharper demarcation between civilian and war production resulted from these reforms. The Ministry of Aviation had temporarily risen in ministerial rank. For the first time, its minister was a senior member of the Cabinet. When Sandys became Secretary of State for Commonwealth Affairs in 1961, he was succeeded as Minister of Aviation by Thorneycroft, who thus returned to the Cabinet after his temporary sojourn in the political wilderness. But with the cancellation of the Blue Streak missile project, much of the political prestige seemed to have gone out of the new creation. Thorneycroft was transferred to the Ministry of Defence in the summer of 1962. The new Minister of Aviation, Julian Amery, was again excluded from the Cabinet.

THIRTEEN

THE ORGANIZATION FOR ECONOMIC POLICY,
1914–1939

The Situation before 1914

Even in the land of the classical economists, the State had never been reduced completely to the exclusive triad—Justice, Defense, and Instruction—to which many in the nineteenth century had wanted to limit it. By 1900, the State had come to control many economic activities, and in practice "gas-and-water" socialism had penetrated deeply.[1] The concept that the State could best serve economic welfare by abstaining from all intervention had also begun to suffer a certain theoretical corrosion. But however much incidental government measures affected economic life, the idea that the government had a central, directing role to play in economic policy was still absent. Trade policy was consciously concerned with little but consular activities and the conclusion of trade agreements. Free-trade principles prevailed against intermittent protectionist agitation. In matters of taxation, both Conservatives and Liberals tended to hold that "money should be left to fructify in the pockets of the taxpayer."[2] Against them, the Labour movement was not yet much of a political force, since it was divided into three groups: the Lib-Labs (Labour representatives who supported the Liberal Party), the supporters of an independent Labour Party, and a turbulent group of industrial unionists who rejected all parliamentary action. Social concerns did lead the government to regulate certain aspects of industrial life. But such intervention did not reach deeply. The mitigation of poverty was to most a question of private philanthropy and not an obligation of the State (except for the provision of workhouses).

The government apparatus naturally reflected this situation. Treasury control was strict. All departments had to submit their estimates to the close scrutiny of the Treasury and seek its permission for every increase in expenditure. Only the Service departments could make proposals to the Treasury "with that sort of jaunty air, which a pugilist wears when he expects to enter the ring at least on equal terms with his opponent."[3] Unlike the other departments, who submitted their budgets to Parliament

---

[1] Sidney Webb's lyrical enumeration of such developments (Chap. 2, *Fabian Essays in Socialism,* 1889) is well worth rereading in this connection.

[2] Bridges, *Treasury Control,* p. 6.

[3] Laski, *Reflections,* p. 184; cf. Asquith, *Memories,* I, 256–57; *Life of Lansdowne,* p. 191.

through the Financial Secretary to the Treasury, they placed their estimates directly before Parliament through their own Financial Secretaries to the War Office and the Admiralty. But in practice this did not relieve the Service ministries from stringent Treasury supervision.

The power of its officials was so great that Sir Charles Trevelyan could dub the Treasury "the department of departments."[4] Traditionally, the Permanent Secretary to the Treasury had enjoyed a salary higher than that of his opposite number in other departments. Much of this is of course still true. Yet actual relations were different. "My Lords of the Treasury" did not hesitate to circulate haughty directives, and even sent young officials to lay down the law to very senior officials in other departments.[5] Before 1914, the Treasury was mighty and hated by many. It was, in Amery's words, "not in the main an economic department but a Department of Economy."[6]

The slight importance attached to economic tasks in the nineteenth century was reflected in the inferior status of the economic departments. Neither the Board of Trade nor the Board of Agriculture was judged, in the political world, to be on a par with the Foreign Office, the Home Office, the Treasury, or even the Colonial Office and the Service departments. The central government had at its disposal practically no assistance from expert economists. There was an abyss between the extremely theoretical economics of the day and the views of officials who were for the most part trained in the classics or the humanities.[7]

Even so, certain significant changes occurred before 1914. Important social reforms were instituted by the Liberal Cabinets between 1906 and 1914. Lloyd George especially (who from 1905 to 1908 preferred the Board of Trade to the Post Office, and who in 1908 compelled Asquith to appoint him Chancellor of the Exchequer[8]) asserted himself strongly. "I am the only Chancellor who ever began by saying and meaning to spend money," he was to declare later on.[9] Germany had had a system of social security for decades, and this was not without influence in England.[10] Controversial bills were passed to provide insurance benefits for the aged, the sick, and the unemployed. New administrative arrangements became necessary. In 1911 and 1912 a National Insurance Commission was set up under the Treasury. Lloyd George knew his political life was at stake He attracted promising young men from various departments to man the new Commission. Many of them later reached the highest official positions; hence, this body is often considered to have been the beginning of the modern civil service.[11]

[4] Greaves, *Civil Service*, p. 146; cf. Mackintosh, pp. 257–60.
[5] Grigg, *Prejudice and Judgment*, p. 36.
[6] 356 H. of C. Deb. (1 February 1940), col. 1359.
[7] Cf. Anderson, *Economic Studies*, pp. 5–6.
[8] Beveridge, *Power and Influence*, pp. 72–73, and *Esher Papers*, II, 303.
[9] Jones, *Diary*, p. 146.
[10] Cf. Beveridge, *Power and Influence*, pp. 55ff, 80; Braithwaite, *passim*.
[11] Anderson, *Administrative Technique*, pp. 7–8; *Life of Anderson*, p. 31ff; Bridges, *Portrait*, p. 11; Salter, *Memoirs*, Chap. 3.

Lloyd George also expanded the activity of the Treasury in more directly economic matters. A Development Commission was instituted to finance development projects, and a Road Board was set up to give government support to roadbuilding.[12] At the same time, Labour Exchanges were established within the framework of the Board of Trade, which also played a part in the application of unemployment insurance.[13] The work of the Board of Trade expanded considerably; of a staff of about 7,500 in 1914, about 4,800 dealt with labor matters alone.[14]

As a whole, however, the organization of the machinery for economic policy remained haphazard. Friction existed between the Board of Trade and the Foreign Office regarding the control of foreign trade. The Home Office and the Local Government Board exercised a number of ill-coordinated powers, especially with respect to safety and health regulations.[15] For no one was economic policy a matter meriting continuous thought or central coordination.

The Influence of the First World War

The war of 1914–18 did not immediately change the situation. When the first financial panic, at the beginning of August 1914, had subsided, many thought special regulations unnecessary. Naturally, the needs of the Army must be met. This would demand special financial provisions and perhaps would affect the Treasury's persistent drive for economy. Almost no one, however, banked on a long war. There was strong resistance to introducing higher taxation, rationing, and conscription. Most regulations during the early part of the war had an air of improvisation. In particular, the Board of Trade clung to the idea that the market mechanism could iron out most difficulties.[16] But in fact, the war of 1914–18 was the first one to be fought not only at the front but also in factory and on farm.[17] Munitions production, shipping, food, labor relations, and conscription could not, in wartime, be left to free agents or regulated by voluntary effort. Elsewhere we have seen how, under Asquith, attempts were made to solve such problems by generally ineffective committees, and how these developments, under Lloyd George, led to the institution of new government departments for Shipping, Food, Labour, National Service, etc., which—in rather irregular ways, with a new élan and ad hoc powers—tried to find a balance between military demands, civilian efforts, and civilian needs.

This development was not without effect on the positions of the Treasury and the Board of Trade. The grip of the Treasury on the departments

---

[12] Chester–Willson, pp. 55–56.

[13] Cf. Beveridge, *Power and Influence,* pp. 61ff, 72ff.

[14] Llewellyn Smith, p. 233; see also J. A. M. Caldwell, "The Genesis of the Ministry of Labour," *Public Administration,* XXXVII (1959), 367–91.

[15] Cf. Chester–Willson, pp. 63–64, 82, 96–97.

[16] *Ibid.,* p. 61.

[17] Cf. Hancock–Gowing, p. 12ff, and Salter, *Memoirs,* pp. 73–104.

loosened. "Treasury control of expenditure . . . became practically non-existent," wrote Austen Chamberlain, who was appointed Chancellor of the Exchequer at the end of the war.[18] As new economic departments were instituted, the Board of Trade lost a number of its tasks. It retained its prestige as "the Doyen of Economic Departments."[19] But after 1918, it could not regain the status of a comprehensive Ministry of Economic Affairs, which it had been approaching in 1914.

The organization of economic policy on the level of the War Cabinet itself remained inadequate. The Committee of Economic Defence and Development and the Home Policy Committee which were finally set up proved makeshift arrangements. The former disappeared quickly. The latter lived on, after 1919, as the Home Affairs Committee, but principally as a technical medium for coordinating legislation.

The years after 1918 were full of administrative confusion. The turmoil of war had brought a certain looseness in the thought about government organization. Certain new ministers, whose main experience so far had been in private enterprise, often took up their tasks in a very unorthodox fashion. Some drafted ambitious plans for a drastic overhaul of economic life. Geddes, for instance, wished to modernize and electrify the railways, and for this reason sought to establish a Ministry of Communications. This became the basis of the later Ministry of Transport.[20]

There were pleas (not only in socialist circles) to modernize or even nationalize the coal mines. It was proposed that a Minister of Mines be appointed to work under the President of the Board of Trade. But the idea met with opposition from the House of Lords, where it was considered that such a half-way office would lead to confusion about parliamentary responsibility: all important decisions would in fact rest with the President; a quasi-independent Ministry of Mines would be an increasingly extravagant money-spender; and it would afford appropriate machinery for future nationalization. The rank of the head of the Mines Department of the Board of Trade was therefore reduced to that of a Parliamentary Secretary.[21] In practice, however, the Secretary of Mines continued to hold a quasi-independent position. In this he resembled the Secretary for Overseas Trade, who administered the Department of Overseas Trade, established in 1917 as a compromise between the Foreign Office and the Board of Trade. According to this agreement, the Secretary for Overseas Trade was Assistant Parliamentary Undersecretary of State

---

[18] Chamberlain, *Down the Years,* p. 132. As was related in Chap. 4, Lloyd George refused in 1918 to admit Austen Chamberlain to the Cabinet as Chancellor of the Exchequer. The official residence of the Chancellor, 11 Downing Street, was not put at his disposal, but reserved for Bonar Law. Therefore the Chancellor (unlike his predecessors) did not enjoy direct access to 10 Downing Street via a connecting door. For similar situations after 1921, see Chap. 16, n. 28.

[19] Chester–Willson, pp. 84, 67–71.

[20] *Ibid.,* pp. 72–77; see also the list of ministers in 112 H. of C. Deb. (February 1919).

[21] Chester–Willson, pp. 78–81.

for Foreign Affairs, and at the same time Additional Parliamentary Secretary to the Board of Trade.[22]

Certain new proposals were also canvassed in regard to more general economic policy. The Permanent Secretary to the Board of Trade, Sir Hubert Llewellyn Smith, set up a General Economic Department of the Board of Trade in 1918. The task of this new body, according to his definition, should be "to anticipate, watch, and suggest means of dealing with important questions and movements likely to arise in commerce and industry and which from their generality or novelty did not fall within the scope of any specialized department." The department would work in close cooperation with other departments. It would have no executive powers. Part of its staff would be on a temporary basis, and qualified economists would be given the opportunity to serve in it on a temporary basis. The new department did not last long; the anti-waste campaign of the early 1920's soon swept it away, leaving behind little but the title of Chief Economic Adviser to His Majesty's Government, which was granted in 1919 to Llewellyn Smith personally.[23]

At the same time, certain new developments affected the relations between the Treasury and the other departments. The rather chaotic state of government finances, coupled with demands from the House of Commons for still further tax cuts, made it urgently necessary to reinforce the influence of the Treasury. But scarcely anyone wished to return completely to the position before 1914, when the Treasury, in the words of Sir Robert Morant, was not only the "head and crown" of the other departments, but also "their most effective repressive master."[24] On forming his Government after the elections of 1918, Lloyd George instituted a Cabinet Committee—composed of himself as Chairman, the Chancellor of the Exchequer, and some other senior ministers—which would seek to arbitrate conflicts between the departments and the Treasury without bringing them before the Cabinet.[25]

The war had profoundly influenced the Treasury's outlook. Treasury officials had learned to consider officials from other departments more as potential equals and not merely as extravagant subordinates. They had come to realize that the greatly increased volume of government business would make it impossible and undesirable for the Treasury to seek to lay down the law to other departments in minute detail.[26] In 1919, the onetime Secretary of the National Insurance Commission, Sir Warren Fisher, was appointed Permanent Secretary to the Treasury. He had himself suffered from the haughty attitude of the pre-1914 Treasury, and hence

---

[22] *Ibid.,* pp. 69–70, and list of ministers in 112 H. of C. Deb. (February 1919).

[23] Reconstruction Papers (Llewellyn Smith), Folios 778–80; Llewellyn Smith, pp. 239–41; Chester–Willson, pp. 294–96; Anderson, *Economic Studies,* p. 7; cf. Cd. 9230 (1918), p. 23.

[24] Reconstruction Papers (Sir Robert Morant), Folio 1080.

[25] 120 H. of C. Deb. (29 October 1919), cols. 744–45, and Chamberlain, *Down the Years,* pp. 134, 138.

[26] Bridges, *Treasury Control,* p. 8; Smellie, pp. 245–47.

consciously worked for reform.[27] Direct financial responsibility was put squarely on the departments themselves. The Permanent Head of a department himself usually became its Accounting Officer, so responsibility for policy and finance was concentrated in one and the same hand. Through these reforms, the Treasury became a little more the center, a little less the censor, of the other departments.

These new relations were accompanied by an attempt to weld the civil service more definitely into a corps. Contacts between the departments became closer and more informal. Shifts of personnel between the departments were encouraged. This could only strengthen the tendency of a closely knit group of officials to exercise a strong collective influence on the making of policy.[28]

For the time being, however, these reforms were limited to issues of financial control, or over-all policy. Neither dominant economic doctrine nor Treasury tradition nor the general political situation was conducive to the Treasury's taking an active role in matters of economic policy proper. The successive Chancellors of the Exchequer between the wars— Sir Austen Chamberlain, Sir Robert Horne, Stanley Baldwin, Neville Chamberlain, Philip Snowden, and Sir John Simon—hardly shone by unexpected initiatives. Even Churchill—according to Lloyd George "the merriest tax collector since Robin Hood"[29]—followed orthodox ways between 1924 and 1929. Hence, until at least 1939, the Treasury's new position had potential rather than effective importance for the machinery of economic policy.

On the whole, whatever enthusiasm for change existed after 1918 was soon washed away by the realities of economic depression. The House of Commons, elected in the Coupon Election of 1918, demanded drastic economies and abolition of government intervention. In 1921, a Select Committee on National Expenditure under Geddes was charged to in-

---

[27] See especially Sir H. P. Hamilton, "Sir Warren Fisher and the Public Service," *Public Administration*, XXIX (1951), pp. 3–38. See also Grigg, *Prejudice and Judgment*, pp. 50–51.

[28] The civil service reforms in 1919 led to more uniformity in Establishment matters and to a division of the civil service into three distinct groups: the administrative class, the executive class, and the clerical class. Sir Warren Fisher officially became Head of the Civil Service. In 1956, the Secretary of the Cabinet became Joint Permanent Secretary to the Treasury and Head of the Civil Service, but in 1962 the Secretaryship of the Cabinet reverted to a separate official. At the same time, two Joint Permanent Secretaries were appointed to head the Treasury. One of them is also Head of the Civil Service, and is especially responsible for the promotion of management services throughout the civil service.

As Head of the Civil Service, the (Joint) Permanent Secretary to the Treasury has always advised the Prime Minister on senior appointments throughout the Home Civil Service, particularly in the case of such senior personnel as Permanent Secretaries and Finance Officers (cf. Greaves, *Civil Service*, p. 172ff). The combination of Permanent Secretary to the Treasury and Head of the Civil Service has sometimes been thought potentially damaging. It has been held that certain officials may have taken insufficiently firm stands against the Treasury, in order not to spoil their chance of promotion (cf. 125 H. of L. Deb. [25 and 26 November 1942], cols. 223ff, 275ff [in particular the views of Hankey]).

[29] Grigg, *Prejudice and Judgment*, p. 199.

quire into the superfluity of any State tasks. To forestall or blunt the Geddes Axe, the Government abolished numerous recently established bureaus. Those that remained, such as the Ministry of Transport and the Ministry of Labour, soon fell off to second or third rank.

Developments between 1924 and 1929

The coming to power of the Labour Government in 1924 gave rise to fearful expectations of revolutionary developments. As insiders had correctly forecast, however, Snowden turned out to be "the most orthodox Chancellor since Gladstone."[30] Snowden willingly followed Asquith's advice "not to divulge the proposals of [the] Budget to [his] Cabinet colleagues until the morning of the day when the Budget was to be presented to the House of Commons."[31] The first Socialist budget hardly betrayed a strong socialist conviction. Nor did it become an instrument of active social or economic policy. It provided something for everyone. It was popular but hardly constructive. At the same time, the Treasury's position was further formalized by a new rule stipulating that no proposals might come up for Cabinet discussion unless the Treasury had had an opportunity to scrutinize their financial implications.[32]

Proposals for innovation in the machinery of government did not come from Snowden or other Socialist ministers, but from the Government's recent recruit, Haldane. Haldane's Machinery of Government Committee had suggested in 1918 "that in the sphere of civil government the duty of investigation and thought, as preliminary to action, might with great advantage be more definitely recognized."[33] The Committee had adduced military experience in evidence. In 1924, Haldane (who in effect chaired the C.I.D. under the first Labour Government) had come to the conclusion that adequate government research could best be stimulated by a committee modeled closely after the C.I.D. He consulted with the Secretary to the Cabinet, Hankey, and the Permanent Secretary to the Treasury, Fisher.[34] Various memoranda were drafted and obtained MacDonald's somewhat lukewarm approval. The purpose of such a Committee of Economic Inquiry would be

a. To ensure that national problems were actually being faced and thought out in advance on a basis of fact;
b. To assist the Government of the day with an organization—stable but not

---

[30] *Life of Haldane*, II, 143, 160.
[31] Snowden, *Autobiography*, II, 617, 641; cf. Keith–Gibbs, pp. 88–89.
[32] For an instance in which this directive meant in practice a Treasury veto of the circulation of an important policy document, see Duff Cooper, *Old Men Forget*, pp. 219–20.
[33] Cd. 9230 (1918), para. 12; for an earlier statement by Haldane, see Hume, p. 348.
[34] Haldane, *Autobiography*, pp. 331–34; *Life of Haldane*, II, 178–79; Anderson, *Economic Studies*, pp. 7–8. Mackintosh (p. 439) also refers to a letter from Lord Esher (*The Times*, 25 May 1924) as a source of inspiration for the proposal.

rigid—for exploring the problems in which it is interested without the need for improvising coordination; and

c. To utilize to the greatest advantage the existing facilities of the government departments under conditions most likely to command the ready cooperation of their officials.[35]

The MacDonald Cabinet fell from office, however, before the new organization was introduced. The "father" of the C.I.D., Balfour, revived the plan. In 1925, a Committee of Civil Research was established. In practice, it differed little from what Haldane had wanted. The Committee was "charged with the duty of giving connected forethought from a central standpoint to the development of economic, scientific, and statistical research in relation to civil policy and administration."[36] Like the C.I.D., it worked mainly through wide-ranging subcommittees. But it gave relatively little attention to economic issues and was much less closely integrated into the government machinery than the C.I.D.[37] Most of all, it was a personal apparatus of Balfour himself. This was as much its weakness as its strength. Apart from Haldane, nobody was more interested at this time than Balfour in how to integrate scientific advice into the determination of government policy. But Balfour was 77 in 1925. And he was himself little interested in economic problems.

The most important economic problems facing the Conservative Cabinet between 1924 and 1929 were whether Britain should return to the gold standard, on the basis of the prewar parity of the pound; continued unemployment; and the revived debate on free trade vs. protection. As Chancellor of the Exchequer, Churchill had an influential voice in such matters. He knew the value of expert advice. According to his then private secretary, P. J. Grigg, Churchill accused the Treasury officials of not consulting enough with R. G. Hawtrey, who occupied the somewhat weak position of Director of Financial Enquiries. "I remember," wrote Grigg, "his demanding from time to time that the learned man should be released from the dungeon in which we were said to have immured him, have his chains struck off and the straw brushed from his hair and clothes, and be admitted to the light and warmth of an argument in the Treasury Boardroom with the greatest living master of argument."[38]

Churchill's decision to return to the gold standard in 1925, later to be so hotly criticized, did not lack expert agreement. On the contrary, J. M. Keynes's was a somewhat lonely voice when he argued in his *The Economic Consequences of Mr. Churchill* (1925) that this step would have calamitous economic and social consequences. Soon, the General Strike of 1926 and the continuously high unemployment figures appeared to prove Keynes right. Particularly in the Liberal Party, new ideas about a pro-

---

[35] Anderson, *Economic Studies*, pp. 9–10.
[36] Cmd. 2440 (1925), quoted by Bridges, *Treasury Control*, p. 11, and Chester–Willson, p. 322; cf. Mackintosh, pp. 439–40.
[37] Tizard, pp. 15–16.   [38] Grigg, *Prejudice and Judgment*, p. 82.

gram for large-scale public works were canvassed. Positive proposals to this end were made in the so-called Liberal Yellow Book, *Britain's Industrial Future* (1928).[39] This report also advocated establishing an Economic General Staff, which was to facilitate and raise the quality of Cabinet decisions through continuous expert study of economic problems, rather like the military staffs did on defense issues.[40]

Many Conservatives were more interested in reviving propaganda in favor of economic protection, however. In the 1924–29 Cabinet, the principal proponent of this was Amery, Secretary of State for the Dominions and the Colonies, who, as a disciple of Joseph Chamberlain, pleaded for Imperial Preference.[41] His desires stranded primarily on the persistent opposition of Churchill and the Treasury. As a result, Amery developed a strong antagonism toward the Treasury, which he accused of being "the master" instead of "the faithful steward of the productive departments."[42] When, in 1929, the second Labour Government succeeded Baldwin's second Cabinet, Amery warned Thomas against assuming responsibility for unemployment as Lord Privy Seal. "I asked how far the Treasury was being put under his control," wrote Amery. "As he seemed vague on the point, I said: 'Jimmy, you are starting your job with a noose around your neck and the other end of the rope in Snowden's hands.' "[43]

Experiments under the Second Labour Government (1929–31)

The second MacDonald Cabinet came into office in 1929, the year of the great financial crisis that began on Wall Street and reverberated throughout the world. The Cabinet succumbed in 1931 to internal disagreement about economic policy. Developments between 1929 and 1931 form as much a part of the general history of the Cabinet as of the government machinery for economic policy; hence most of it was treated in Chapter 4. As we saw, the experiment to make Thomas, as Lord Privy Seal, responsible for employment matters was not very successful. Lansbury was later to describe the meetings of Thomas and his assistants as gatherings "in a sort of semi-dungeon high up in the Treasury Offices." "We were surrounded," he wrote, "by the reputed élite of the civil service. . . . There was always present one faithful watchdog of the Treasury, who could always be counted on to find good and excellent reasons why nothing should be done."[44]

In January 1930, MacDonald replaced the Committee of Civil Research

[39] Cf. *Life of Keynes*, p. 392ff; Harrod, *The Prof*, p. 68.
[40] Sir William Beveridge had made a similar proposal before 1928 (Beveridge, *Power and Influence*, p. 214; Beveridge, *Full Employment in a Free Society*, London, 1953, pp. 259–60).
[41] Amery, *My Political Life*, II, *passim*, and especially 503–4; cf. Vansittart, *The Mist Procession*, p. 354.
[42] Amery, *Constitution*, pp. 94–97, and *Constitution*, 2d ed., p. 186; Amery, *Forward View*, p. 444.
[43] Amery, *My Political Life*, II, 502.   [44] Quoted from Dalton, *Memoirs*, I, 260.

of 1925 with a new Economic Advisory Council. This body was composed of the Prime Minister, the Chancellor of the Exchequer, the Lord Privy Seal, the President of the Board of Trade, the Minister of Agriculture and Fisheries, other ministers as required, and a maximum of eight other persons "chosen in virtue of their special knowledge and experience in industry and commerce."[45] MacDonald chose rather carefully; among the outside members were economists like Keynes, G. D. H. Cole, and R. H. Tawney; employers of the quality of Sir Andrew Duncan and Sir Josiah Stamp; and trade unionists like Bevin and Citrine.[46] The Council was not given executive powers and was not to interfere with the administrative and parliamentary responsibilities of ministers and departments. It was served by a special secretariat under the Deputy Secretary to the Cabinet, Tom Jones, which included some other economists, notably Hubert Henderson as Assistant Secretary. It is generally felt, however, that the experiment of the Economic Advisory Council failed. To quote Jones:

> MacDonald . . . called for "scientific government" at the same moment as he had to conform to his party's electioneering manifesto, *Labour and the Nation,* and to the economics of a democratic capitalist State. MacDonald had a suspicious nature and . . . disliked admitting his ignorance of a problem even to the expert whom he had summoned to unravel it—in contrast with Lloyd George, who wanted to understand the problem quickly, and with Baldwin, who was content that the expert should understand it. In MacDonald's day I more than once took Sir Hubert Henderson . . . to No. 10 to discuss measures for dealing with unemployment, only to be dismissed unheard after twenty minutes occupied by the Prime Minister in waffling.[47]

A major problem, however, was disagreement among the experts themselves. It was in this period that there began to circulate the famous quip: "Where five economists are gathered together there will be six conflicting opinions, and two of them will be held by Keynes."[48] The Economic Advisory Council set up a small subcommittee to examine the economic situation and report on plans for action. It soon broke up, because the employers' representatives resisted the desire of Cole and Keynes to investigate the possibility of relieving unemployment by a program of capital development. A later subcommittee charged to study the issue of free trade vs. protection also failed to agree.[49] No amount of study or deliberation could solve disagreement or uncertainty about policy. Bridges and Anderson gave some additional reasons why the Economic Advisory Council proved unsatisfactory. "From the outset," wrote Bridges, "the Council was rather cut off from the main stream of government activity by the exalted position given to it, and by the fact that its members were busy people engaged in activities outside the government work."[50] In the words of Anderson, "It bore the appearance of an auxiliary engine not geared

[45] Cmd. 3478 (1930); Anderson, *Economic Studies,* p. 11.
[46] *Life of Bevin,* p. 436. [47] Jones, *Diary,* p. xxxi.
[48] *Ibid.,* p. 19. [49] *Life of Bevin,* pp. 437–39.
[50] Bridges, *Treasury Control,* pp. 11–12.

to the main shaft. . . . Ministerial responsibility was too diffuse. There was no effective minister in charge."[51]

The worse the crisis became, the more MacDonald sought recourse in organizational experiments. After Thomas resigned, MacDonald himself took charge of unemployment matters. He was aided by the new Lord Privy Seal, Vernon Hartshorn, the Chancellor of the Duchy of Lancaster, Attlee, and a group of senior civil servants under the then Permanent Undersecretary at the Home Office, Anderson.[52] Various committees were established to study the financial and economic situation. The Committee of Inquiry into Finance and Industry, which was headed by Lord Macmillan and reported in 1931, had especially great influence. A committee under Sir George May was charged with inquiring into the possibilities of further economies in expenditure. The Treasury and the Bank of England spoke with still different voices.[53] Meanwhile, the depression sank in further. It sapped the confidence of the country and destroyed the cohesion of the Cabinet.

The Great Depression (1931–39)

Nominally, the Economic Advisory Council remained in existence under the National Governments of the 1930's. Certain subcommittees continued to work. But the parent body itself in effect sank into oblivion.[54]

In September 1931, Britain went off the gold standard. The most important economic measure after that was the introduction of Imperial Preference, to which the Government agreed in Ottawa in 1932, in consultation with members of the Commonwealth. An attempt was made to insulate the imposition of import duties from political pressures by forming an Import Duties Advisory Committee. It was hoped that this body would be able to work out objective rules, which the Treasury would simply have to apply. The Committee disappeared in 1939 after a rather fruitless existence.[55] Numerous incidental regulations were made for special sectors of the economy. Agriculture, for instance, was given a large number of Marketing Boards, which sought to regulate the disposal of agricultural products.[56] Again, it was attempted to isolate these organizations (like other bodies, such as the Unemployment Assistance Board) from the central organization of government, so that they might be less subject to the pressure of day-to-day politics. In these as in other sectors, the widening scope of the Government's economic policy led to closer formal and informal contacts with private enterprise.[57]

---

[51] Anderson, *Economic Studies*, pp. 16–17; cf. Smellie, pp. 253–54; Salter, *Memoirs*, p. 230.

[52] Anderson, *Economic Studies*, p. 11.   [53] Cf. Bassett, pp. 26–60.

[54] Chester–Willson, p. 323; Sir Richard Hopkins, Introduction to D. N. Chester, ed., *Lessons from the War Economy*, p. 3.

[55] Cf. Vernon–Mansergh, pp. 117–20, 137–38; Tivey–Rendel, pp. 7–8.

[56] Street, pp. 166–68.

[57] *Ibid.*, p. 163, Smellie, pp. 250–52; Chester–Bowring, pp. 93–94. Cf. S. E. Finer, *Anonymous Empire: A Study of the Lobby in Great Britain* (1958).

Uncertainty about economic policy persisted throughout this period. Some came to advocate a measure of planning. In 1936, Keynes published his *General Theory of Employment, Interest and Money,* which was to have a revolutionary influence on economic policy after 1939, and to bring a drastic change in the Treasury's position towards economic life. But the Government itself showed little initiative during this period. Henderson was persuaded by friends to leave his post in the Cabinet Office in 1933 and return to academic life, as he found little useful work in government employment.[58] It happened, Jones wrote in his diary in 1934, that MacDonald

summoned the Trade and Employment Committee, and the Secretaries with great difficulty conjured up an agenda. There was, as usual, much talk and few decisions, and the Prime Minister announced that the Committee would meet again in a week's time. This was done with the same result, and when he suggested meeting again for a third time, the Chancellor protested against the waste of a morning.[59]

During the 1930's, the dole was more typical of Government policy than the creation of employment through public works. After all, was not the situation in Britain more favorable than in other capitalist countries? Leading officials such as the Permanent Secretary to the Treasury, Fisher, and the Chief Industrial Adviser, Wilson, preferred work on defense or foreign-policy matters. Few politicians were eager to take on any of the economic departments. When Eden complained to Baldwin about the Cabinet's frequent intervention in matters of foreign policy, Baldwin told him to "remember that out of [his] twenty colleagues there was probably not more than one who thought he should be Minister of Labour and nineteen who thought they should be Foreign Secretary."[60]

[58] Jones, *Diary,* p. 116.   [59] *Ibid.,* pp. 121–22.
[60] Eden, *Facing the Dictators,* p. 319.

FOURTEEN

THE PLANNING MACHINERY DURING THE SECOND WORLD WAR

Preparations before 1939

In 1916 and again after the Armistice of 1918, all British government departments were directed to commit their war experiences to paper.[1] Afterwards, numerous interdepartmental committees, under the auspices of the C.I.D. held discussions on the problems future governments might face in the event of war. For a long time, such discussions were carried on in desultory fashion. Not until the so-called Ten Year Rule was rescinded in 1932, and especially after 1935, did they acquire substance and directness.[2] Planning for war had its center in the departments and in the offices of the Cabinet Secretariat, alias the Secretariat of the C.I.D. In addition, a Committee for Economic Information played some part. Formally a subcommittee of the Economic Advisory Council, it was guided by Stamp, a prominent railway director, who simultaneously served the government in various high-level advisory functions. Experts outside the civil service were sometimes commissioned to carry out special investigations. Beveridge, for instance, was requested to design a food-rationing scheme. In his final report, he went beyond this precise assignment, stressing the urgent need for a detailed study of the *general* problem of civil mobilization.[3] Plans were elaborated for controlling scarce resources, industry, prices, and war finance. Certain new government departments were proposed for the eventuality of another war. In contrast to the situation in 1914, the Government prepared to take the fullest possible powers immediately if war should break out.[4]

For understandable reasons, most of these investigations and deliberations took place in secret. Consequently, various groups outside the immediate circle of civil servants concerned could not but feel that too little was being done. Again, Parliament and the Press exerted pressure for the establishment of an Economic General Staff. At the same time, a number of leading industrialists advocated forming a special Department of Economic Planning. Such plans found little favor with the Government at first. But shortly before the Second World War, the Government

---

[1] Hankey, *Supreme Command*, pp. 569–70.
[2] Hancock–Gowing, p. 45ff.
[3] Beveridge, *Power and Influence*, pp. 240–47, 389–95.
[4] Hancock–Gowing, pp. 52, 84.

requested three economists—Stamp, Henry Clay, and Henderson—to screen the departments' existing plans and determine whether they were realistic and compatible with considerations of over-all economic policy.[5]

The First Year of the War

This 1939 inquiry came to be known as the Stamp Survey. It gave birth, shortly after war broke out, to an interdepartmental committee for economic policy, meeting under the chairmanship of Stamp, who was given the personal title of Adviser on Economic Cooperation.[6] The Labour Opposition criticized the arrangement, partly because Stamp simultaneously occupied numerous functions in private industry. The Opposition also attacked the Treasury's overbearing influence on economic policy. It demanded the appointment of a separate Minister for the Coordination of Economic Affairs, who would take over the general supervision of economic planning from the Chancellor.[7] Such criticisms led the Government to introduce a ministerial Economic Policy Committee, to which Stamp's interdepartmental committee would report. But this new Cabinet committee continued to be guided by the Chancellor of the Exchequer, Simon. Over-all economic policy, Simon argued in the House of Commons, was a matter for the Cabinet. The implementation of policy, on the other hand, faced ever-changing problems that could never be satisfactorily handled in a logical, neatly devised committee structure. The divorce of planning from execution and the appointment of a new super-minister above the departments could therefore only create confusion.[8]

The Labour Party continued to regard finance as the wrong yardstick for war planning and attacked Simon and the Government on this point.[9] The Opposition disliked and distrusted Simon, and disliked even more his newly appointed Permanent Secretary, Sir Horace Wilson, Chamberlain's confidant. Socialist rancor is still apparent in Dalton's graphic description of Wilson's last appearance in 10, Downing Street, in May 1940:

In Chamberlain's time, Sir Horace Wilson occupied the small room opening out of the Cabinet Room at No. 10 Downing Street, facing towards the Horse

[5] Anderson, *Economic Studies*, pp. 12, 13; Hancock–Gowing, p. 47; Robinson, pp. 37–38.

[6] 352 H. of C. Deb. (9 October 1939), cols. 28–29.

[7] 351 H. of C. Deb. (26 September 1939), cols. 1247–48 (Attlee) ; 352 H. of C. Deb. (18 October 1939), cols. 905–6, 913–15 (Shinwell); 356 H. of C. Deb. (1 February 1940), col. 1309 (Morrison). For similar criticism by the Liberals, see 352 H. of C. Deb. (18 October 1939), cols. 925–32 (Sinclair), and cols. 946–50 (Davies). Cf. Chester, *Machinery*, p. 5.

[8] 352 H. of C. Deb. (18 October 1939), cols. 932–46.

[9] The official British historians have rendered an unfavorable verdict about the Treasury's preponderant place before 1940. In their view, the Treasury's position was partly responsible for the fact that "the economic effort of war was commonly assessed in terms of finance rather than of physical resources" (Hancock–Gowing, p. 93; cf. 94–97). Cf. also Chester, *Machinery*, p. 6; *Hore-Belisha Papers*, pp. 243, 245; Ironside, pp. 129–30; Eden, *Facing the Dictators*, p. 498.

Guards Parade. There every morning he reported for duty. But when he came, as usual, in good time on the morning of May 11, he found that the paratroopers had arrived before him. On the couch, opposite the door through which he entered, sat Brendan Bracken, the new Prime Minister's Parliamentary Private Secretary, and Randolph Churchill, the new Prime Minister's son, the latter in uniform. They stared at Sir Horace, but no one spoke or smiled. Then he withdrew, never to return to that seat most proximate to power.[10]

The Planning Organization during Total War (1940–45)

The end of the "phony war"—which brought Churchill to the helm at the same time—caused vast changes. "The other war"—the total mobilization of the home front—now enveloped the entire British nation.[11] The chairmanship of the two most important new economic committees of the Cabinet, the Economic Policy Committee and the Production Council, was given to the new Socialist minister without portfolio, Greenwood. The new Chancellor of the Exchequer was left outside the new War Cabinet for the time being.[12] It was soon clear to all that manpower, military production, and shipping were the decisive factors in the war. Programming on the basis of the total available production factors and directing them into the right channels became the government's most important tasks on the home front. To enable the government to acquire a full inventory of resources and to follow developments in the more important sectors of the economy, the assistance of trained economists and statisticians became imperative.[13] Many departments appointed their own experts. Apart from these, a Central Economic Information Service was established within the Cabinet Office in 1940.[14]

For the first time in British administrative history, economists were now drawn directly into the determination of central economic policy. In January 1941, the Central Economic Information Service was split into a Statistical Section and an Economic Section (the latter under Lionel Robbins). The reason for this division was a desire to guarantee the objectivity of statistical data and analyses. The economists were to give expert advice to ministers. "If they were to be of any use," Keynes' biographer has written, "[they] would naturally be expected to have strong views of their own, and there was the human danger that such views might influence the form in which the statistics were presented."[15]

---

[10] Dalton, *Memoirs*, II, 320–21.

[11] The term is taken from Beveridge, *Power and Influence*, p. 273.

[12] The Chancellor of the Exchequer, Sir Kingsley Wood, was again a member of the War Cabinet between October 1940 and February 1942. In September 1943 Anderson became Chancellor of the Exchequer, *as a member of the War Cabinet*. It is symptomatic that under Chamberlain in 1939 the Permanent Secretary to the Treasury often attended Cabinet meetings; under Churchill after 1940 the Permanent Secretary to the Foreign Office took his place.

[13] For the confusion in the statistical services before 1940, see Smellie, pp. 252–53.

[14] Harrod, *The Prof*, pp. 181, 186.

[15] *Life of Keynes*, p. 502; Harrod, *The Prof*, pp. 212–13; MacDougall, p. 67.

In addition to the experts in the Cabinet office, the Treasury appointed its own economic advisers, Keynes, Henderson, D. H. Robertson, and Lord Catto, who carried the "high-sounding but indeterminate position of Economic Adviser to the Chancellor of the Exchequer."[16]

A very powerful influence was also exercised by the Prime Minister's Statistical Office, headed by Cherwell ("The Prof") and staffed by a number of scientists, among them such economists as Donald MacDougall, G. L. S. Shackle, and Roy Harrod.[17] According to Harrod, one should think about certain aspects of the war effort, particularly the over-all allocation of resources, "in terms of a Churchill–Prof–MacDougall triangle, with the Prof as the go-between." He described their cooperation as "joint thinking, the initiating spark for which might, according to the occasion, come from any one of the three." Cherwell had not acceded to Churchill's suggestion to create a large department, because he preferred to be "selective, not comprehensive, in his range."[18] This did not make "S Branch" any more popular in Whitehall. Cherwell "detested bureaucrats," and they reciprocated "with suspicion, if not disfavor and fear."[19] Cherwell was, moreover, exceedingly self-assured and often vindictive, regarding "those who disagreed with him" as "perfect fools."[20] Enjoying Churchill's full confidence, Cherwell had, in the words of C. P. Snow, "more direct power than any scientist in history."[21]

Friction also tended to arise between the other central services. But the Cabinet Office and the Treasury economists were soon housed in one building, and in practice there developed a definite division of labor. The Central Statistical Office occupied itself primarily with coordinating and interpreting departmental statistics, a most complicated task because heretofore the departments had been wont to collect and present their statistics in greatly different fashion. The Economic Section had as official terms of reference:

to receive all economic intelligence collected by various governmental agencies; to cover, by their own researches, any gaps in that intelligence; to make or procure specific studies in those spheres which are not covered by any one department; to appraise economic intelligence, both general and particular; and to present coordinated and objective pictures of the economic situation as a whole and the economic aspects of projected government policies.[22]

But in practice the Economic Section became mainly the personal staff of the Lord President of the Council, Anderson, whom Churchill charged in February 1941 with a "special responsibility for the economic side of the home front."[23]

---

16 *Life of Keynes,* p. 498, n. 1.
17 MacDougall, *passim;* Harrod, *The Prof,* pp. 179–237; cf. Churchill, I, 468; II, 684 (minute of 8 November 1940).
18 Harrod, *The Prof,* pp. 181–87; cf. pp. 197–99.
19 *Life of Cherwell,* p. 216; Morrison, *Autobiography,* p. 191.
20 Harrod, *The Prof,* p. 5.   21 Snow, p. 63.
22 Anderson, *Machinery,* p. 20.   23 Anderson, *Economic Studies,* p. 15.

The entry of economists into the central government apparatus had important consequences. Thereafter, systematic study was made of the main determinants of national income and national production.[24] With the help of Keynes, Wood (as Chancellor of the Exchequer) published the first National Income White Paper in 1941. In 1940, Beveridge drew up a Manpower Survey, the forerunner of the important Manpower Budgets, which were to form the basis of general planning in later war years.[25] In 1942, for the first time, a careful inventory was made of the resources and requirements of military production.[26] At the same time, the basis was laid for the later investment surveys, balance-of-payments prognoses, etc. Better, more quantified data made it possible to determine priorities with greater precision and to control individual sectors of the economy with more certainty. Government economic policy practically became the total control of production and distribution.

Following the advice of the C.I.D., new departments were instituted in 1939 for shipping, food, supply, and economic warfare. The Ministry of Aircraft Production was established in May 1940. In October came the Ministry of Works, which was given increasing powers over building. In 1941, the Ministries of Transport and Shipping were joined in the Ministry of War Transport. In 1942, a Ministry of Production followed, and in the same year all energy matters were concentrated in a new Ministry of Fuel and Power. These new departments, like the older ones, represented competing claims on national production. Ultimately, only the Prime Minister and the Cabinet could decide between the contestants, since in the final analysis priorities depended on the ends and strategy of the war itself. Between the Cabinet and the executive organs for particular sectors of the war economy, there developed a complicated network of committees. It was their task to estimate total needs and weigh them against the available manpower, shipping, imports, material resources, factory space, etc., all of which were in short supply. Sir Oliver Franks, a one-time Oxford don who became a leading official in the Ministry of Supply during the war (and since then has held many other posts of the greatest importance), gave the following picture of this committee system in 1947:

Decisions were reached after open discussion and argument between those concerned, whether as suppliers or users. Each member of these committees had to make his case in the presence of his rival claimant or claimants. All on each committee had the same statistical information, and all claims were subject to ruthless cross-examination by interested parties.[27] This argumentative process was an essential condition of success. No lonely individual, however excellent the scheme of allocation he had worked out, could have presented it

[24] Bridges, *Treasury Control,* p. 14; see also Robinson, pp. 37–57, and Stone, pp. 83–94.
[25] Beveridge, *Power and Influence,* pp. 276–88; Hancock–Gowing, p. 284ff.
[26] Scott–Hughes, p. 455.
[27] But see Robinson, p. 50, for a somewhat less optimistic view.

with any hope of acceptance to one of these committees. This type of central planning only works if those who are involved in the decision feel bound by it and convinced by rational considerations that what is proposed is as fair and reasonable as can be in the circumstances. A general plan of allocation is not only a theoretical exercise in distributive justice but a practical directive for ensuing action. It is necessary that the principal agents should acknowledge a commitment to the decision.[28]

The Civil Histories of the Second World War give an elaborate description of these committees in a variety of fields. Hence, there is more information about the administrative history of the Second World War than of any other period in British history. But these studies are often unreadable. The picture they represent is frequently confused, which is a testament to their truthfulness.[29] Each committee had a fixed base in the existing departments and in other organizations that controlled or stimulated a particular sector of the economy. But personal factors continued to play a considerable role, and the higher the level, the more important this factor became. At the top of the hierarchy decisions were no longer taken solely on the basis of predetermined administrative procedures, but according to the informal relations between those whose influence was ultimately decisive. D. N. Chester, who worked in the Cabinet Office during the war, wrote:

Time and again, committees which appeared well on paper and to the public, which had clear terms of reference and well-balanced membership, would splutter out after a short, uneasy, and unfruitful life, while other committees would go from strength to strength. It was almost uncanny on occasion to see the rise and fall of particular committees, almost as though they had a life of their own. Some would start out with apparently rosy prospects, with a flourish of announcements, perhaps even with a public statement; they would have several regular meetings, minutes and papers would be circulated, and then even though the work for which they were originally set up still continued, they would become less active, they would cease to meet, to all intents and purposes they were dead even though not formally wound up. Decisions in this field would still be taken, but probably in another committee or in the Cabinet, or might even be largely working understandings without any formal committee decision. Broadly speaking, if the ministers (and their advisers) who really held the power were in agreement, the precise committee machinery was of little importance; if they were not in agreement, then the committee would not work anyhow.[30]

Perhaps the best illustrations of such developments at Cabinet level were the successive failures of the Production Council under Greenwood and the Production Executive under Bevin, and, in contrast, the decisive growth of the Lord President's Committee under Anderson. By 1941,

---

[28] Franks, p. 12.
[29] In a letter to Marshall, Ismay described the British wartime machine as "an apparently shapeless mass of committees" (Johnson, p. 289).
[30] Chester, *Machinery*, pp. 26–27.

the Lord President's Committee was in charge of such questions as wages, prices, inflation, and concentration of industries, and was very influential in determining priorities of manpower and materials. At the beginning of 1942 it drew to itself such additional domestic problems as social insurance and rationing.[31]

It is easy to overestimate the element of rationality in the planning process. The War Cabinet relied on figures for its directives. "The figures were often out of date before they were approved, and as soon as the general directive was issued, it was whittled away by one small decision after another, taken somewhere far down the hierarchy. In time these small decisions mounted up until there was a new crisis, a new program, and once more an ineffective directive from above."[32] Numerous government offices worked aloof from and sometimes against one another. The Ministry of Production, for instance, demanded full authority in questions of economic policy, at least with regard to physical factors of production. But it could not break down the resistance of such a venerable department as the Board of Trade, which maintained its authority over civilian production.[33]

The final organization for economic policy, therefore, was far from settled. Through Bevin the Ministry of Labour had acquired a very special position. The Lord President had become the main coordinator of economic policy. But when Anderson became Chancellor of the Exchequer, in 1943, the Treasury's position started to rise again. The relation between the Lord President and the Chancellor of the Exchequer became one of the crucial problems of the future. Neither the government organization for economic policy nor the problem of the place of economists in government had found a definite solution. In the field of economic policy, as elsewhere, the war had complicated rather than simplified interdepartmental relations.

[31] Hancock–Gowing, p. 220; cf. Chester, *Machinery*, pp. 10–11; Robinson, p. 48.
[32] Ely Devons, *Planning in Practice—Essays on Aircraft Planning in Wartime*, (1950), reviewed by W. J. M. Mackenzie in *Public Administration*, XXIX (1951), 180.
[33] Scott–Hughes, pp. 499–501.

FIFTEEN

THE ORGANIZATION FOR ECONOMIC POLICY
AFTER 1945

From War to Reconstruction (1945–47)

More people—men and women from all walks of life—worked in British factories in 1945 than ever before. But precious machinery was worn out. A large part of the merchant navy had been sunk, and the greater part of overseas investments had been sold. The American Lend-Lease plan had saved the British effort from a financial breakdown during the latter part of the war. But in August 1945, only a few days after the Japanese surrender, the plan was suddenly and unexpectedly terminated. Britain's economic position was dangerous. To invest and to export became matters of life and death for a country that was dependent on imports even for its food. Demobilization and the changeover from war production to civilian production created vast administrative and economic problems. Many who remembered the bleak days after 1918 were full of fear and foreboding.

The experience of war had wrought a considerable change in prevailing views about economic policy, however. In the famous White Paper of 1944, the National Government had in effect publicly committed future governments, of whatever party, to full responsibility for "the maintenance of a high and stable level of employment" and "the production and equitable distribution of essential supplies," while guarding against inflation and balance-of-payment difficulties.[1] The government did not lack powers. War legislation had given it complete authority over the allocation of important raw materials. It controlled the locating of new industries. New investments needed its approval. Taxation and rationing enabled it to regulate both the level of general demand and the consumption of particular articles. It controlled imports and exports and laid down the lines of control over all financial transactions with non-residents of the sterling area. Through the practice of bulk-buying, the government itself had become the largest British trader. Nationalization was soon to bring such key industries and enterprises as the Bank of England, the mines, railways, airlines, and gas and electricity under government ownership. But great power also created great responsibility. "By 1945 over two-thirds of the

---

[1] Cmd. 6527 (1944).

national resources were directly employed for work for the government."[2] This situation made the smooth and correct functioning of the government machinery of even greater importance to British society than before.

As Lord President of the Council, Morrison inherited in 1945 the main coordinating tasks in economic policy.[3] He continued to be assisted by the staff of the Economic Section in the Cabinet Office. Cripps was appointed President of the Board of Trade, especially charged with increasing the efficiency of British industry and stimulating exports.[4] His main instruments were special working parties for individual branches of industry. They consisted of representatives of employers and employees together with a number of specialists, and had as terms of reference:

to examine and inquire into the various schemes and suggestions put forward for improvements of organization, production, and distribution methods and processes in the industry, and to report as to the steps which should be taken in the national interest to strengthen the industry and render it more stable and more capable of meeting competition in the home and foreign markets.[5]

The Treasury, under Dalton, also played a considerable role in economic policy through its control of the budget, its influence on the rate of interest, its control over borrowing money via a Capital Issues Committee, and its international financial policies. According to Morrison, however, it was "a matter of some doubt how far the Treasury was subject to the machinery of economic coordination."[6] At times between 1945 and 1947, the Lord President as the coordinator of domestic economic policy, the President of the Board of Trade as the stimulator of the export trade, and the Chancellor of the Exchequer as the minister responsible for the country's financial situation pursued conflicting policies. Apart from objective differences in tasks and views, personal rivalries between Morrison and Dalton may have worsened these divergencies.

Two ministers had acquired positions of prominence that they had not enjoyed before 1939: the Minister of Agriculture and Fisheries and the Minister of Labour. The responsibilities and political importance of the Minister of Agriculture had risen substantially since the government

---

[2] Robinson, p. 35.

[3] See especially Morrison, Chaps. 2, 3, and 13; Bridges, *Treasury Control,* p. 17ff; Anderson, *Economic Studies,* pp. 20–25; Smellie, pp. 304–6; Milne, pp. 406–21; Beer, pp. 66–106; Beloff, p. 34ff; Chester–Willson, pp. 108–22, 326–30; Chester, *Planning,* pp. 336–64; Chester, *International Social Science Bulletin,* pp. 217–28; Marris, pp. 759–83; Trend, pp. 239–52; and Morrison, *The Peaceful Revolution* (1949), Part I.

[4] Like his predecessor in Churchill's Caretaker Cabinet, Cripps was also Minister of Production. The Ministry of Production "had few friends and disappeared amidst the rival claims of at least three senior ministers—the Lord President, Chancellor of the Exchequer, and President of the Board of Trade—to be regarded as the major force in economic coordination" (Chester, *Planning,* pp. 340–41).

[5] 414 H. of C. Deb. (15 October 1945), cols. 693–94; *Life of Cripps,* pp. 336–37; Tivey–Rendel, pp. 133–37.

[6] Morrison, p. 308; *The Times,* 3 December 1947; *Life of Cripps,* pp. 356–57, 362–64. For the considerable independence Dalton had in framing his budgets, see Dalton, *Memoirs,* III, 24–25.

had committed itself to keeping up agricultural production in the British Isles by various supports. Labour's Minister of Agriculture, Tom Williams, also enjoyed high personal prestige. Bevin had raised the Ministry of Labour to great heights. It continued to occupy a key place even after his departure, because of the vital importance of manpower for total economic planning, the political and economic significance of employment policy, and the political weight of government consultations with both sides of industry. Even after he became Foreign Secretary, Bevin maintained a strong interest in labor: until 1947 he remained chairman of a Cabinet committee on manpower. His influence was such that for a time his successor, George Isaacs, was thought to be little but his shadow.[7]

Immediately below the various Cabinet committees were four high-level interdepartmental committees of civil servants, for manpower, raw materials, capital investments, and balance of payments, respectively. They were knit together by a steering committee composed of the permanent secretaries of the main economic departments under the chairmanship of the Permanent Secretary to the Treasury.[8] As in wartime, these committees had to measure the total needs of all sectors of the economy against the limited resources available. Ultimate priorities were determined by ministerial committees or by the Cabinet itself acting "as a kind of court of appeal."[9] It was felt that each industry should be represented in these final consultations by one department only. For this reason, the Ministry of Supply, for instance (which Attlee merged with the Ministry of Aircraft Production in 1945), was made the regular sponsoring department for engineering and heavy industry.[10]

The continuous interdepartmental struggle about priorities increased the desire of many departments to have their own economic and statistical services. Whether the recently established central statistical and economic sections of the Cabinet Office could compete with these centrifugal forces seemed somewhat doubtful, especially since many of their highly competent "temporaries" returned to the universities in 1945 and 1946. For this reason, the Permanent Secretary to the Treasury, Bridges, and others strongly resisted the proposal that these central services be transferred to the Treasury. They feared that this would put the central services under the heavy mortgage of anti-Treasury sentiment, which many of the economic departments continued to harbor. Such a transfer could therefore only augment the risk of a war of figures between the departments.[11] For somewhat similar reasons, however, others continued to press for a strong production general staff, which, directly under the political leaders and free from departmental pressures, would be responsible for over-all eco-

[7] G. G. Eastwood sought to dispel this impression in his *George Isaacs* (London, 1952).

[8] Chester, *Planning,* p. 341.

[9] Morrison, p. 301; cf. *Economic Survey for 1947,* Cmd. 7046, pp. 4–9.

[10] Chester–Willson, p. 108.

[11] Cf. *ibid.,* pp. 327, 329; Chester, *Machinery,* pp. 17–19.

nomic planning. The main ministerial coordinator, Morrison, rejected this proposal. Such an organization, he argued in the House of Commons in 1946, would have to become almost as large as the government itself, and would inevitably introduce endless friction with the existing departments.[12]

The Labour victory in 1945 had been greeted with great enthusiasm in the Labour ranks. "That first sensation, tingling and triumphant, was of a new society to be built," Dalton wrote, "and we had power to build. There was exhilaration among us, joy and hope, determination and confidence. We felt exalted, dedicated, walking on air, walking with destiny."[13] The elation lasted for some time. After a year, the Labour Government still looked back with satisfaction on its honeymoon in office.[14] The demobilization of men and industries, and their transition into a peacetime economy, had gone smoothly. Nationalization bills were making good progress. New social-insurance benefits could be financed, yet taxation lowered. For the time being, the big Dollar Loan from the United States, which Keynes had negotiated for Britain in 1946, relieved pressure on the balance of payments. Exports and investments rose quickly.

The Crises of 1946 and 1947 and Their Consequences

Satisfaction did not last long, however. Three serious crises destroyed the initial optimism during 1946 and 1947: the food crisis in 1946, which led to bread rationing; the fuel crisis, which paralyzed British industry for some time in early 1947; and the convertibility crisis of the summer of 1947, which once again confronted Britain with the full gravity of the balance-of-payments problem.

The fuel crisis in the winter of 1946–47, in particular, provoked a serious crisis in public confidence. It soon became known that warnings against likely fuel shortages had been of little avail against the buoyant obstinacy of the Minister of Fuel and Power, Shinwell.[15] If such a fundamental problem as fuel and power could not be handled properly, many asked, what likelihood was there that the Labour Government could plan the economy as a whole with any chance of success?[16] Immediate measures were required to restore confidence. Morrison was seriously ill at the time. Cripps announced a strengthening of the planning apparatus in the House of Commons on 10 March 1947.[17] Each department, said Cripps, had been ordered to institute a full-time planning staff under a senior officer. But at the same time, it was necessary to strengthen the interdepartmental planning arrangements. The government therefore proposed to appoint a Joint Planning Staff somewhat on the lines of the Joint War

[12] 419 H. of C. Deb. (28 February 1946), col. 2130.
[13] Dalton, *Memoirs,* III, 3.
[14] Chester (*Planning,* pp. 341–42) rightly points out that the word "planning" does not figure in the Index to Hansard in 1945 and 1946.
[15] Dalton, *Memoirs,* III, 203–5; but see also E. Shinwell, *The Labour Story* (London, 1963), pp. 182–84.
[16] Chester, *Planning,* pp. 343–44.
[17] 434 H. of C. Deb. (10 March 1947), cols. 969–71.

Production Staff of the Second World War. The main strength of this staff would be made up of departmental planning officers. But to ensure effective direction from the center, a full-time executive head of the inter-departmental staff would be appointed. Each departmental planning officer would have on his staff at least one officer whose duties were to be so arranged that, while he kept in contact with his own department, he could devote a considerable part of his time to the central work of the joint staff. In addition, the head of the planning staff would be assisted by "a small picked staff of persons with programming experience and a small secre-tariat." The new staff organization would deal with both the preparation of long-term plans and the day-to-day adjustment of existing plans to changing circumstances. "The arrangements," said Cripps, "are a de-velopment or evolution, and will be calculated to ensure strong direction from the center, where it is needed, without interference with departmental responsibilities."

Some weeks after Cripps's announcement, Attlee informed Parliament that Sir Edwin Plowden had been appointed Chief Planning Officer. The Chief Planning Officer, Attlee told the Commons, would work directly under the Lord President and would have access to all ministers concerned with production. But all decisions on planning policy would continue to be made by the Cabinet, not the Chief Planning Officer, and ministers would continue to be wholly responsible.[18]

Shortly afterwards two more bodies were established to strengthen liaison with the public. An Economic Information Unit was set up to coordinate and stimulate information on economic issues.[19] In addition, an Economic Planning Board was instituted "to advise His Majesty's Government on the best use of . . . economic resources, both towards the realization of a long-term plan and on remedial measures against . . . immediate difficulties." The members of this board were Plowden, who was Chairman (Morrison informed the Commons to ironic cheers that he himself might take the chair from time to time) ; three representatives of the Federation of British Industries and the British Employers Associa-tion ; three representatives of the Trade Unions Congress ; three members of the Central Economic Planning Staff ; the Permanent Secretaries to the Board of Trade, the Ministry of Labour, and the Ministry of Supply ; and the Director of the Economic Section of the Cabinet Office.[20] It was

[18] 435 H. of C. Deb. (27 March 1947), cols. 1412–13. Plowden's appointment caused some criticism. The Communist Piratin asked whether the new Chief Planning Officer really sympathized with socialist principles (435 H. of C. Deb. [1 April 1947] cols. 1831–32). A Conservative landholder demanded that besides an industrial planner, a high-level agricultural consultant should be appointed, to preserve the balance between agriculture and industry (435 H. of C. Deb. [3 April 1947], col. 2212).

[19] S. C. Leslie, "The Economic Information Unit," *Public Administration,* XXVIII (1950), 17–26.

[20] 439 H. of C. Deb. (7 July 1947), col. 1804. Morrison refused to include rep-resentatives of agriculture and also resisted pressure to admit special representatives of smaller enterprises, organized in the National Union of Manufacturers.

publicly announced that the purpose of these bodies was to promote contact and understanding between the government and private enterprise. Undoubtedly, they were also symbolic of the Government's desire to restore its greatly diminished prestige by "public information" and "consultation."[21]

But only a few months later, in August 1947, England faced a new crisis. Under the terms of the Dollar Loan of 1946, the Government had reluctantly agreed to restore free convertibility between the pound and the dollar after a year. Even before the end of this period, the import program from dollar areas was drastically curtailed. The introduction of convertibility, on 15 July 1947, nevertheless led to a fast drain on the dollar reserves, notably by third countries, including those who used their sterling balances to buy "Packards for Pashas." General revision of economic policy was inevitable. Food imports had to be cut further, domestic investments tempered, and exports increased. Even so, convertibility could not be maintained, and was abandoned on 21 August 1947.

The Labour Government's prestige suffered further from these happenings. It was now clear to all that it was impracticable to put financial policy under the Chancellor, domestic economic policy under the Lord President, and international economic policy under a Cabinet committee that had met under Attlee since early 1947. The Government seemed to fumble through sheer weariness (both Morrison and Bevin were seriously ill in 1947, and Dalton felt completely exhausted). "Self-confidence weakened, collectively and individually," and tempers within the Government ran high. Cripps in particular insisted that a fundamental political change was necessary. As early as April 1947 he had wished Bevin to return to the home front, and to take charge of planning and publicity. In August and September 1947 he went further, and wished to substitute Bevin for Attlee because under Attlee "there was no leadership, no grip, no decision," and Morrison "didn't understand what planning meant." As Prime Minister, Bevin should act as Minister of Production, while Cripps himself might be his Chief of Staff, and Attlee, perhaps, Chancellor of the Exchequer. Dalton was willing to join in a pilgrimage to face Attlee with an ultimatum, provided Morrison would cooperate. But the revolt failed because Bevin refused to take part in the conspiracy, and Morrison thought himself the better alternative Prime Minister. Cripps then intended to resign individually, but Attlee countered by proposing that Cripps himself take over a new post of Minister for Economic Affairs. Cripps accepted, and eventually Morrison, too, yielded and thus lost his coordinating tasks in economic policy.[22]

Unlike the wartime Minister of Production, said a public announcement on 29 September 1947, the new Minister for Economic Affairs would not have a special department at his disposal. Instead, he would have only a small office and, for the rest, would be assisted by the existing Central

[21] Cf. Chester, *Planning*, p. 345.
[22] Dalton, *Memoirs*, III, 236, 240–41, 245–47.

Economic Planning staff, the Economic Information Unit, and the Economic Section of the Cabinet Office. At the same time, the committee system was overhauled at Cabinet level. No longer would there be two committees operating side by side, one for international and the other for domestic economic policy. Instead, the committee system was to have two tiers. Attlee himself took the chair of a new Economic Policy Committee, which included all the more important ministers of the Labour Cabinet: Dalton (Chancellor of the Exchequer), Cripps (Minister for Economic Affairs), Bevin (Foreign Secretary), Morrison (Lord President), and Addison (Lord Privy Seal). Under this committee, which was to determine over-all policy, an executive Cabinet committee was organized, the so-called Production Committee. It met under Cripps and included all ministers who headed economic departments that had to turn general directives into concrete measures. These structural reforms were soon followed by changes in personnel. Older ministers with a political standing of their own, such as Shinwell, were replaced by younger men. In practice, coordination by Cabinet committee gave way, to quote Morrison, to "the direct economic administration by one leading economic minister (in addition to the necessary coordination through committees)."[23] Cripps "asked particularly that a group of younger men should be given an opportunity in the production ministries whose work he had to coordinate." Once a week Cripps dined with them: "Wilson of the Board of Trade, Strauss of Supply, Gaitskell of Fuel and Power, Douglas Jay, Economic Secretary to the Treasury, Marquand, the Paymaster-General, who [had] special economic duties, and perhaps one or two others . . . a round-table talk over dinner, a pooling of ideas . . . perhaps a little like a social evening with the headmaster."[24]

Immediately after Cripps's appointment, many observers wondered how far the new Minister for Economic Affairs would be able to carry through his will in matters of economic policy against the Chancellor of the Exchequer. Dalton promised full cooperation.[25] But the relations between the new Minister for Economic Affairs and the Treasury were inevitably delicate. "It seems clear," wrote the parliamentary correspondent of *The Times* on 30 September 1947, "that the Minister for Economic Affairs will not exercise supervision over Treasury policy. It will be necessary for the new Minister and the Chancellor of the Exchequer to work in close association so that economic and financial policy may march in step." A few weeks later, the problem was suddenly and unexpectedly solved. Dalton prematurely disclosed to a lobby correspondent a tax change he was about to propose in the House of Commons, and was forced to resign in November 1947.[26] Attlee appointed Cripps Chancellor. Cripps retained the general supervision of economic policy, taking the Central

[23] Morrison, p. 299.   [24] Williams, *Triple Challenge*, pp. 84–85.
[25] Dalton, *Memoirs*, III, 247.
[26] Milne, p. 411, speaks of "one of the most persuasive examples of chance in politics." For details, see Dalton, *Memoirs*, III, 276–86.

Economic Planning staff, the Economic Information Unit, and the Regional Boards for Industry with him to the Treasury.

For the first time, control over the import program, overseas finance, the investment program, national incomes policy, and the Budget was concentrated in one hand.[27] The task of the Chancellor became more comprehensive and of greater moment than ever before. His duties were intolerably heavy. An attempt was made to relieve him by strengthening ministerial personnel at the Treasury. In December 1947, an Economic Secretary to the Treasury was appointed next to the Financial Secretary. This position was further raised in status in 1950, when Gaitskell was appointed Minister of State for Economic Affairs. When Cripps's health deteriorated, Gaitskell acted practically as Deputy Chancellor of the Exchequer. So strong was his position that Attlee found it feasible to pass over various older claimants and appoint Gaitskell Chancellor of the Exchequer in October 1950, even though until that time Gaitskell had not even been a member of the Cabinet. Cripps had worked hard. He had been the symbol of austerity. His death seemed to many symbolic of the fatal pressure of modern government.

The Organization in the Later Years of the Labour Government

In the meantime, prosperity slowly returned. The worst shortages were overcome. Reconstruction went ahead with the aid of the Marshall Plan. As the pattern of consumption widened, economic policy developed more and more from a system of direct control to one of a more global control of imports, investments, and the over-all level of consumption. The road was difficult. In 1949, the pound was devalued. In 1950, Korea again caused serious strains on the balance of payments, as well as difficulties in the supply of raw materials. Strict controls were reimposed over basic raw materials; in 1951 a separate Ministry of Materials (placed initially under the Lord Privy Seal, R. R. Stokes) was established to administer these controls. But the trend continued toward a freer economy.

The new developments had a considerable impact on the machinery for economic policy. The Central Economic Planning staff did not develop at all along the lines Cripps had so persuasively sketched in the House of Commons in March 1947. He had suggested that the Planning Staff would bring about a new form of coordination in which both central guidance and departmental experience would be utilized to the full. In practice, the Planning Staff became little but a division of the Treasury. Its main task was to scrutinize the possible consequences of specific departmental plans for the economy as a whole. But the number of officials who served in it was small, and they had rarely had specific economic training. The Planning Staff could of course avail itself of the advice of the Economic and Statistical Sections of the Cabinet Office, which included a number of well-

[27] Bridges, *Treasury Control,* p. 19; *Life of Cripps,* pp. 363–65.

trained economic experts. But neither the Planning Staff nor the Economic Section developed into a truly directive organ. The Economic Section advised, and the Central Economic Planning Staff studied and tried to harmonize and coordinate. Both "planners" and economists served on numerous interdepartmental committees and often acted as their chairmen or secretaries. As Treasury officials they had influence. They advised and warned but did not take decisions and might not be supported by ministers in the face of conflicting political and financial considerations adduced by other divisions of the Treasury or other departments.

The Economic Planning Board declined in importance in similar fashion and became an advisory agency rather than a planning instrument. It was consulted *ad hoc*, and increasingly *post hoc*. It came to meet less often, and even saw its official duties curtailed in 1950. The references "towards the realization of long-term plans" and "remedial measures against . . . immediate difficulties" were deleted, and its new function described as simply "to advise His Majesty's Government on the best use of . . . economic resources."[28] Henceforth, the Economic Surveys were to speak of "trends" rather than "targets," "programs," or "plans."[29]

During the latter part of the Labour Government, in other words, economic planning had a short-term orientation. Planning was neither continuous nor detailed, except in specific sectors. It was remedial rather than forward-looking. Ministers intervened, if politically necessary, when developments seemed to get out of hand. But if at all possible, "a habit of discussion and a disposition to seek agreement" took precedence over considerations of long-term targets and programs.[30] The once optimistic belief in over-all planning receded before the realities of administration. In Chester's words, "Perhaps the revulsion . . . against the wide range of governmental control of and interference in any manner of economic and social affairs was helped by the tiredness of those called upon to administer the vast machine."[31]

The Conservative Reaction after 1951

Churchill returned to office definitely intending to clip the Treasury's wings. The explanation of this attitude must be based on various factors. His period at the Treasury, between 1925 and 1929, probably was one of the least satisfactory in his many-faceted life (it is the only one he has never fully described in any of his autobiographical writings). At various crucial periods he had suffered under the niggardly attitude the Treasury commonly showed towards defense expenditures. (It also did so, one must add, under Churchill himself, but then his foot was in the other camp, and international politics were relatively peaceful.) The Treasury's rise to a new position of dominance after 1947 must have seemed to Churchill a

28 Tivey–Rendel, p. 137.   29 Milne, p. 407.
30 Trend, pp. 241–42; cf. Milne, p. 410; Beer, pp. 80–81; Marris, pp. 778–79.
31 Chester, *Trends*, pp. 19–20.

manifestation of socialist (or Crippsian) nonsense. It is unlikely, more-over, that he wished Butler (who became Chancellor of the Exchequer in 1951) to inherit any political claims from Cripps's position.

Whatever the motives, there is no doubt that by various expedients Churchill sought to restrain the influence of the Treasury. In vain he tried to persuade Anderson to become the Overlord of the Treasury, the Board of Trade, and the Ministry of Supply. Then he invited Salter to become Minister for Economic Affairs, but Salter thought it unwise to accept the position, which in his view could never be sufficiently powerful against the Treasury.[32] Various coordinating duties in the economic field were then delegated to the other Overlords. Cherwell, too, regained much of the strong position he had had during the war. With the aid of his war-time assistant, MacDougall, who had returned with him to official duty, he succeeded in persuading Churchill and the Cabinet to stop convertibility, on which the Treasury and the City had set their minds in 1952. A power-ful committee of senior ministers was formed to hedge further about the position of the Chancellor of the Exchequer.[33] Churchill also disliked the system of two-tier committees with identical terms of reference, on the ministerial level and on the civil service level, through which the Labour Government had been wont to operate. For a time he even attempted to do away with the existing structure of official committees altogether, and to substitute purely ministerial control of business.[34]

But Churchill's reforms eventually proved to be little but a passing phase. Official committees soon came into their own again. The Over-lords experiment failed, and Butler regained a considerable part of the coordinating powers that the Chancellor had exercised since 1947. Apart from personal and political factors, economic policy itself played a strong role in this. The Conservative Government quickly abolished many of the remaining controls. This could only increase the importance of monetary weapons for central economic policy, which, in turn, could only bolster the position of the Treasury against other departments. An external symptom of this new development was the transfer of the Economic Section from the Cabinet Office to the Treasury in 1953. Apparently, the Treasury's position as an "interdepartmental department" was thought to be suffi-ciently consolidated to allow it to make the transfer without the objections that had been raised in 1945. For a long time, the Treasury, the Cabinet Office, and the Ministry of Defence had shared the same premises in Great George Street. Gaitskell had spoken without contradiction of the "econo-mists in the Treasury" in 1951.[35] Perhaps the actual changes were not so great, after all?

During most of the 1950's, economic development seemed to offer a rosy picture in Britain. Incomes rose, and goods of all kinds came to fill British shops and homes. Butler held out the happy vista of doubled

[32] Salter, *Memoirs*, p. 339.   [33] Woolton, *Memoirs*, pp. 371–75.
[34] Beloff, pp. 26–27.
[35] 494 H. of C. Deb. (21 November 1951), col. 440.

living standards within twenty-five years. Prosperity brought powerful electoral support to the Conservative Party and tended to silence criticism about the machinery for economic policy, or at least to reduce it to a purely theoretical exercise. Economists and some students of public administration might engage in a post mortem about wartime planning experiences or dispute the economic policies of the immediate postwar era. They might differ in their appreciation of the contemporary scene and prescribe varied remedies for the future. But on the whole there was little urgency behind these discussions. Monetary weapons seemed to be able to achieve all that was necessary. And what other department could handle these weapons but the Treasury?

The Treasury Burden

If there was satisfaction about concentrating both economic and financial responsibilities in one hand, there was less agreement about whether this accumulation of duties was becoming excessive for the men most directly concerned, i.e., the Chancellor of the Exchequer and his senior officials. The number of interdepartmental committees on which they were expected to sit was oppressive, and this difficulty was compounded by the growing impact and number of international organizations.[36] Of even greater weight was the psychological burden of responsibility. During the entire period, the balance-of-payments problem "obtruded continuously; exasperating, monotonous, and inescapable."[37] There was continuous inflation, which a number of sophisticated measures were unable to control. The very technicality of such measures did little to improve the response of the population, or even of most other ministers in the Cabinet. At the same time, the spending proclivities of departmental ministers did not abate. Increasingly, the Chancellor became a somewhat lonely figure in the Cabinet.[38] Butler resigned his post in 1955, partly for personal reasons, and partly because he was physically exhausted. Macmillan spent only a relatively short period at the Treasury before being elevated to the Prime Ministership. But of the three Chancellors since 1957, one (Thorneycroft) resigned in 1958 in the face of inadequate Cabinet support for his wish to keep expenditures down to a predetermined level, and another (Lloyd) was dismissed in 1962, without even the compensation of the Woolsack that he had coveted.

In the light of such powerful political factors, certain adjustments at the top of the Treasury could be little but palliatives. After 1951, Salter acted for a short while as Minister of State for Economic Affairs under the Chancellor of the Exchequer. Both the Financial and the Economic Secretaryships to the Treasury continued to be posts of considerable importance over the period. But their status was not high enough to basically relieve the Chancellor of any but detailed administrative and parliamentary

---

[36] A special section on this subject in the Dutch edition of this book has been left out, in view of Professor Beloff's much fuller treatment in his *New Dimensions of Foreign Policy* (1961).

[37] Eden, *Full Circle,* p. 276.   [38] Heasman, p. 468.

duties. Various ingenious proposals were elaborated to relieve the Chancellor further. Sir Geoffrey Crowther, former Editor of *The Economist,* proposed, for instance, to sever the Prime Ministership from the post of the First Lord of the Treasury, and to appoint to the latter a senior minister in charge of economic policy; under him the Chancellor of the Exchequer would remain in charge of financial policies of a more detailed and technical nature.[39] Other observers continued to plead for the appointment of a separate Minister for Economic Affairs, but they did so somewhat hesitantly because they were well aware of the crucial problems that were bound to arise between such a minister and the Chancellor of the Exchequer.[40]

Various ministers were at one time charged informally to lend a helping hand to the Chancellor of the Exchequer; in 1958, for instance, Maudling (then Paymaster-General) was charged to assist the Chancellor over a wide range of duties in the economic field. In 1961 ministerial aid to the Chancellor was further formalized. According to an official announcement of 9 October 1961, the Prime Minister, "after discussion with the Chancellor of the Exchequer, [had] agreed that the Chancellor should have the assistance in the Treasury of a senior Cabinet minister." The Chancellor would keep full responsibility for the Budget and also continue to deal with the administration of the revenue departments. A Chief Secretary to the Treasury and Paymaster-General "should, under the general direction of the Chancellor, deal with the whole range of public expenditure, both current and prospective, including the scrutiny of departmental estimates and the framing of forward surveys." The new minister was to be in the Cabinet. According to one official publication, it was "understood that departmental ministers will not in general be able to 'appeal' to the Chancellor about a decision made by the Chief Secretary."[41]

Much must in practice depend on personalities. The first Chief Secretary was a former Minister of Housing, Henry Brooke, who occupied a high place in the ministerial hierarchy; he was appointed Home Secretary during the Cabinet reshuffle of July 1962. His successor, on the other hand, was a new entrant to the Cabinet who previously had served a term of unparalleled length at the Ministry of Pensions and National Insurance.

A strengthening of personnel was also attempted at the level of officials. In 1953, the Permanent Secretary to the Treasury was given a deputy, who, in addition to his other duties, was in charge of the Central Economic Planning Staff. "Still too much has been concentrated in the State, to which I must say—and I alone—'Yes' or 'No,' " Bridges said, however.[42]

[39] For a slightly different proposal with the same intentions, see *The Economist,* 27 April 1957.

[40] Morrison, p. 308; Chester, *Machinery,* p. 19; Chester, *Planning,* pp. 351–53, 363–64; Chester, *Treasury,* p. 20; Chester, *International Social Science Bulletin,* pp. 225–26.

[41] United Kingdom Information Service, *Economic Record* (Toronto), November 1961, p. 2 (quoted by Heasman, p. 477).

[42] As reported by Herman Finer in a review of Beer's *Treasury Control,* in *American Political Science Review,* LI (1957), 523.

When Bridges retired in 1956, it was decided to appoint two Joint Permanent Secretaries. The official announcement of 20 July 1956 read:

Sir Roger Makins will have charge of the financial and economic work of the Treasury and will be responsible wholly to the Chancellor of the Exchequer, Sir Norman Brook, in addition to his duties as Secretary of the Cabinet, will take charge of all other Treasury work, including that which falls within the responsibility of the Prime Minister in his capacity as First Lord of the Treasury. He will be the official head of the Home Civil Service.

Some commentators attached considerable importance to these appointments. *The Economist*, for instance, interpreted them as clearly a "shift from No. 11 to No. 10" in the making of economic policy and civil service control.[43] Personal factors seemed equally important, however.[44] Sir Norman Brook had been appointed Chief Planning Officer and Deputy Permanent Secretary of the Treasury in 1951. But at Churchill's request he had stayed on as Secretary of the Cabinet. When Bridges finally retired in 1956, Brook was willing to remain Secretary of the Cabinet as well as Permanent Secretary to the Treasury. The appointment of another Joint Permanent Secretary, wholly available for financial and economic matters, was therefore indicated.

In 1960, Makins was replaced by Sir Frank Lee. Only two years later, health reasons forced Sir Frank to give up his post and accept the appointment of Master of Corpus Christi College, Cambridge. His premature retirement (he was only 58) occasioned new concern about the heaviness of the burden on the Permanent Secretaries to the Treasury. At the same time, more stress was being laid on the importance of management services and long-term planning of government expenditures; this increased the duties of the Treasury and shifted the prevailing accent of Treasury policies. In July 1962, it was decided to appoint three new officials to succeed Brook and Lee. The Secretaryship of the Cabinet again became a full-time job; Sir Burke Trend, who had been Deputy Secretary, was appointed to the post. A new Joint Permanent Secretary to the Treasury was appointed to manage the public service, and at the same time another Joint Permanent Secretary was put in charge of the financial and economic work of the Treasury. Ultimately, such reforms could relieve the Chancellor's personal burden only slightly. *The Times* sadly commented when the appointments were announced: "In administration, men and methods go hand in hand. Good men can make a bad system work. The best organization in the world cannot in the long run save inadequate men."[45]

The Place of Professional Economists in Government

The role of professional economists in the British civil service tended to be very modest in the 1950's. The number of top-ranking economists

[43] *The Economist,* 28 July 1956.   [44] Cf. Chester, *Treasury,* pp. 18–23.
[45] *The Times,* 30 July 1962.

available in Britain was small by any reckoning, and the respective amenities of employment in the civil service and the universities were heavily
in favor of the latter. Methods of recruitment and promotion in the administrative class of the civil service were dominated by the traditional preference for the gentleman-amateur, which was hardly conducive to an increase
of the number of government economists. Even in 1962, the Economic
Section counted, according to the Imperial Calendar, no more than the
Economic Adviser, a Deputy, one senior Adviser, five economic advisers,
and seven economic assistants. Outside the Economic Section, there were
practically no professional economists serving in any branch of the
administration.

The Economic Adviser was undoubtedly a member of the policy-
making group in the Treasury. But his position with respect to other
sections of the Treasury was not very strong, and his influence was limited
by traditional civil service insistence on regular lines of responsibility and
outward unanimity. Sir Robert Hall, who had been Director of the Eco-
omic Section since 1947 and Economic Adviser to H. M. Government
since 1953, was highly conscious of the need of economic experts to work
"in an administrative setting." In a public lecture in 1955, he argued that
"there should be a fairly intimate connection between those who formulate
and administer economic policy and those who are advising on the technical aspects of it. Thus it is advantageous if some administrators have had
an economic training and that economists should have some experience of
administration."[46] He felt that economists often could not obtain administrative experience, because they tended to think too abstractly and were
inclined to generalize on inadequate data. Hall's deputy between 1953
and 1955, I. M. D. Little, was on the other hand "sometimes shocked by
the naïve sureness with which very questionable bits of economic analysis
were advanced in Whitehall." Little granted that "economists may be too
academic . . . they may not appreciate administrative difficulties, or may
lack a sense of political possibility. But then, there is no danger of these
things being overlooked."[47]

The Retreat from Complacency

Toward the latter part of the 1950's, concern about economic policy
and the possible inadequacy of its available instruments revived and spread
more widely. Three factors were chiefly responsible for this: a sense of
defeat in the face of continuing inflation; a growing interest in long-term
planning in private industry, nationalized industry, and government in
general; and comparisons with foreign countries.

Throughout the 1940's and 1950's, the rise of personal incomes in
Britain greatly exceeded the rise of national productivity, causing a considerable rise in the price level and a steady threat to the ever-sensitive

[46] Hall, p. 126; cf. Beloff, pp. 172–73.   [47] Little, p. 36; Marris, pp. 780–83.

balance of payments. The persistent pressure for higher wages made the place of the trade unions a burning political issue, no less serious because it was especially difficult for a Conservative Government to grapple with it. Once more, but in very different fashion from 1940, the post of Minister of Labour became a focus of considerable weight. The Government stressed the need for continuous consultation with the Trade Union Movement; but such contacts were complicated by political distrust and by the inability of the Trades Union Congress (T.U.C.) to develop much strength against the particularist interests in its midst. Various expedients were tried to enhance the element of national economic policy considerations in the operation of specific industrial contracts. The government sought to manipulate the wages of its own employees as a means of restraining private employers from being too ready to grant wage increases. But the vista of a continuing boom and the threat (actual or potential) of strikes blunted the concept of a "guiding light" in the nationalized undertakings as much as in private industry. Independent courts of inquiry and arbitration tribunals were not very effective, since such bodies could do little but seek the golden mean between what the unions asked and what the employers offered, rather than make decisions based on the rise of productivity in the industry concerned or on government policy as a whole.

In 1957, the Government decided to establish an independent Council on Prices, Productivity, and Incomes. Staffed by three high-ranking experts, this Council was charged with reporting annually on the level of prices and wages and developments in labor productivity. Its reports were to be binding on no one, but it was hoped that they would prepare public opinion for possible anti-inflationary measures, and have a moderating effect on the distribution of profits and the raising of wages.[48] The quality of the reports of the "Three Wise Men" proved greater than their practical influence.

Consequently, the British economy remained in a rather unstable and nervous state, necessitating an assortment of highly intricate measures to preserve the value of the pound and to prevent inflation from running wild. In the long run, this proved upsetting to both private and nationalized industries. Such large industries as iron, steel, and chemicals felt frustrated in their own long-term planning because of the constant "stop-and-go" policies of the government. The word "planning," which for a decade or more had tended to be a dirty word to Conservatives, paradoxically came to be upgraded by such bodies as the Federation of British Industries. The need to take long-term views was also expressed in government circles. In particular, a report from the Select Committee on Estimates, *Treasury Control of Expenditure* (July 1958), followed by a report of the (Plowden) Committee, *Control of Public Expenditure* (1961) did much to focus attention on the potentially wasteful effect of

[48] Cf. *The Economist,* 2 November 1957.

piecemeal decisions on the long-run development of important government services.[49] There was a definite retreat from the view that the government should seek to use its own expenditure policies for anti-recession purposes. In a series of carefully argued White Papers, it was admitted that such policies might be applicable in case of a large-scale recession, but that they could not be used effectively for marginal adjustments during a period of full employment.[50] In particular, the investments of the nationalized industries could not be accelerated or retarded on short notice without causing considerable harm and financial waste to the industries concerned. A concern with "the forward looks" into government expenditures came to replace, or at least to be equal to, the traditionally short-term orientation of Treasury policies.

As an outward sign of these new concerns, the internal organization of the Treasury was recast in July 1962, when two new Permanent Secretaries were appointed. Three new groups were established within the general division of financial and economic policy. One was concerned with financial and monetary policy, another with resources and expenditure, and a third with "the balance of the national economy as a whole, dealing with short-term economic trends, long-term reviews of resources, problems of economic growth, and incomes policy." According to the official announcement, the third group would

comprise divisions in which economists from the economic section, under the professional supervision of the Economic Adviser, will work together with administrators in an integrated staff. As a central part of the organization it will provide services for the other two main groups, and it will work closely under the direction of the permanent secretary in charge of the financial and economic work of the Treasury.[51]

But perhaps the most decisive factor of all was the malaise caused by statistics comparing the economic growth of the Common Market countries and Britain. It was mortifying to find that the British economy lagged far behind that of most countries in Western Europe. What had hitherto been mainly a question for professional experts suddenly became a national issue of explosive importance, threatening the self-esteem of every Briton and eroding the prestige of the Government in power. Both the issue of joining or not joining the Common Market and attempts to diagnose and remedy British economic illnesses became a matter of popular debate, carried on in the Press, the pubs, the clubs, the colleges, and private homes. Delegations composed of businessmen, Members of Parlia-

---

[49] Cmnd. 1432 (1961) ; see also Ursula Hicks, "Plowden, Planning and Management in the Public Service," *Public Administration*, XXXIX (1961), 300–302.

[50] *Public Investment in Great Britain*, Cmnd. 1203 (1960), paras. 5–10; *The Financial and Economic Obligations of the Nationalized Industries*, Cmnd. 1337 (1961), paras. 24–28; *Control of Public Expenditure*, Cmnd. 1432 (1961), para. 13ff.

[51] *The Times*, 30 July 1962. See also D. N. Chester, "The Treasury, 1962," *Public Administration*, XL (1962), 419–26, and the series of articles on the Plowden Report in the same journal, XLI (1963), 1–50.

ment, civil servants, and journalists traveled to the Continent, and particularly to France, to probe the secret of Government organization for long-term economic growth.[52] This eventually resulted in the fashioning of new machinery for economic development.

The Establishment of the National Economic Development Council and of the National Incomes Commission

The first sign of things to come appeared in a Commons debate on economic policy on 25 and 26 July 1961. In a somewhat groping statement, the Chancellor of the Exchequer said on 26 July:

At the moment, we have these various bodies whose function is to take stock of the present situation, to comment on what is happening, on what has happened, and to advise. These bodies do very valuable work within their terms of reference. I say frankly to the House that I want something more purposeful than that. I envisage a joint examination of the economic prospects of the country stretching five or more years into the future. It would cover the growth of national production and distribution of our resources between the main uses, consumption, Government expenditure, investment, and so on. Above all, it would try to establish what are the essential conditions for realizing potential growth. That covers, first, the supply of labor and capital, secondly, the balance-of-payments conditions and the development of imports and exports, and, thirdly, the growth of incomes.[53]

Lloyd invited both sides of industry to separate meetings with him on 22 and 23 August 1961. According to contemporary reports, he gave them a choice of two rather distinct proposals:

(1) an independent planning body which would make economic forecasts and projections, entirely free of Government control. . . .

(2) A two-tier tripartite body. The top tier would consist of a council of employers' representatives, trade union leaders, representatives of nationalized industries, and possibly some outsiders; it would be presided over by the Chancellor, and would be responsible through him to Parliament. The lower tier would consist of an "office" which would be semi-independent of the Government and staffed by experts. Its task would be to provide the council with collated information.[54]

The employers' representatives greatly preferred the second alternative, and the Chancellor decided accordingly, formalizing his proposal in a letter of 23 September 1961 to the employers' and workers' organizations. Various other interest groups such as farmers, consumers, white-collar workers, and professional and public-service organizations pressed in vain for inclusion in the new council, officially baptized National Economic

---

[52] Cf. P.E.P. "Economic Planning in France," *Planning*, 27, No. 454 (1961), 207–37.

[53] 645 H. of C. Deb. (26 July 1961), col. 439.   [54] Keesing, p. 18330.

Development Council, but soon popularly known as "Neddy."[55] The T.U.C. General Council, on the other hand, remained skeptical and suspicious, because it regarded the new body as yet another attempt by the Government to sell a policy of wage restraint. The Chancellor had to soft-pedal the role of the N.E.D.C. in incomes policy. Even so, when the T.U.C. General Council finally agreed, by a vote of 21 to 8, to join, it did so only after making a number of explicit reservations. In a letter to the Chancellor, the T.U.C. stressed the right of the N.E.D.C. to initiate discussions and make recommendations on any subject. It re-emphasized that it attached great importance to the right of the delegates to the N.E.D.C. to report to their organizations, and that it would not regard association with the new Council as debarring those organizations from expressing in public such reservations as they might have about government decisions on economic policy.[56]

In December 1961, even before the T.U.C. had agreed to cooperate, the Government appointed Sir Robert Shone Director-General of the new organization.[57] As an executive member of the Iron and Steel Board, he had long been an articulate advocate of the need for long-term planning. In February 1962, the Government designated ten other members of the new Council.[58] It included six representatives of the employers' organizations, publicly hailed as representative of the younger, more forward-looking kind of British managers;[59] two representatives of the nationalized industries, one of whom had formerly been associated with the Labour Movement, and another who had played a prominent role in private enterprise; and two members who were authorities in their own right, Sir Oliver (soon Lord) Franks and Professor H. Phelps Brown, who had been one of the Three Wise Men. They were joined soon afterwards by six members delegated by the Trade Union Movement. Both the Economic Planning Board and the Council on Prices, Productivity, and Incomes lapsed.

Below the Council was formed an expert staff, composed of a section of professional economists headed by MacDougall and a section of industrialists. Recruitment did not run smoothly: in the early summer of 1962, one could meet many economists in Britain "going to work for Neddy." But very few of them did so full-time or without the safe backing of a leave of absence from another post. Staffing of the industrial side also seemed to meet with obstacles.

On 7 March 1962, the Council met for the first time. The Chancellor warned that the new body was not a panacea, "the cure-all for our eco-

---

[55] This is evident from questions in the House of Commons on 27 February; 1, 12, and 13 March; 3 and 19 April; and 24 May 1962.
[56] Letter from the T.U.C. General Council to the Chancellor of the Exchequer, 24 February 1962.
[57] 651 H. of C. Deb. (18 December 1961), col. 981.
[58] 653 H. of C. Deb. (8 February 1962), reply to a written question, col. 88.
[59] Cf. *Financial Times,* 6 March 1962.

nomic troubles and diseases." But he hoped that it would be "more than a façade of cooperation, a form of window-dressing." He then defined the tasks of the Council as follows:

(a) To examine the economic performance of the nation with particular concern for plans for the future in both the private and the public sectors of industry.

(b) To consider together what are the obstacles to quicker growth, what can be done to improve efficiency, and whether the best use is being made of our resources.

(c) To seek agreement upon ways of improving economic performance, competitive power, and efficiency; in other words, to increase the rate of sound growth.[60]

In his statement, Lloyd strongly emphasized that he "would not seek to exclude any subject from our discussion," nor "arrogate to ministers the right to fix the agenda." But a subject that had been a main point in Lloyd's statement in Commons on 26 July 1961 was conspicuously absent in the terms of reference—i.e., "the growth of incomes." One commentator spoke scathingly of "another example of *Hamlet* with a missing Prince."[61]

The Government sought to divert some of the criticism. On 26 July 1962, Macmillan informed the House of Commons that the Government intended to establish a National Incomes Commission (popularly called "Nicky," as a companion to Neddy.)[62] The proposal was elaborated in a White Paper of 5 November 1962. For the time being, the Commission was to consist of two full-time members and two part-time members, charged with the following terms of reference:

(1) The parties immediately concerned may refer to the Commission for inquiry any current claim or specific question relating to pay or other conditions of service or employment.

(2) The Government may refer to the Commission for review any matters relating to pay or other conditions of service or employment where the cost is met in whole or in part from the Exchequer. [The White Paper made clear that this did not include the nationalized industries, or any specific current claims that could be referred to arbitration.]

(3) The Government may refer to the Commission for retrospective examination any particular settlement relating to pay or other conditions of service or employment [other than an award at arbitration].

[60] N.E.D.C. information sheet, n. d.
[61] Graham Hutton, "Evolution or Revolution," *National Provincial Bank Review*, No. 58 (May 1962), 8.
[62] 663 H. of C. Deb. (26 July 1962), cols. 1759–63. Lovers of horoscopes might wish to note that the birth of Nicky was announced exactly one year after the first intimation of the future arrival of Neddy. They will find equal significance in the fact that the first conversations about Neddy between the Chancellor and the two sides of industry (on 22 and 23 August 1961) were held on the thirtieth anniversary of the debacle of MacDonald's Labour Government, which, if anything, had excelled in improvising machinery for economic policy.

The Commission was empowered to take evidence from the parties concerned, from any other parties that appeared "to have a substantial interest in the issues arising, or from or on behalf of the Government." In considering its cases, the Commission was "required to have regard both to the circumstances of the case concerned and to the national interest." Apart from its inquiries into wage settlement, the Commission was also instructed to report from time to time on the need for the Government to honor its pledge that "if any undue growth in the aggregate of profits should result from restraint in earned incomes, that growth would itself be restrained by fiscal or other appropriate means."[63] But the new Commission was not given the power to set aside wage agreements. Its only effect could be through public opinion or further government action. In December 1962, the Government referred its first case to the new Commission.

Some Problems Inherent in the New Arrangements

At the time this book was completed, the N.I.C. had not, and the N.E.D.C. had hardly begun to work. Most observers had refrained from comment, suspending judgment, though showing signs of skepticism.[64] The following problems might be mentioned as warranting a somewhat pessimistic outlook.

One complication is, undoubtedly, the somewhat anomalous position of the Chancellor of the Exchequer. Under the new arrangement, he is both the minister responsible for economic policy, and, as chairman of the N.E.D.C., the leading member of a high-powered advisory body to himself. No difficulties need occur on that score if prevailing opinions in the Treasury and the new Council are virtually identical. Things will run equally smoothly as long as the N.E.D.C. is willing to function mainly as a passive sounding-board for the Chancellor in power. Neither assumption seems realistic, however. The aggregate weight of the membership of the N.E.D.C., the quality of its expert staff, and its deliberate orientation towards long-term growth are liable to make for divergent views. The N.E.D.C. was founded in an atmosphere of widespread skepticism about Treasury policies. It was deliberately placed outside the regular bureaucracy to allow non-official groups and persons a share in framing as-yet-undefined new policies, which, at any rate, should be different from the present ones. Conflicts are therefore likely to arise between the advice given by the N.E.D.C. and that given by the regular Treasury staff. If so, what is to be the place of the Chancellor? Is he, as chairman of the N.E.D.C., to be given a brief by the Treasury staff? Will he seek to steer the deliberations of the Council only into channels that are congenial to him and to the Treasury? In case Neddy wishes to report in a direction

---

[63] Treasury Press Release, 5 November 1962.
[64] See Hutton, *op. cit.*, and Michael Shanks, "What Future for 'Neddy,'" *Political Quarterly*, XXXIII (1962), 348–59.

antagonistic to existing government policies, are its views to be made public? According to an official statement in the House of Commons on 13 February 1962, the decision about this would rest with the Council itself. But would the Chancellor, as chairman, allow himself to be over-ruled in case the Council (or perhaps only its majority) wished to issue a report that was damaging to himself, or to the Government generally, or wished to advise measures he could not accept because of political considerations? Conversely, is not the N.E.D.C.'s advice likely to be greeted with profound skepticism in Whitehall? Will not government departments reiterate the traditional complaint that advice is easy to give if not joined to actual responsibility for execution? Will not the very aloofness of the new Council, placed in an exalted position, frustrate both the practicability and the acceptability of its recommendations?

A second complication results from the somewhat uncertain position of the staff of the N.E.D.C. According to Lloyd's official letter of invitation on 23 September 1961:

This staff, which would work under a Director to be appointed from outside the civil service, although under the aegis of the Government, would not be part of the ordinary Government machine. It would act under the general direction of, and be responsible to, the Council.[65]

The Council (and presumably its staff) has the right to initiate any discussion or investigation. But it has no executive duties, and its staff is not directly represented in interdepartmental committees. To facilitate the work of the N.E.D.C., departments have appointed special liaison officers. N.E.D.C. officials are bound by the Official Secrets Act. But they are dependent to a considerable extent on whatever information the departments give them. Short-term departmental interests may well result in damaging selectivity here and there.

A third difficulty springs from the specific place of professional economists in the organization. It has apparently been the intention to recruit a considerable number of economists for the N.E.D.C. staff. It is therefore not unlikely that the Council alone will employ more high-class economists than the government as a whole. They are headed, moreover, by MacDougall, who proved an artist in personal influence both in World War II and in the early 1950's.[66] (A cynic might even find some significance in the fact that Sir Donald always seems to be returning to government service when there is a definite disenchantment with the role of the Treasury in economic policies, as was the case in 1940 and in 1951.) The Treasury is not likely to look favorably on any sign of the (presumably highly competent) N.E.D.C. staff's becoming an effective alternative source of economic advice. Possibly in an attempt to counter this threat, the Treasury seems to be showing somewhat more respect for its own professional economists; as we saw, they were singled out for special mention

[65] Treasury Press Release, 23 September 1961.
[66] See especially Harrod, *The Prof,* pp. 181ff, 197–99.

in the public announcement when the Treasury was reorganized in July 1962. If this means that the economic experts will have greater influence, it offers no guarantee for greater unanimity among the experts themselves, or about economic policies, whether in a short-term or a long-term perspective.

A fourth point concerns the relations between the N.E.D.C. and the N.I.C. The N.I.C. is primarily an extension of existing wage-fixing and arbitration machinery; in addition, it is an instrument designed to make the Government's policy of wage restraint more appealing to the public. Its establishment may have helped to reconcile the trade unions to the "lesser" evil of the N.E.D.C. But as the Conservative Government correctly argued when it set up Neddy, incomes policy is of decisive importance to economic growth. Either Neddy will succeed in getting the policy under its purview, or it will be precluded from considering the issue. If Neddy obtains control, there will be little for Nicky to do, at least in the area of general economic policy. And if Neddy does not obtain control, it is difficult to see how Nicky could effectively grapple with an issue that its more powerful brother could not even tackle. Both organs, moreover, can do little in themselves to solve the underlying problems of British industry—old-fashioned management and outdated commercial and labor-relations policies.

Finally, both Neddy and Nicky lack teeth. For all the new appeal of "planning," neither the Conservative Government nor private enterprise is prepared to adopt or reimpose new economic controls. But economic growth cannot be produced solely by expert calculations or monthly meetings of leading industrial representatives, no matter how indicative or persuasive they may be.[67] It demands appropriate action by the government and private economic agents. The establishment of the N.E.D.C. was unmistakably, a political step. It was caused by the Government's wish "to do something" (or at least to appear to do something) about economic growth. It was intended to take economic policies out of politics, as seemed to have been achieved so successfully in France. As Macmillan said in a speech in Leicester on 5 March 1962, "It could help us to get rid of what has been for far too long one of our biggest hindrances: the idea of 'the two sides' in industry. All this talk of 'us' and 'them.' I prefer the slogan of 'working together.' "

Such views were hardly agreeable to the Labour Party and the Trade Union Movement, which first attempted to keep incomes policy out of the N.E.D.C., and then virtually sought to cold-shoulder the N.I.C.[68] A

[67] The new Chancellor of the Exchequer, Maudling, said during the Conservative Party Conference at Llandudno on 10 October 1962: "Inflation is always with us. It is an endemic disease of democracy." And after expressing his gladness that no one at the Conference had demanded that the National Incomes Commission be given the power to determine wages, he said: "Our solution is based on the pressure of public opinion in a responsible democracy" (*The Times*, 11 October 1962).

[68] Cf. 648 H. of C. Deb. (7 November 1961), cols. 804–932, 651 H. of C. Deb. (18 December 1961), cols. 955–1074, and Michael Foot's column in the *Daily Herald*, 6 March 1962.

further deterioration of the economic situation by the end of 1962 seemed to drive home the point that even attractive machinery is no substitute for a satisfactory economic policy. The real test of Neddy and Nicky is therefore yet to come. Perhaps they will overcome their own explicit limitations and develop into powerful pressure groups of their own in favor of entirely new economic policies. If so, the Conservative Government may have bought some short-term political gain by creating a future Frankenstein that will devour their traditional economic tenets. Or perhaps, as seems more likely, these agencies will go the way of their predecessors, slowly declining under a lack of prestige and work, failing to agree because of internal dissension, and eventually being taken into the protective if somewhat oppressive custody of a regular department of government.[69]

[69] Neddy enthusiasts would do well to study more closely the records of the Economic Advisory Council of 1930 and the Economic Planning Board of 1947.

[PART THREE]

CABINET REFORM IN BRITAIN

SIXTEEN

CABINET CHANGES SINCE 1914:
A RECAPITULATION

Since 1914, the place of the Cabinet in the British political system has not fundamentally changed. The Cabinet is now, as it was then, a committee of leading parliamentarians who, with the general support of the majority party in the House of Commons, in permanent debate with the Opposition, responsible to King and Parliament, and constantly in the public eye, take or approve the main political decisions—in the process reacting to impulses from the civil service and from social forces outside the immediate government institutions.

But changes in the scope of government have resulted in definite shifts within these terms. Sometimes these shifts implied only slight changes in atmosphere; at other times they brought considerable modification in structure and operation. Even a hasty perusal of the preceding chapters makes one conclusion inescapable: these changes cannot be regarded as an unequivocal adjustment of the organization of British central government to changed administrative duties. New tasks did require special administrative arrangements. But personal factors and existing departmental divisions and loyalties threw up serious obstacles;[1] new administrative organs, or sections, often encountered suspicion; and political considerations demanded their toll. In many cases only the emergencies of war could break down irrational opposition.[2] But wartime, in turn, introduced numerous administrative improvisations. The administrative machinery was complicated with new departments, which mortgaged corporate loyalties just as heavily as did older departments.

It is nevertheless possible a posteriori to distinguish certain trends in the development of British central government over the last fifty years. These may be conveniently grouped into six categories: the effects of the increase of government tasks on the existing interdepartmental structure; attempts to improve coordination between departments; further differentiation in the ministerial hierarchy; changes in the relation between

---

[1] Of these, formal ones were the less important. The Prime Minister had long ago acquired a substantial say in attributing different tasks to his ministerial colleagues; his political ascendancy over Parliament assured the necessary legislative and budgetary approval for most changes he thought desirable. The availability of the sinecure offices and the theoretical indivisibility of the office of Secretary of State offered him further flexibility for introducing changes. In the Ministers of the Crown (Transfer of Functions) Act of 1946, provision was formally made for allowing the transfer of statutory powers from one minister to another by Order in Council.

[2] Cf. Robson, pp. 1–7.

ministers and civil servants; the increasing involvement of experts and scientific advisers in central government; and changes in the relation between ministers and Parliament.

The Effects of the Heavier Burden of Government on the Existing Interdepartmental Structure

Since 1914, the burdens on the central government machinery have vastly increased. This is evident even from the sheer quantitative angle. The number of civil servants employed in the service of the central government—excluding the personnel of the armed forces and the nationalized industries—increased fourfold, from a little more than a quarter million in 1914, to about a million forty years later.[3] At the same time public expenditure rose considerably. Supply expenditure, which was only 6 per cent of the gross national product in 1910 and 12 per cent in 1930, had risen to 22 per cent by 1960; total public expenditure of all kinds, including that of local authorities, national insurance funds, and the capital expenditure of the nationalized industries, now represents about 42 per cent of the gross national product.[4] The size of the higher civil service increased even more: the administrative class grew from less than 500 in 1914 to about 3,500 in 1955. The number of Treasury personnel grew almost ten times, from about 140 in 1914 to about 1,300 in 1955, while over the same period the size of the Foreign Office increased thirty times, from 190 in 1914, to 5,710 in 1955.[5]

But changes cannot be measured in quantitative terms alone. Since 1914, government business has become more complicated and interrelated. The borderline between the public sphere of government and the private one of the individual and society has increasingly disappeared as government policies and popular demands in close interaction have resulted in increasing State intervention. The civil service has moved out of the restricted environment of Whitehall, as service functions have come to be added to regulatory ones. International factors too have complicated even national decision-making processes.[6]

The ensuing change in the tasks of government had various consequences for the interdepartmental structure.

Individual ministers and existing departments were burdened more heavily. This was more true for some ministers than for others. While some departments saw their powers increase rapidly, others grew only slowly. Not every new government task brought an equal addition to the task of the minister and his highest administrative advisers. Some depart-

---

[3] See Moses Abramovitz and Vera F. Eliasberg, *The Growth of Public Employment in Great Britain* (1957), Table I, p. 25.
[4] Cmnd. 1432 (1961), para. 10.
[5] Cf. Chester, *Trends*, pp. 13–16; P.E.P., "The Growth of Government," *Planning*, XXIII (1957), pp. 232–35, 247–48.
[6] Beloff, *passim.*

ments managed to absorb new functions more easily than others.[7] But the accumulation of tasks became in certain instances so heavy that some duties had to be relinquished at all costs.

New departments were instituted. The reason for their establishment might vary. Sometimes a new department became necessary because of a sudden expansion of government authority over a new field. But more usually, new departments had their basis in government functions that already existed. If so, the *raison d'être* for a departmental split-up might be the political interest that a specific field of government suddenly acquired in the constant tussle between the Government and the Opposition. Or a new department might be the result of a desire of a heavily burdened ministry or department to surrender some of its powers to others. Or a particular range of tasks that had hitherto been dispersed over various departments might be concentrated into one department, for efficiency's sake. Whatever the specific cause, the number of government departments increased considerably. This had immediate consequences for the size of the Cabinet.

There was constant pressure to enlarge the Cabinet. As we saw in Chapter 2, this force was at work even before 1914. Ministers at the head of new departments have never gladly suffered exclusion from the Cabinet. The Cabinet increased from 12 to 14 members around 1875 to 23 in 1915. It changed again from 16 members in 1922 to 23 in 1939, and from 16 in 1946 to 21 in 1962. Many politicians have judged this inflation of the Cabinet to be detrimental to the value of Cabinet discussion. "Six are fully as many as can usefully converse on any subject," an experienced Lord Chancellor sighed more than a hundred years ago.[8] A council of some twenty members tends to degenerate into a public meeting. Factions may form, and considerations of prestige may block agreement. Parkinson has thought it possible to fix "the coefficient of inefficiency" between 19 and 22.[9] So, apparently, thought the designers of the Cabinet room, in 10, Downing Street, which can hardly hold more than 22. Prime Ministers have usually found it desirable but difficult to keep the number of Cabinet members below that limit. This, in turn, had two further consequences:

The principle that every minister at the head of an important administrative department has a claim on Cabinet membership was perforce abandoned. Even in the nineteenth-century Cabinets this principle had not always been respected. Before 1914, however, those who were not admitted to the Cabinet usually occupied offices that were not really comparable to a large department of government. Ever since the War Cabinet of Lloyd George, however, heads of important departments have been excluded from the Cabinet. Conversely, the removal of the direct link between the Cabinet and individual departments has removed a brake on

---

[7] Chester–Willson, pp. 343–45.   [8] Aspinall, p. 163, n.1.
[9] *The Economist*, 3 November 1956; reprinted in C. N. Parkinson, *Parkinson's Law and other Studies in Administration* (1957), pp. 33–44.

the further increase in autonomous departmental units. Non-Cabinet ministers have usually had all the formal trappings of their more fortunate Cabinet colleagues. They have "Cabinet rank."[10] They receive the same salary. They are made Privy Councillors. They are sent the most important Cabinet papers and are invited to attend parts of Cabinet sessions. But they have remained outside the Cabinet as such. Whatever the arguments in favor of this situation, few have found it really satisfactory in practice. Hence:

It was also consciously attempted to decrease again the number of independent departments. This number rose particularly rapidly during the two world wars, when the government assumed many new tasks and when the institution of the War Cabinet had removed the normal link between the Cabinet and the departments. The re-establishment of the traditional Cabinet was generally accompanied, on the other hand, by the deliberate dissolution of various new departmental units. Since 1951, attempts have also been made to decrease the number of departments in charge of ordinary civilian tasks by amalgamating them with other departments. Some of the traditional ties between the Cabinet and the departments have thus been restored.

Attempts to Improve Coordination between Departments

As government tasks became more interdependent, new instruments of coordination became vital.

The increased pressure of business made it necessary to hold more formal Cabinet meetings. The number of Cabinet sessions per year rose from about forty before 1914, to about sixty after 1918, to an average of eighty-nine between 1946 and 1957.[11] There is, however, an absolute limit to the time and thought that ministers can give to Cabinet business. It was therefore necessary to resort to other expedients if business was not to become clogged at Cabinet level.

Cabinet procedure was further formalized.[12] This was true of both the preparation and the execution of Cabinet decisions. The Cabinet Secretariat was charged with keeping off the Cabinet agenda all business that was not absolutely essential. The agenda itself acquired greater importance. New rules were adopted for the composition and the timely circulation of Cabinet memoranda to all departments concerned, before certain problems could be raised in the Cabinet. Officials were instructed

---

[10] The title "Minister of Cabinet Rank" has officially lapsed (Mackenzie–Grove, p. 337).

[11] Data provided by the Treasury Library; cf. Jennings, *Cabinet Government,* p. 249.

[12] *Ibid.,* pp. 242–64; Jennings, *Constitution,* p. 179ff; Chester, *Cabinet,* pp. 37–41; Hewison, pp. 36–41; Mackenzie–Grove, pp. 338–42; Beloff, pp. 165–66; Johnson, pp. 239–42.

to solve interdepartmental controversies on the lowest possible hierarchical level. Issues were to be brought to the Cabinet only when all other means of settling them had been exhausted, and when the points of contention had been so well defined that the alternatives were clear. Cabinet minutes came to stay. The Cabinet Secretariat introduced a detailed register of business that was still under consideration, as well as an index of decisions taken. It was charged to notify all departments concerned of Cabinet decisions, and, if necessary, to draw attention to omissions in execution. "Much Cabinet business is now almost formal," two British authors wrote recently.[13]

At the same time it was tried to lighten the Cabinet's burden by introducing an extensive system of Cabinet committees. Cabinet committees were known in the eighteenth and nineteenth centuries, but at that time they were usually nothing but an expedient for settling specific problems. Only the C.I.D. introduced a *system* of permanent committees, which, like the parent committee, were initially not technically Cabinet committees. When Lloyd George severed the Cabinet from the departments, the Government attempted to bridge the threatening gap by holding special Cabinet sessions, establishing the Cabinet Secretariat, and introducing Cabinet committees. Lloyd George's rather chaotic methods did little to rationalize the system. Nor did his successors do much in this direction. Between 1919 and 1939 there existed many committees, but hardly a committee system. Only the War Cabinet of the Second World War and the Labour Government consciously built a pyramid of committees that were to facilitate decision-making below Cabinet level. Depending on the temperament of successive Prime Ministers, such a committee system has since been more or less formal, and more or less extensive. But under all of them the number of committees has been considerable. An inquiry in the early 1950's revealed the existence of at least 700 interdepartmental committees, of which more than 100 were technically Cabinet committees.[14]

The complexity of the committee system has created a new coordination problem. When numerous conflicts of confidence flared up in 1950, during a period of active rearmament and great economic stress, a special Coordinating Section was instituted within the Cabinet Secretariat. It was charged

to follow the work of the many committees dealing with defense and economic questions and to ensure that there is no duplication; in cases of doubt to suggest which particular committee should consider a particular question; and generally to see that the new problems emerging are dealt with smoothly and efficiently.[15]

---

[13] Mackenzie–Grove, p. 339.

[14] Bosworth Monck, *How the Civil Service Works* (London, 1952), p. 100. Whether an interdepartmental committee is a Cabinet committee is "not defined by membership but whether or not it is served by the Cabinet Office" (Beloff, p. 27).

[15] Hewison, pp. 38–39; for a similar duty of Hankey, even in 1914, see his *Supreme Command*, pp. 226–27.

This formal Coordinating Section has since disappeared. But even now it is the task of the Cabinet Secretariat not only to service but also (if at all possible) to kill committees—provided the Prime Minister and ministers concerned consent.

The existence of Cabinet committees has made it possible to reduce the time normally spent on Cabinet sessions to two sessions of two hours each per week. But for some ministers, notably the Chancellor of the Exchequer, the great number of Cabinet committees has posed an extra burden. This is one reason why an attempt has been made to reduce their number by charging individual ministers rather than committees with special coordinating tasks.

Special coordinating ministers were appointed. These ministers were charged with relieving the Prime Minister and the Cabinet as much as possible of the responsibility for coordinating groups of departments in certain specific fields of policy. Sometimes, as in the case of the Minister of Defence, the coordinating minister was given a department of his own. Occasionally, the duties of a coordinating minister were publicly announced, as in the case of the Minister of Production. At other times, only a vague indication of his tasks was given in Parliament, as in the case of the Overlords and ministers like Morrison, Richard Stokes, and Charles Hill, who in 1945, 1951, and 1957, respectively, were charged with the general coordination of government information services. But more often, coordination duties have been kept secret. Normally, a coordinating minister exercises his duties as chairman of a Cabinet committee, the composition of which is also not disclosed. Whether he occupies a sinecure office or heads one of the more important departmental posts in the ministerial hierarchy will depend on personal and political factors rather than on formal ones.

Less official agents also play a considerable role in improving interdepartmental coordination. Prime Ministers have often relied on informal meetings to resolve interdepartmental disputes. Occasionally, they have asked ministerial colleagues to act for them on incidental matters without attributing any formal authority to them. An important part is played by unofficial means of communication: telephone conversations, casual notes passed by one minister to another on the Treasury Bench or during a Cabinet session, informal talks over luncheon and dinner tables, short chats in the lobbies of Parliament, etc. In addition, the network of private secretaries serves to smooth out many less important problems and to ensure ready communication.[16] In the Prime Minister's immediate environment there have always been a few high-placed civil servants—technically residing in the Cabinet Office, the Treasury, the Foreign Office, or in a somewhat more formalized Prime Minister's Secretariat—who by long experience have become "masters of . . . institutional understanding . . . able to prod and stroke, caress and jab, the relevant parts of the

---

[16] Jones, *Diary,* pp. xix–xxi; Mackenzie–Grove, pp. 191–94.

English organism, so that somehow or other, in a way that [makes] organizational diagrams look very primitive," certain vital matters are seen through.[17]

Finally, some formal agencies play a coordinating role. Certain agencies have been deliberately placed in a central position because they represent some high-level *expertise* useful to the entire government or because they supply common services. Economic advice, statistical coordination, certain defense matters, and central information and intelligence services have thus at various times been concentrated in a non-departmental central coordinating agency. In addition, certain departments have always provided special services for other parts of the government machinery in such matters as office buildings and office requirements; legal, actuarial, and audit services; etc.[18]

Further Differentiation in the Ministerial Hierarchy

Since 1914, the ministerial hierarchy has become further differentiated in various ways.[19]

The position of the Prime Minister has been reinforced. Various factors have contributed to this. The increased importance of foreign affairs and defense matters (both nationally and internationally) has led to a more constant intervention of the Prime Minister in these sectors. The growing complexity and interdependence of government has enhanced his role of supreme coordinator. The House of Commons and the public have become more prone to appraise government acts not as measures of individual ministers or departments but as parts of government policy as a whole. This has tended to raise the Prime Minister's stature over that of both his party and his colleagues. The Government, in other words, is judged as much by its Prime Minister as the Prime Minister is by his Government. Since the days of Lloyd George, the right to advise the King to dissolve Parliament has become in practice the Prime Minister's alone rather than the Cabinet's. Elections have tended to be a competition between alternative Prime Ministers as well as between rival parties or

---

[17] Snow, p. 61.   [18] Chester–Willson, pp. 274–80.

[19] The following discussion refers, of course, to a ranking according to *political* criteria. Since 1914, ministers have tended *formally* to become more equal. This is apparent, for example, in the use of the title "Minister" for many offices that formerly had more archaic designations. Salaries, too, have been equalized to a great extent. This process began during the First World War, when it was temporarily decided that all ministers would pay their salaries into a common fund, and draw equal amounts from it. The Ministers of the Crown Act (1937) provided for a salary of £5,000 for all ministers who headed a government department except the Postmaster-General and the First Commissioner of Works, who were to get £3,000, and the Minister of Pensions, who was thought worth only £2,000. Since then, the salary of the Postmaster-General has been raised to £5,000. The Lord President, the Lord Privy Seal, and the Chancellor of the Duchy of Lancaster are entitled to £3,000 if they are not in the Cabinet, and £5,000 if they are. See Ministers of the Crown Act (1937), and Wade–Phillips, pp. 139–40.

programs. The increased length of the ministerial hierarchy has augmented the Prime Minister's powers of patronage and heightened a sense of dependence on the part of his appointees. Those at the bottom of the ladder know that they can move up only by the grace of the Prime Minister. Those on the highest step must often ponder the fact that below them are many who would be only too happy to shed crocodile tears over their possible dismissal, but who are yet ready to take their place immediately at the Prime Minister's bidding. Some observers have also stressed the enduring importance of the Prime Minister's having his own staff in the Cabinet Office. This might conceivably (but in practice not too frequently) brief him against proposals of his departmental colleagues, and enhances his powers over the Cabinet agenda and the circulation of Cabinet papers and Cabinet minutes.

It is somewhat farfetched, however, to conclude from this that the British system of government is, in fact, tending towards a presidential system.[20] Nor should one accept without question the statement that "Britain is not governed by the Cabinet but by the Prime Minister, his senior colleagues, junior ministers, and the leading civil servants, with the Cabinet acting as a coordinating body and clearing house for business."[21] This sentence is either a truism or an underestimation of the Cabinet's role as a political as well as an administrative agency. No Prime Minister is fully independent of the Cabinet or its most influential members. Each Prime Minister governs at the mercy of party; and notwithstanding superficial affirmations to the contrary, a British political party is more than a group of the Prime Minister's friends and idolaters. The tradition of collective responsibility and the corporate strength of vested departments is too strong to allow easy control by one central minister, let alone by his non-departmental private secretariat. Even the sheer burden of office prevents any Prime Minister from intervening at all closely except in the most urgent matters. If he can make his will prevail in any matter he chooses, he can only do so by leaving most things alone.

In recent times, a Deputy Prime Minister has become a more regular feature of British Cabinets. The first person to bear this unofficial title was Attlee, who was termed Deputy Prime Minister in 1942. Morrison was recognized as Deputy Prime Minister from 1945 to 1951. In the autumn of 1951, Churchill nominated Eden "Foreign Secretary and Deputy Prime Minister." The King refused to agree to the latter title, however, because it might interfere with his free choice of Churchill's eventual successor.[22] But whatever the nomenclature, many Cabinets have

[20] See the correspondence in the *Daily Telegraph,* touched off by a provocative letter on 2 August 1960 from Professor Max Beloff; cf. *The Economist,* 13 August 1960.

[21] This statement appeared on the jacket of Mackintosh's *The British Cabinet* (1962). For a good critical review, see D. N. Chester, "Who Governs Britain?" *Parliamentary Affairs,* XV (1962), 519–27.

[22] *Life of King George VI,* p. 797.

had one minister who was expected to take the chair at Cabinet meetings in the Prime Minister's absence. This minister was sometimes, but not necessarily, the Prime Minister's logical successor. In a real coalition government, for instance, the two are not likely to coincide. No one expected that Attlee might be appointed Prime Minister of the National Government after 1942 if Churchill should die. On the contrary, in June 1942, Churchill formally recommended that the King entrust the formation of a new government to Eden, in case he himself should die on a journey to the United States.[23] Again, in 1944, Churchill formally advised the King to send for Anderson if both he and Eden should be killed on their journey to Yalta.[24] Bevin, Dalton, and Cripps were not likely to conclude from Morrison's unofficial title of Deputy Prime Minister (Morrison presumably was so designated because he was the officially elected Deputy Leader of the Labour Party) that he was the only possible choice as Prime Minister of the Labour Cabinet after 1945, in case something happened to Attlee. Between 1951 and 1955 Eden was both the unofficial crown prince and the actual Vice–Prime Minister of the Cabinet.[25] Under Eden himself, Butler acted as Deputy Prime Minister, but it did not prevent the appointment of Macmillan over his head in 1957. Butler has remained in the number two position since then. In October 1961, when he relinquished his Leadership of the House of Commons but remained Home Secretary, it was officially announced that he was "to give special assistance to the Prime Minister over a wide field of public duties, and, in particular, to head the ministerial group charged with the oversight of the Common Market negotiations." In March 1962, Macmillan still refused to nominate a Deputy Prime Minister, holding that the office did not technically exist under the constitution.[26] But after the ministerial upheaval of July 1962, Butler gave up the Home Office to accept the new post of First Secretary of State. It was intimated that he would act as Deputy Prime Minister, even though again that title was not formally conferred by the Queen. According to *The Times* of 18 July 1962, the new title lent "an appropriate dignity to Mr. Butler's position, the title Deputy Prime Minister having an insufficiently archaic ring about it by British standards." But even as First Secretary, Butler could be far from certain that he would, after all, become Prime Minister.

Other leading ministers, too, have seen their positions strengthened. For a long time past in British history, a connection had been noted between the growth of the Cabinet and the disposition of leading ministers to prepare and at times to take important decisions in informal meetings outside the Cabinet. If Peel "had started upon a more limited scale, he would have had no difficulty in keeping out its deformities," Lord Ripon

[23] Cf. Eden, *Full Circle,* p. 266.
[24] *Life of King George VI,* pp. 544–45; *Life of Anderson,* pp. 315–18.
[25] When both Churchill and Eden were ill in 1953, Salisbury directed foreign policy, and Butler "assumed authority for Home Affairs" (Eden, *Full Circle,* p. 52).
[26] 655 H. of C. Deb. (13 March 1962), col. 1117; Heasman, pp. 467–68.

stated over a century ago. "He must now only take care that they have no power or influence."[27] The appointment of coordinating ministers who at the same time preside over the more important Cabinet committees has perhaps led to a certain institutionalization of an Inner Group. However important personal factors continue to be, it is now practically unthinkable that such officeholders as the Chancellor of the Exchequer, the Foreign Secretary, to a lesser extent the Minister of Defence, and (if they are important committee chairmen) the Lord President and the Lord Privy Seal, can be kept outside the privileged circle of actual Cabinet leaders for long.

The development of the committee system has also had an impact on the position of the sinecure offices. Instead of being honorific advisers or ministers incidentally charged with specific tasks, the most important sinecure holders have often become essential links in the complex policy-making mechanism. Many factors have caused this process. The existing sinecures regained some of their earlier political influence when Lloyd George utilized them to form a non-departmental War Cabinet above the departments, thus establishing a precedent that was also followed for a time during the Second World War. The occurrence of coalition government in 1915, 1931, and 1940 enhanced the position of a second man in the Cabinet, who owed his rank not to an important ministerial portfolio or a strong political position within the Prime Minister's party but to his place as Leader of a party that represented an independent force within the coalition. Such politicians have often preferred a sinecure office to a large department.[28] Bonar Law, for instance, abandoned the Treasury for the Privy Seal in 1919, and Austen Chamberlain followed this example in 1921. Baldwin similarly preferred the Lord Presidency to the Treasury in 1931. Attlee became Lord Privy Seal in 1940, Deputy Prime Minister and Secretary of State for the Dominions in 1942, but again Lord President of the Council in 1943. In addition, the evolution of the Cabinet-committee system has done much to raise the status of sinecure-holders acting as chairmen of important standing committees. A sinecure post has also often served as an office for the Leader of the House. At times, however, various ministers who have resembled the

---

[27] Aspinall, p. 163.

[28] Another indication that the ministerial status of the sinecure offices has risen is that since 1916 various holders of these offices have been able to claim the house at 11, Downing Street, which is normally the home of the Chancellor of the Exchequer; in other cases they have at least shared these quarters with the Chancellor. In 1919, for instance, Bonar Law continued to occupy the house when he exchanged the Exchequer for the Privy Seal. When Clynes was Lord Privy Seal and Deputy Leader of the Labour Party, he worked at No. 11 in 1924. As Lord President of the Council, Baldwin lived there from 1931 to 1935; Neville Chamberlain did the same in 1940. Attlee and Cripps shared the house with the Chancellor of the Exchequer, Sir Kingsley Wood, when they held the office of Privy Seal in 1941 and 1942, respectively. Morrison worked there between 1945 and 1951 as Lord President, and in 1951 Cherwell moved in as Paymaster-General. (Data provided by the Treasury Library.)

traditional "elder statesmen" rather than directors of the central government machinery have still been appointed to the Lord Presidency or the Privy Seal. The fact that Butler thought it necessary to assume the Home Secretaryship in addition to the Privy Seal in 1957 has often been regarded as proof that even a powerful coordinating minister cannot wield sufficient political strength from a sinecure office against the main departments of government.[29]

As we saw in Chapter 8, recent developments have also served to increase the actual burden on the holders of sinecure offices. Two of them (the Lord Privy Seal and the Paymaster-General) have in fact become second Cabinet ministers in the Foreign Office and in the Treasury, respectively. The office of the Duchy has been assigned to the Leader of the House of Commons, who is also party chairman. And the Lord President of the Council, Hailsham, has collected such an assortment of duties that his post can hardly be described as a "sinecure." A confirmation of this development may be seen in the reappearance of ministers without portfolio in the Cabinet.

The separation between Cabinet ministers and ministers of Cabinet rank outside the Cabinet has led to further differentiation within the ministerial hierarchy. Membership in the Cabinet, by itself, has never implied equality of status. The remark of a former Socialist minister that "the youngest and most junior member can sometimes get his colleagues to change their minds" conveys more of a sense of hierarchy among Cabinet members than of a prevailing egalitarianism.[30] But even so, the cleavage between the least important minister within the Cabinet and the most important one outside it has become deep, whatever the personal influence of the ministers concerned.[31]

The appointment of Ministers of State has added a new category of ministers between heads of departments and parliamentary secretaries. The first Minister of State was Beaverbrook, who was appointed to this newly created office in 1941. He was a member of the War Cabinet, as were Lyttelton and Richard Casey, who were successively appointed Minister of State Resident in the Middle East. Since then the office of

[29] Cf. *The Economist,* 27 April 1957, and Dogan–Campbell, pp. 342–45.
[30] Gordon Walker, p. 20.
[31] A recent, somewhat perfectionist study (Heasman, pp. 327–28) has even attempted a rather fanciful division of non-Cabinet ministers into five categories:

"First, heads of autonomous departments that are concerned with the formulation of important policies who might, therefore, in other circumstances, be in the Cabinet (for example, the Minister of Pensions and National Insurance and the Minister of Health); secondly, heads of essentially administrative departments whose responsibilities do not warrant their presence in the Cabinet (specifically, the Minister of Works and the Postmaster-General); thirdly, holders of minor sinecures and ministers without portfolio whose assignments are of an auxiliary nature; fourthly, the three Service ministers, the importance and expenditures of whose departments exceed, by far, those of (say) the Minister of Works (since 1946 the list of "ministers not in the Cabinet" has been headed almost invariably by the three Service ministers), yet who are clearly subordinate, as the Minister of Works is not, to a member of the Cabinet; and finally, Ministers of State."

Minister of State has declined in rank. In 1943 a son of Bonar Law, Richard Law, was appointed Minister of State at the Foreign Office. As such, he was subordinate to the Foreign Secretary. Ministers of State have been appointed particularly when a minister's burden threatened to become unduly heavy but to divide his duties among separate departmental ministers seemed impossible or undesirable.[32] In the Foreign Office, for instance, a second Minister of State has been appointed since 1953.[33] In the Treasury an Economic Secretary was joined to the Financial Secretary in 1947. For a time in 1950 and again in 1951, this minister carried the personal title of Minister of State, and since 1957 both the Financial Secretary and the Economic Secretary have been paid the same as the Minister of State (but they are less often Privy Councillors and are included under the heading "junior ministers" in the official list).[34]

When the Board of Trade absorbed the Department of Overseas Trade in 1946, it was still found necessary for a special Minister of State to occupy himself full-time with problems of overseas commerce under the general direction of the President of the Board of Trade.[35] In 1948, when the emancipating of colonies began to gain momentum, a separate Minister of State was appointed to the Colonial Office. The development of various areas toward self-government greatly increased the tasks of the Secretary of State for the Colonies until each colony gained independence.[36] Eventually, however, the work of the Colonial Office began to shrink, while that of the Commonwealth Relations Office increased *pari passu*. A separate Minister of State for Commonwealth Relations was added. Finally, in July 1962, Macmillan appointed Sandys Secretary of State at both offices, thus leaving the Minister of State and the Undersecretary of State at the Colonial Office as the sole full-timers in that department. The Secretary for Technical Cooperation, appointed in 1961, also ranks as Minister of State, although he is not statutorily responsible to any other minister.[37] A Minister of State has also been appointed in the Scottish Office, which is responsible for a range of government tasks that in England are the

---

[32] The half-way position of Ministers of State between senior ministers and junior ministers was, as it were, arithmetically fixed in 1957, when they were awarded a salary of £3,750. A minister normally receives £5,000, a parliamentary secretary £2,500.

[33] After Eden returned to the Foreign Office in 1951, he told Morrison that he found his duties twice as heavy as they had been in 1945 (Morrison, *Autobiography*, pp. 297–98, and Morrison, p. 63). For graphic descriptions of the very heavy burden on the Foreign Secretary, see Grey, *Twenty-Five Years*, II, 251ff and Strang, *Home and Abroad*, pp. 298–300. Eden himself thought that in normal times, the Foreign Secretary and the Chancellor of the Exchequer bore heavier burdens than the Prime Minister (*Full Circle*, p. 317).

[34] Heasman, p. 328.

[35] According to the Ministers of the Crown Act (1937), the Secretary for Overseas Trade, the Secretary of Mines, and the Financial Secretary to the Treasury enjoyed a salary of £2,000—i.e., £500 more than the other junior ministers.

[36] Cf. Sir Charles Jeffries, *The Colonial Office* (1956), p. 118. Parkinson's Law is partly based on the "experiences" of the Colonial Office (*ibid.*, pp. 10–11).

[37] Willson, *Supplement*, p. 177.

responsibility of various departments. In December 1957, finally, a Minister of State for Welsh Affairs was appointed, largely as a concession to nationalist sensitivities; he is under the Minister of Housing and Local Government, who is technically also Minister for Welsh Affairs, and works mainly in Wales, as his Scottish counterpart does in Scotland. Both Ministers of State are peers.[38]

It is difficult to generalize about the extent to which Ministers of State have been able to relieve the burden on more senior ministers. In practice, much depends on the personalities concerned, and on the willingness of Parliament to transact business with the Minister of State rather than the senior minister in charge, which depends largely on political circumstance. The Ministers of State have not become substitute ministers; as we saw, in the two vitally important cases of the Foreign Office and the Treasury, Cabinet ministers rather than ministers below the line have recently been added to help shoulder the impossible tasks of the ministers in charge. Thus, increasingly, a system of having two senior ministers in a department has been found necessary, rather than a further strengthening of subordinate staff. This has posed new problems of dividing responsibility at the highest level of government, as well as further differentiation within the Cabinet.

At the same time, the number of parliamentary secretaries has increased. In 1914, there were only 14 undersecretaries and parliamentary secretaries. In 1919 this number had increased to 27. In 1939 the number had declined to 23, but it now stands at 32. This increase partly reflects the increase in the number of departments that were given their own parliamentary secretary. But in addition, more than one parliamentary secretary has sometimes been appointed to a single department; statutory limitations on the number of parliamentary secretaries who could serve in any particular department were removed in the Ministers of the Crown (Parliamentary Secretaries) Act of 1960. From 1939 to 1958, the number of Joint Undersecretaries in the Scottish Office increased from one to three, and since 1961 there have been three parliamentary secretaries at the Ministry of Transport. There are now two Joint Parliamentary Secretaries in five other departments: Home Affairs, Foreign Affairs, Commonwealth Relations, Agriculture, and Pensions and National Insurance. In such ministries as the Foreign Office and the Treasury, the grading of ministers at lower levels has become quite complicated: in addition to the First Lord and the Chancellor of the Exchequer, the Treasury now houses a Chief Secretary (who is in the Cabinet), an Economic Secretary and a Financial Secretary (who practically rank as Ministers of State), and the Parliamentary Secretary and the junior Lords (who serve as whips and as such do not deal with Treasury busi-

---

[38] The Home Secretary acted as "Minister for Welsh Affairs" from 1951 to 1957; since that time, the position has been filled by the Minister of Housing and Local Government.

ness). Similarly, the Foreign Office has its Foreign Secretary (who is in the House of Lords, and for whom both the Prime Minister and the Lord Privy Seal answer in the House of Commons), the Lord Privy Seal (who is a Cabinet member especially concerned with European problems), two Ministers of State, and two Joint Undersecretaries.[39]

Considerable pressure has been exerted on the House of Commons to be satisfied with junior ministers as spokesmen on various matters of departmental policy. On less controversial issues, this seems to have had some effect. Civil servants, too, have learned to regard the desk of the senior minister as a potential bottleneck and hence have been more ready to clear business with lower-ranking ministers (always providing that personalities, politics, and the parliamentary responsibility of the senior minister permit this). Junior ministers would thus seem to have gained some prestige on the administrative and parliamentary level. But at the same time, the ministerial ladder has become steeper and the intermediate steps more important. To hold office as a junior minister is more necessary for further promotion than ever before. But remuneration is low, and at times concern has been expressed about whether persons of sufficient quality are readily coming forward to undergo this testing.

A more subtle but no less real differentiation grew between the older departments and the newer ones. As we saw, this distinction was not unknown before 1914. In Chapter 4 attention was drawn to the strong resistance encountered by such departments as the Ministries of Labour, Health, Transport, and Air, which were established after 1916. Similar obstacles confronted various departments that originated during World War II, including the Ministries of Supply, Town and Country Planning, Fuel and Power, Civil Aviation, and National Insurance. The more powerful politicians generally continued to prefer the long-established departments. New departments were therefore often given to politicians who could not expect or demand higher office: older politicians who had reached the top of their pole, or younger ones who considered such posts as no more than a steppingstone. Thus these newer departments often became part of a vicious circle. They were not important enough to attract politicians of the first rank. And because they were not led by first-rate ministers, they often did not become really influential in the ministerial hierarchy.

Symptomatic of the lesser prestige of the newer departments were the more frequent reorganizations they had to undergo. There were various drastic shifts, for instance between the Ministries of Health, Works, and Town and Country Planning. The Ministry of Supply was tossed about, and finally disbanded in 1959. Such departments as Pensions and National Insurance, Transport and Civil Aviation, and Food and Agriculture were

[39] Cf. Peter Bromhead, "The British Constitution in 1961," *Parliamentary Affairs,* XV (1962), pp. 148–49.

joined together without much ado. Others simply disappeared. Such occurrences were hardly likely among the older departments (the Service departments forming a notable exception) : their traditional prestige, their corporate pride, and the political power of their ministerial heads made them to a large extent inviolate.

But all these status differences were in their turn affected by other factors, such as personality, or the political or administrative importance that a department might assume at a particular period. Powerful politicians—Morrison or Hore-Belisha at the Ministry of Transport, Bevin at the Ministry of Labour, Bevan at the Ministry of Health, Dalton at Town and Country Planning, Macmillan at Housing and Local Government, Sandys at Aviation—were able to enhance the repute of their departments. The political importance of the Ministries of Labour and Agriculture increased in conjunction with the rising political importance of their clienteles. Technical factors for a time enhanced the prestige of the Cinderella of the Service departments, the Air Ministry. In a crisis, the political importance of a particular ministerial post might even soar overnight.

In other words, traditional differences in prestige, considerations of status, personal influences, political circumstances, and the relative significance of particular government tasks at any given time make the ministerial structure into a complicated hierarchy, the pattern of which may differ considerably from one moment to the next.

The Relation between Ministers and Civil Servants

The relation between ministers and officials, too, underwent substantial changes as a result of the development of modern government.

The entire administrative apparatus grew considerably in size and complexity.[40] It therefore became more and more difficult to direct it. This increased both the burden of ministerial work and the strain of nervous tension. As a former Labour minister wrote, "The real strain arises not from what ministers do but from what they feel they ought to be doing." Or in the words of Sir Ivor Jennings, "It is not work, but worry."[41]

Ministerial control over the civil service therefore became more problematical. This is as true of ministers individually as of the Cabinet as a whole. Thousands of decisions about which ministers do not and could not know are taken daily in their name. The measure of leadership that ministers give cannot but differ from person to person. But in practice, ministers can do little more than initiate certain proposals, decide controversies that proved impossible to settle at lower levels of the civil ser-

---

[40] Cf. P.E.P., "The Growth of Government," *Planning,* XXXIII (1957), pp. 232–35, 247–48; Chester, *Trends,* p. 17.

[41] "On Being Out of Office," by a Fallen Cabinet Minister, *Sunday Times,* 11 November 1951; Jennings, *Constitution,* p. 156.

vice hierarchy, and intervene in issues that touch a political nerve or happen to have their special interest. "Ministers," Franks has written, "criticize, they reject, they alter, they judge and decide."[42] They are far from being the only springs of policy.

The position of the higher civil servants has acquired correspondingly greater importance. Even more than before the highest officials have become "permanent politicians," serving as alter egos of their ministers.[43] The institution of the Cabinet du Ministre as France knows it did not develop in Great Britain. Nor is there any inclination to adopt the American practice of changing the highest officials when a new party arrives in office. On the contrary, even now the parliamentary secretary sometimes enjoys less contact with his minister than do the main permanent officials; and the career private secretary is more frequently found in his minister's company than is his parliamentary private secretary.

The higher civil servants seem to be becoming less anonymous than they were in 1914. No longer can it be said of civil servants that "like the Fountains in Trafalgar Square, they play from ten to five, with an interval for lunch." The urgency of coordination and the fact that ministers can be challenged in Parliament on every issue within their general competence compel senior officials to occupy themselves personally with a large variety of government business. Work in evenings and on weekends is the rule rather than the exception. One can ask, with Wilfrid Harrison, "Why do they do it?" and reply, with him, in the simple statement, "Because the work would not get done if they did not." Harrison formulates the dilemma in one sentence: "As government activities increase and work multiplies, the load that converges on them increases; and the process is cumulative because with the constant pressure and absence of relief the working tempo becomes reduced."[44]

It is a moot point whether ministers or senior civil servants are the harder pressed by the burdens of modern government. A minister has many responsibilities outside his departmental duties. To quote Chester:

The work is likely to be more strange to him and therefore more difficult. He has the ultimate responsibility for all decisions and must face any public criticisms. He has also many other claims on his time—attending the House of Commons, speaking on public occasions of all kinds. And he is constantly in the public eye with the possibility that any public utterance of his may get widespread publicity.[45]

But ministers have the *ultimum remedium* of leaving much real work to the civil servants. The latter are permanent, and can never take their leave, even at the hands of an ungrateful electorate or Prime Minister.

---

[42] Franks, p. 52; Milne, p. 410; cf. Jennings, *Queen's Government,* p. 114: "The civil service governs, the Ministers control the process of government."
[43] The term "permanent politicians" is taken from Kingsley, p. 269.
[44] Harrison, p. 149.   [45] Chester, p. 19.

The Increasing Role of Experts in the Making of Policy

The growing complexity of government tasks has made it more necessary than formerly to include experts in the policy-making process. This has come about on various levels:

The number of experts within the departments has increased considerably. The scientific civil service now is about four times as large as the administrative class of the civil service; the professional, scientific, and technical classes *in toto* include about one and a half times the number of persons of the administrative and executive classes jointly.[46]

Special advisers and advisory organs have been added to the machinery of government. Apart from the desire of ministers and departments to obtain the expert advice of government scientists, the Cabinet itself has sometimes wanted to have special advisers at its disposal so departmental proposals could be tested from angles not influenced by specific departmental loyalties. To this end, various persons and agencies have been established in staff positions at the top levels of central government. Such central advisory agencies often found their origin in the modest staff of the C.I.D., which served as model for the Cabinet Secretariat and for the many joint bodies under the Chiefs of Staff Committee. These agencies, in turn, stimulated the demand for similar organizations elsewhere in the government. Personal factors sometimes led to the appointment of experts to such specially created posts as Economic Adviser to H.M. Government and Chief Industrial Adviser. During World War II, the Economic Section and the Statistical Office were established in the Cabinet Office. After 1945, a number of these specialist posts and agencies were drawn into more departmental orbits. The Treasury absorbed the economists of the Cabinet Office. The military members of the Cabinet Secretariat formed the nucleus for the Ministry of Defence in 1946. All this had little effect, however, on the formation of policy at the highest levels. High-level economic experts, the top of the Treasury, the leading professional and scientific staff in the Service Departments and the Ministry of Defence, and the members of the Cabinet Office remain in immediate contact with one another and with the Prime Minister and leading Cabinet ministers. They form a small, closely knit group that exercises an immediate influence on policy in a measure determined as much by personality as by the position each member may formally occupy in the hierarchy.[47]

At the same time advice was also increasingly drawn from circles outside the immediate government apparatus. The complexity of modern government is such that the state cannot hope to appoint its own expert staff in all fields into which the government enters. Particularly when government begins moving in unexplored terrain, it tends to be highly

---

[46] See annual data in *Britain: An Official Handbook,* H. M. Stationery Office; see also Laski, *Reflections,* pp. 204–12; Brundrett, pp. 245–56; Tizard, *passim.*
[47] Snow, pp. 54–57.

dependent on available outside knowledge. Close consultation with interested parties, to obtain advice and consent, is indicated. Various means have evolved to ensure the service of non-governmental experts for government purposes. Special regulations have made it easier for academic experts to serve in the government for a short period (and, conversely, for a few civil servants to spend a period of study and reflection in the universities). Advisory committees are playing an increasingly important role.[48] They many range from formally instituted Royal Commissions to casually arranged discussion groups. Some are only temporary, others permanent. According to a recent study, there were some two hundred standing committees attached to the central government in 1939. This number had increased to almost five hundred in 1958, of which no less than 60 to 70 per cent were expert committees rather than consultative or administrative ones.[49] Undoubtedly, many such advisory bodies have served more than one purpose; they have been instruments for the government to get its case across to interest groups and interested experts. But, in turn, these groups have also obtained a more ready influence on government policies.

The Government has also become increasingly aware of the importance of both pure and applied research for the military strength, economic prosperity, and social welfare of the British people. Since the First World War, support for research has been increasing. It ranges from block grants to the universities to highly specialized subventions or government research contracts. As long as such sponsorship did not clearly reside under any one department, such activities were promoted under the aegis of a number of agencies under the Privy Council. Among them were the Department of Scientific and Industrial Research (established in 1916), the Medical Research Council, the Agriculture Research Council, and the Nature Conservancy, which nominally reported to the Lord President of the Council.[50] In 1959, however, the importance of research had become so much of a political issue that the Conservative Party included the appointment of a special Minister for Science in its election program. The new minister was duly appointed in October 1961. But as we saw in Chapter 8, not much changed in practice.

But the increasing role of science has also affected the extent of ministerial control. The ideal image of the ever-wise, triumphantly commonsensical amateur has come in for increasingly skeptical comment. More and more concern is being expressed about whether modern science and democratic control are even compatible. Various expedients have been tried to preserve political supervision. Parliamentarians have formed their own specialized scientific committees. Ministers have more readily concentrated on certain fields. Both through advisory committees and through the appointment of rival experts in government service, the government

[48] Cf. Vernon–Mansergh, *passim*; Tivey–Rendel, *passim*; S. E. Finer, *Anonymous Empire: A Study of the Lobby in Great Britain* (1958).
[49] Tivey–Rendel, pp. xi, 10–11.   [50] Cf. Chester–Willson, pp. 249–73.

has tried to lower political dependence on any one scientist. But no final solution has been found, or seems possible. Especially in certain fields where national security seems to dictate "closed politics," the prestige of function and personality allows a few experts a preponderant influence. "Court politics" has sometimes led to the elevation of advisers to ministerial status, as in the cases of Cherwell and Mills.[51]

Ministers and Parliament

Considerable change has come about in the relation of ministers to Parliament. The pressure and complexity of administration has forced successive Governments to ask for increased power. Apart from the issue of delegated legislation, this has also led to certain problems for the ministerial hierarchy.[52]

It has strengthened the element of individual ministerial responsibility, both in a legal and in a political sense. Numerous government powers are legally no longer vested in the Crown but in individual ministers.[53] The heavy burden of modern government makes it imperative that ministers accept sole responsibility over a wide field, without burdening their colleagues. The extension of government powers has increased the number of issues on which ministers can be technically challenged in Parliament. This burden has not hit all ministers equally. The introduction of the rota system in question time, for instance, has had the effect of lessening ministerial answerability for a considerable number of ministers.[54] Oral questions have become increasingly a political game, which may require debating skill as much as a thorough grounding in a particular issue. Nevertheless, parliamentary questions pose a considerable burden on some ministers and their senior official advisers. Also, the M.P.'s increased practice of asking written questions and using private correspondence to seek information or redress about particular official decisions has considerably augmented the burden of ministerial office.[55]

This has strengthened the tendency to seek to lessen ministerial responsibility for a number of tasks. Devolution of powers to autonomous organs of government —e.g., public corporations, administrative committees, and administrative tribunals—has absolved ministers from certain responsibilities in specific fields or at least has narrowed the scope of their answerability to general direction, rather than to day-to-day administra-

---

[51] Snow, *passim*; Tivey–Rendel, pp. 94–95.

[52] See, e.g., Sir Cecil Carr, *Delegated Legislation* (1921) ; Lord Hewart of Bury, *The New Despotism* (1929) ; Sir C. K. Allen, *Law and Orders* (1956) ; *Report from Committee on Ministers' Power*, Cmd. 4060 (1932) ; *Report from the Select Committee on Delegated Legislation*, H. C. 310-I (1953) ; W. A. Robson, *Justice and Administrative Law* (1951).

[53] Jennings, *Queen's Government*, pp. 95–96. But cf. S. E. Finer, "The Individual Responsibility of Ministers," *Public Adminsitration*, XXXIV (1956), 377–96.

[54] Chester–Bowring, p. 145ff.   [55] *Ibid.*, pp. 96–108.

tion.[56] The existence of such bodies as well as of advisory committees has given ministers the opportunity to disclaim responsibility or at least to defer it until such time as these bodies may decide or issue a report.

At the same time, the element of collective responsibility toward Parliament has increased as well. In many cases it became impossible to divide government tasks neatly among separate departments; in the making of policy various interests merged. "The Government" became for both parties and for the electorate a collective body, which must accept responsibility for the welfare of the entire nation and for each individual citizen.

The increase of State tasks demanded more efficient legislative procedures.[57] No longer could the quiet tempo of legislation be preserved. Parliamentary business has become more complicated and time-consuming. More and more mornings are given over to committee meetings. The Government has had to resort to stricter procedures such as the closure and the guillotine to expedite legislation. Stricter rules have been adopted about the parliamentary agenda, and question time has been further rationed. Private Members' Time has sometimes been taken over for Government Business. The task of piloting bills through Parliament has come to require more concentrated attention, the more so because each bill that has not been adopted before the end of the session automatically lapses.

No longer is the Prime Minister able to combine his increased duties with the Leadership of the House of Commons. During the two world wars, Lloyd George and Winston Churchill had set the precedent of delegating this function to other ministers. In 1942, Churchill appointed Cripps Leader of the House, as Lord Privy Seal. Since then Eden has acted as Leader from 1942 to 1945 as Foreign Secretary, Morrison from 1945 to 1951 as Lord President of the Council, Chuter Ede in 1951 as Home Secretary, Crookshank as Minister of Health and Lord Privy Seal until 1955, Butler as Lord Privy Seal and Home Secretary till 1961, and since then Macleod as Chancellor of the Duchy of Lancaster. Personalities, not portfolios, determined these choices. But at all times, one leading minister has had to concentrate on parliamentary business. Morrison has deemed it necessary that this minister should, at the same time, preside over the Legislation Committee of the Cabinet.[58]

With the government's growth in size, the percentage of parliamentarians of the majority party directly tied to the government has increased as well. This increase has taken place on the level of ministers, Ministers of State, parliamentary secretaries, and parliamentary private secretaries. In 1947, only 49 members of the House of Commons enjoyed a paid office

[56] *Ibid.*, pp. 92–96.
[57] For details, see Lord Campion, *An Introduction to the Procedure of the House of Commons* (1947) ; Campion, *Parliamentary System,* pp. 28–29 ; Morrison, p. 221ff.
[58] Morrison, p. 117.

under the Crown. This number had risen to 68 in 1962.[59] Including the parliamentary private secretaries, just over a hundred members of the governing partly in the Commons now hold some kind of office.

From time to time, traditional concern about "placemen" was resuscitated. A Select Committee on Offices or Places of Profit under the Crown, appointed during the session of 1941–42, recommended that the number of ministers who could sit and vote in the House of Commons be limited to sixty; that the proportion between ministers and parliamentary secretaries as specified in the Ministers of the Crown Act in 1937 be maintained strictly; and that the convention of having only one parliamentary private secretary per department be adopted.[60] At the time, few of these recommendations were effected. But in 1957, a House of Commons Disqualification Bill was passed. It limited the number of senior ministers in the House of Commons to twenty-seven and the number of all ministers to seventy. Pressure on these limitations continues, however. Somewhat pessimistically, Ross has proposed to increase the number of parliamentarians, rather than to seek to restrain the number of officeholders.[61]

As the position of the most senior ministers was enhanced, the psychological distance between them and the backbenchers in Parliament became wider. Becoming more occupied with departmental duties, ministers have found less opportunity to maintain informal contacts with backbenchers. They have come to Parliament to speak rather than to spend part of their day listening to the debates or talking politics in the lobbies or the smoking room. Even more so than formerly, they appear on the scene as prima donnas rather than as colleagues in a club. Backbenchers have felt frustrated by this and have found inadequate compensation in the increased committee work of the House. More and more, they have come to feel themselves ill-paid and little-esteemed numbers in a Parliament where others dispose of their votes and their political future. Their frustrations have sometimes broken out in two psychologically closely connected attitudes: rebellious eruptions against the party leadership and attempts to somehow gain a place on the ministerial ladder. To maintain constant and cordial relations between party leaders and party followers has thus become more vital and more difficult. The importance of the whips has increased, and so has their number. In each party, small liaison committees between leaders and backbenchers have been established—department by department or between backbenchers and frontbenchers generally—to supplement the more formal proceedings of the meetings of the Parliamentary Party as a whole.[62] But no arrangement has been able to close the gap.

---

[59] Cf. the table in Richards, p. 214; the number of parliamentary private secretaries in the House of Commons has risen from 16 in 1910 to 36 in 1960. There are also a number of unpaid Assistant Whips.

[60] H. C. 120 (1941); cf. H. C. 349 (1956).

[61] Ross, *Elections and Electors*, p. 123.

[62] Morrison, pp. 121–33; cf. Richards, pp. 93–107, 143–56.

Complaints about the Functioning of
British Central Government

These varied adjustments notwithstanding, complaints continue to be heard about the malfunctioning of the central government apparatus. This phenomenon is not new. Ever since Balfour argued that "democracy threatens to kill its servants by the work it requires of them,"[63] ministers and high officials have constantly warned, irrespective of political persuasion, that the machinery threatened to break down. Haldane spoke of Asquith's Cabinet as "a congested body of about twenty in which the powerful orator secured too much attention," a system in which the Prime Minister "knew too little of the details of what had to be got through to be able to apportion the time required for discussion" and whereby "business was not always properly discussed and the general point of view that vitally required decision almost never."[64] In Chapters 3 and 4, the strains of the period from 1914 to 1922 were dealt with *in extenso*. Lloyd George's experiments ended in chaos rather than a new system. The Cabinets of Bonar Law and Baldwin restored some peace and order in the higher ranges of government but suffered from indecisiveness. MacDonald declared in 1924 that his duties were so heavy "that if you stopped to go much beyond the surface of things, you got caught up in doubts that were like nightmares and that the only thing to do was to plunge boldly in the knowledge that the next man would have to do the same."[65]

Lord Robert Cecil, who served under Asquith, Lloyd George, and Baldwin, was equally pessimistic in 1932. The pressure of government business, he argued, affected the health of leading ministers, resulting in breakdowns and early deaths, insomnia, exhaustion, indecisiveness, and an inclination to postpone or not to shoulder responsibilities. Cecil spoke of "the Prime Minister's disease . . . an instinctive refusal to decide anything if decision could by any means be avoided."[66] Jones, who was Deputy Secretary of the Cabinet until 1931 and a close companion of Baldwin and many other leading politicians in the 1930's, gave in his diary many examples that substantiate Cecil's general picture. He reported that Baldwin and Neville Chamberlain refused in 1932 to heed a summons for the Cabinet in vacation time because of the fatigue they had suffered at the Ottawa Conference of that year. He gave extensive information about the poor health of MacDonald and Baldwin between 1931 and 1937. He suggested that Hoare suffered from fainting fits because of overwork when he was Foreign Secretary.[67]

During this period the Cabinet Office under Hankey was accused of being partly responsible for overburdening ministers with an excess of

---

[63] Broad, *Winston Churchill*, p. 78.   [64] Haldane, *Autobiography,* pp. 216–18.
[65] *Holmes-Laski Correspondence*, p. 628.   [66] Cecil, pp. 11–13, 19.
[67] Jones, *Diary* pp. 56, 158, and above, Chap. 4; see also H. J. C. L'Etang, "The Health of Statesmen and Affairs of Nations," in *The Practitioner* (1958), pp. 113–18.

activities. But Hankey himself was to write thirteen years after he resigned as Cabinet Secretary: "An imperative necessity is to reduce the paralyzing strain of overwork on ministers, Parliament, and public servants, which threatens the country's constitution of all its strength." In the light of the "proliferation of Coordinating Commissions, Boards, Councils, Committees, Subcommittees, Working Parties, Panels, and the like," he deemed "a drastic and immediate overhaul" urgently necessary.[68]

In earlier chapters we treated the criticisms that were leveled against Churchill's administrative habits, both from 1940 to 1945 and from 1951 to 1955. Churchill had little sympathy for committees. However, in 1942, Cripps complained that Churchill tolerated such inefficient ways of administration as a needless proliferation of the committee system, inadequate delegation of authority, and old-fashioned ways of communication.[69] After 1947, Cripps himself became the classic example of a minister who practically met with death through insufficient delegation of duties to others. In 1947, Bevan proposed to postpone the discussion about nationalizing iron and steel because ministers "were all too tired to size up all the points."[70] The fate of Bevin and Cripps, the exhaustion of Butler as Chancellor of the Exchequer, of Eden as Foreign Secretary, and of other ministers made one member of Parliament, Martin Lindsay, brand in 1954 the system one of "Government by Endurance."[71] The Lord Chancellor, Kilmuir, declared in April 1956 in a Rectoral Address at St. Andrew's University that it was doubtful "whether a minister ever has sufficient time to consider the most profound problems of his country's future."[72] In that same month an article appeared by a former Socialist minister, Patrick Gordon Walker, who argued that "the rush of affairs is so tumultuous that the fine machinery of the Cabinet is in constant danger of getting clogged up with a surfeit of business."[73] Only six months later came the Suez crisis and Eden's resignation. Again the problem of the physical strain of ministers was painfully brought home. Desmond Donnelly, Labour member of the House of Commons, requested Macmillan to appoint a Select Committee to investigate the entire problem of the heavy burden that rested on ministers. For the time being, Macmillan refused the suggestion. But he asked Attlee and some other Privy Councillors to hold an informal inquiry. Their report apparently brought little solace.[74]

Whatever the reforms in the organization of central government, therefore, the complaint is still being made that ministers are seriously overworked, with the inevitable result that insufficient attention is given to matters of long-term policy, that business is not transacted efficiently, and that hurried compromises often take the place of well-thought-out decisions.

[68] Hankey, *Science and Art*, p. 23.   [69] *Life of Cripps*, pp. 313–14.
[70] Dalton, *Memoirs*, III, 250; cf. p. 264.   [71] *Sunday Times*, 18 July 1954.
[72] *The Times*, 21 April 1956.   [73] Gordon Walker, p. 21.
[74] 568 H. of C. Deb. (11 April 1957), cols. 1296–98; cf. the letter from Desmond Donnelly M.P. in *The Times*, 14 December 1956.

Proposals for General Reform of the Cabinet Structure

Criticism has generally been accompanied by proposals for further reform. These proposals have evoked discussions that are interesting for a number of reasons. They throw light on some basic problems of central government and give some indication of the direction in which public-administration thought has been developing over the last decades in Britain. And they offer an opportunity for a critical appraisal of the politics and the political theory that would seem to form the basis of public administration doctrines that are common in this field. One caveat seems in place here. These various reform proposals are not fully representative of British thought and experience in this matter. Proposals for changes from inside the government are either reflected in the actual changes that have taken place or have not been disclosed so far. This study therefore restricts itself in the following chapters to the thoughts of some British writers who have played a prominent role in actual politics or have strongly influenced contemporary academic thought about central government.

Reform proposals have been made by different persons in a wide variety of settings. They show many nuances. Nevertheless, three themes recur with great frequency in the debate: (a) there should be a fundamental redistribution of tasks among departments; (b) a small, non-departmental Cabinet chiefly concerned with policy-making should be established; and (c) Cabinet membership should be restricted to the most important ministers, while an extensive system of Cabinet committees should be utilized.

In reviewing these proposals, one should remain constantly aware of the tasks the Cabinet should perform in the British political system. These can be summarized as follows:

1. The Cabinet should be able to decide the most important policy questions encountered by the central government both in day-to-day practice and in long-term perspective. This implies that ministers should have the time to concentrate on such questions; that they should have at their disposal the best expert advice available from departmental and non-departmental advisers; and that they must remain aware of the more important ideas and social movements found in the country at large.

2. The Cabinet should supervise the machinery and processes of administration and make sure that the bureaucracy functions effectively and in unison. To do this, the Cabinet must have adequate insight into actual administrative procedures. It must be able to intervene in specific issues and to ensure coordination where necessary. But it must not be burdened to such an extent that the normal flow of administration becomes hampered and insufficient attention is given to long-term policy considerations. Decisions must be effectively prepared, and once taken they must be fit for execution *and* be recognized as such by the departmental and other official organs that will have to implement them.

3. The Cabinet should be able to make valid its claim to represent the political desires of at least the majority of politically articulate groups in the population. This requires that the relations between the Cabinet and the Parliamentary Party and its constituent groups be so close that steady support is secured; that enough voters continue to view the Government as effectively promoting their articulate or inarticulate interests; that the nation as a whole (notwithstanding group and party differences) be willing to abide by the leadership of the Cabinet; and that the internal relations within the Government allow a softening of political and personal conflicts to such an extent that external homogeneity can be preserved and a constant clearance of political, policy, and administrative decisions can be effected.

4. In all its functions—as decider of policy, administrative coordinator, and focus of political desires—the Cabinet should be able to proceed without impairing the legal and political responsibility of individual ministers and of the Government as a whole toward Parliament. This requires that Parliament remain able to hold individual ministers responsible for the efficient discharge of their duties; that collective responsibility remain intact; and that, in addition, Parliament be able to judge the more general question of whether the process of decision-making is that of an efficient and responsible government.

SEVENTEEN

PROPOSALS TO RATIONALIZE
THE INTERDEPARTMENTAL STRUCTURE

The Argument

"There is much overlapping and consequent obscurity and confusion in the functions of the Departments of executive Government," reported the (Haldane) Machinery of Government Committee, which inquired into the central government organization in 1917 and 1918. The Committee sought an explanation for this unsatisfactory state of affairs:

This is largely due to the fact that many of these departments have been gradually evolved in compliance with current needs, and that the purposes for which they were thus called into being have gradually so altered that the later stages of the process have not accorded in principle with those that were reached earlier. In other instances, departments appear to have been rapidly established without preliminary insistence on definition of function and precise assignment of responsibility.[1]

Many students of public administration have concluded from this diagnosis that a more systematic distribution of government tasks among the various departments would lead to a considerable improvement in the working of government. Related functions, so they have argued, should be combined as much as possible within one and the same department. This would give each minister a more homogeneous field of duties. Many matters now requiring interdepartmental consultation could then be settled at intradepartmental levels. This would relieve the Cabinet of numerous coordination problems and would help to prevent duplication.[2] Furthermore, a redistribution of functions among departments would also make it possible to decrease their number. This, in turn, might lead to the restoration of the traditional link between ministerial control of a department and Cabinet membership. Collectively, the ministers would represent all fields of government in the Cabinet, and yet the Cabinet would not become so large as to become indecisive. Both the preparation and the execution of government decisions would improve. At the same time, internal re-

---

[1] Cd. 9230 (1918), para. 4.
[2] Salter called "the proliferation of time-wasting departmental committees an automatic measure of an obsolete differentiation of functions" (*Personality in Politics*, p. 118). Cf. Smellie, p. 241.

sponsibility within the government apparatus and external responsibility toward Parliament would be clearly established. This would ensure a better insight into the weaker spots in the organization of government. Each important field of government would be, to quote the Haldane Committee, "under separate administration, the Cabinet being in a position of supreme executive direction, and Parliament holding the various ministers directly responsible to it for the efficiency of the service with which they were respectively charged."[3]

Since the publication of the Report of the Haldane Committee in December 1918, many have argued for a complete overhaul of the inter-departmental structure. The idea received particularly strong support during the Second World War. In 1941, for instance, the National Committee on Expenditure explicitly criticized the Government for paying insufficient attention to the problem of government organization.[4] And again, in 1947, the Select Committee on Estimates held:

What is needed is not a sporadic shifting of duties which . . . may well result in equally bad overlapping elsewhere. The necessity is rather for a modification of the present pattern of the administrative machine. . . . The part played by O. and M. technique and knowledge in this redesigning must be that of planning the structure and machinery of government rather than that of attending to its plumbing and maintenance.[5]

In spite of such affirmations the practical influence of this body of thought has been limited. This can be explained by a number of both theoretical and practical objections with which the proposal has met.

Theoretical Objections to the Proposal

The proposal seems a simple and obvious one: departmental functions are assessed and redistributed in such a way that a more logical organization chart emerges. In reality, it is much more ambiguous than it appears at first sight. For it is not at all evident in which direction reorganization should take place. At least three possibilities exist: (a) departments can be combined in such a way that the number of departmental ministers can be reduced to some ten or fifteen, or any other a priori number; (b) the tasks of each department can be so ordered that any one department will have as homogeneous a set of functions as possible; and (c) each department can simply be given that size which allows its minister and his highest official advisers to handle its business most effectively.

These three proposals by no means lead to the same result. The first aims consciously at a *decrease* in the number of autonomous departmental units. In view of the present burden of governmental tasks, the other two criteria, if applied consistently, would presumably lead to an *increase* in

---

[3] Cd. 9230 (1918), para. 19.   [4] H. C. 120 (1942).

[5] H. C. 143 (1947), paras. 48–49. "O & M" refers to the work of the Organization and Methods Division of the Treasury, which is discussed below, pp. 278–79.

the number of departments. These different proposals can be reduced to a common denominator only if no distinction is made between *amalgamating* departments into a small number of super-departments and *grouping* a large number of independent departments under the indirect guidance of special coordinating ministers.

The Amalgamation of Departments

Proposals under this general heading may be divided roughly into two categories: those that aim at an over-all reorganization of the departmental structure and those that try to improve the existing situation by incidental readjustments and amalgamations.

The Haldane Committee itself clearly belonged to the first category. It advocated one general principle according to which government functions should be redistributed: the "class of service" a particular department performs.[6] Its Report divided the tasks of government into the following groups: Finance; National Defence and External Affairs; Research and Information; Production (including Agriculture, Forestry, and Fisheries), Transport and Commerce; Employment; Supplies; Education; Health; and Justice.[7] The rearranging and criticizing of this scheme, the scrapping and adding of functions, have become a cherished pastime of teachers and writers on public administration. We shall not follow in their steps, for one basic reason. Whatever reorganization is proposed, the joining of existing departments would inevitably imply a heavier burden for the ministers in charge of the new, larger departments. A minister more heavily loaded with departmental duties would have little time to concentrate on active planning of policy. Ministerial control over the bureaucracy would tend to become precarious. The regular dispatch of business might be held up in many cases because of the special sphere of interest of the minister, or simply because undecided affairs piled up on his desk. The appointment of junior ministers or Ministers of State who might act for him can have only limited effect as long as Parliament continues to hold the minister himself responsible.[8] It could be argued that the super-departmental minister should be exempted as much as possible from his departmental responsibilities—for example, by charging him only with the general supervision of a group of departments, but leaving each department to a low-ranking departmental minister, who would continue to be fully responsible to Parliament. But in that case, one in fact discards the proposal to amalgamate departments in favor of that of a Cabinet in which non-departmental Overlords direct groups of departments without assuming actual control or responsibility for execution. This proposal will be treated in Chapter 18.

Incidental amalgamations have often been proposed and carried through. Long before 1946, the combining of the Service ministries into

[6] Cd. 9230 (1918), para. 18ff.   [7] *Ibid.*, para. 55.
[8] Schaffer, p. 362ff.

one Ministry of Defence had often been advocated. This evoked similar proposals in other spheres. Laski, for instance, advocated in 1938 the establishing of a Ministry of Production that would absorb the Board of Trade, the Ministry of Agriculture, and the Ministry of Labour.[9] After the Second World War, Laski came to reject this plan (without mentioning that he himself had proposed it in 1938) because of the novel political importance the Ministries of Labour and Agriculture had acquired. Laski then pleaded for a Ministry for the Nationalized Industries, which would bring together the Ministries of Transport, Fuel and Power, and Supply.[10] Other writers have suggested forming one Ministry for Social Security, or Social Welfare, which would make superfluous separate departments for Pensions, National Insurance, Health, and the like. Some amalgamations have indeed taken place in recent times. They meet with less objection, but also fall far short of the complete overhaul that some so strongly advocate.

The Ideal of Homogeneity

The notion of self-contained departments was put forward particularly by two members of the Haldane Committee, Beatrice Webb and Sir Robert Morant. Before the Haldane Committee first met in 1917, Beatrice Webb drafted a memorandum in which she catalogued the then-existing administrative organization, while testing it against her own definition of efficiency, which was that "each department ought as an ideal to be self-contained; that is, it should include the whole of its subject matter, and no part of any other subject matter, while no other department should interfere with its work."[11] Morant, too, desired a fundamental reorganization, because only in this way could conflicts of interest be fairly assessed instead of condemned as "atrocious departmental jealousy, or the mere pugnacity of obstructive interests."[12]

During the hearings of the Haldane Committee, this "self-containment" criterion met with strong criticism from the Permanent Under-secretary for Home Affairs, Sir Edward Troup, and from the Permanent Secretary to the Board of Trade, Sir Hubert Llewellyn Smith, both heads of government departments that have sometimes been irreverently characterized as "rag bags." According to Troup, "It was not generally possible or even desirable to secure that every department should be completely self-contained. . . . The administration was an organic whole and could not be cut up into watertight compartments. Each department should regard itself, both in theory and in practice, as standing in some relation to the other departments of the Public Service and not as an isolated unit."[13]

---

[9] Laski, *Parliamentary Government*, p. 249.   [10] Laski, *Reflections*, p. 153.

[11] *Conspectus of Existing Government Departments* and *Notes on Conspectus*, Reconstruction Papers, Folios 378–93.

[12] *Draft Addendum to Report of Machinery of Government Committee*, Reconstruction Papers, Folios 1077–78.

[13] Reconstruction Papers, Folios 699–700.

Llewellyn Smith was of the opinion that it was possible to devise logical proposals, but that it was not possible to carry them into effect at present. In many cases they would even be undesirable, for instance, if one should try to reabsorb Agriculture and Fisheries into the Board of Trade, which would be the department concerned with productivity. One advantage of larger departments, he said, was that they could preserve more independence from special-interest groups.[14] One could go further than this, and deny that homogeneity is attainable in the present-day world where the business of government is becoming increasingly complex and interdependent. Or one could argue that, if attainable, homogeneity would tend to invite every department to view its tasks in an egocentric fashion at a time when coordination and adjustment of special considerations to general policy are more desirable than ever.

Since the Haldane Committee put forward the criterion of "class of service" as the guiding principle for allocating departmental functions, both theoretical inquiry and practical experience have amply shown that a single criterion is not compatible with the requirements of modern government. Work processes, geographical considerations, and the interests of special social groups do have, and must have, as great an influence on the distribution of functions among departments as the main service each department is supposed to render.[15]

The Utilitarian Principle of the Size of the Job

"The ideal size for a ministry," according to a Study Group of the Royal Institute of Public Administration, "is the size that throws up no more business than can flow smoothly across the desks of the Minister and his Permanent Secretary."[16] The practical effect of this criterion must vary with the tasks for which a department is responsible, the qualities of individual ministers and officials, and the political pressure to which a particular field of government activity is exposed at any given moment. If it is true, however, that ministers and higher officials are seriously overworked, application of this principle would lead to a further increase in the number of departments. This would meet with the usual objections against an increase in the number of ministers such as its adverse effect on the size of the Cabinet as well as on the relations between ministers. Moreover, the most heavily burdened departments—e.g., the Foreign Office, the Treasury, and, to a lesser extent, the Board of Trade and the Home Office—would seem to be exactly those that would be the most difficult to split up.

Those who advocate this principle therefore tend to regard it as only one of the many factors that might be taken into account when particular

14 *Ibid.*, Folios 774–80.
15 Cf. Chester–Willson, pp. 350–62; Mackenzie–Grove, pp. 363–64; L. Petch, "The Study of the Machinery of Government," *O & M Bulletin,* V (1951), 3–4.
16 Chester–Willson, p. 343.

problems are raised about the distribution of tasks among departments. To quote anew from the Study Group's Report: "Perhaps the only thing that can be said with certainty is that sometimes in the life of a ministry there comes an increasing recognition that it has become so large that either it is no longer a candidate for new functions, or that it is time that it lost some to another ministry."[17]

Practical Difficulties of the Proposal

The Report from which we have just quoted is the result of an inquiry into changes in the organization of British central government since 1914. The inquiry was held between 1953 and 1957 by a group of high officials and academic experts in public administration. The Group began its work with the intention of first investigating how far certain administrative norms (such as the principle of homogeneous services advocated by the Haldane Committee) had influenced actual developments. Initially, the Group felt that this factor might have caused the establishment of certain new departments, such as the Ministry of Transport (1919) and the Ministry of Health (1919). Inspection of the actual documents and hearings with the surviving principals, however, soon proved this proposition untenable. The single most important factor in the establishment of a separate Ministry of Transport was, as discussed above, the personal ambition of Eric Geddes to build a national electrified railway system. Similarly, the setting up of a Ministry of Health was far from being a consequence of rational administrative considerations alone. Above all, it was born under the pressure of a few leading ministers and high civil servants, including the then Minister of Reconstruction, Dr. Christopher Addison, and Morant himself, whose advocacy of the principle of homogeneous services may have been couched in general terms, but whose real interest lay in segregating the field of social services from traditional civil service loyalties.[18]

In the preceding pages we have seen similar instances. New departments were instituted to please particular strata of the population, as was the case with the Ministry of Labour and the Ministry of Pensions during the First World War. Or they found their origin in public clamor, as was true when a special Minister for the Coordination of Defence was appointed in 1936, and when a Ministry of Supply was finally introduced shortly before the Second World War. Or a new ministry resulted when a particular field of government suddenly became important, as aircraft production did in 1940. Shifts occurred because of specific demands by powerful ministers: Bevin, who finally broke through the traditional refusal of the Home Office to transfer the Factory Inspectorate to the Ministry of Labour; Beaverbrook and Lyttelton, who demanded control over the

[17] *Ibid.*, p. 344.
[18] Addison, *Politics from Within*, II, 221ff; Chester–Willson, p. 152.

allocation of scarce materials as Ministers of Production; Hugh Dalton, who returned to the Cabinet in 1948 by a back door, and who by 1950 saw his influence as Minister of Town and Country Planning greatly extended. Financial considerations also played an important role. Wartime opened the door for numerous new administrative experiments, irrespective of cost. But the return of peace soon evoked a drive for economy, which resulted in a death warrant for a number of new departments.

If impulses for establishing new departments were therefore often not mainly organizational in character, the reverse might be equally true. Certain desirable administrative reforms were often blocked by resistance from ministers. A transfer of duties readily suggests the incompetence or diminished prestige of those from whom the tasks are taken. Strong ministers are therefore likely to resist any diminution of their authority. Transfers and reorganizations have often been postponed until new political and personal forces made their influence felt. By the latter part of the 1940's, organization experts had long advocated a general reshuffle of duties between the Ministry of Health, the Ministry of Town and Country Planning, and the Ministry of Works. But such an overhaul had to wait until 1951, when Bevan left the Ministry of Health.[19] Similarly, particular amalgamations of departments have often occurred only when a new Cabinet came into power. The Ministries of Transport and of Civil Aviation, and of Pensions and National Insurance, for example, were not put under one minister until the advent of the Churchill Government of 1951.

The strategic moment for a general overhaul soon passes. Each new Prime Minister receives from his highest official advisers a list of ministerial offices that exist by law or convention. A new Prime Minister may choose to deviate from this list in that he may decide to combine particular offices, create new departments, or leave certain sinecure offices open. But at the critical moment, most Prime Ministers will have other things in mind. In any event, they will be more interested in personnel than in administrative considerations. Once a new Cabinet is formed, personal and political forces come into their own again. Moreover, few ministers have a genuine interest in matters of administrative organization. "Nearly every minister is so intent upon using the instrument at hand for an immediate purpose," wrote Lord Salter, "that he will do little except by tampering and trivial adjustments to improve it."[20]

High civil servants also resist drastic changes. They too are accustomed to the existing structure. They have their habits, their expectations of promotion, their prestige considerations. Through personal relations, contacts with particular groupings in the society, and material factors such as the building in which it is housed, each department develops a special

[19] Dalton, *Memoirs*, III, 349–50.
[20] Salter, *Personality in Politics*, p. 119; see also "Principles of the Haldane Report," *The Times*, 8 and 9 October 1943. The author was Charles H. Wilson.

atmosphere. Redistribution of functions is therefore a far more complicated process than is generally realized. Numerous officials fulfil duties not only in sections that are to be transferred but also in those that remain with the old department. A separation of tasks, therefore, does not necessarily lead to an economy in personnel, which may have been the rationale of the reform in the first place. Similar difficulties may occur in departments that have to absorb new functions. Every reform threatens to disturb continuity. Unlike private firms, the Government cannot shut its doors and post a sign: "Closed for Remodeling."

These factors would seem to explain why redistributions of functions among departments have always been of limited character. Even so, it would be wrong to minimize their effect. Problems of coordination and overburdening often concern details. Specific reforms may therefore bring considerable relief in the aggregate. But they do not affect the basic structure of the governmental organization. Particular reorganizations have been important only to the extent that they have prevented the workload on ministers from becoming even more excessive.

The Background of the Proposal; The Report of the Machinery of Government Committee (1918)

Before 1914, only incidental proposals had been made for a fundamental reorganization of the interdepartmental structure. The slow pace and the restricted scope of government, the clear separation that still prevailed between most tasks of the State, permitted a calm development of the government structure. After 1900, this situation changed drastically under the impact of two factors: the growing demand for active State interference in social and economic affairs, and the outbreak of the First World War. The rapid increase of government tasks and the administrative improvisations that accompanied it threw the existing interdepartmental structure out of joint. New departments were often demanded for new government tasks. At the same time, a demand developed for a total reconstruction of the government apparatus. Such a desire, moreover, was often nourished by a drive for economy.

These several currents flowed together in the Haldane Committee.[21] In 1916, the Treasury presented a memorandum to the then Financial Secretary to the Treasury, Edwin Montagu, in which attention was drawn to the financial waste resulting from a bad distribution of functions among departments.[22] After the political crisis at the end of that year, Lloyd George appointed Montagu Vice-President of the Reconstruction Committee, which was to inquire into problems of postwar rehabilitation.[23] In

---

[21] See especially the essays of Bridges, *Haldane*; Wilson, *Haldane*; and Hume. For a fuller treatment of this subject, see my essay "The Haldane Committee and the Cabinet," *Public Administration*, XLI (1963), 117–35.

[22] Bridges, *Haldane*, p. 260; Chester–Willson, p. 293.

[23] Beatrice Webb's *Diaries, 1912–24*, pp. 6, 82, 84–86.

this capacity, Montagu drafted a memorandum in which he rejected both the prewar and the wartime Cabinet systems. In his opinion, the first had suffered from protracted discussions and irrational confusion of the functions of political councillor and departmental administrator. The War Cabinet, on the other hand, had introduced an untenable divorce of the Cabinet from the most important departments. He therefore suggested forming a Cabinet composed of a limited number of Secretaries of State, each of whom would supervise a number of satellite departments in a particular field.[24]

Montagu's memorandum resulted, in July 1917, in the establishment of a subcommittee of the Reconstruction Committee, the so-called Machinery of Government Committee, of which Haldane became Chairman. In addition to Haldane and Montagu, Sir Robert Morant, Sir George Murray, Alan Sykes, J. H. Thomas, and Beatrice Webb were appointed members. The Committee's terms of reference were "to enquire into the responsibilities of the various departments of the central executive Government and to advise in what manner the exercise and distribution by the Government of its functions should be improved."[25]

There was some difference, therefore, between the immediate cause and the final scope of the Committee. Whereas Montagu's note had especially dealt with the Cabinet, the terms of reference referred mainly to the distribution of departmental duties. This subtle difference also played a role within the Committee. The politician Haldane had a great interest in questions of Cabinet organization. Beatrice Webb, Morant, and Murray, on the other hand, laid more stress on the need for efficient administrative organization. Perhaps the atmosphere of the discussions is captured most clearly in Beatrice Webb's diary: "We sit twice a week over tea and muffins in Haldane's comfortable dining room discussing the theory and practice of government. I try to make them face the newer problems of combining bureaucratic efficiency with democratic control; they are forever insisting that the working of Parliament makes sensible, leave alone scientific administration, impracticable."[26]

The Committee collected a great deal of material in the form of memoranda and oral evidence.[27] From documents preserved in the British Library of Political and Economic Science in London, it is clear that different opinions were voiced from the outset about the most desirable Cabinet structure. Officials from the Cabinet Secretariat such as Hankey and Tom Jones pleaded discreetly for maintaining something like the War Cabinet structure in peacetime.[28] Others rejected such a "directory or tribunal."[29] Various proposals were made for retaining some form of

[24] Reconstruction Papers, Folios 227–35.
[25] Cd. 9230 (1918), para. 2.   [26] Beatrice Webb's *Diaries, 1912–24*, p. 98.
[27] Beatrice Webb, *Methods of Social Study*, pp. 149–52; cf. Vernon–Mansergh, pp. 54–55; Mackenzie, *Administration*, pp. 57–60.
[28] Reconstruction Papers, Folios 949ff, 967.
[29] Including the Secretary of the Reconstruction Committee, Vaughan Nash (*ibid.*, Folios 1004–1005).

committee system after the war. Officials such as Llewellyn Smith were prepared to exclude some of the new departments from the Cabinet, provided that the most important older departments were sure of Cabinet representation. G. M. Young (who also worked in the Cabinet Secretariat at the time) toyed with the idea of dividing ministers into two categories: permanent Cabinet members and ministers who would voluntarily refrain from attending the Cabinet, except when its business would directly concern their departments.[30]

Ideas were many, therefore, and the diversity was reflected in both the deliberations and the recommendations of the Committee. In its report, it demanded a small Cabinet, preferably of ten, or at most twelve members, who would meet frequently and be supplied with all the information necessary for arriving at expeditious decisions. The Cabinet would have to consult personally all the ministers whose work was likely to be affected by its decisions. The Cabinet Secretariat would have to be maintained and be charged with supervising the execution of Cabinet decisions.[31] But the Committee did not pronounce on the vital issue, as appears from a paragraph that is too little noted:

Whether the new type of Cabinet should consist of ministers in charge of the principal Departments of State, or of ministers "without portfolio" able to concentrate their whole attention upon the problems submitted for their consideration, or of ministers of both kinds are questions which we do not propose to discuss here.[32]

The refusal to enter into this matter is important: it enabled the Committee to advocate potentially conflicting ideas such as that of a smaller Cabinet and that of specialized, selfcontained departments, at one and the same time.

The Committee was less wary in advocating a redistribution of departmental functions according to one, overriding criterion.[33] Due partly to his German-philosophic training, Haldane was a strong believer in "first principles."[34] His temperament was radical, systematic, unemotional. He was driven by the desire to guarantee Britain the fruits of the rapidly developing sciences in all sectors of social life. At an early age, he had pressed for a "scientific approach" to administrative problems.[35] As Secretary of State for War, he had had a considerable influence on the development of the General Staff and the improvement of War Office and Army organization generally. He advocated the establishment of a separate

---

[30] Reconstruction Papers, Folios 777–78, 1012–13, 989–90.
[31] Cd. 9230 (1918), para. 7.   [32] *Ibid.*, para. 10.
[33] *Ibid.*, paras. 18–27.
[34] In addition to Haldane's autobiography and the biographies by Maurice and Sommer, see Beatrice Webb's *Diaries, passim*; Salter, "Haldane, the Capacious Intellect," *Personality in Politics,* pp. 113–19; Lloyd George, *Memoirs,* II, 1010–11; Markham, *Friendship's Harvest,* p. 43ff; Wells, *Autobiography,* II, 766–68; the Haldane Centenary Essays, *Public Administration,* XXXV (1957), 217–65; and Wilson, *Haldane, passim.*
[35] Cf. 139 H. of C. Deb. (2 August 1904), col. 634.

Ministry of Labour before the turn of the century, and favored a Ministry of Justice. Moreover, he was one of the leading instigators in the establishment of the (now Royal) Institute of Public Administration in 1922.[36] His entire career was dominated by a concern for specific policies rather than personal loyalties. "Political success," Haldane said, "is not to be an admired minister surrounded by a devoted group of adherents. It is to have a belief that is true and leads others to follow it."[37]

Somewhat similar elements played a role in the activities of Beatrice Webb and her husband, Sidney Webb. Both had a strong belief in the future bureaucracy of an egalitarian state, an ineradicable confidence in the value of their own visions and social investigations, a somewhat unimaginative concentration on government affairs alone. The Webbs had virtually no emotional allegiances to person or party. Men were to them, so it seemed, objects rather than individuals.[38]

Morant was of a much more emotional nature.[39] But he too had a characteristic detachment from, not to speak of distaste for, politics. His entire life had been determined by a struggle for social reforms, particularly in matters of education, social insurance, and health. In this, he had clashed with existing departments and developed a strong dislike for "the archaic machinery of government by means of which the pressing social problems of [this] country are at present supposed to be envisaged and handled."[40]

The cooperation of Haldane, Morant, and Beatrice Webb hence made the report of the Haldane Committee into a revolutionary document, which strongly emphasized first principles, the need for fundamental reorganization, and the desirability of adequate study of administrative questions. Efficient organization was a credo to all three. But behind this seemingly objective belief simmered an intense desire for *specific* social and administrative reforms.[41] This helps to explain why they attached such importance to the principle of organizing departments so that they could devote themselves fully to promoting particular government services. Typically, they paid little attention to the fact that far-reaching specialization of administrative functions is likely to be confusing to the ordinary citizen as he faces a considerable array of authorities bent on their efficiency rather

---

[36] *Life of Haldane*, I, 58–59; II, 62–63, 120–22, 176, 250; Bridges, *Haldane*, pp. 259, 263–64; Cd. 9230 (1918), chap. 10; Earl Jowitt, "Haldane and the Law," *Public Administration*, XXXV (1957), 222–31.

[37] Anderson, "Haldane the Man," *Public Administration*, XXXV (1957), 220–21; cf. Haldane, *Autobiography*, pp. 216, 343–44; Sommer, *Haldane*, p. 348.

[38] See Beatrice Webb, *My Apprenticeship* (1938); *Our Partnership* (1948); *Diaries, 1912–24* and *1924–32*; Margaret I. Cole, *Beatrice Webb* (1945); Margaret I. Cole, ed., *The Webbs and Their Work* (1949); H. G. Wells, *The New Machiavelli*, *passim*.

[39] See for Morant for example, B. M. Allen, *Sir Robert Morant: A Great Public Servant* (1934); Markham, *Friendship's Harvest*, pp. 167–207; Beatrice Webb's *Diaries, 1912–24*, pp. 97–98, n. 6. An unfavorable portrait of Morant is given by Braithwaite, *passim*.

[40] Reconstruction Papers, Folio 1072.

[41] Mackenzie, *Administration*, p. 58ff; Schaffer, p. 354.

than his sense of comfort.[42] It also explains the scant attention, not to say contempt, they had for the role of persons and party in politics, and for the strong influence of tradition and traditional *esprit de corps* on daily administration. In the Report can be found traces of the thought that "homogeneous services" would automatically produce the "right" policies, so that parliamentary criticism could become exceptional and even unnecessary, or, at most, a matter for experts only.[43]

Their ideas were hardly representative of the outlook of ordinary civil servants. They clashed with those of at least one active member of the Committee, Sir George Murray, a former Permanent Secretary to the Treasury, whom Violet Markham described as "wise, cynical, humorous, a realist without illusions."[44] Murray and Haldane restrained the Committee from advocating more extreme ideas, as appears in a letter from Morant to Beatrice Webb of 6 December 1918. Morant wrote that he found the Report's conclusions "terribly weak." He enclosed a draft addendum that he had wanted to add to the Report as a minority note and continued:

Murray said at once that if I were to do an addendum in the "ginger" direction he would feel bound to do an addendum in the opposite direction; this at once made Haldane miserable and he begged me to refrain, adding that if I did one, and Murray, then no doubt you, also, would want to do an addendum, pressing points of yours that were too mild or were omitted from the Report.[45]

Beatrice Webb's final judgment appeared in her diary: "The Report embodies all the right ideas and follows closely the lines laid down in the Webb document. But these ideas appear in nebulously phrased, hesitating propositions: a concession to Murray's vested prejudices and Sykes' vested interests and Haldane's incurable delight in mental mistiness."[46]

Developments since 1918

The Report of the Machinery of Government Committee was published a few days before the Khaki Elections of 1918. It received little publicity at the time and found support mainly in academic circles.[47] During the following decades it served as an inexhaustible source for exhortation to decrease expenditure by "more efficient government."

During the 1920's and 1930's, however, American management literature began to filter into Britain. It found a measure of practical application in business, especially in the 1930's, when the Depression forced economies and rationalization of procedures and machinery. At the same

---

[42] Cf. Hume, pp. 350–51.

[43] Cf. the lecture by C. H. Wilson, *Haldane and the Machinery of Government* (1956), p. 10ff, and Mackenzie, *Administration*, pp. 57–60. See also Hume, pp. 348–52; Schaffer, pp. 362ff; L. F. Urwick, "Management and the Administrator," in A. Dunsire, ed., *The Making of an Administrator* (1956), pp. 52–59.

[44] Markham, *Return Passage*, p. 147.   [45] Reconstruction Papers, Folio 1071.

[46] Beatrice Webb's *Diaries, 1912–24*, 8 December 1918, p. 137.

[47] Bridges, *Haldane*, p. 262.

time, Britain witnessed the increasing influence of public administration experts in the Federal Government of the United States. In 1937, the famous Report by the President's Committee on Administrative Management (composed of Louis Brownlow, Charles Merriam, and Luther Gulick) was published in Washington. It laid great stress on the need to concentrate the approximately one hundred existing government offices into a smaller number of departments, "the smallest possible number without bringing together in any department activities which are unrelated or in conflict with each other."[48] Roosevelt presented this report to Congress with a message that heralded the struggle for efficiency in administration as the highest task of modern democracy. Such thought also came into vogue in England, where notably left-wing circles watched the New Deal with avidity and envy. After 1935, rearmament also increasingly affected the distribution of tasks among existing departments. Defense experiences were often thought applicable to problems of civilian government.

But not until the Second World War did organization doctrines find practical application in central government in Britain.[49] Recommendations by the Haldane Committee (1918) and the Tomlin Commission on the Civil Service (1931) notwithstanding, the Treasury had deemed the appointment of a few "Treasury Investigating Officers versed in the use of office machines and appliances" sufficient until 1939. But the fast development of administrative tasks after 1939 threatened to get out of hand. An Advisory Panel of Businessmen recommended the establishment of an effective Organization and Methods Division in the Treasury. Faith in planning and the very turmoil the war had brought about were conducive to the conception that the State of the future would need a new organization.[50] The Select Committee on National Expenditure also urged a change of approach. In 1942, the Organization and Methods Division was definitely established in the Treasury. After that, O & M work developed apace. Organization experts soon came to argue that organizational principles applied not only to lower levels of Government, but also to the work of the Cabinet itself.[51] Reforms, so they argued, could result in vast improvements.

This conviction found a sympathetic ear in the Select Committee on Estimates, which investigated the control of the civil service in 1947 in an attempt to ensure the greatest possible economy in Establishment matters. "It is now a matter of urgency," stated the Committee's report, "that these questions should be attacked scientifically and not as a series of piecemeal adjustments." The Committee asked whether the Machinery of Government Division in the Treasury—a body that, until then, had investigated incidental frictions in the government apparatus and reported

---

[48] *Report of the President's Committee on Administrative Management,* 1937, p. 34.
[49] Chester–Willson, pp. 333–38.
[50] *Fifth Report from the Select Committee on Estimates,* 1946–47, H. C. 143, paras. 3–8.
[51] *Ibid.,* paras. 1492–1553 (evidence by Mr. N. Baliol Scott).

on them to a special Cabinet committee—drew sufficient profit from the vast experience of the O & M experts. The Committee regarded with satisfaction the establishment of a special committee for machinery-of-government questions, composed of permanent secretaries and certain other experts. But it preferred that a special body of full-time outsiders be charged with constantly scrutinizing the over-all organization of the government.[52]

In agreement with the recommendations made by the Select Committee on Estimates, the Machinery of Government Division was brought under the O & M Division of the Treasury in 1947. The O & M Division drafted a number of voluminous reports about possible reforms in the interdepartmental organization.[53] They had little influence. Before the Select Committee on Estimates, the Permanent Secretary to the Treasury, Bridges, had contested the suggestion that "vast improvements can be made if the problem is treated as an engineering problem."[54] There was, Bridges said, a considerable difference in matters of organization between the lower and higher ranges of government. "You want to bring into play not only an experience of organization and of the operations carried out by the departments," Bridges held, "but also, I think, experience of the way ministers approach these questions and of the working of Cabinet committees, and so forth."[55]

Ministers and high civil servants refused to be told how to do their jobs by organization specialists. The experts were soon reduced again to minor advisory positions, while the responsibility for interdepartmental organization questions was again moved up to *ad hoc* committees of Permanent Secretaries. The Machinery of Government Division shrank to one part-timer who mainly carries out secretarial duties for the special committees just mentioned. The philosophy of O & M work itself also changed. The complexity of daily administration was more readily appreciated. Organization theory itself came to put more stress on factors of informal organization.[56] Organization experts learned that imposition from outside was a less promising technique than persuasion from within. Consequently, O & M work was decentralized to a considerable extent to individual departmental units, the O & M Division acting as stimulus and adviser rather than as chief or controller for all but the less-important departments.

Management doctrine therefore had little success in central government. This seems to be due, above all, to a *vitium originis*. It deems the experiences of army organization and private enterprise directly applicable to the public service, without giving enough attention to the different tasks the government administration fulfills, the public pressures to which it is exposed, and the very special factors that enter into the recruitment of the highest government leaders.

[52] *Ibid.*, paras. 49, 50. [53] Chester–Wilson, pp. 336–37.
[54] H. C. 143 (1947), para. 1500. [55] *Ibid.*, para. 1608; cf. Schaffer, pp. 355–56.
[56] Cf. Mackenzie–Grove, pp. 361–64.

EIGHTEEN

PROPOSALS FOR A POLICY CABINET

The Argument

The proposal to establish a purely non-departmental Cabinet, oriented above all toward the framing of policy, was strongly advocated by L. S. Amery. Of the numerous passages he devoted to the proposal in debate or in writing, the following of 1936 is perhaps most characteristic of his thought:

It is my profound conviction, based on a good many years of practical experience, that a Cabinet consisting of a score of overworked departmental ministers is quite incapable of either thinking out a definite policy, or of securing its effective and consistent execution. . . . We attempt to direct the affairs of a great nation by weekly meetings between departmental chiefs, all absorbed in the routine of their departments, all concerned to secure Cabinet sanction for this or that departmental proposal, all giving a purely temporary and more or less perfunctory attention to the issues brought up by other departments. Every Cabinet meeting is a scramble to get through an agenda in which the competition of departments for a place is varied by the incursion of urgent telegrams from abroad or of sudden questions in the House of Commons for which some sort of policy or answer must be improvised. The one thing that is hardly ever discussed is general policy. Nothing, indeed, is more calculated to make a Cabinet Minister unpopular with his colleagues, to cause him to be regarded by them as "Public Enemy No. 1," than a tiresome insistence on discussing general issues of policy, often controversial, when there are so many urgent matters of detail always waiting to be decided. The result is that there is very little Cabinet policy, as such, on any subject. No one has time to think it out, to discuss it, to coordinate its various elements, or to see to its prompt and consistent enforcement. There are only departmental policies. The "normal" Cabinet is really little more than a standing conference of departmental chiefs where departmental policies come up, from time to time, to be submitted to a cursory criticism as a result of which they may be accepted, blocked, or in some measure adjusted to the competing policies of other departments. But to a very large extent each department goes its own way, following its own bent and its own tradition, fighting the "Whitehall War" to the best of its ability.[1]

---

[1] Amery, *Forward View*, pp. 443–44. Amery particularly objected to the power of the Treasury in the Cabinet: "The Treasury has always pursued its own policy, however inconsistent with the general policy of the Cabinet. It enjoys immense powers of holding up and frustrating, in detail, policies sanctioned by the Cabinet and by Parliament and exercises them to the full" (*ibid.*, p. 444; Amery, *Constitution*, pp. 94–97).

Amery saw the root of these evils in the confusion of responsibility for the making of policy with that for the day-to-day management of large administrative departments. To quote another passage:

It is a commonplace of scientific organization, long since recognized in the Fighting Services, that where the same persons are responsible for day-to-day administration as well as for the planning of policy to meet the remoter needs and uncertain eventualities of the future, the latter duty is bound to be neglected. Routine business is always more urgent and calls for less intellectual effort than sitting down to think seriously about something that may happen "next year, sometime, never."[2]

Amery concluded that a special policy Cabinet should be instituted.[3] This would consist of six or seven ministers, all of whom would be free from departmental duties. It would exercise administrative control and coordination by inviting the ministers concerned to special Cabinet sessions, or by organizing permanent or *ad hoc* committees to be presided over by Cabinet members. But such necessary tasks would not be its main preoccupation. Separate sessions would be set aside for reviewing long-term policy. Furthermore, policy committees should be instituted for special fields. They would be separate from the administrative Cabinet committees and concentrate exclusively on policy issues. Each policy committee would be assisted by a research and planning staff composed of members of intelligence staffs of the departments concerned. The Prime Minister would always act as chairman of these committees. But under him, one Cabinet member would act as his substitute. He would be the recognized policy minister for the departments in that particular sector.

In this way, Amery argued, it would be possible to arrive at well-considered policy directives, which would differ basically from the hasty decisions that now arise under the influence of interdepartmental bargaining or sudden political crises. The proposed system should remain entirely flexible so that it could be adjusted at any time to the personalities involved. Since the Cabinet and the departments would be assigned separate functions, the departmental structure need no longer create difficulties. On the contrary, departmental duties would become susceptible to further rationalization and specialization. Departmental ministers would have more time for their specific tasks. But at the same time, they would still be able to influence general policy by belonging to policy committees and administrative committees and by attending Cabinet meetings whenever matters in which they had an immediate interest were discussed.[4]

All these arguments recall the views put forward in the Report of the War Cabinet of Lloyd George on the year 1917. The idea also found its

---

[2] Amery, *Constitution*, p. 88.

[3] Amery used the term "policy Cabinet" to describe his proposed arrangement. One should not conclude that by adopting his terminology I am granting his argument, or that all Cabinets do not perforce deal with policy questions.

[4] Cf. Amery, *Forward View*, pp. 445–47; Amery, *Constitution*, pp. 86–96.

strongest support during both world wars. During World War II, for instance, the plan was advocated by many, especially Beveridge and *The Times*. In peacetime it was especially popular among Socialist politicians in the early 1930's, and since 1945 it has found a measure of support from Lord Samuel, Christopher Hollis, and others.[5] Its attractive simplicity and challenging character probably explain why the proposal found more support, as well as stronger criticism, in circles of politicians and political scientists than did suggestions for a fundamental overhaul of the inter-departmental structure. Among ministers, Churchill, Anderson, and Morrison have emphatically rejected the concept of a non-departmental Cabinet for peacetime purposes. In academic circles it has been criticized especially severely by Laski and Chester, but also by many others.[6] We shall review these criticisms according to the four main functions of the Cabinet: the making of policy, administrative coordination, ministerial responsibility, and the articulation of political life.

The Proposal and the Determination of Policy

The argument that a small, non-departmental Cabinet is best suited to devise and decide policy rests in particular on three propositions: First, a small Cabinet can meet more frequently; hence it will grow quickly into a closely knit team and thereby expedite discussions and increase the decisiveness of the Cabinet. Second, because the members of the Cabinet will have no direct departmental responsibilities, they will have more time to concentrate on fundamental issues of Cabinet policy. Third, the departments will fit in better in the decision-making process: interdepartmental conflicts will fall more easily into place if they are regarded against the background of long-term policy considerations. Because only policy ministers are members of the Cabinet, and because they have the support of special planning staffs, their authority over the departments will be greater than that of present-day coordinating ministers.[7] Because the departmental ministers can exercise their influence in special Cabinet sessions and Cabinet committees, a serious gap between the Cabinet and the departments need not arise.

The Economies of Small-Scale Deliberation

Most critics accept the view that a small body will more readily come to decisions than a larger one, albeit with two reservations. Jennings has rightly argued that in the last analysis everything will depend on per-

---

[5] Beveridge, *Power and Influence*, pp. 269–70, 332; Lord Samuel in *The Times*, 9 September 1947, 3 February 1950, and 9 February 1950; Hollis, pp. 89–94.

[6] Anderson, *Machinery*, pp. 11–13; Morrison, pp. 32–35, 52–56; Laski, *Reflections*, pp. 120–52; Laski, *Government in Wartime*, pp. 9–15; Chester, *Cabinet*, pp. 51–55; K. C. Wheare, *The Machinery of Government* (1945), pp. 10–11; Jennings, *Queen's Government*, pp. 116–18; Wiseman, pp. 168–70; Smellie, pp. 307–8; Finer, *Theory and Practice*, pp. 596–97; Carter, p. 340ff; Harrison, pp. 138–42.

[7] Cf. Amery, *My Political Life*, II, 93.

sonalities: "The length of a discussion in the Cabinet or a Cabinet committee must depend primarily on the people present, whether they have ideas of their own, or ambitions of their own."[8] It is possible that in a smaller group ministers will size up their colleagues sooner and better; if so, this is likely to promote the rapid dispatch of business. In a larger Government, ministers have an opportunity to press their views during formal Cabinet sessions only; *ceteris paribus*, this tends to slow up decisions. But it is equally possible to argue the reverse. The more formal character of the larger Cabinet limits the opportunity to discuss ideas prematurely, and gives less license to gossip or personal pressure. Generalization is therefore difficult.

A second footnote is of more critical importance: in a small Cabinet, the proceedings are more dependent on the special preoccupations of individual ministers, or of Cabinet members collectively. Elaborate consultation with persons and groups tends to make government a slow process. But it minimizes the possibility that important aspects of a problem will be overlooked.

Freeing the Leading Ministers from Departmental Responsibilities

Amery's proposition that non-departmental ministers have more time to consider fundamental problems is not easily acceptable. If the policy minister is to preserve his influence, he must remain *au courant* of the more important business being transacted in the departments under his supervision. This forces him to read numerous documents, to consult continuously with other ministers and civil servants, and to be readily available for endless deliberations.[9] Amery argued that the policy ministers concerned would normally have had extensive experience in the departments under their supervision.[10] But his critics challenge this statement, since one-time experience rapidly becomes obsolete at the present pace of government. And they point out, in addition, that the policy ministers would not have the administrative and expert assistance with which large departments so readily provide their ministers.[11]

The Cabinet and the Departments

The view that a policy Cabinet would improve relations with the departments is generally rejected. A policy formed without the direct and constant participation of the departments, many critics have argued, will generally be unrealistic. As Laski has written: "Policy is the expression of an accumulation of minutiae, with which the non-departmental minister does not concern himself."[12] He also wrote: "The men who make the decisions must be those through whose hands the pivotal papers pass.

---

[8] Jennings, *Queen's Government*, p. 116.
[9] Cf. Laski, *Reflections*, pp. 142–43; Chester, *Machinery*, pp. 28–29.
[10] Cf. Amery in *The Manchester Guardian*, 29 April 1954.
[11] Harrison, pp. 140–41.   [12] Laski, *Parliamentary Government*, p. 248.

They do the work of selection out of which principles emerge; and the work of selection is itself the necessary ground upon which alone right decisions can be taken."[13]

Others have agreed with Laski. Policy should be determined inductively, Salter has written.[14] Or, in the words of Anderson, any long-term planning should, after all, "be fed, or at least refreshed, in practice from the departmental dynamos."[15] The War Cabinet of 1916–18 is usually adduced in evidence. Lloyd George also attempted to exclude the departments as much as possible from the formation of long-term policy, so the critics of a policy Cabinet argue. But in practice, realistic decisions could not be reached without the constant presence of a large number of departmental ministers. The system therefore led to endless friction and to a loss of time and energy, which could easily have been avoided if departmental ministers had been included from the start. Either the policy Cabinet meets alone, so the critics continue, and its members tend to become "just a group of backroom boys brooding over future policy"; or it generally meets with most departmental ministers present, in which case it is difficult to see what advantage the policy Cabinet has over the existing system.[16] Another objection raised against excluding the departmental ministers is that it does not leave the departments free to look after their business in a presumably detached and neutral fashion, but invites them to pursue their interests in highly egocentric ways—much more so, in fact, than when all ministers are members of the supreme policy-making body. A non-departmental Cabinet, Laski has written, becomes "not a maker of policy but a corrector of mistakes."[17]

Various proposals have been put forward to meet these objections, at least partially. In 1941, the Liberal Leader, Clement Davies, advocated establishing a (War) Cabinet composed of three ministers without portfolio, who would be assisted by five super-ministers: the Chancellor of the Exchequer and four ministers controlling internal and external affairs, defense, and production, respectively.[18] In 1947, Samuel devised a scheme for a Cabinet of ten members. According to his proposal, the Prime Minister and five other Cabinet members would not be charged with departmental duties. Instead, they would act as chairmen of sub-Cabinets for defense, trade and commerce, external affairs, social services, and industry, agriculture, and transport. The Foreign Secretary, the Chancellor of the Exchequer, the Home Secretary, and the Lord Chancellor would also be included.[19] The scheme deliberately subordinated the

---

[13] Laski, *Government in Wartime*, p. 10.
[14] Salter, *Cabinet*, p. 116. Cf. Churchill in 368 H. of C. Deb. (22 January 1941), cols. 258–59.
[15] *The Times*, 11 February 1950.
[16] Morrison, p. 34; cf. Smellie, p. 293: "A naked athlete can never move in comfort among armed men"; Chester, *Cabinet*, p. 55; Wiseman, p. 169.
[17] Laski, *Government in Wartime*, p. 10.
[18] 368 H. of C. Deb. (21 January 1941), cols. 224–25.
[19] *The Times*, 9 September 1947; see also *The Times*, 3 February 1950 and 9 February 1950.

Foreign Secretary and the Chancellor of the Exchequer to the sub-Cabinets. For this Samuel was publicly taken to task by Anderson, who questioned the practical possibility of subordinating the Chancellor of the Exchequer and the Foreign Secretary to non-departmental committee chairmen. Anderson held that there was no logical principle on which to include those ministers in the Cabinet and to exclude the ministers of Labour, Trade, Health, Housing, Scotland, the Commonwealth, etc.[20]

Salter had somewhat similar views. He therefore proposed that the special policy committees of the Cabinet and the joint planning staffs serving these committees should be directed by the most important *departmental* ministers, e.g., the Minister of Defence, the Foreign Secretary, and the Chancellor of the Exchequer. With the Prime Minister, these ministers should form the Inner Cabinet. In directing their own departments, they should be assisted by Ministers of State, who would relieve them of part of their departmental duties.[21]

Amery himself conceded part of the argument to his critics when he wrote, in a review of Morrison's *Government and Parliament*:

What is important is that the policy ministers should form a definite collective group and enjoy a priority of authority in matters of general policy. . . . Whether they alone are called the Cabinet or whether that title is retained by a wider body including a dozen departmental ministers is a matter of detail.[22]

The Proposal and the Process of Daily Administration

The proposal for a policy Cabinet can be criticized further from two angles: first, the preparation of Cabinet decisions and, second, their execution.

The Preparation of Cabinet Decisions

For a smooth functioning of the decision-making process, a great deal depends on whether the policy ministers would work through the staff of the existing departments, would have a staff of their own, or would be assisted by joint staffs, drawn from the departments, but working under the control of the policy ministers.

In the first case, Morrison and others have argued, "the civil servants would tend to have a dual responsibility to [the departmental minister] and to the supervising minister," which might imply that "the civil servants may be confused, if not resentful."[23] The system would throw a new burden on already hard-pressed civil servants, who would have to serve two masters instead of one. If the policy ministers were to be given their own staff, all classic conflicts between line and staff agencies would be provoked on a much larger scale. "A proposal having been discussed

---

[20] *The Times*, 6 February 1950, and 11 February 1950.
[21] Salter, *Cabinet*, pp. 114–16.
[22] *The Manchester Guardian*, 29 April 1954.   [23] Morrison, p. 52.

by one set of officials and settled by one minister," said Jennings, "is then discussed by another set of officials and settled by another minister. It is always easy to add to the work without adding to the work done."[24] Amery's compromise suggestion for joint staffs—composed of representatives from all the departments concerned, but working directly under the policy minister—presupposes considerable harmony between the departments. As we have seen, the joint-staff principle has in practice covered little more than institutionalized interdepartmental consultation. In the case of the defense organization, these staffs developed into a coordinating department. The Central Economic Planning Staff, on the other hand, became a mere division of the Treasury. In both cases, these joint staffs tended to fulfill secretarial rather than policy-making functions. Neither would seem to accord with the kind of distinction between day-to-day administration and policy planning that Amery wished to see established. Moreover, any governmental machinery, if good, will tend to be increasingly charged with urgent business. This is likely to drive out the orientation toward the more distant future that was the aim of Amery's original proposal.[25]

The Implementation of Decisions

Many critics have pointed out difficulties that are likely to arise in the stage of execution. In the absence of direct links between the departments and the policy-making center, departmental policies are likely to diverge from the Cabinet's intentions. Or, to use a more telling metaphor of Jennings, there is a danger that ministers will "go joy-riding with departmental policy."[26] Others have feared conscious opposition from the departments. Laski eagerly quoted a passage from Sir Henry Taylor's *The Statesman* (1836) : "He who has in his hands the execution of measures is in truth the very master of them."[27] Did not Churchill consider one of the main advantages of a Cabinet composed of "chiefs of organizations" to be that only this kind of machinery would ensure that decisions were executed "with alacrity and with goodwill"?[28] Franks, too, based his argument in favor of a committee system mainly on the view that depart-

---

[24] Jennings, *Queen's Government*, p. 117.   [25] Beloff, p. 120.
[26] Jennings, *Constitution*, p. 154; cf. Laski, *Government in Wartime*, p. 10; Jennings, *Queen's Government* p. 116.
[27] Laski, *Government in Wartime*, p. 9. Amery also adduced Taylor in evidence: "It is one business to do what must be done, another to devise what ought to be done" (Amery, *Constitution*, pp. 89–90). Apparently, Taylor considered both active daily administration and detached contemplation essential for a Cabinet. He wrote: "This, then, is the great evil and want—that there is not within the pale of our government any adequately numerous body of efficient statesmen, some to be more externally active and answer the demands of the day, others to be somewhat more retired and meditative in order that they may take thought for the morrow" (Sir Henry Taylor, *The Statesman* [1836; Mentor Books ed. 1958], p. 105; cf. Wilfrid Harrison, "Sir Henry Taylor and 'The Statesman'," *Public Administration*, XXX [1952], 61–70). On the basis of a similar argument, Morrison advocated including both departmental and non-departmental ministers in the Cabinet (*op. cit.,* p. 43).
[28] 368 H. of C. Deb. (22 January 1941), col. 261.

ments would acknowledge a commitment to decisions only if they had been given sufficient opportunity to influence them before they were taken. Others have spoken outright of the danger of deliberate sabotage. A supervising minister, Morrison has suggested, "would, I think, live a lonely life in his little office, faced with the dilemma of doing little or nothing on the one hand, or fighting his way through resistance and friction on the other."[29]

An additional objection to the proposal is that the special preoccupations of Cabinet members might well block the progress of business in which the policy ministers happened to be less interested. Anderson has also called it "a very questionable benefit" to deprive the departments of the services of the most experienced ministers.[30]

The Proposal and Ministerial Responsibility

Chester has given the following succinct definition of the principle of ministerial responsibility:

Briefly stated, ministerial responsibility means that for every act of a government department and for every omission to act (where departments have legal power to do so), responsibility can be placed on a particular minister. . . . It merely implies that any matter falling within the power of the central government can be laid at the door of a particular minister, not of the government as a whole nor of a corporate body known as a department.[31]

It has often been argued that Amery's proposal is in basic conflict with this principle. A policy minister, it is held, cannot but deprive his subordinate ministers of full authority in their own departments, and hence the proposal for supervising ministers is "inconsistent both with the parliamentary responsibilities of ministers and with departmental control."[32] Many writers have thought this argument alone sufficiently decisive to reject both a non-departmental Cabinet and the appointment of supervising ministers with specified tasks over subordinate departmental ministers. Actually, this almost universal disapproval hides a number of rather heterogeneous views.

Conflicting Motives

Some authors have based their rejection of the proposal on the fact that ministers usually have definite *statutory* duties for which they are responsible to Parliament. They see no great difficulty where ministers have *prerogative* powers. Others have pointed to the difficulty of distinguishing between policy and administration. They have consequently thought a supervising minister acceptable in fields where such a distinction *can* be made. Still others have used a moral argument: they think it unfair to

---

[29] Morrison, p. 53.   [30] *The Times*, 11 February 1950.
[31] Chester, *Ministerial Responsibility*, p. 1; Chester–Bowring, p. 167.
[32] Anderson, *Machinery*, p. 12.

burden ministers with the responsibility for matters that are not within their undivided control.

These various arguments are needed to explain away the Ministry of Defence, which has functioned as a policy ministry over the three Service ministries. Defense, some say, is to a very considerable extent a matter of prerogative powers. The merit of the relation between the Minister of Defence and the Service ministers, others argue, is that special legislation has provided a clear demarcation of responsibilities. Other observers hold that it is easy to distinguish defense policy from the mere administration and equipping of the three Services. And others put forward a more opportunistic argument: the task of the Service ministers is so heavy—even when they concentrate only on their own administrative tasks—that they can have but little ambition to deal also with policy matters. There is a very strong streak of special pleading in such arguments.

Implicit or Explicit Functions for the Policy Ministers?

The element of confusion is also noticeable in the fact that considerable difference of opinion exists on the question of which system would most erode parliamentary responsibility: a non-departmental Cabinet in which the duties of the ministers are not specified, or a Cabinet in which each minister has clearly defined supervisory powers over a group of departments. As we saw, Beveridge rejected a specific grouping of departments under a supervising minister because it was in conflict with ministerial responsibility. For this reason, he demanded a War Cabinet of ministers without portfolio; though there might be some division of labor between them, ministers should have no exclusive spheres. Anderson, on the other hand, said that one of the basic advantages of Churchill's War Cabinet over Lloyd George's was that Churchill's Cabinet ministers had well-defined departmental duties. He called it a "misconception . . . that certain ministers who were members of the [Churchill] War Cabinet had an overriding responsibility in respect of matters within the competence of ministers of Cabinet rank, not in the War Cabinet." Churchill, for one, had a different opinion about this.[33]

Individual and Collective Ministerial Responsibility

Fundamental to the argument that ministerial responsibility is infringed by a policy Cabinet is the view that there are clearly marked spheres in government for which ministers have sole responsibility. Its defenders point out that ministers are given definite statutory responsibilities by Acts of Parliament. The very existence of the principle of collective responsibility implies, however, that such a specific field of responsibility can be neither exclusive nor clearly delineated. Ministers are wont to determine for themselves which issues to decide on their own responsibility and which to refer to the Cabinet. The pressure of modern

[33] Anderson, *Machinery*, p. 11; cf. Churchill in 500 H. of C. Deb. (13 May 1952), col. 1112.

government makes it inevitable (and desirable) that ministers shoulder responsibility for matters of substantial importance without always consulting their colleagues. But each minister knows that these colleagues, and especially the Prime Minister, can at any time disown a policy that they refuse to endorse (albeit with the possible penalty of resignation of the minister concerned).

Precisely because a minister can normally rely on the political support of his colleagues, even when they have had no direct voice in the matter, he should retain their confidence. No legal borderlines prevent them from holding him accountable for all his *faits et gestes*. Consequently, the dividing line between individual and collective responsibility is flexible. Where this line is drawn in any specific situation is dependent on a number of factors. The political weight of a particular minister can enlarge his freedom of action. The need for specialization that logically follows from the highly complicated and cumbrous character of modern administration works in the same direction. The political importance of a particular issue, on the other hand, can make a minister's entire field of responsibility an object of Cabinet concern. The dividing line differs, in other words, from period to period, from function to function, from person to person, and from political situation to political situation.

The real question of a policy Cabinet is therefore not whether it infringes on individual ministerial responsibility (every Cabinet does) but whether the policy Cabinet does not so divide *political* responsibilities that the unity of the Cabinet and the possibility of forming a judgment about the process of policy formation are jeopardized. Amery thought his proposal would force Parliament to distinguish more clearly than hitherto between matters of policy and execution. He could also have drawn support from Jennings' view that "the more ministerial responsibility is divided by adding to the number of ministers," the more specific and effective parliamentary responsibility becomes.[34] Yet Amery did not deal with the basic dilemma posed by his critics. Either the policy ministers accept full responsibility or they do not. If they do, does it not follow that they will be so heavily burdened that the very justification for their appointment is bound to disappear? And if they do not, what guarantee is there that the departmental ministers will not go their own ways?

The Proposal and Political Realities

Many critics have found unacceptable a scheme by which five or six ministers would have final authority on all important government issues. In Amery's view, it would be up to the members of the policy Cabinet to send a constant stream of policy directives through the entire governmental service. The status and experience of these ministers, their "wider outlook as well as the abler brain," would ensure that departmental ministers would freely follow these directives and so implement Cabinet

[34] Jennings, *Constitution*, pp. 152–53.

decisions.[35] Is this at all probable? Most politicians owe their places to their own ambitions, capacities, and political influence. Almost every minister wishes to belong to the inner circle. Some politicians are bound to have such an important position in the party that they *must* have a place in the Cabinet lest the coherence of the government and party should suffer. But this political qualification is not identical with that of judgment or administrative experience; really decisive is the reserve power a particular politician could wield against the Cabinet if he were excluded from it. Any Prime Minister must also consider other factors in forming his Cabinet: personalities, administrative skill, debating strength, and representation of interest groups, religious creeds, and special regions such as Scotland. As Bagehot has written:

The difficulty of making up a Government is very like the difficulty of putting together a Chinese puzzle: the spaces do not suit what you have to put into them. And the difficulty of matching a ministry is more than that of fitting a puzzle because the ministers to be put in can object, though the bits of a puzzle cannot.[36]

And unlike an ordinary jigsaw puzzle, Cabinet-making becomes more difficult when there are fewer pieces.

The great danger of restricting the effective right of decision to a very small circle is, therefore, that those excluded will not concentrate on their jobs but on political maneuvers, on forming groups and cliques, and on forcing palace revolutions.[37] However influential five or six Cabinet members may be, they can hardly afford to treat important departmental ministers in a brusque fashion. Departmental ministers can weaken the Cabinet's grip on Parliament even by little asides that might suggest a lukewarm attitude toward Cabinet policy. Some have enough resignation value to force access to Cabinet sessions at any time. The entire system would therefore seem to lead to "a loss of goodwill and camaraderie."[38] There may be many in a normal Cabinet who seem mere passengers. As Laski reported to Oliver Wendell Holmes after a conversation with Mac-Donald and Haldane in 1924:

There are some who literally cannot do any business at all and merely repeat the advice of their permanent officials. There are some, again, who do their own work most competently but refuse to budge an inch beyond purely departmental questions. There are others who carry their weight on all subjects. There are others also who insist on butting in with the clearest inability to understand. I gathered that in a Cabinet of twenty you can expect four or five who are really generally useful; that ten will bear their own burdens so long as they are not expected to go beyond their province; and the remainders are dead weights, who are there for political reasons not justified in the event.[39]

[35] Amery in 356 H. of C. Deb. (1 February 1940), col. 1362; Beveridge in *The Times*, 14 February 1942.
[36] Bagehot, p. 157; *Webb Memorandum*, pp. 15–16.
[37] Laski, *Reflections*, pp. 151–52.   [38] Morrison, p. 53.
[39] *Holmes-Laski Correspondence*, p. 628.

But is it really possible to speak of "political reasons, not justified in the event"? Everyone may have his own thoughts about what is political ballast and what not. One might even defend the paradox that only adequate ballast will keep the Cabinet on an even keel, so that a few ministers on the bridge can determine its course with some freedom of action.

A further objection advanced against Amery's proposal is that five or six persons cannot easily carry the psychological burden of all important national issues. Intellectual inbreeding is likely to jeopardize a small Cabinet's relation to Parliament, party, and country. It is argued, finally, that country and Commons will support and recognize the moral leadership of a Cabinet only if it includes the ministers whose departments are most subject to political conflict.[40]

The Background of the Proposal for a Policy Cabinet

Agitation for a non-departmental Cabinet first arose during World War I, when the traditional Cabinet failed in decisiveness, and the departmental structure proved ill-suited to the unprecedented demands of total war. The loss of life, the sapping of will, the evasion of victory created political unrest. New leaders were demanded irrespective of party, new forms of government irrespective of traditional structures. Once established, Lloyd George's War Cabinet was to exercise a profound intellectual influence. Many came to attribute victory to this administrative device, while others rejected it violently as the epitome of political immorality. The emotional debate about Lloyd George, in other words, came greatly to affect the academic discussions about a non-departmental Cabinet.

After 1918, the proposal was given a more definite theoretical grounding. It was suggested that a non-departmental Cabinet might improve its working if the departments were grouped together under specialized policy ministers. They should be given a special staff organization for the elaborating of policy directives to be implemented by the departments. Military analogies exercised a considerable influence on the terminology and theory of the proposal.[41] It was also in the military sphere that the institution

---

[40] Cf. Wiseman, pp. 170–71; K. C. Wheare, *The Machinery of Government* (1945), pp. 10–12.

[41] The Report of the Esher Committee (Cd. 1932 [1904]), in particular, became a *locus classicus*. Amery referred to the great influence Sir Gerald Ellison, its Secretary, exercised on him: "He made me realize that in an Army which exists for an eventuality of war, uncertain in time as well as in character, but which also has to live its routine life meanwhile, the more urgent and intellectually easier tasks of that routine life will inevitably thrust aside and smother all serious planning for war itself, unless those who are to do the planning and training are entirely freed from all routine administrative duties and responsibilities" (*My Political Life*, I, 193–94; cf. L. S. Amery, *The Problem of the Army* [1903], pp. 122–24, 215, 217, 228).

Ellison's "lucid brain and massive knowledge" also came to be of use to Haldane, when Ellison became his Military Secretary at the War Office in 1905 (Amery, *My Political Life*, I, 206, 212; Haldane, *Autobiography*, pp. 199–200, 206–7; *Life of Hal-*

of staff organizations (the C.I.D., the Imperial General Staff, and the Naval War Staff) and the appointment of a coordinating minister above existing departments (the Minister of Defence) were first advocated and applied. These precedents stimulated the view that similar patterns of organization could also be used profitably outside the defense field, either in a specific sector of government responsibilities or in devising the machinery of government as a whole.[42]

The essence of the argument in favor of a policy Cabinet is that in the long-term view, satisfactory policies can be achieved only if the responsible ministers are kept free from departmental pressures and routine administration, and instead are able to form their decisions with the aid of separate expert staffs. In this view the national interest is apparently imperiled at present by political maneuvers and the vested interest of departments. Underlying this attitude is indignation about non-realization of certain policies that their advocates had regarded as manifestly in the national interest. Consciously or unconsciously, they represent the "real" national interest against the failings of the nation itself. Thus it is no wonder that the proposal has been particularly defended by politicians in opposition, and by politically uncommitted (if far from dispassionate) experts.

The life of Amery, for instance, was one pugnacious exertion on behalf of particular policies that were often in opposition to the policies of his own Conservative Party. As a young man, before 1914, Amery agitated for army reform and conscription when the great majority of Liberals and Conservatives were well satisfied with the existence of a small regular army and an intricate, inefficient, but colorful local reserve. At the same time, he favored a progressive social policy when even the thought of this was anathema to most in his party. He belonged to a small but highly active group of opponents of the National Government of 1915, which he rejected as in conflict with the nation's real interest.[43] In the 1920's he

---

dane, I, 172; Falls, pp. 246–47). After that, Haldane became the most articulate advocate of the General Staff, both within the Services and for the Cabinet generally. He later sought to extend the General Staff principle to the civilian field (cf. his *Memorandum* to the members of the Machinery of Government Committee, Reconstruction Papers, Folios 781–86, partly reprinted in Wilson, *Haldane*, p. 7; Cd. 9230 [1918], paras. 12–14; *Life of Haldane*, II, 14).

Amery applied the General Staff principle to Cabinet organization as such; in advocating the policy Cabinet, he constantly used military analogies (e.g., *My Political Life*, III, 361–62), as did Attlee (356 H. of C. Deb. [1 February 1940], col. 1416). Ellison died in 1947, a rather forgotten man. For Ellison's own ideas, see Ellison, "Lord Roberts and the General Staff," *Nineteenth Century*, CXII (1932), 722–32, and Ellison's letters to the Editor of *The Times*, 9 September 1939 and 12 October 1943.

[42] This view is criticized by Mackenzie–Grove p. 353ff.

[43] Cf. for instance his philippic against the Asquith Cabinet, which he reproached for "unanimity in procrastination, unanimity in shirking the issues, unanimity in postponing decisions." Instead, he wished "a single will, expressing the will of the nation; a thinking, foreseeing, planning mind; a purpose ardent, masterful, inflexible; an enthusiasm drawing inspiration from the inexhaustible wellspring of the nation's patriotism, kindling the nation's spirit to flame by the contagion of its own utterance and example" (*My Political Life*, II, 69, 73).

continued to agitate, both inside and outside the Cabinet, for protection when even Baldwin (who had risked a dissolution and lost an election on that issue) thought it unwise to pursue the issue further. He regarded the National Governments of the early 1930's as a conspiracy of party caucuses instead of a consistent outcome of a deliberate choice on policy.[44] In 1935, he defended Italy and shrugged off the League of Nations at a time when almost the whole of England cried out against Mussolini and called for sanctions. He fought for a tough line against Germany when his own leaders were negotiating "peace in our time" in Berchtesgaden, Godesberg, and Munich. Like Churchill, Amery felt slighted when Baldwin appointed Inskip in 1936 to the office of Minister for the Coordination of Defence. He was disappointed when he was not included in the Government even in 1939. In May 1940, he was pleasantly surprised when some in all parties thought him the best possible Prime Minister. He felt sidetracked when Churchill offered him only the India Office without a seat in the War Cabinet.[45] Throughout his life, in other words, he met with frustrations of a personal or policy nature. His effectiveness in the Cabinet was never equal to the strength of his beliefs: Amery is often adduced as the classic example of a man who spoiled his case by talking too much in Cabinet sessions.[46] If he was often in opposition to his own party, he was ready to work with opponents on the other side of the House. He even advocated the regular participation of opposition representatives in government councils.[47]

Similar elements can be found in other proponents of a policy Cabinet. Beveridge, one-time journalist, ex-official, academician and researcher, the architect of the Welfare State (who was kept away from its construction by his political patrons), "wandering voice" during the Second World War, even went so far as to rationalize his frustrations into political philosophy. In his autobiography, he construed a basic dichotomy between power and influence as "the chief alternative ways by which things get done in the world of affairs." He defined power as "ability to give to other men orders enforced by sanctions, by punishment, or by control of rewards," influence as "appeal to reasons or to emotions other than fear or greed."[48] Underlying these definitions is the view that power is justified only if guided by influence, or, in other words, that politicians on their own apparently lack the knowledge, the time, and the rationality that should vindicate their exercise of power.[49] No wonder Beveridge was one of the

[44] Cf. Bassett, p. 281; cf. Amery, *My Political Life*, III, 10.
[45] Amery, *My Political Life*, III, 196, 318–19, 370, 375.
[46] Mackintosh, p. 416.   [47] Amery, *Constitution*, p. 93.
[48] Beveridge, *Power and Influence*, p. 3; cf. pp. 14, 182–83, 251.
[49] Beatrice Webb once described all politicians as "mendicants for practicable proposals" (*Our Partnership*, London [1948], p. 402, and a similar passage in her *Diaries, 1924–32*, p. 142). Before World War I, Beveridge had set his mind on a newly created post of Director of Labour Exchanges in the Board of Trade; when he was only offered a position as general adviser, he refused, because he did not wish to become "an expert celebrating *in vacuo*" (*Power and Influence*, pp. 77–78). Bev-

most consistent advocates of an Economic General Staff, of intelligence organs, of using in the war such experienced thinkers as the "old war-horses" or the "old dogs" from Oxford and Cambridge—Keynes, Layton, Salter, and Beveridge himself.[50] In his memoirs, he showed a noticeable dislike of the departments, which might interpose themselves between the leading politicians and the experts. His explicit ideal, at least during World War II, was the rule of a few unencumbered politicians clothed with power and directly assisted by uncommitted experts, who should rule over departments that were assigned purely executive functions.

It seems significant that the idea of a policy Cabinet has been particularly attractive to Liberal politicians generally. What did the Liberals have but influence when they lost political power? Equally typical is the reverse development among Socialist politicians. As long as Labour was still in a weak minority, the only reserve left to them (apart from eschatological expectation) was personal influence through research and publications, a field in which the Webbs in particular excelled. The unhappy ending of the two Labour minority governments, in 1924 and in 1931, resulted in a definite distrust of the traditional institutions of government. The idea of a political directorate that should, on the one hand, take complete powers, but on the other be explicitly tied to policy programs, prepared by party specialists and sealed by party congresses, was easily born in these circumstances. Neither Attlee nor Cripps, Strachey nor Bevan maintained such schemes once Labour was effectively in power. Equally typically, most insistence on the need for thorough study and intelligence staffs is found among those who think Labour failed between 1945 and 1951, either because the Government was not socialist enough, or because dogma led it to pursue harmful policies, to the disadvantage of both country and party.

The influence of the propaganda for specialized policy staffs has therefore been slight. Some intelligence organs or research divisions were introduced within certain departments, but they have occupied a somewhat weak position against the ordinary line divisions. Most successful were such staffs in the defense sphere, where strategic planning is a must and secrecy can keep conflicts within the confines of a theoretical national interest. In addition, plans for a policy Cabinet and policy staffs had a certain appeal in periods of national crisis, when it became necessary to take rapid decisions without elaborate consultation and exchange of papers, and the nation as a whole was prepared to submit willingly to decrees from above. For the rest, their influence was slight. The application of military organization schemes to the civilian sphere generally ended in failure, both in the case of general and joint staffs and in the case of supervising ministers.

---

eridge clearly hoped (and even expected) that the Liberal Party would regain a measure of political power in 1945 through the force of his personal reputation (*ibid.*, pp. 348–51).

[50] Beveridge, *Power and Influence*, p. 268ff.

Experiments with small emergency Cabinets (as undertaken from 1916 to 1919, in 1931, and from 1939 to 1945) were discontinued as soon as conditions reverted to normal. They met with the strong antagonism of the politicians and the departments that were excluded from the lonely heights. In short, the axiom of an "objective policy" was powerless and unreal in the actual world of personal and group conflict.

NINETEEN

PROPOSALS TO RESTRICT THE CABINET TO THE MOST IMPORTANT MINISTERS

The Argument

If an effective decrease in the number of ministers by means of a rationalization of the interdepartmental structure cannot be achieved; if a complete divorce between the Cabinet and the departments as proposed by the advocates of a policy Cabinet is rejected; if yet it is thought desirable to keep the size of the Cabinet down to a manageable number, then the only way out is to restrict Cabinet membership to an elite among ministers and to introduce special procedures to ensure adequate coordination with those excluded from the Cabinet. The main advocates of this proposal (which closely reflects government practice since 1945) were Anderson and Morrison. Their views rested on four arguments:

First, each peacetime Cabinet should be sufficiently representative.[1] This makes it imperative that the most important departments—e.g., the Foreign Office, Home Office, Treasury, Ministry of Defence, and Board of Trade—be included. At the same time, it militates against excluding those departments that are particularly important to influential clienteles. This means, for example, that the Ministers of Labour and Agriculture and the Secretaries of State for Scotland and for Commonwealth Relations must also be included. The constitutional place of the House of Lords demands that at least some ministers be chosen from that chamber, notably the Lord Chancellor and at least one other senior minister who can act as Leader of the House of Lords. When certain fields of governmental activity (e.g., housing or education) are subject to political tension, it is unwise and undesirable to leave the ministers in charge outside the Cabinet. Consequently, in normal circumstances it should be regarded as unfeasible to form a Cabinet of less than fifteen to eighteen members.[2] A Cabinet composed of more than twenty members, however, would tend to degenerate into a public meeting, impair secrecy and efficient consulta-

---

[1] Cf. Morrison, pp. 29–30; Anderson in *The Times*, 11 February 1950; cf. Laski, *Reflections*, pp. 156–58.

[2] Cf. Chester, *Cabinet*, p. 55; Morrison, p. 56.

tion, and affect ministerial *esprit de corps*.[3] Inevitably, a number of ministers cannot be regular members of the Cabinet; they can only be invited to attend when business that directly concerns their departments is discussed.

Second, the increased pressure of government business affecting ministers in both their departmental and their Cabinet duties makes it desirable to free the Cabinet as much as possible from matters that could be settled on a lower level. But at the same time, collective responsibility and the interdependent character of much government business continue to demand interministerial consultation. "If either the Prime Minister or the Cabinet collectively had tried to do this work directly, the men and the machine might have broken down within six months," Morrison concluded after a survey of the manifold duties that confronted the Labour Government after 1945.[4] The only way out of this dilemma is to use a system of permanent and, where necessary, *ad hoc* committees to which the Cabinet can delegate the authority to settle as much business as they could handle. Such committees can also serve to associate non-Cabinet ministers with questions of general policy.[5]

Third, the complicated process of deciding on general policy and on specific interdepartmental disputes can be guided properly only by a small number of ministers, who, in constant personal contact, can take charge of the main coordinating tasks under the ultimate responsibility of the Prime Minister. They can best do this as chairmen of the Cabinet committees concerned. Although they would have a strong influence on the determination of policy through their position as committee chairmen and their more diversified political experience, nevertheless they should not be given the authority to issue directives to other ministers. Moreover, the structure and composition of committees should be kept secret, in order not to interfere with the principle of ministerial responsibility. Otherwise, there is a danger that the overlords will be held more responsible than either the Cabinet collectively or the responsible departmental ministers individually. This would abrogate the prestige of the departmental ministers concerned and would make the coordinators responsible for specific decisions for which they lack both the necessary detailed knowledge and the legal authority.[6]

Finally, and most important, the system should be flexible. The Prime Minister should not be impeded in his right to select that committee system and that membership of committees which he deems most suitable to the problem in hand, given the particular political and personal relations of the moment. A Prime Minister should ponder the use of the sinecure offices for appointing suitable coordinating ministers. But he should not be tied to this practice; it might be equally advisable, in particular circum-

---

[3] Morrison, pp. 30–31.   [4] *Ibid.*, p. 36.
[5] *Ibid.*, pp. 16–27; Anderson, *Machinery*, pp. 13–18.
[6] Anderson, *Machinery*, pp. 17–18.

stances, to appoint as coordinator a minister whose department occupies a predominant place in the field to be coordinated.[7]

This argument is obviously strongly colored by the existing state of affairs. This is both its strength and its weakness. Daily practice proves that it can work. Hence the proposal is, of necessity, relevant and realistic. But at the same time, it is subject to all the criticisms that are leveled against the present Cabinet system. These criticisms can again be broken down into four categories regarding, respectively, the determination of policy, the mechanics of daily administration, ministerial responsibility, and the reality of the political process.

The Proposal and the Determination of Policy

Doubt has often been expressed about the value of ministerial committees for the making of policy. A Socialist ex-minister said in the House of Commons in 1940:

I can imagine these meetings of ministers. You come with tiredness to a committee after a heavy day in the department. . . . All of you, and you know it, are wanting to get back to your own job, where you are masters of ceremonies once more, when the talking is finished, so that you can get on with your own job. You cannot govern by committees of ministers . . . you are bound to get a compromise between rival views on the basis that some minister has to get something out of it in order to preserve his self-respect.[8]

The former minister who spoke these words was Morrison, then a leading figure on the Opposition front bench. He argued that instead of "reconciliation, coordination, settlement," the urgent need was for "direction, decision, drive" under the inspiration of "a minister with knowledge and advice" who, in exceptional cases, should be in a position to say, "With respect, you are all wrong, every minister is wrong, every one of these civil servants is wrong."[9] As a former coordinating minister, speaking ex cathedra in his *Government and Parliament,* Morrison was in later years to give a much more optimistic picture of the system of "government by committee" and a much more modest impression of the influence any coordinating minister might hope to wield.[10] The contrast in his statements is more than the difference between a debating speech of an Opposition leader and the mature and considered opinion of an insider. It reflects a contradiction inherent in the problem itself.

[7] *Ibid.,* p. 16. Anderson particularly stressed the value of a *departmental* coordinating minister (see, e.g., *The Times,* 6 and 11 February 1950). Morrison (pp. 37, 307–8), on the other hand, tends to prefer a *non-departmental* coordinator.

[8] 356 H. of C. Deb. (1 February 1940), col. 1322.

[9] *Ibid.,* cols. 1312–13. In this debate he also said: "If there is one word in the English language in the administration of public affairs with which I am utterly sickened and disgusted, it is the word coordination. . . . Coordination has its uses, but it is no substitute for government. . . . The machinery that ministers have got is machinery of discussion, consultation and mediation and not machinery of executive Government" (col. 1321).

[10] Morrison, pp. 54–55.

The greatest objection to a minister who is placed above the departments rather than in charge of a single one is, indeed, that he will determine policy without sufficient regard for departmental experiences, and that, consequently, he may take decisions that are impossible to implement, or are at least regarded as impossible to implement, by the departments that have to execute them. But it is equally true that decisions by committees of interested departments tend to be more the result of the pressure of departmental interests than of a careful consideration of all the factors involved.

Characteristically, attempts have been made to evade this dilemma by means of hybrid arrangements. A coordinating minister is placed over the departments; but, in order to placate departmental sensitivities, he is not given a large staff of his own nor the right to issue directives, and ministers under him maintain the right at all times to appeal to the full Cabinet. Or recourse is sought in the establishment of a policy staff that is deliberately isolated to some extent from the day-to-day business of the executive branches of departments. But in order to retain liaison with the departments, this staff is recruited from the personnel of the very departments that are to be coordinated. Or an attempt is made to lessen the pressure of departmental *parti pris* by combining a group of leading ministers into an "Inner Cabinet." But again, in order not to rupture the ties with the departments, other departmental ministers are included in the Cabinet, and some, as of right, in the Inner Cabinet itself.

None of these makeshift arrangements seem to have been very successful. However large the number of overworked coordinators, complaints are still made about the lack of coordination. Even the most influential coordinating ministers—Anderson, Morrison, Butler—were soon reduced from a motor to a pivot in the governmental machinery, both through the burden of their tasks and through the persistent pressure of departmental interests. Joint Staffs either became anemic or became the personal staff of one minister who soon acquired effective authority over the field. The concept of an Inner Cabinet also gives little solace. Either it is nothing but a complicated term for the powerful role of leading ministers, in which case there is no self-evident guarantee that they will of necessity arrive at a considered and harmonious stream of policy decisions; or it refers to a group of ministers who enjoy the special confidence of the Prime Minister, which again implies no guarantee for the purposefulness, acceptability, or comprehensiveness of their directives. Or it stands for the pinnacle of a deliberately organized Cabinet pyramid: if so, the problem again enters of the relation between coordinating and departmental ministers.

The question whether a fairly large Cabinet can ever be a good policy-making instrument is, therefore, the reverse of the question whether a small policy-making Cabinet can do better. A large Cabinet lacks informality. It is forced to pay more attention to departmental interests. But at the same time, it is more securely anchored in the world of day-to-day government and in political controversies that cannot be exorcised by incantation about "objective" policy needs.

The Proposal and the Process of Daily Administration

An extensive committee system may be of great use. Both those who propose to rationalize the interdepartmental structure and those who propose a policy Cabinet expect important advantages from it. But they regard a committee system not as an alternative but as a supplement to their proposals for general reorganization. In particular, advocates of an interdepartmental rationalization feel that a satisfactory committee system can operate only on the basis of a more rational distribution of functions among departments, and not as a palliative to minimize the problems resulting from an irrational allocation of departmental responsibilities.

An extensive, hierarchical committee system is justified by the need to decide as much business as possible at the lowest interdepartmental level.[11] This presupposes a pyramid of committees highly specialized at the base, but becoming more comprehensive as they approach the top. Anderson, Morrison, and others have made specific proposals for the organization of committees at Cabinet level.[12] They desire, in particular, a defense committee, a committee on foreign affairs, a committee on economic policy, a committee on social affairs, and a legislation committee. In addition, they ask for *ad hoc* committees whenever necessary. Reality shows a more ragged picture. The delimitation of functions, the allocation of new tasks, and the coordination of business between committees create constant problems. Once formed, committees may continue to meet even after the reason for their establishment has long disappeared. Nevertheless, what Chester has called an "inverted Gresham's Law of committees" may be seen at work. "Ministers and officials [direct] their topics to the committees where they [are] likely to get an adequate and firm decision and so the more powerful and able chairman [attracts] items to his agenda."[13]

This cannot but affect the position of coordinating ministers. Smellie has rightly stated that the most important tasks come perforce to rest on the shoulders of the most important ministers. The committee system may therefore relieve the Cabinet, but at the expense of placing an even heavier burden on leading ministers.[14] As Bacon said: "It is one thing to abbreviate by contracting, another by cutting off; and business so

---

[11] Cf. Bridges, *Portrait*, pp. 23–24; Anderson, *Machinery*, p. 13.

[12] Anderson, *Machinery*, pp. 14–17; Morrison, pp. 17–27; Salter, *Cabinet*, pp. 114–16; Chester, *Cabinet*, pp. 51–52; Cecil, pp. 15–16; Smellie, pp. 308–9.

[13] Chester, *Machinery*, p. 17. Public administration also has a Gresham's Law, proposed by Don K. Price ("Staffing the Presidency," *American Political Science Review*, XL [1946], 1161). It runs, "Responsibility for a quantity of specific routine work makes it impossible to handle more general and important problems."

[14] Smellie, pp. 238; Dalton, *Memoirs*, III, 198–99; cf. Chester, *Machinery*, pp. 28–29.

handled at several sittings or meetings goeth commonly backward and forward in an unsteady manner."[15] To refer a question to a committee may well be to place it in a situation in which ministers discuss matters not once or twice but a great many times. Again and again, rationalization of the committee system itself has been demanded. But how can this be achieved? By a rigid system of permanent committees, with a hard and fast division of duties among them? On the basis of his rich experience in the matter, Hankey has doubted the feasibility of this system: "Each departmental issue is usually found to concern a different group of government departments." Hence, the more flexible the system, the better it may be expected to work.[16] But how can an overgrowth of constantly changing specialized committees be controlled? The Cabinet Office has tried to devise systems for this. But the complaint about committee work that was made both before and after the Second World War, both when Hankey was Secretary to the Cabinet and later, is still made: the burden it places on ministers and senior officials is too heavy.

The Proposal and Ministerial Responsibility

The Cabinet structure advocated by Anderson, Morrison, and others is based on a definite hierarchical principle. This implies a certain differentiation in the political responsibility of ministers. Anderson has suggested a new concept of "corporate responsibility" in addition to the existing concepts of individual and collective responsibility, in which all ministers (both inside or outside the Cabinet) share. The new concept would refer to the specific responsibility of those who, as members of the Cabinet, share in the determination of general policy.[17] Does this further differentiation provide any solution to the controversial problem of the responsibility of those hybrid ministerial figures that the Anderson model produces, e.g., the coordinating minister and the non-Cabinet minister? Obviously, both share in the collective responsibility of the government. As members of the Cabinet, coordinating ministers also share in corporate responsibility. But insofar as their tasks are kept secret, they apparently cannot be held individually responsible for these duties. Ministers outside the Cabinet do not share in corporate responsibility; they do share in collective responsibility; and, at the same time, they are individually accountable for their own departments, even though coordinating ministers or the Cabinet may have taken decisions on which they were consulted only inadequately or not at all.

Are such distinctions real? Or should one say again that collective and individual responsibility cannot be clearly differentiated? Parliament, and

---

[15] Essay 25, "Of Dispatch," in *Essays of Francis Bacon* (1625), Nelson Classics ed., p. 125.

[16] Hankey, *Control*, p. 41.   [17] Anderson, *Machinery*, pp. 8–9.

particularly the Opposition, will not refrain from attempts to probe the internal structure and divisions of the Cabinet simply out of respect for any formal categories of ministerial responsibility. The government team, in turn, will appeal to the principle of collective responsibility in all cases where a breach in its front may threaten. Individual ministers will seek to avoid the blame for unpopular policies as much as possible, but they will be eager to get their share of the credit for any popular ones. It is therefore legitimate to query whether the discussion is as important as some have thought it, particularly since the Overlords controversy. And it is also permissible to ask whether Anderson and Morrison, who raised the question of ministerial responsibility with such conviction against the proposal for a policy Cabinet, should not have paid more attention to the question of the possible erosion of effective responsibility for ministers outside the Cabinet. With Churchill, one may be of the opinion that "hashing it all up" is not very elegant, so that the advocates of this plan can scarcely parade as the censors of constitutional mores.

The Proposal and Political Realities

The political complications of the proposal differ according to the place a minister occupies in the ministerial hierarchy. The most important coordinating ministers face a crucial dilemma in choosing their office. Should they work from an important departmental post or from a sinecure office? Control of a major department of government ensures a minister the support of a powerful apparatus. It gives him recognized status in the eyes of all concerned. It brings him ministerial credit for all meritorious departmental acts. But it can also impose such a heavy burden that it may destroy his health. He may well meet with serious suspicion on the part of the other departments he is to coordinate; they will view him not as the impartial referee, but as the spokesman of a powerful rival interest. All this is less true of the coordinating minister who occupies a sinecure office. But he, too, suffers from many anomalies. It is not necessarily true that the personal burden is lighter. The minister is likely to be a continuous attender of meetings. He has to familiarize himself with constantly shifting business without the aid of a departmental staff, whereas he contends with ministers who will be thoroughly briefed by their departments. Secrecy deprives him of most opportunities to obtain laurels for the work he sees through. Even worse, he may soon become known as little but the drafter of compromises, as nothing but a political broker. In an open parliamentary system, an influential politician has less reason to be satisfied with the status of *éminence grise* than in an absolutist setting.[18]

---

[18] *The Economist* suggested on 27 April 1957 that Morrison and Butler lost their chance to become Party Leader and Prime Minister, respectively, when they took charge of a sinecure rather than a heavy-weight departmental office.

For ministers lower in the hierarchy, there arises the problem of their attitude toward the authority of the coordinating ministers. On the one hand, subordinate ministers will have the understandable inclination to seek the support of influential coordinators who may help them to see through projects at Cabinet level. But on the other hand, they will also attempt to limit the role of coordinators to strictly circumscribed tasks. This explains the strong emphasis that is placed again and again on the right of all ministers to appeal to the full Cabinet. Professor W. A. Robson has clearly indicated the drawbacks of a further hierarchical differentiation. As he wrote in 1948:

It may lead—and has led in certain instances—to other ministers jockeying for the support of this or that key figure. It tends to destroy equality of discussion both in Cabinet and Committee. . . . It may promote factions within the Cabinet régime. It may lessen the possible range of choice for the party leadership. . . . It means that a minister tends to be less interested in the work of his department than in the status which he enjoys as political chief of that department. It may mean that the weight attached to ministers' views and policies depends more on the position which they occupy in the hierarchy than on the wisdom and knowledge which those who impress them possess.[19]

The problem of whom to include and whom not to include in the Cabinet continues to cause difficulties. Admittedly, the larger Cabinet gives more room to meet ambitions. It is also true that there will always be borderline cases. But in all cases, there is an arbitrary element in the decision to include some ministers and to exclude others. The older departments may succeed in obtaining Cabinet representation because they traditionally attract the more prominent politicians; but they can do so only at the expense of the potential importance of the newer departments that remain outside the Cabinet.[20] That the problem of who should be included will remain insoluble as long as the actual number of independent ministerial departments is, of necessity, larger than the desirable maximum of the Cabinet, is well illustrated in a proposal G. M. Young made to the Haldane Committee in 1918. Called as a witness, he proposed a system by which all ministers would formally be members of the Cabinet and receive all documents and minutes. Normally, Young suggested

only those who were known to be interested in the subject under consideration, or expressed a wish to attend, were expected to take part in the ordinary meetings. The full Cabinet would meet at stated intervals for discussions of policy in which it was essential to have political interests and tendencies as well as administrative considerations represented.[21]

This proposal obtained a measure of support from Haldane himself.[22] Is it realistic? It would seem a misapprehension to believe that British

[19] Robson, pp. 11–12.   [20] Cf. Chester, *Cabinet*, pp. 35–36.
[21] Reconstruction Papers, Folio 989.
[22] Reconstruction Papers, Folios 1013–14.

ministers would attach so little importance to their personal attendance in Cabinet that they would refrain from sitting in for reasons of administrative comfort. On the contrary, actual pressure has been such that successive Prime Ministers have thought the political utility of an increased Cabinet to outweigh any inconveniences of size.

The Background of the Proposal

The idea of uniting only the most prominent ministers in an informal, supreme policy-making body is at least as old as, if not older than, the word "cabinet" itself. The Cabinet technically still is what it has always been, an informal gathering of ministers, invited by the Prime Minister to deliberate on the more important issues of State in order to present agreed decisions to King and Parliament. The nineteenth century witnessed a constant increase in the number of Cabinet members, so much so that practically all heads of independent departments eventually acquired membership. But this never fully destroyed the view that the Prime Minister ought to have absolute discretion in the choice of ministers he wanted to invite to the Cabinet. As we saw, an extensive debate on the most desirable composition of the Cabinet first arose at the time of Lloyd George's War Cabinet. Some advocated severing the direct link between the Cabinet and the departments once and for all by forming a non-departmental policy Cabinet, while others advocated restoring the connection by cutting down the number of independent government departments.

A compromise proposal was first submitted to the Haldane Committee by Llewellyn Smith, then Permanent Secretary to the Board of Trade.[23] He rejected the existing system of a non-departmental War Cabinet for peacetime purposes because it reduced ministers to "appellants before a tribunal" and destroyed collective responsibility. He thought a concentration of functions in fewer and larger departments desirable, even if it might involve some system of subordinating certain ministers to others. Hence he argued in favor of a Cabinet of twelve, composed of the most important departmental ministers and three holders of sinecure offices, who could act as chairmen of permanent Cabinet committees in the fields of Imperial Defence, External Affairs, and Economic and Social Policy, respectively. Non-Cabinet ministers and leading civil servants would participate in the committees' proceedings. Llewellyn Smith's proposal had little effect for the time being: the Cabinet grew constantly between 1919 and 1939, and the Cabinet committee system was hardly developed. Only a few, such as Lord Cecil of Chelwood in 1932 and Laski in 1938, put forward schemes that resembled Llewellyn Smith's.[24] They

[23] Reconstruction Papers, Folios 774–80, 1012–13.
[24] Cecil, p. 16ff; Laski, *Parliamentary Government*, pp. 249–52; cf. *Holmes-Laski Correspondence*, II, 1385. Cecil advocated, on the one hand, that the number of departmental ministers be cut down and, on the other hand, that the strengthening of the element of long-term policy be made possible by forming a General Purposes Committee, to be composed of the Prime Minister and the chairmen of permanent Cabinet committees.

based these schemes on the desire to improve the efficient working of the Cabinet, without accepting the alternative arrangements of a policy Cabinet or a total overhaul of the interdepartmental structure. Because their proposals differed only in degree from the existing situation, they had less popular appeal than the proposal for a policy Cabinet. When Neville Chamberlain decided to re-establish a War Cabinet in 1939, there was general clamor for it to be non-departmental in character.

During the Second World War, however, a definite change occurred. Churchill lashed out with conviction and oratorical vigor against the proposal for a non-departmental directorate, which could only weaken his position as supreme war leader. His philippics against "that exalted brooding over the work done by others," against "more and more theoretical supervisors and commentators, reading an immense amount of material every day, but doubtful how to use their knowledge without doing more harm than good," and against "a disembodied Brains Trust" found their way into the literature in which they were soon elevated to the status of decisive argument.[25]

Below Churchill's War Cabinet there developed, in the meantime, an elaborate committee system in which departmental claims on scarce resources were assessed and arbitrated. Under ministers who had the required political standing and the suitable temperament, these committees developed into antechambers of the Cabinet. Most departmental ministers lost the direct access to the Cabinet that they had frequently maintained under Lloyd George. But they kept in closer touch with the determination of policy, and on the whole the cleavage between Whitehall and the Cabinet was less deep than it had been during the First World War. To a considerable degree, the new system was the work of Anderson, who often acted as *trait d'union* between the departments and the Cabinet.[26] Anderson's appointment to a ministerial post in 1938 had in itself been a striking step since, until rather recently, he had only occupied positions in the civil service. He had been Secretary to the English National Insurance Commission in 1912, organizer of the Ministry of Shipping during the First World War, and right hand to Addison and Morant, "relieving [them] of all the 'things' " in the difficult period of the establishment of the Ministry of Health after 1919. He had occupied the highest official post in Ireland between 1920 and 1921, when conflict between the Irish and British rose to unprecedented heights. Soon afterwards, he became Permanent Secretary to the Home Office. In this capacity, he organized the Government's action during the General Strike of 1926 in such authoritative fashion that a number of ministers could devote themselves to the more spectacular sideshows of this serious conflict.[27] In 1932, Anderson

[25] Churchill, I, 320, 327; IV, 499.

[26] See *Life of Anderson, passim,* and the obituary of Lord Waverley, *The Times,* 6 January 1958.

[27] *Life of Anderson, passim*; Addison, *Politics from Within,* II, 15; Braithwaite, pp. 18–19; Markham, *Friendship's Harvest,* p. 199; Templewood, *Nine Troubled Years,* pp. 31, 82, 84; Grigg, *Prejudice and Judgment,* p. 188.

had been appointed Governor of Bengal, a region then riddled by terrorist activities. On his return from India, he had been taken into the Government as Lord Privy Seal, with the thorny task of organizing civil defense. Afterwards he was appointed Minister of Home Security and Home Secretary (1939–40), Lord President of the Council (1940–43), and Chancellor of the Exchequer (1943–45).

His most outstanding qualities were his Olympian calm, which earned him the nickname "Jehovah"; his sure judgment and intellectual grasp; his demand for absolute efficiency; and his unsurpassed feeling for the personalities and sensitivities of Whitehall, which had ripened through his long official career.[28] With Churchill's backing, he made the Lord President's Committee the pivot of the administrative machinery below the Cabinet, which it largely continued to be under Attlee (1943–45) and Morrison (1945–51).

Anderson's influence on the development of the Cabinet system was theoretical as well as practical. During the latter part of the Second World War, he presided over a Machinery of Government Committee of the National Government, charged with the duty of investigating and reporting on the problems of postwar government organization. The reports of this committee have never been published, but there is reason to believe that Anderson's Romanes Lecture of 1946 contained its main conclusions. Churchill and Attlee closely followed its recommendations. Also, the advice given in 1945 by the leading officials of the Cabinet Office—the Secretary to the Cabinet, Bridges, and his future successor, Brook—pointed in the same direction.[29]

Thereafter, the actual development of Cabinet organization under Attlee seemed to bring Anderson's ideas into practice. Attlee was a committee chairman *par excellence*. Morrison, Bevin, and Cripps had also learned to work through committees during the war years, and together they formed a tight if not very harmonious inner circle in the Cabinet. Toward the end of the Labour Government, its structure admittedly showed serious cracks due to the disappearance of the personalities that had given it strength. But this did not essentially affect its image, because shortly afterwards Churchill's attempt to revive his war team in peacetime misfired and pushed aside any criticism of the structure of the Labour Government. In addition, the Overlords controversy offered the Socialist Opposition the opportunity to patent the apparent structure of the Labour Government as a norm for good government. Morrison's *Government and Parliament,* published in 1954, became through its detailed exposition and authoritative tone somewhat of a *locus classicus.*[30] The transition from idea to fact, from fact to norm, was complete.

---

[28] *Life of Anderson, passim.* Cf. Attlee, *As It Happened,* pp. 128, 140; Chester, *Machinery,* p. 10; Hancock–Gowing, p. 223; Braithwaite, pp. 36–39.

[29] Chester–Willson, p. 334; *Life of Anderson,* pp. 392–93; Morrison, p. 18.

[30] The noticeable similarity in the views of Anderson and Morrison should, of course, mainly be attributed to their rather similar experiences as coordinating ministers. But a subsidiary factor may also have had some influence. The main academic

Other factors also contributed to this development. The number of separate departments had increased so greatly, especially when the War Cabinets were in power, that it was impossible to include all ministers in the Cabinet. The desire of many parliamentarians to acquire office put a large number of ministerial posts at a premium. Once departments had again achieved Cabinet representation, it became more difficult politically to exclude them except in definite emergencies. The advocates of the system also point rightly to the fact that a number of other political factors cannot but work in the direction of a larger and more representative Cabinet. In the later 1950's, the tasks of government were less subject to alteration or extension than before. The increased size of government, and of the government budget, made it easier to accommodate changes without fundamental reforms.

Hence, this proposal has tended to dominate for the time being. It carries the imprint of a useful compromise. It seems businesslike, not the product of a non-British logic or fantasy. But is there not an element of profound truth in R. N. Spann's remark that "the elevation of an uneasy compromise into an ideal type is peculiarly the work of men like . . . Herbert Morrison, who think that it is the British birthright to have the best of inconsistent worlds"?[31]

Since 1956, however, the Suez troubles, uncertainty about defense and economic policy, the changing fortunes of Macmillan and his Cabinet, and the almost traumatic debate about the Common Market have done much to affect the element of complacency on which the thesis has long rested.

---

writer who is identified with their ideas is D. N. Chester, now Warden of Nuffield College. During the war, Chester worked as a "temporary" under Anderson in the Cabinet Office. After 1951, he urged Morrison to write his *Government and Parliament* (cf. Morrison's Preface, pp. v, viii). Would it be too farfetched to suppose that Morrison profited not only from Nuffield's amenities but also from the pertinent views of its Warden? In addition to his own rather extensive and important writings on the subject, Chester also helped to shape, and undoubtedly greatly influenced, the report entitled *The Organization of British Central Government, 1914–56* (Royal Institute of Public Administration, London, 1957). The writer of the report, F. M. G. Willson, was a fellow at Nuffield for a considerable time.

[31] R. N. Spann, "Reith and the B.B.C.," *Public Administration*, XXVIII (1950), 211.

TWENTY

CABINET ORGANIZATION AND THE BRITISH POLITICAL SYSTEM

In this concluding chapter, the arguments of the three preceding chapters will be briefly summarized, and proposals that seek to improve the working of the Cabinet indirectly through reforms elsewhere in the political system will be briefly discussed.

The Historical Roots of the Reform Movements

In spite of their differences the reform proposals have two things in common: the climate in which they originated, and the belief that improvements can be obtained through administrative reorganization.

Around 1900, three developments came to undermine the confident British belief that a simple empiricism in matters of government would create the best possible of British worlds: (a) the growing military and economic strength of Germany; (b) the serious military reverses of the Boer War; and (c) a stream of revelations about the actual misery in which many Britons still lived after "a century of progress." By the end of the nineteenth century, active State intervention was being widely demanded. Varying pleas were heard for the protection of industry and agriculture, army reform, improvement in education, the encouragement of scientific research, the introduction of new social insurance and new instruments of employment policy, and organization and planning. In some circles, these demands evoked a lively interest in Imperial Germany, where military organization, scientific invention, and an extensive system of social security seemed to flourish. Such demands also kindled interest in reorganizing the central government.

Most active Cabinet reformers were associated with a few select circles (of mixed political and official composition) in which demands for reform were eagerly discussed and canvassed well before World War I. In the first place, an important role was played by some colonial "proconsuls," notably Curzon and Milner (whom *The Times* described even in 1954 as "the most powerful administrative genius that Britain has produced to this day.") During his eventful administration in South Africa (1897–1905), Milner surrounded himself with a nucleus of brilliant young men, soon nicknamed "Milner's Kindergarten."[1] This included

---

[1] *The Times*, 23 March 1954; *Life of Milner* and *Life of Dawson, passim*; Halpérin, pp. 198–220. Milner and Curzon acquired the greater part of their political and

Lionel Curtis, Philip Kerr (Lord Lothian), Geoffrey Dawson, and (somewhat less prominently) Starr Jameson and L. S. Amery. Each one was destined for an important if divergent career in British politics and administration.

Secondly, the Army reformers—most importantly Esher and Balfour, but also Haldane, Hankey, and Amery—had leading roles.[2] In 1903, Sir Gerald Ellison, Secretary to the (Esher) War Office Reconstitution Committee, drafted the first well-reasoned plea for introducing a General Staff in Britain and for providing effective coordination between the three Services, on the ministerial, planning, and executive levels. The General Staff doctrine inspired the establishment of specific planning staffs in both the defense and the civilian fields, and also evoked plans for a non-departmental policy Cabinet. Haldane and Amery were notably active in advocating the extension of the Staff principle in the civilian sphere (and both explicitly acknowledged Ellison's influence on their thoughts.) Hankey built up the organization of the C.I.D. and transferred its experiences in committee organization and secretarial services to the central government machinery as a whole.

Thirdly, one encounters a small group of radical Tories, liberal Imperialists, and intellectual Socialists who, in the first decade of the twentieth century, met in a dining club, typically named the Co-efficients. In spite of different motivations and political allegiances, its members tended to agree on the need for a forward-looking, nationalistic foreign policy and a socially progressive domestic policy. This circle included Amery, Hewins, Haldane, Lord Robert Cecil, F. S. Oliver, H. G. Wells, Sidney Webb, and others.[3] The Webbs, at the same time, were the prime movers behind numerous social investigations and concrete demands for administrative reforms. "Mrs. Webb," Samuel has written, "held . . . on a small scale the nearest approach to one of the intellectual salons of the eighteenth century that we have had in our days."[4] She brought together politicians and officials to discuss problems of administration and social policy. In 1911, Wells published his famous satire *The New Machiavelli*, in which he depicted the Webbs as "amateur unpaid precursors of the bureaucratic administrative class of the future."[5] Those who met with the Webbs were also often active in Toynbee Hall, a settlement established in 1884 in the East End of London, where young officials and writers, often fresh from Oxford, lived and spent part of their free time on adult

---

administrative experience as unchallenged leaders of colonial bureaucracies that were hardly subject to parliamentary supervision. This could not but influence their views on political life and on the tasks of government. Samuel and Anderson lived part of their lives in somewhat similar atmospheres—in Palestine and India, respectively. In this connection see also Wells, *The New Machiavelli*, pp. 302–3, 328–29.

[2] See also *Life of Roberts*, pp. 411–63.

[3] Amery, *My Political Life*, I, 222ff; Wells, *The New Machiavelli*, pp. 302–6; Wells, *Experiments in Autobiography*, II, 761ff; Halpérin, pp. 155–56; and Bernard Semmel, *Imperialism and Social Reform: English Social Imperial Thought, 1895–1914* (1960), pp. 72–82.

[4] Samuel, *Memoirs*, p. 29; Wells, *The New Machiavelli*, pp. 183–86.

[5] Wells, *The New Machiavelli*, p. 191.

education and other social work. Among those associated with Toynbee Hall were Milner, Morant, Anderson, Beveridge, Llewellyn Smith, Salter, and Attlee.[6]

All these groups exercised influence through writings and speeches. A number of them were drawn into active government service between 1906 and 1914, when Haldane carried through his military reorganizations and Lloyd George fastened on social reforms as a new stage in his kaleidoscopic political career. Notably, the National Insurance Commission, in many ways the first truly executive government department working outside the confines of Whitehall, symbolized a drastic breakthrough of traditional official loyalties and beliefs. Lloyd George knew his political future was dependent upon the success of the new social security legislation. From all departments and from outside the civil service, he brought together an unusual team of competent younger administrators, persons of the quality of Anderson, Warren Fisher, Salter, G. M. Young, Claud Schuster, and Tom Jones, who—under the ultimate responsibility of Morant—built up the new administrative machinery for the social insurance system.

Not long afterwards, the First World War broke out. This forced a drastic reorganization of the Cabinet and the central government machinery. Opposition to Asquith's traditionalist methods and indifferent leadership crystallized in such protest movements as the Ginger Group (1915–16), which did much to suggest the possibility of alternative leaders and organizational procedures at a time when normal political life was largely suspended. Once Lloyd George was in office, persons such as Milner, Curzon, and Hankey were given the opportunity to carry through actual administrative reforms. Many of the persons mentioned were given employment in political office, the Cabinet Secretariat, or the Garden Suburb. Others acted as initiators or organizers of important new departments including Shipping, Food, and Health, or served in advisory capacities. Central administration became highly fluid and even chaotic. A Machinery of Government Committee was set up. It offered Haldane, Morant and Beatrice Webb a platform for advocating the total reorganization of the interdepartmental structure.

Once included in the government, each person followed his own career. It was no longer possible to speak of certain nuclei, even though many former members of such groups found one another again in such organizations as the Institute of Public Administration, established in 1922. But their hand is easily discovered in a considerable number of administrative reforms. Warren Fisher, Permanent Secretary to the Treasury from 1919 to 1939, drastically reshaped the relationship between the Treasury and the other departments and was active in many other organizational innovations. Morant and Anderson helped to launch the

---

[6] Beveridge, *Power and Influence,* p. 15ff; Janet Beveridge, *Beveridge and His Plan* (1954), p. 52ff; Braithwaite, pp. 13, 282.

Ministry of Health. Esher and Haldane conceived the idea of the Committee of Civil Research, which was implemented by Balfour.[7] Haldane also introduced considerable changes in the organization of the C.I.D. and the Lord Chancellor's department in 1924. Samuel was instrumental in bringing about the small National Cabinet of 1931 and remained an ardent proponent of other organizational reforms. Amery, Beveridge, and Dawson became persistent advocates of a small, non-departmental Cabinet. Anderson was to be the most influential civil servant of his time, the administrative coordinator of the War Cabinet during the Second World War, and the initiator of the new Cabinet system that Attlee and Morrison consolidated after 1945.

As time went by, a certain divergence became apparent between those who had achieved a successful career and those who were somewhat frustrated in their ambitions for personal advancement or for certain concrete objectives of policy. The former found themselves fairly well satisfied with the existing situation or, at most, incidental reforms. The latter continued to demand basic changes in the machinery of government. They invoked precedents set by Lloyd George or recalled the precepts of the Haldane Committee. They found ready support from scattered groups who wished to have better (and presumably cheaper) government through administrative reforms: the economizers, the advocates of "more business efficiency in government," the Organization and Methods experts, the protagonists of effective government planning. Their campaigns had little influence on actual developments. But in periods of national emergency or national uncertainty such as the depression of the 1930's, the military reverses of 1941 and 1942, the economic crises of 1946 and 1947, the Suez affair, and the deep-seated malaise of the early 1960's, they gained a renewed popularity. In the main, however, traditional forms of organization, personal factors, and *ad hoc* reactions to political and administrative problems determined the direction in which Cabinet organization developed.

The Essence of the Three Proposals

The Proposal to Rationalize the Interdepartmental Structure

The leitmotiv of this proposal is the belief that a correct reorganization of the interdepartmental structure can, in itself, solve all the major problems of the functioning of the Cabinet. A well-thought-out reallocation and specialization of tasks, so the argument goes, guarantees balanced and deliberate government action in all fields for which the government is responsible. The problem of coordination is lessened because it is henceforth restricted to essential issues. This, in turn, decreases the workload on ministers, who need be involved only in matters requiring ultimate sanction, and therefore have more time to consider matters of over-all policy.

---

[7] Mackintosh, p. 439.

To a considerable extent, moreover, policy will be evolved automatically by experts and bureaucrats from the nature of things. Typically, this body of thought tends to concentrate more on the Prime Minister than on the Cabinet.[8] The Prime Minister is depicted not as part of the Cabinet but as Supreme Commander. Other ministers merely assist him in the implementation of a strategy that he determines. The composition of the Cabinet itself is therefore of secondary importance. If, after a rational redistribution of functions, the number of departments becomes too large and hence the "span of control" too wide, then a new hierarchical level of super-ministers may easily be fitted in between the Prime Minister and the departments.

No clear reply is given to the question whether these ministers will be mere coordinators among equals or actual chiefs of super-departments. Apparently, the question is not considered to be very important; the only real issue is whether there are clearly defined lines of authority and responsibility from top to bottom and vice versa. Little attention is paid to the relation between the Cabinet and Parliament. Parliament should mainly judge the results of particular policies and should not meddle with administrative organization, which is a matter for expert judgment only; if Parliament presses for further influence in administrative matters, it actually becomes a harmful force adversely affecting the efficiency of government. Ultimately, the entire government apparatus is thought to be largely self-contained. Little attention is paid to the pressures of outside forces; they can only disturb the smooth running of a perfect machine.

Various motives may be discerned for this kind of reasoning. Sometimes such views spring from a technocratic, apolitical mentality that wishes to run the body politic as a private firm: efficiently, effectively, cheaply. Significantly, many of its advocates refer to the supposedly shining examples of military organization or private enterprise. Administration is conceived as a *passe partout* that fits any keyhole, irrespective of differences in purpose, accountability, or environment. Many of its protagonists draw their inspiration from the United States, the mecca of scientific management, where the cry for "more business in government" was first heard and from which a torrent of writings on organization theory keeps pouring forth. They point particularly to the voluminous reports of the President's Committee on Administrative Management (Brownlow Committee, 1937) and the Hoover Commission (reporting since 1949), which pleaded for a drastic remodeling of the Executive. Insufficient attention is paid to the fact that these reports were pervaded by a spirit that is alien to British experience, that they had but little effect in the United States, and that they were strongly influenced by factors that are

[8] Cf. Haldane's Memorandum to the Machinery of Government Committee, 11 January 1918 (Reconstruction Papers, Folios 781–86). It is interesting to find that Mackintosh, too, tends to overstress the leading role of the Prime Minister, and, at the same time, to regard the Cabinet as chiefly an administrative agency (see, e.g., p. 381ff).

not applicable to the British situation : the existence of a single Executive, the complicated relations between the President, Congress, and the independent Executive Commissions, the absence of strongly disciplined political parties, and the anti-political tradition of much American thought on public administration.

Other factors would also seem to have played a role, notably in the case of members of the Haldane Committee. They hoped for a number of political and social reforms that could be realized only with the aid of new bureaucratic organs. Once instituted, these organs would, hopefully, evolve the desired policies by their own momentum. Definite political passions thus lay at the root of the demand for "rational" reforms. The allegiance of persons such as Haldane, the Webbs, and Morant was not directed toward persons or party, however, but toward concrete policies, not necessarily to be identified with any political grouping. If one may dub the previously mentioned school of organization theorists "administrative technocrats," the latter may well be called "technocrats *in politicis.*"

The Proposal for a Policy Cabinet

The essence of this proposal is that if leading politicians are relieved of routine duties and are assisted by adequate staffs, correct policy decisions will readily be taken. The reverse side of this argument is that this cannot be achieved as long as vested interests in the political parties and the departments play so large a role. Amery and his followers sought to insulate the Cabinet from political and administrative forces. The Cabinet would be composed of only the most experienced and authoritative ministers, hence of only a few members. The remaining ministers would then hold purely departmental positions and would execute rather than shape policies. At the same time, the Cabinet would be largely detached from the complications of politics. Throughout his life, Amery was a persistent advocate of the doctrine that Cabinet and Parliament are basically distinct organs of government, having their own history, their own tasks, and their own responsibilities.[9] He applauded the idea of a National Government, provided that it rested on objective policy needs, not on the desire of "dexterous parliamentary advocates" or "party caucuses" to retain their privileged positions by obscuring basic differences of political opinion.

No satisfactory answer is given to the objection that such a small Cabinet would hardly be rooted strongly enough in the party, the bureaucracy, or the country at large to make its policy directives acceptable or feasible. In fact, the proposal rests on a high degree of impatience with the influence of personalities and interests, as well as on an underestimation of the administrative complexities and obstacles that are encountered in the formation and execution of any policy. It represents an intellectual

---

[9] Amery, *Constitution,* pp. 1–32; Amery, "The Nature of British Parliamentary Government," in Lord Campion *et al., Parliament: A Survey* (1952), pp. 37–71.

protest against the realities of political and bureaucratic life and reflects the increasingly important challenge that the growing influence of scientific experts poses for traditional political thought. Its philosophical outlook is pervaded by a yearning for a Platonic government of the best. This desire is most readily found among those who have not been successful in the rough life of actual politics.

The Proposal to Restrict the Cabinet to the Most Important Ministers

Anderson, Morrison, and their followers use the existing departmental divisions (which they readily recognize as the product of history rather than logic) as the starting point for their proposal. They repudiate the possibility of drastic administrative reforms, believing that such reforms would break up the coherence and continuity of administrative life. At the same time, they reject the proposal of a policy Cabinet as being in conflict with both political and administrative exigencies. They conclude that only a division between ministers in the Cabinet and ministers outside it, together with a full-grown committee system, can relieve the burden on central government.

Those who advocate this proposal do not deal very extensively with any of the criticisms leveled against it. If it is argued that the system leaves insufficient room for the discussion of long-term policy questions, the proponents point to the Inner Cabinet. If it is said that policy-making is too dependent on interdepartmental compromises, they counter by asking whether a policy formed without the contribution of departmental experience can ever hope to be realistic. If the existing administrative structure with its large number of departments and countless committees is depicted as topheavy and disorderly, the only reply is that only insiders can truly assess this, and that at any rate the existing state of affairs has the great merit of flexibility. If the present state of things is attacked, it is defended as the best that is humanly possible. If total reorganization is demanded, it is argued that the maximum attainable has already been achieved by incidental reforms.

This theory, in other words, freely generalizes into a norm something that has developed only from many unrelated incidents. Its main advocates are, in the first place, those who at one time occupied central positions in the existing system: coordinating ministers such as Anderson and Morrison and senior civil servants such as Bridges; and, in the second place, a great number of academic observers who rely primarily on the authority of the former. Occupying the key places, those politicians and officials understandably were well satisfied with the existing state of affairs. They have tended to minimize the problems inherent in the system. The heavy strain on leading ministers, the unsystematic character of policy formation, the unsatisfactory position of ministers and departments outside the Cabinet are considered minor blemishes at most. But they strongly attack alternative proposals, which they reject as wanton destruction of living organisms, as the apolitical dreams of planners and quasi-rationalists. And they emphatically stress the importance of such political factors as the natural desire of parliamentarians to gain office and to climb in the ministerial hierarchy, and the need to form a government that is sufficiently representative of the existing subgroupings within the majority party. Ultimately, they reject any generalizations about an abstract, "best" model of the Cabinet or the Cabinet committee system, because in the final analysis the personalities at the top are the only decisive determinants. The advocates of this view give the impression of having the wider view and the wiser outlook. Yet there is a decided streak of complacency in their theories. They stand foursquare on the status quo. But they can hardly offer any terra firma in a crisis situation.

The conclusion that specific political experiences and attitudes underlie each of these proposals therefore seems inescapable. Those who favor a rationalization of the interdepartmental structure regard the Cabinet above all as a supreme administrative coordinator, to be shaped by the needs of bureaucratic action, which itself should be insulated as much as possible from outside pressures. The advocates of a non-departmental policy Cabinet believe that the chief duty of politics is to promote the "objective" national interest through policies that will become self-evident if politicians are given sufficient time to profit from expert opinions. The more empirical school conceives of politics as the ever-changing reactions of party politicians and leading civil servants to pressures from official and outside forces. But in fact the Cabinet has at least a threefold function: It is, *at one and the same time,* administrative coordinator, the clearinghouse of policy, and the focus of the chief politically articulated forces in a society. Partial proposals do insufficient justice to the many-sided character of Cabinet tasks. Hence they cannot but neglect important elements in them.

Shifts, Hesitations, and Compromises

The inherent bias in each of these proposals may also be illustrated in two other ways. It can be shown that those politicians and officials who had the most varied political careers were also those who most readily changed their views on Cabinet organization. And it can be proved that the more academically oriented politicians have been the most hesitant and ambiguous on the subject.

The first point may be illustrated by reference to Churchill, Morrison, and Hankey. In 1917 Churchill declared himself willing to take office as a general counsellor in Lloyd George's War Cabinet. When he became "only" Minister of Munitions, he condemned the very principle on which that Cabinet was erected.[10] He rejected non-departmental overseers when

---

[10] Beaverbrook, 1917–18, pp. 126, 358; *Life of Lloyd George,* p. 495.

he himself became Prime Minister during the Second World War. But he was the first to abandon this "principle of good government" when the governmental structure as it had developed after 1945 seemed to offer no proper niches for some of his wartime collaborators. There is a remarkable oscillation in his views on whether the Service ministers should be in the War Cabinet, depending on whether he coveted one of these posts. We have already referred to the drastic shift in Morrison's evaluation of the Cabinet committee system, which he denounced in 1940 and extolled in 1954.

Equally typical is the change of opinion of Hankey, who was Secretary of the Cabinet beween 1916 and 1938. In 1918, Hankey thought the basic War Cabinet model applicable in principle to peacetime government.[11] After twenty years of experience, he concluded that "a small Cabinet of planners" should not be recommended. "The planners do not know enough of the detail and form plans that are not administratively workable," Hankey wrote in 1957. "Long-range planning must always include those who will be responsible for execution, and in these days, when so many departments are affected directly or indirectly in the planning, it is best done in Cabinet or Cabinet Committee." And he added, "Otherwise the ministers left out and their departments become suspicious and teamwork becomes difficult."[12]

The doubts and hesitations of more academically inclined insiders are exemplified by Haldane and Samuel. Haldane was the outstanding advocate of the doctrine of the General Staff. At the same time, he was convinced that modern society required large-scale bureaucratic organizations. In addition, he was deeply involved in politics. In his writings, one can find defenses of both the General Staff doctrine and the Joint Staffs concept. At various times he was both an advocate and an antagonist of a Minister of Defence. He pleaded for the appointment of a separate Minister of Research in 1918 and yet was the chief instigator of a basically interdepartmental Committee of Civil Research in 1924. Sometimes he appeared to defend the politics-administration dichotomy that he rejected at other times. As to the Cabinet itself, he denounced the unorganized ways of the period before 1914. But one finds little indication of what he desired as a substitute. The Haldane Committee, as we saw, preferred "a Cabinet small in number—preferably ten, or at most, twelve," but refused to pronounce on whether these ministers should head departments.[13] During the Committee's hearings, Haldane agreed to a suggestion, first put forth by G. M. Young, to divide ministers into two categories. All ministers would have Cabinet rank, but it would be understood that out of a total number of some twenty-five, only some ten might take "part in every meeting of the Cabinet, the remaining fifteen being entitled to ask for a

[11] Reconstruction Papers, Folio 949.
[12] Letter from Lord Hankey to the author, 10 November 1957.
[13] Cmd. 9230 (1918), paras. 7, 10.

Cabinet meeting to discuss business affecting them, and being summoned to any meeting at which business with which they were concerned was to be taken."[14]

Such wavering opinions can also be traced in the utterances of Samuel. In 1916, he did not join Lloyd George's War Cabinet because he objected to both its monopoly of political power and its specific personnel. In the fall of 1917, he devised a scheme for a Cabinet of fourteen members, all ministers heading regrouped departments. In 1931, he was the main instigator of the formation of a concentrated, fully departmental emergency Cabinet of some ten members. Having lost the opportunity to regain power, his evaluation changed. He came to advocate a non-departmental, functional Cabinet, judiciously diluted by a few of the more important departmental ministers who would take a definitely subordinate place. "Planning staffs" and "sub-Cabinets" came to dominate his thought. Politics, so it seemed, was now mainly a disturbing factor that might threaten the satisfactory working of his "Power House of Planning."[15]

Proposals to Improve the Working of the Cabinet Indirectly through Reforms Elsewhere in the Political System

The heavy ministerial burden can be only partially attributed to Cabinet work. Consequently, any reforms that could lessen the other tasks of ministers might favorably affect the workings of the Cabinet. In this concluding section, we can do little but catalogue these proposals, and in passing provide only marginal comment.

Proposals to Ease the Parliamentary Duties of Ministers

It has been suggested, in particular, that ministers should be freed from electoral burdens or from duties to their constituents, or both.[16] This could be achieved by allowing ministers to be represented by a substitute Member of Parliament for their constituency while in office, or it could be institutionalized on a more permanent basis, for instance, by allowing both the Government party and the Opposition party to keep some forty members out of the normal district elections, and to have them chosen instead by proportional representation, rather in the way that English municipal councils elect their aldermen.[17]

Somewhat less fanciful are proposals that seek to free ministers from the need to attend debates and to trot through the division lobbies, simply to register the known majority of the Government party over the Opposi-

[14] Reconstruction Papers, Folio 1013.

[15] Samuel, *Memoirs*, pp. 125–26; Reconstruction Papers, Folio 595; *The Times*, 9 September 1947.

[16] In 1919, the traditional requirement that each newly appointed minister should subject himself once more to re-election was abolished. Cf. 112 H. of C. Deb. (17 February 1919), cols. 614–64.

[17] Cf. letter by H. B. Jenkins in *The Economist*, 25 May 1957.

tion party. This could be done by introducing proxy voting or mechanical voting, by holding important divisions at pre-arranged hours, or by limiting the total number of divisions in any one parliamentary session. Such proposals were particularly canvassed in the period between 1950 and 1951 when the Conservative Opposition sought to exhaust Labour ministers through all-night sittings. Of the same character but more drastic is Baldwin's proposal to return deliberately to longer parliamentary recesses, in order to obviate the real danger of "government by tired men."[18]

These proposals might have much greater effect than some of their protagonists seem to realize. They might introduce rather basic changes in the relation between ministers and backbenchers in ways not likely to be agreeable to everyone concerned, and weaken the influence of Parliament even more than tends to be the case today.

Proposals to Relieve Ministers from Part of Their Responsibilities to Parliament

The pressure on ministers can be attributed largely to the fact that Parliament can force a minister to occupy himself at any moment with any matter within the responsibility of his department. In particular, parliamentary questions and business correspondence place a heavy burden on certain ministers, their private offices, leading civil servants, and the departments at large.[19] So does the need to defend detailed clauses of bills in Parliament or in parliamentary committees.

Proposals that seek to lessen these charges may be categorized as quantitative and qualitative. The first category comprises the proposition to limit further the number of questions that can be asked of any one minister during a parliamentary session.[20] In the same category may be placed the suggestion to divide ministerial responsibilities among more people, either vertically, by allowing Ministers of State and parliamentary secretaries to have a more independent responsibility, or horizontally, through a further division of tasks among a greater number of independent ministers. Future Prime Ministers might well wish to follow Macmillan's habit of delegating certain particularly thorny issues to special ministers, irrespective of traditional departmental boundaries. All in all, however, such proposals often tend to shift rather than solve existing administrative complexities.

Consequently, the discussion generally centers on proposals that aim at a substantial, qualitative change in ministerial tasks. Effective relief, so it is held, can be achieved only if ministers are actually exempted from

---

[18] *Parliamentary Reform*, pp. 109, 121–25.

[19] Chester–Bowring, *passim.*

[20] *Parliamentary Reform,* pp. 117–20; but see Chester–Bowring (p. 92ff) for the extent to which many ministers are already relieved by the very congestion of question time.

certain responsibilities. This can be done either by transferring the responsibility to other bodies that are directly, and independently, responsible to Parliament or by transferring it to bodies who have no direct responsibility to Parliament.

In the first case, there would be a return to the earlier practice whereby fairly independent administrative boards reported directly to Parliament, often through one or more of their members who sat in Parliament, not through a directly responsible minister. Specialized parliamentary committees might supervise the work of these independent commissions. The great disadvantage of such proposals is that they destroy the unity of administration. In the second case, certain ministerial tasks are transferred to bodies that have no immediate responsibility to Parliament, as is the situation with the public corporations and administrative tribunals.[21] Ministerial control over such bodies is limited at most to matters of over-all policy or some financial control. But day-to-day management and specific decisions are fully within their discretion, and hence not a matter on which Parliament can challenge ministers. These reforms have had some effect, and it seems likely that the principle may be pushed further. There is a real limit, however, to what they can achieve. The increased interdependence of government makes it difficult to isolate certain governmental activities. Moreover, whenever the electorate feels sufficiently disturbed on a particular issue, no minister can afford to act like Pontius Pilate. The experience of the nationalized industries has shown only too well that parliamentarians seek to push their influence to the maximum possible, whatever the statutory arrangements.[22]

Proposals to Lighten the Ministerial Burden by Delegating Additional Tasks to the Civil Service

These proposals concentrate on three points in particular : more direct aid by officials to ministers; further improvement in the instruments of administrative coordination below the Cabinet level; and greater deconcentration and delegation of authority to subordinate administrative agencies.

Appointment of more top-level civil servants has the undoubted danger of an even greater undesirable fragmentation of tasks than is found at the present time. Moreover, is it not true that the more people there are on the highest level, the more work they make for one another?

Improvement of coordination procedures and more delegation of

[21] Chester–Bowring, pp. 92–96; *Chester, Ministerial Responsibility,* pp. 3–4; Tivey–Rendel, p. 6ff.

[22] There is very extensive literature on this subject. See, e.g., the reports of the Select Committee on the Nationalized Industries, H. C. 332 (1952) ; H. C. 235 (1953) and H. C. 120 (1955) ; Morrison, pp. 247–86; Chester, *The Nationalized Industries: An Analysis of the Statutory Provisions* (1951) ; W. A. Robson, ed., *Problems of Nationalized Industry* (1952) ; Robson, *Nationalized Industry and Public Ownership* (1962) ; Raymond Nottage, "Reporting to Parliament on the Nationalized Industries," *Public Administration,* XXXV (1957), 143–67.

authority to lower administrative levels have often been advocated. But one important factor prevents such changes from having much, if any, effect in practice. Possible conflicts and problems can be settled lower down in an administrative hierarchy only when all parties concerned refuse to refer them to a higher authority or when those higher up refuse to occupy themselves with such issues. Experience proves that such conditions rarely prevail. Even though Britain generally has a one-party Cabinet, this offers no guarantee that leadership at Cabinet level will be unified. In England, too, emotions may run high between departments and ministers, over personal as well as material issues. Unity, in other words, is not given, but has again and again to be forged by long consultations and difficult compromises. Departmental *esprit de corps* and interdepartmental tensions ensure that few decisions are taken without a fight, which generally results in an appeal to a higher authority for decision. Delegation of authority meets with one more paradoxical obstacle. The ministers who complain most about their heavy burden are often those who are least prepared to let things go.

Proposals That Might Preserve the Health of Ministers

"Men of ordinary physique and discretion cannot be President and live, if the strain be not somehow relieved. . . . We shall be obliged always to be picking our chief magistrates from among wise and prudent athletes—a small class," Wilson said. His complaint was echoed by Baldwin, who sighed in 1932 that ministers ought to be thirty-five, not seventy.[23]

The heavy strain on ministers may well have serious effects on their health, and ministers in poor health may well take poor decisions. As *The Economist* wrote shortly after Eden resigned in January 1957:

The problem was first posed after the First World War, and has recently become sadly familiar in practice. A statesman falls ill through overwork; there follows a period when he is making many wrong decisions because he is ill, but he himself does not recognize the fact and his colleagues are too embarrassed to tell him; then his illness overpowers him and he retires, his mistakes made, into the shadow.[24]

The list of ministers who were seriously ill in office is a long one: It includes MacDonald, Baldwin, Neville Chamberlain, Churchill, Attlee, Morrison, Dalton, Cripps, Bevin, Butler, and Eden, to mention only the most prominent. The age at which parliamentarians are normally recruited is higher now than it was in the more aristocratic era of the eighteenth and nineteenth centuries.[25] But the probationary period of a potential minister is hardly shorter. Cabinet members become older, and

[23] Woodrow Wilson, *Constitutional Government in the United States* (1917), pp. 79–80; Jones, *Diary*, p. 69; cf. *Esher Papers*, III, 249.

[24] *The Economist*, 27 April 1957.

[25] Cf. Dogan–Campbell (p. 813) listing the ages at which British politicians were first appointed to each category of ministerial posts from 1945 onwards.

so do members of the shadow Cabinet, who often pass their best years out of office. The party spirit nevertheless generally militates against any attempt to replace them by younger ones, until well past the time the older leaders are too old to lead.

Hence, it has been proposed to introduce age limits, periodical health checks, compulsory rotation of at least the most grueling government posts, and periodical leaves of absence.[26] Such proposals have been rejected by *The Manchester Guardian,* among others.[27] In the *Guardian's* view, they conflict with the democratic tenet that only the people and their constitutional representatives should decide who is fit to rule. Is this a valid argument? The leaders' confident belief that they cannot be spared is often defended with an appeal to an alleged popular will. One need not deny the importance of a feeling of psychological trust between the grateful people and their known leaders in order to believe also that these very people easily adjust to new faces. It is incorrect, moreover, that doctors would be put in the place of electors. Their medical opinion would be only negative: they would declare particular political leaders physically unfit, not politically desirable.[28]

The Burden of Modern Government

If proposals for the reorganization of the Cabinet structure can have no more than limited effect, and if proposals for changes elsewhere in the system are for the time being little but brainwaves, then the ultimate question is whether the burden of modern government is not becoming unmanageable in any case. Three schools of thought tend to coexist on this issue.

An optimistic school holds that the problem has really been exaggerated under the combined influence of the posturing of ministers and the quasi-rationality of ardent Cabinet reformers. Laski, for instance, has pointed to the element of affectation that might lie at the base of some ministers' complaints about their oppressive workload. The mask of the irreplaceable servant of the State, threatened with breaking down under the mass of duties he carries, hinting at but never realizing the desire to retire from politics, often covers what is really strong ambition. Would-be Cabinet reformers have little inducement, moreover, to view the existing situation optimistically: "One sometimes wonders," Harrison has written, "whether the dimensions of the problem presented by the Cabinet have not been exaggerated in order to allow an opportunity for suggesting an attractively neat solution."[29]

An element of optimism may also be found in the second school of

[26] Cf. Dalton, *Memoirs,* III, 19–21.
[27] *The Manchester Guardian,* 31 December 1957.
[28] The proposal is less extreme, at any rate, than one made by Ross, who has advocated that all candidates for elective office should voluntarily submit to psychological, intelligence, and aptitude tests, the results of which would become public property (Ross, *Parliamentary Representation,* pp. 230–31).
[29] Harrison, p. 141; Laski, *Reflections,* pp. 147–52.

thought, which holds that the existing organization of government may be easily relieved of its admittedly excessive tasks by a drastic devolution of powers to lower administrative organs. Even at the time of the Haldane Committee, Morant, Beatrice Webb and others argued in favor of decentralizing the government. Morant advocated the establishment of separate territorial authorities for Scotland and Wales.[30] The Webbs devised various schemes to split up the duties of central government along more functional lines. A Social Parliament was to be established as a supplement to the existing Political Parliament. Or, according to a later scheme, the United Kingdom Government was to deal only with matters of foreign affairs, defense, finance, trade, and justice; all other tasks were to be delegated to lower National Governments for England, Scotland, and Wales, which were to be provided with their own Executive and their own Parliamentary Assembly.[31] Since then, the doctrine of decentralization has grown into an ethos, but not into an effective force in day-to-day government.[32] The proposal is logically related to the federalist view, which advocates a transfer of certain duties to supranational bodies as well as internal decentralization. If it is true that much of the present administrative burden derives from the manifold links of national administration with international organizations, such a shift, if drastic enough, would undoubtedly lighten the central machinery of government.

Finally, a pessimistic school argues that there is a human limit to the accumulation of functions that a government can carry. According to neo-Liberals like Hayek, this point has long since been reached. But even a former Socialist minister could write:

The incessant press of meetings has an important but little remarked effect upon the nature of modern government. *It sets a strict upper limit upon the extent of democratic planning.* Planning presupposes the careful coordination of policy between those men who have the powers to carry the plan into effect.

[30] Reconstruction Papers, Folio 1074.

[31] *A Constitution for the Socialist Commonwealth of Great Britain*, pp. 108–46; *Passfield Papers*, section 4, item 24: "A Scheme of Devolution" (March 1930); cf. Beatrice Webb's *Diaries*, 1924–32, 7 March and 30 April 1930; and Beatrice Webb, "A Reform Bill for 1932," *Political Quarterly*, II (1932), 1–22. According to Beatrice Webb, a drastic devolution of powers would free the National Cabinet from a large number of duties. Thus the Cabinet might be composed only of the Prime Minister, the Secretaries of State for Foreign Affairs, Home Affairs, Dominions and Colonies, War, Air, and India; the First Lord of the Admiralty; the President of the Board of Trade; and the Lord Chancellor.

One commentator has characterized the suggestion to divide the government tasks between a Political Parliament and a Social Parliament as follows: "The Political Parliament was to retain all the present trappings and so enable the young gentlemen from Oxford and Cambridge to continue their Union Debates in the traditional manner on foreign affairs and other matters that Webb was not greatly interested in. Meanwhile the Social Parliament was to be an enlarged L. C. C. [London County Council] for all England, where the graduates of the London School of Economics might do the real business of governing England" (Alan M. McBriar, in Margaret Cole, ed., *The Webbs and Their Work* [1949], pp. 95–96).

[32] For a survey, see *Parliamentary Reform*, pp. 38–60; cf. Keith-Gibbs, pp. 247–68, especially p. 262ff; Vernon–Mansergh, pp. 63–72.

There can only be a relatively few such men, or administrative confusion will result. But coordination of policy consumes much of the time and energy of these few men. Every hour spent in meetings must be subtracted from the exiguous ration of hours that a minister has left for the task of direct administration. Beyond a certain point—the more you plan, the less you do. Ministers conceive a deep distaste for embarking upon projects that will entail more and longer meetings with their colleagues. This means that even Socialist ministers are selective about the sectors of the national life that they can attempt to plan.[33]

A realistic analysis of the functioning of the British Cabinet cannot restrict itself to questions of organization. Such ever-changing personal factors as the mental and physical condition of leading ministers and relations between ministers must be taken into account. Political pressures both at home and abroad must be considered. So must the fact that the Cabinet's role and operation are largely determined by a specific political system, of which the Cabinet is but one part. And before any definite judgment can be made, subjective views about how much government intervention is "right" must be clarified.

[33] Gordon Walker, p. 22; cf. Chester, *Planning*, p. 363; Chester, *Trends*, pp. 19–20.

POSTSCRIPT 1963

The Decline of the Macmillan Administration

Fortune did not smile on Macmillan during the last stages of his political career. The Cabinet reshuffle of July 1962 had symbolized his paramount position. But it was evident that this transformation of the Government Front Bench was the last Macmillan could politically afford. Notwithstanding the new crop of "managerial" ministers, the Macmillan administration did not succeed in rehabilitating its electoral prospects. In fact, nearly everything seemed to go wrong.

The decline in Macmillan's reputation must be attributed in part to the failure of the Common Market negotiations. Entry into the Common Market was thought likely to produce the catalysis British industry apparently needed so badly, as well as to give a modern face to British foreign policy. Macmillan staked his personal authority on persuading Britain to join, in the face of the twin forces of British insularity and imperial nostalgia. For a time, the strategy seemed politically rewarding, since it allowed the Conservatives to identify their party with the cause of modernization, bequeathing to Labour the mantle of the Little Englanders. Then an imperious foreigner vetoed British admission, leaving the Government bewildered and the British people resentful.

Defense policy, too, became increasingly bedeviled. The scrapping of the Blue Streak and Skybolt missiles painfully brought home the unmanageable character of independent weapons-development policies. The inevitable alternative of reliance on the United States was not popular even among those who were most concerned with maintaining Britain's military posture: rather than let Britain be a dependent ally with an independent deterrent, some preferred to retain the semblance of independence with no deterrent at all.

On top of all this came the essentially trivial but politically dramatic Profumo affair. This must be seen in relation to the Vassall case of September 1962. The arrest on a charge of espionage of Vassall, a relatively low-ranking official who worked in close proximity to Admiralty secrets, threw a further burden on British security, which was already under suspicion of laxity. For a time T. G. D. Galbraith, a Civil Lord of the Admiralty, seemed to be involved, and he resigned from the Government. A special tribunal chaired by Lord Radcliffe exonerated him of damaging but ill-established newspaper charges, and shortly thereafter he was given a new office.

The incident must have influenced the attitude of Macmillan and other Conservative ministers when it was rumored that no less a figure than the Secretary of State for War, John Profumo, had shared a mistress with a Russian diplomat. Profumo was questioned closely by five Conservative leaders and denied the allegations. Subsequently, in the House of Commons, Profumo threatened to bring suit against anyone who might repeat the story outside the House. When, after further investigation, the story was proved true, the spectacle of a Minister of the Crown lying to his colleagues, lying to the House of Commons, and falsely suing and obtaining damages from foreign journals, dealt the Government a staggering blow.

Matters were not improved when it became known that Macmillan himself had not been informed about the affair in its early stages, even though the security forces knew of it: the Head of the Civil Service, Sir Norman Brook, had apparently thought it unnecessary to acquaint the Prime Minister with certain facts reported to him. When, at last, Macmillan did know, he sought no personal confrontation with Profumo, preferring to believe in the word rather than in the guilt of a Government colleague. The affair would have been awkward for any Government. For a Government faced with the prospect of fighting an election against the tide of popular feelings, it was damaging in the extreme. However unfairly, Macmillan became the symbol of the inept complacency and anachronism that seemed to lie at the roots of Britain's problems.

With difficulty, Macmillan quelled a storm in the Cabinet and among backbenchers. But some withheld their support. The impression was widespread that Macmillan had agreed to resign in order to unite the party, and support was already building up for Reginald Maudling, the Chancellor of the Exchequer, to succeed him. It seemed generally agreed that Macmillan's distinguished career should not appear to be cut short by a chance collision with the operations of a prostitute. The signing of the Test Ban Treaty seemed to offer the possibility of a more dignified withdrawal from office. In this fashion Macmillan stayed, and stayed on. Gradually, the speculations about the succession lost their confident ring.

Finally, on the eve of the Annual Conference of the Conservatives, held in October 1963 at Blackpool, Macmillan let it be understood that he definitely intended to lead the Conservatives during the next election. Although some may have been dispirited, the stage was set for a closing of the ranks. Then, suddenly, Macmillan became ill, and had to undergo surgery. He announced his intention to resign, expressing the hope that it would "soon be possible for the customary processes of consultation to be carried on within the party about its future leadership."[1]

The Selection of Home as Prime Minister

Macmillan's announcement converted the Blackpool Conference into something resembling an American Presidential convention. Conflicts

[1] *The Times,* 11 October 1963.

arose over who was to be the keynote speaker in Macmillan's place. Lapel buttons appeared flaunting a "Q" for Quintin Hogg (Lord Hailsham), who dramatically cast his hat into the ring for the Leadership. Applause was measured in length and loudness, informal canvassing and negotiations were held in smoke-filled rooms, and rivals appeared frequently on television screens. The Conference disbanded before the final decision was made, and the scene shifted back to London. From the most exciting intra-party maneuverings since 1923, if not 1916, finally emerged the Earl of Home.

Obviously, at the time of this writing (26 October 1963), no objective academic evaluation of Home's selection can be made, since many facts are not yet known, possibly unreliable newspaper reports as yet providing the only information.[2] The full flavor of the story could only be conveyed by the pen of a Beaverbrook. However, some comments might be in order.

First of all, Home owed the possibility of his selection, paradoxically, to the joint endeavor of a Labour politician and certain disaffected Conservatives in the House of Lords. If it had not been for Anthony Wedgwood Benn's efforts to secure the right to renounce his title, the 1963 Peerage Bill would scarcely have been introduced in time, if at all. Though constitutional lawyers differed on whether a peer could constitutionally be appointed Prime Minister, it is most unlikely that in 1963 a member of the House of Lords would have emerged as Leader of the Conservative Party, had he not had the possibility of going over to the Commons.[3] Moreover, the original Peerage Bill sponsored by the Government would have postponed this opportunity until the next general election. Home therefore indirectly owes his selection to an amendment of the House of Lords (pushed through against the Government's wishes) that made immediate renunciation possible.[4] The Peerage Act has transformed the intricate power structure through which the Conservative party leadership is "evolved." Candidates once thought to be above the struggle can now enter it with all the prestige of their noble styles and titles. The influence of "political families" may well have gained a new importance in ministerial recruitment.

It should also be noted that Macmillan did not resign immediately, but merely announced his intended resignation at some future unspecified date. This left less room for independent action on the part of the Crown than had been the case in 1923, or 1957.

[2] I have relied mainly on *The Times, The Observer* (13 and 20 October 1963), *The Sunday Times,* and *The Sunday Telegraph* (20 October 1963).

[3] The doubt about the actual inconstitutionality (as distinct from the political difficulties) of the selection of a peer as Prime Minister has been intensified by various disclosures suggesting that Curzon was passed over in favor of Baldwin in 1923 for personal reasons, the argument of his peerage having been advanced only to soothe his disappointment. (See especially Amery, *Constitution*; Amery, *My Political Life*, II, 259–61; *The Manchester Guardian,* 29 April 1954; and *Life of Bonar Law,* Chap. 32; but see also *Life of King George V*, pp. 376–77.) In 1940, Lord Halifax himself, rather than the King or various other political leaders, thought it would be impossible for him to lead the Government from the House of Lords.

[4] *The Times,* 17 July 1963.

It is evident that Macmillan did nothing to facilitate a succession by the Deputy Prime Minister, R. A. Butler, who seemed the logical if not the popular choice. Once again the position of Number Two in the Cabinet was shown to have little real substance. Butler was acting Prime Minister while Macmillan was hospitalized. He was not the first to be informed of Macmillan's intention to resign. He was at no time personally consulted by the Queen. He did not preside over the informal consultation within the party that preceded the appointment of the new Prime Minister. Newspaper reports even suggest that Macmillan refused to take a telephone call from Butler at a crucial moment, when it is said that Butler's main rivals had indicated their willingness to serve under him if this could prevent Home's accession.[5] Macmillan advised the Queen to send for Home within a few hours of this incident.

The consultations involved some aspects peculiar even to the somewhat unique procedures of the Conservative Party.[6] Unlike his opposite number in the Labour Party, the Leader of the Conservative Party is not directly elected by the Parliamentary Party. According to Conservative beliefs, he must "emerge" as the undisputed choice of the Party, after due consultation with its main constituent parts, the Cabinet (if Conservatives are in power), the members of both Houses, prospective parliamentary candidates, and the constituency associations. Apparently, opinions were extensively collected by the Lord Chancellor, the Chief Whip, and other party dignitaries, with Macmillan acting as the final arbiter of the process. But from the outset, the questions asked of the main participants in the process—the members of the Cabinet and of the Conservative Party in the Commons—tended to be loaded against more controversial, if more obvious, candidates, like Hailsham and Butler. Those consulted were asked to indicate not only their first preference but also their second, and to indicate whom, if anyone, they would not serve under. The last question served as a definite invitation for vociferous anti-Hailshamites and anti-Butlerites to cancel one another out, and thus to make the eventual choice of a less controversial figure all the more likely. (Butler's case was further weakened by the continued preference of some potential supporters for the similarly "modern Conservative" Maudling, who remained in the ring until the last gasp.)[7]

Home was not immediately appointed Prime Minister, but only invited to form a Cabinet. Even so, his position against any competitors was strongly enhanced. Those who now refused to serve under him would invite the odium of dividing the party in an election year without the certainty of a following adequate to form a Government themselves. The situation for them was made even more difficult when the bogey was raised that the Queen might turn to Harold Wilson, charging him to form a Cabi-

---

[5] See *The Sunday Times,* 20 October 1963.
[6] For a full description, see McKenzie, *passim.*
[7] See *The Observer,* 20 October 1963.

net and dissolve Parliament. History offered the example of the trouncing of the badly divided Conservative Party in 1906; this was enough to scare into thinking twice even those Conservatives who needed the lessons of history more than the lessons of Gallup polls.

Hence, it is poor reasoning to conclude from Home's success in forming a Cabinet that his appointment was the best possible. To borrow a phrase Balfour used in 1916, Butler and the others had, in fact, a pistol held against their heads. But, one might ask, would not Butler's antagonists have yielded equally rapidly if *his* hands had been on the trigger? In this light, it also seems doubtful that Macmillan's decision to advise the Queen to send for Home could really be justified by the need to save the Crown from embarrassment. If Butler had been given the opportunity to form a Cabinet, success on his part could equally have "proved" his nomination correct. A failure by Butler, on the other hand, followed by a successful formation of a Cabinet by Home, would not have been any more dangerous to the Crown than a failure by Home, inducing either a party split or the formation of a Cabinet by some other Conservatives.

Home's choice (and the events preceding it) exposed the many unresolved divisions in the Conservative Party. At the last minute, a small group of influential "modern Conservatives" met in the home of Enoch Powell to block Home's accession. The group included Iain Macleod (then Leader of the House of Commons and Chairman of the Conservative Party Organisation), Reginald Maudling (Chancellor of the Exchequer), F. J. Erroll (President of the Board of Trade) and Powell (Minister of Health). They apparently felt that all past endeavors to give the Conservative Party a modern outlook would be jeopardized by the selection of an Earl, who seemed to owe his choice largely to anti-Butler machinations, engineered by what seemed to them a reactionary minority, aided and abetted by all traditional forces in the Conservative Party of family and the Establishment.[8] Their move was both too late and too weak, and in the end only Macleod and Powell refused to serve under Home. Consequently, Home had to find only two replacements in the ministry Macmillan bequeathed to him. He chose Selwyn Lloyd, who became Leader of the House, and Maurice Macmillan, a son of the outgoing Prime Minister, who became Economic Secretary to the Treasury. Yet for all its similarity of personnel, a Cabinet led by Home and Selwyn Lloyd would be different from one led by Butler and Macleod.

There were many accidental ironies in the situation. Home's appointment was a curious reversal of the one made in 1923. Then a relatively inexperienced commoner (Baldwin) was preferred over one of the most experienced statesmen of the day (Curzon). Now the most experienced commoner was passed over for a peer who, until 1960, had been practically unknown in British politics, except to insiders. Personal factors played a predominant role in both cases, but whereas in 1923 sickness was instru-

[8] Cf. *The Times* (20 October 1963) and sources given in n. 2.

mental in silencing the outgoing Prime Minister (Bonar Law), now all threads came together in the sickroom of Macmillan, who only a short time before had seemed likely to be driven from office. One result of the selection was the shift of Butler, whose reputation had been made in home affairs, to the foreign field, while Home, who apart from a period as Minister of State in the Scottish Office had had only international experience, was now to preside over the home front, at a time when Britain's domestic problems seemed the predominant political issue. A second-generation Labour peer had paved the way for a Fourteenth Earl to become Conservative Prime Minister. It is ironic that the banner of equality of opportunity should now be waved by those Conseratives, who answer Labour's accusation of class bias with the counter-argument that in modern times peers should not be denied the rights accorded to commoners. Finally, the unexpected appointment of Home gave the Conservatives the new face they needed badly. If nothing else, the spectacle of an aristocrat who only shortly before had candidly admitted his need for a box of matches to help him with his economic calculations, pleading the case of Britain's economic modernization, had the appeal of the unexpected.[9]

Cabinet Changes in 1963[10]

With the transfer of Butler to the Foreign Office, the office of First Secretary of State lapsed again. But at the same time three new ministers appeared in the Cabinet. Home readmitted the Ministers of Power and of Public Buildings and Works (who had been excluded in 1959 and 1957, respectively). Among major offices, only the Minister of Aviation, the Minister of Pensions and National Insurance, and the Postmaster-General were left outside the Cabinet. At the same time, Lord Carrington was appointed a second Minister without Portfolio to act as Leader of the House of Lords and to assist Butler in the Foreign Office.

The departure of both Home and Hailsham from the Lords threatened to strip the Government of its official power in that House : in a large Cabinet, the exit of these two peers left only the new Minister without Portfolio and the Lord Chancellor to preserve the link between the Cabinet and the Upper House. The flexibility available through the use of the sinecure offices once more became apparent. Macleod's refusal to serve led Home to make two new appointments : Hare, who had been Minister of Labour, was appointed to the Duchy, named Chairman of the Conservative Party Organisation, and raised to the peerage to help restore the balance in the Lords. Selwyn Lloyd became Leader of the House of Commons as Lord Privy Seal. On vacating the Privy Seal, Heath returned to the administration of domestic policies with a new title (Secretary of State for Industry, Trade, and Regional Development) but at the head of an old office,

[9] Cf. the editorial in *The Guardian,* 19 October 1963.
[10] See *The Times,* 21 October 1963.

the Board of Trade. With the disappearance of the office of First Secretary of State, the office of Central African Affairs returned to Sandys, who continued to combine the Commonwealth Relations and Colonial Offices. These two offices had previously been even more closely integrated, when subordinate ministers in each office were given the authority to occupy themselves with matters within the competence of the other.

Home's Cabinet of twenty-three was the largest since Asquith's in 1915 and Neville Chamberlain's in 1939. For someone like the Minister of Aviation, Julian Amery, exclusion from an enlarged Cabinet must have been doubly painful. At various times pressure has been exerted for the appointment of new ministers of Cabinet rank. In October 1963, the Robbins Committee on Higher Education made a strong plea for the establishment of a separate Ministry of Arts and Science.[11] The proposal was strongly criticized by those who feared that the separation of the universities from other educational institutions (which would remain under the Ministry of Education) would lead to invidious discriminations. But only a short while earlier, at the Scarborough Conference of the Labour Party, Harold Wilson had acclaimed the marriage of science and socialism as the prelude to Britain's modernization. The issue was too explosive to ignore, and Home consequently gave Hailsham (who had stayed on as Lord President of the Council and Minister for Science) the task of implementing the Robbins proposals.

A casual perusal of the 1963 Hansard reveals pressure for such different offices as a senior Minister for Overseas Trade (calculated to undo the feared effects of Britain's continued exclusion from the Common Market), a more powerful Minister for Welsh Affairs, a Minister for Security, and even a Minister for Tourism.[12] Not everyone was satisfied with the intended ministerial monopoly of one Secretary of State in the defense field. Ruminating at a meeting of the Fabian Society at Scarborough, Harold Wilson suggested that a new Labour Government might wish no less than five new Government departments: for Production and Economic Planning, Higher Education, Disarmament, Overseas Development, and Science.[13] Among all these pleas for an increase in ministerial portfolios, there was only one lonely voice in favor of an amalgamation: A. Lewis, M.P., advocated the merger of the Foreign Office, the Commonwealth Relations Office, and the Colonial Office into a new Ministry of External Affairs.[14]

Signs of dissatisfaction among junior ministers continued to appear. In a question addressed to Macmillan in the Commons on 7 March 1963, R. Gresham Cooke advocated changing the name of parliamentary secretaries to "Deputy Ministers," in order to make it explicit that junior ministers were ministerially in charge of their office when Ministers (or Min-

11 *The Times* (24 October 1963) and Letters to the Editor on succeeding days.
12 See 671 H. of C. Deb. (7 February 1963), cols. 663–64; 675 H. of C. Deb. (11 April 1963), cols. 1476–77; and 680 H. of C. Deb. (2 July 1963), cols. 191–92, 193.
13 *The Times,* 1 October 1963.
14 675 H. of C. Deb. (2 April 1963), cols. 247–49.

isters of State, when appropriate) were absent.[15] Macmillan resisted both
the nomenclature and the substance of the suggestion. A junior minister,
he had declared earlier, is

not a Minister of the Crown under the Constitution, because he is not appointed
by the Queen. . . . Constitutionally, of course, the Parliamentary Secretary,
theoretically, cannot give orders to the Permanent Secretary. If there were
some division of opinion, then that must be resolved only by the Minister.
Apart from that, he normally deputizes for the Minister.[16]

And later, in reply to Harold Wilson, Macmillan said, "The Permanent
Secretary is responsible for the organization and discipline of his Department, and he has the right for any question to be settled by the Minister
in charge of his Department."[17] But to check the criticism, Macmillan instructed the departments to print the names of junior ministers above the
names of the most senior officials.[18]

Further Centralization in the Defense Organization

In July 1962, the Select Committee on Estimates had publicly queried
the continued existence of five defense ministries. Such doubts were shared
in many circles inside the organization itself, and they received powerful
reinforcement from the malaise induced by the scrapping of the Skybolt
missile and the Nassau Agreement. In January 1963, the Minister of Defence, Thorneycroft, invited Lord Ismay and Sir Ian Jacob to investigate
the problem anew, and to tender advice on improving the organization.[19]
Shortly afterwards, Sir Frank Lee was asked to return temporarily to
Whitehall from his cloister in Cambridge to study the relation between
the Ministry of Defence and the Ministry of Aviation. In a defense debate
in the Commons on 4 March 1963, Thorneycroft publicly acknowledged
the current complaints:

First, there is doubt as to the effective power of the Ministry of Defence to
make the defense budget a real synthesis of defense problems rather than a
carving up of the cake among different claimants. The second doubt is whether,
when resources are under pressure, the interests of individual Services do not
prevent the formulation of what could be called a real central policy. The third
is whether research and development can really be effectively devised and controlled, and I may say that that is one of the most difficult problems of all.[20]

Thorneycroft then developed some general principles of reform, which
were elaborated in detail in a Defence White Paper of July 1963.[21] The

[15] 673 H. of C. Deb. (7 March 1963), cols. 641–42.
[16] 672 H. of C. Deb. (26 February 1963), cols. 1078–79.
[17] *Ibid.*
[18] 673 H. of C. Deb. (7 March 1963), col. 642.
[19] 670 H. of C. Deb. (23 January 1963), col. 70.
[20] 673 H. of C. Deb. (4 March 1963), col. 38.
[21] Cmnd. 2097.

paper was debated in the Commons on 31 July.[22] The Government announced that it would introduce the necessary legislation in the fall to give effect to its proposals, and that the changes would go into effect formally on 1 April 1964.

The White Paper announced the following reforms. Under the Prime Minister and the Cabinet, a Committee of Defence and Overseas Policy, composed of the Foreign Secretary, the Chancellor of the Exchequer or the Chief Secretary to the Treasury, the Secretary of State for Commonwealth Relations and the Colonies, the Defence minister, and other ministers when invited, will be responsible for major questions of defense policy.

The Admiralty, the War Office, and the Air Ministry will be abolished, and the offices of the present Service ministers will disappear. All statutory powers for national defense will be vested in a new minister, the Secretary of State for Defence. Thorneycroft stated in the Commons that nothing short of this would enable the minister to appreciate fully both the weaknesses and the strength of the arguments presented by the individual services; central responsibility, he felt, was not enough, unless one heard the conflicting arguments before policy was defined.[23]

Although the new organization foreshadows a unified Ministry, it will be "one Ministry on a Service basis with Service ministers subordinate to the Minister of Defence."[24] No amalgamation of the independent Services is envisaged, and the traditional rights of the Chiefs of Staff as professional heads of their Services, having access to the Cabinet and the Prime Minister, are to be fully respected. The powers of the Board of Admiralty, the Army Council, and the Air Council will be abolished, and their powers absorbed into a new Defence Council. This Council will consist of the Secretary of State for Defence, three Ministers of State, the Chief of the Defence Staff, the Chief of the Naval Staff, the Chief of the General Staff, the Chief of the Air Staff, the Chief Scientific Adviser to the Secretary of State, and the Permanent Undersecretary of State. Each Minister of State will act mainly for one Service, but occasionally will discharge whatever duties the Secretary of State will delegate over the entire defense field. While the Defence Council will deal with major defense policy, the Navy, Army, and Air Force Boards will be responsible for management. These Boards will officially be chaired by the Secretary of State, but the appropriate Minister of State will be asked to act for him in normal circumstances.

In addition to the concentration of all legal powers in the hands of the Secretary of State, the central organization will be further strengthened by the establishment of three parallel central staffs. First, the Naval, Army, and Air Staffs, together with the joint Service staffs of the present Minister of Defence, will constitute the Defence Staff, which will be responsible

---

[22] 682 H. of C. Deb. (31 July 1963), cols. 465–578.
[23] *Ibid.*, col. 467.
[24] 673 H. of C. Deb. (4 March 1963), col. 42.

to the Chiefs of Staff Committee and through its Chairman to the Secretary of State. To quote the White Paper: "The Defence Staff must take into account the views of the individual Services and ensure that plans are based on a realistic assessment of their capabilities. But their principal corporate duty will be to find the best Defence solution to the problems with which they are faced."[25] To promote a common outlook on defense problems, these staffs will work in the same building. Connected with the Defence Staff will be a new Defence Operations Centre (as has been evolving in practice since 1961), a Defence Operational Requirements Staff, a Defence Signals Staff, and a Defence Intelligence Staff.

Second, increased influence is to be given to the Scientific Adviser, who will be in charge of a new Defence Scientific Staff, and will be given increased powers over defence research and weapons development. To this end, the existing Defence Research Policy Committee will be split into two Committees, for research and weapons development, respectively.

Third, a Defence Secretariat will be concerned with the entire defense program, the defense budget, and other matters of major policy, including overseas matters in consultation with the Foreign Office, the Commonwealth Relations Office, and the Colonial Office.

Practical considerations, announced Thorneycroft, had decided against a merger of the Ministry of Aviation with the new Ministry of Defence. Such a merger would be damaging to the interests of civil aviation, and would load the Secretary of State with more responsibilities than one man could bear. To achieve close liaison, however, the Minister of Aviation and his senior officials who are mainly or exclusively concerned with defense projects will be housed in the same building with the central staffs of the Ministry of Defence.[26] In addition, the Secretary of State will enjoy the right to call in for consultation officials of the Ministry of Aviation and its establishments. Arrangements will be made for the regular interchange of staffs between the two Ministries.

Thorneycroft described these intended reforms as "the largest administrative change that has taken place, or is proposed to take place, in Whitehall for many a year."[27] The reorganization will directly or indirectly affect some 25,000 civil servants in the various defense ministries, and will also force the Board of Trade to seek new quarters. It was only possible, Thorneycroft replied to all advocates of additional reforms, to move step by step, because the show would have to go on during the transitional period. While not denying the force of this argument, the Labour Opposition could easily point to many half-way measures and forecast that the new reforms would be merely one more passing effusion of the traditional desire for streamlining the defense organization. Criticism in the Commons during the debate of 31 July focused in particular on the following points.

First, the continued independence of the three Services was attacked,

[25] Cmnd. 2097, para. 32.
[26] *Ibid.*, paras. 75–82, and 682 H. of C. Deb. (31 July 1963), cols. 469–71.
[27] *Ibid.*, col. 568; cf. cols. 477–78.

and with it the principle on which the Chiefs of Staff would maintain their authority. This, said the Labour spokesman, Denis Healey, made the proposed organization seem "more . . . like a penthouse than a Pentagon."[28]

Second, it was felt that the demotion of the Service ministers, unaccompanied by that of their Service chiefs, meant in fact an undesirable upgrading of the chiefs, who would now become the heads of their organizations in earnest. But whereas some speakers concluded from this that the Service ministers should be retained, others felt that it was actually an argument for downgrading the Chiefs of Staff.

Third, concern was expressed that the reforms would result in a lessening of civilian control over the military. In summing up Labour's objections, Gordon Walker said, "The basic defect of the White Paper is that the Secretary of State will be in lonely eminence divorced from proper ministerial support." The new Minister would be very high, his nearest colleagues very low down, while the professional heads of departments would stand between him and his ministers.[29] The Opposition therefore advocated the appointment of at least two new Ministers of Cabinet rank, not necessarily in the Cabinet, who would be concerned with defense integration through the defense budget and with the international-policy aspect of British defense organization, respectively.[30] Thorneycroft rejected the suggestion, because neither "the presence of eight ministers round" him nor of "other Ministers of Cabinet rank beside" him would do very much to strengthen the authority of the Secretary of State, which was the purpose of the new proposals.[31]

Fourth, some doubts were expressed on the position of the Chief of the Defence Staff under the new organization. Would not his supreme position result in practice in that "finished advice" which was a danger to any Minister served by a sole military adviser? Consequently, would he not wield immense and dangerous power? Conversely, others argued that the selection of the Chief of the Defence Staff was likely to be governed by "the principle of Buggins's turn," with the chairmanship of the Chiefs of Staff simply rotating among the Services.[32] In either case, would it not be far better for ministerial control to have a Chief Staff Officer on the Ismay model, ready to give the full implications of conflicting opinions rather than the personal ones of a supreme chief?

Fifth, some critics recalled that Julian Amery had once called the traditional belief that difficulties might be eased by housing concurrent and conflicting authorities in the same building the "propinquity fallacy."[33] Even the Pentagon had demonstrated that no amount of physical concentration would do anything to lessen interservice rivalry. They thought it ironic that Amery himself should fall victim to this belief. They pointed to the anomalies of his position: here was a minister, outside the Cabinet but of higher rank than the Ministers of State in the Ministry of Defence,

[28] *Ibid.*, cols. 492, 494.   [29] *Ibid.*, col. 564.
[30] *Ibid.*, cols. 499–500.   [31] *Ibid.*, col. 569.
[32] *Ibid.*, col. 554.   [33] *Ibid.*, col. 495.

who had no power to intervene in general defense matters, but was forced to agree to constant intervention by others in matters of his own Ministry.

When Home formed his new Cabinet, two of the three Service ministers moved on to new Cabinet posts. He did not take the opportunity to reduce the rank of their successors immediately to that of Minister of State. As a touch of poignant irony Earl Jellicoe, the son of a well-known figure in the Admiralty Board in the first two decades of this century, was to preside over the dissolution of that august body. Some thought it small compensation that the Queen agreed to assume the title of Lord High Admiral, thus preserving the title of the office which the Board of Admiralty had for centuries exercised in commission.

The Organization for Central Economic Policy in 1963

During 1963, the National Economic Development Council seems to have found a firmer footing in British Government. At the beginning of the year, its position was still far from established. The fact that one of its reports was prematurely leaked to *The Guardian* cannot have endeared it to the powers that be. As long as the economic situation was slack, Neddy's long-term growth target of 4 per cent seemed a political liability for the Government. Cairncross, the Economic Adviser, once testified to the National Incomes Commission that in the Government's view an annual increase in personal incomes of two to two and a half per cent was the maximum tolerable. This statement gave the Opposition the opportunity to ask whether the Government should not have chosen a minister rather than an official to admit publicly its failure to reach the Neddy target.[34]

But an upturn in the economy made it possible for the Government to revise its pessimistic estimates. As confidence returned, the establishment of Neddy itself seemed to be vindicated as an act of progressive statesmanship. Its long-term growth plan became a standard of reference, both parties vying to see which one could best equal or outrun the pace set by Neddy. Its increased popularity allowed Neddy to extend its organizational substructure. More personnel was attracted, and closer liaison with specific industries was attempted.

The Government also began to pay more attention to problems of regional economic development. The disparity in economic development between the south-east and the rest of Britain and continued heavy unemployment in certain pockets of the country was electorally damaging to the Government. In January, Macmillan charged Hailsham with a special responsibility for the north-east region. It was announced that his main task would be to inquire into the local situation, and to see that special measures for generating new economic activity were rapidly implemented by the various Government departments directly responsible. Hailsham was given a

[34] 672 H. of C. Deb. (26 February 1963), col. 1082.

small staff, and for the rest worked mainly through an interdepartmental committee of civil servants.[35] He still had time to carry out his many other public duties, including the negotiation of the Test Ban Treaty in Moscow.

Labour regarded such organizational expedients as inadequate and amateurish. Harold Wilson pledged a future Labour Government to the establishment of a new Ministry for Production and Economic Planning.[36] The proposal was not very clearly defined, and was partly soured in anticipation of the spoils of office by some internecine strife between the Shadow Chancellor of the Exchequer, James Gallaghan, and the Deputy Leader of the Party, George Brown, who would be the new Production Minister. In forming his new Cabinet, Home countered the propaganda element of the Labour proposal by creating the post of Secretary of State for Industry, Trade, and Regional Development. As such, Heath took over Hailsham's duties in connection with the north-east, and accepted special responsibility for all problem areas generally.[37] Home also brought the Minister of Public Building and Works (G. Rippon) and the Minister of Power (F. J. Erroll, who had previously been President of the Board of Trade) into the Cabinet, ostensibly to signal the great importance which the Government attached to the work of the ministries responsible for economic modernization.[38]

Heath was explicitly appointed as a coordinating minister. During a television interview on 24 October, he said that he felt his task was to coordinate the work of the seven departments most directly involved. Apparently, his main instruments are to be a special Cabinet committee together with a small staff and as much assistance as can be obtained from a conscious upgrading of that venerable but somewhat shackled department, the Board of Trade. At the time of this writing, no precise indication of Heath's powers or of his relations with the Treasury and the National Economic Development Council had been given. However, it was made clear that Maudling would retain the supreme coordinating powers in economic policy. As President of the Board of Trade, Heath will automatically be a member of the National Economic Development Council, which presumably will continue to meet under the Chancellor of the Exchequer. Heath's new post must have increased the importance of the industrial side of Neddy's office. But only time will tell whether the traditional role of the Treasury and the new approaches to economic planning and modernization will still be compatible.

---

[35] 672 H. of C. Deb. (25 February 1963), col. 1078.
[36] *The Times,* 1 October 1963.   [37] *The Times,* 21 October 1963.
[38] Cf. *The Observer,* 2 October 1963.

APPENDIX, BIBLIOGRAPHY, AND INDEX

APPENDIX

The following table lists the names and portfolios of ministers in successive administrations between 1914 and 1962. Boldface type indicates that the minister concerned was a Cabinet member, italics that he was raised to the Cabinet during the period he served in a particular office, lightface roman that he was not a Cabinet member as holder of a particular office.

The table does not normally include such ministerial posts as the Chief Secretary for Ireland before 1922 or the Minister of Materials between 1951 and 1954, which were of minor importance during the period under study. Therefore the total of names in boldface and in italics is not necessarily equal to the number of Cabinet members at any given time.

In preparing the table for the Dutch edition of this book, I drew mainly on the data in the bound volumes of Hansard. For this edition I have checked it against the much fuller tables in David Butler and Jennie Freeman, *British Political Facts, 1900–1960* (London, 1963). I am grateful to Dr. Butler for allowing me to see their data in proof.

BRITISH MINISTERS, 1914–1929

Office	Asquith (1914–15) *Liberal*	Asquith (1915–16) *Coalition*	Lloyd George (1916–22) *Coalition*	Bonar Law Baldwin (1922–24) *Conservative*	MacDonald (1924) *Labour*	Baldwin (1924–29) *Conservative*
Prime Minister	H. H. Asquith	H. H. Asquith	D. Lloyd George	A. Bonar Law Stanley Baldwin	J. Ramsay MacDonald	Stanley Baldwin
Lord Chancellor	Lord Haldane	Lord Buckmaster	Lord Finlay *Lord Birkenhead*	Lord Cave	Lord Haldane	Lord Cave Lord Hailsham
Lord President of the Council	Lord Morley Lord Beauchamp	Lord Crewe	Lord Curzon A. J. (= Lord) Balfour	Lord Salisbury	Lord Parmoor	Lord Curzon Lord Balfour
Lord Privy Seal	Lord Crewe	Lord Curzon	Lord Crawford A. Bonar Law Austen Chamberlain	Lord Cecil	J. R. Clynes	Lord Salisbury
Chancellor of the Exchequer	D. Lloyd George	R. McKenna	A. Bonar Law Austen Chamberlain Sir Robert Horne	Stanley Baldwin Neville Chamberlain	Philip Snowden	Winston S. Churchill
Secretary of State for the Home Department	R. McKenna	Sir John Simon Herbert L. Samuel	Sir G. (= Lord) Cave *E. Shortt*	W. C. Bridgeman	Arthur Henderson	Sir W. Joynson-Hicks
Secretary of State for Foreign Affairs	Sir Edward Grey	Sir Edward Grey	A. J. (= Lord) Balfour Lord Curzon	Lord Curzon	J. Ramsay MacDonald	Sir Austen Chamberlain
Secretary of State for the Colonies	L. Harcourt	A. Bonar Law	W. H. Long *Lord Milner* Winston S. Churchill	Duke of Devonshire	J. H. Thomas	L. S. Amery
Secretary of State for the Dominions						L. S. Amery
Secretary of State for India	Lord Crewe	Austen Chamberlain	Austen Chamberlain *E. S. Montagu* Lord Peel	Lord Peel	Lord Olivier	Lord Birkenhead Lord Peel

Secretary of State for Scotland	T. M. Wood	T. M. Wood H. J. Tennant	*R. Munro*	**Lord Novar**	W. Adamson	Sir J. Gilmour
Secretary of State for War	**Lord Kitchener**	**Lord Kitchener** **D. Lloyd George**	Lord Derby Lord Milner *Winston S.* *Churchill* **Sir L. Worthing-** **ton-Evans**	Lord Derby	S. Walsh	Sir L. Worthington- Evans
Secretary of State for Air			(Lord Cowdray) Lord Rothermere Lord Weir *Winston S.* *Churchill* F. E. Guest	*Sir Samuel Hoare*	C. B. (= **Lord**) **Thompson**	Sir Samuel Hoare
First Lord of the Admiralty	Winston S. Churchill	A. J. (= **Lord**) Balfour	Sir Edward Carson Sir Eric Geddes *W. H. Long* **Lord Lee of** **Fareham**	L. S. Amery	**Lord Chelmsford**	W. C. Bridgeman
Minister of Munitions		D. Lloyd George E. S. Montagu	C. (= **Lord**) Addison *Winston S.* *Churchill* Lord Inverforth			
President of the Board of Trade	John Burns W. C. Runciman	W. C. Runciman	Sir Albert Stanley *Sir Auckland* *Geddes* **Sir Robert Horne** **Stanley Baldwin**	Sir P. Lloyd-Greame (= **Lord** Swinton)	**Sidney Webb** (= **Lord** Passfield)	Sir P. Cunliffe-Lister (= **Lord** Swinton)
President of the Board of Agriculture	W. C. Runciman Lord Lucas	**Lord Selborne** **Lord Crawford**	R. Prothero *Lord Lee of* *Fareham* Sir A. G. Boscawen	**Sir R. A. Sanders**	N. Buxton	E. F. L. Wood (= **Lord** Halifax) W. Guinness (= **Lord** Moyne)
President of the Board of Education	J. A. Pease	Arthur Henderson Lord Crewe	*H. A. L. Fisher*	E. F. L. Wood (= **Lord** Halifax)	**Sir Charles** **Trevelyan**	Lord Eustace Percy

343

BRITISH MINISTERS, 1914–1929 (*Continued*)

Office	Asquith (1914–15) *Liberal*	Asquith (1915–16) *Coalition*	Lloyd George (1916–22) *Coalition*	Bonar Law Baldwin (1922–24) *Conservative*	MacDonald (1924) *Labour*	Baldwin (1924–29) *Conservative*
President of the Local Government Board (Minister of Health)	Herbert L. Samuel	W. H. Long	Lord Rhondda W. Hayes-Fisher Sir A. Geddes C. (= Lord) *Addison* Sir A. Mond	Sir A. G. Boscawen Neville Chamberlain Sir W. Joynson-Hicks	J. Wheatley	Neville Chamberlain
Minister of Labour			J. Hodge J. H. Roberts *Sir Robert Horne* T. J. Macnamara	Sir M. Barlow	T. Shaw	Sir A. Steel-Maitland
Minister of Transport			*Sir Eric Geddes* Lord Peel Lord Crawford	Sir J. Baird	H. Gosling	W. Ashley
Minister of Pensions			G. H. Barnes J. Hodge Sir L. Worthington-Evans J. I. MacPherson	G. C. (=Lord) Tryon	F. O. Roberts	G. C. (= Lord) Tryon
First Commissioner of Works	Lord Beauchamp Lord Emmott	L. Harcourt	Sir A. Mond *Lord Crawford*	Sir J. Baird	F. W. Jowett	Lord Peel Lord Londonderry
Postmaster-General	C. E. Hobhouse	Herbert L. Samuel J. A. Pease	A. H. Illingworth F. G. Kellaway	Neville Chamberlain Sir W. Joynson-Hicks Sir L. Worthington-Evans	V. Hartshorn	Sir W. Mitchell-Thompson
Paymaster-General	Lord Strachie	Lord Newton Arthur Henderson	Sir J. Compton Rickett Sir J. Tudor Walters	Sir W. Joynson-Hicks Neville Chamberlain A. B. Boyd-Carpenter	H. Gosling	Duke of Sutherland Lord Onslow

Chancellor of the Duchy of Lancaster	G. F. G. Masterman E. S. Montagu	Winston S. Churchill Herbert L. Samuel E. S. Montagu T. M. Wood	Sir F. Cawley Lord Beaverbrook Lord Downham Lord Crawford Lord Peel Sir W. Sutherland	Lord Salisbury J. C. C. Davidson	J. C. Wedgwood	Lord Cecil Lord Cushendun
Minister without Portfolio		Lord Lansdowne	Lord Milner A. Henderson Sir Edward Carson J. Smuts G. H. Barnes Austen Chamberlain Sir L. Worthington- Evans C. (= Lord) Addison Sir Eric Geddes			

BRITISH MINISTERS, 1929-1945

Office	MacDonald (1929–31) *Labour*	MacDonald (1931–35) *"National"*	Baldwin Chamberlain (1935–39) *"National"*	Chamberlain (1939–40) *"National"*	Churchill (1940–45) *Coalition*	Churchill (1945) *Caretaker Government*
Prime Minister	J. Ramsay MacDonald	J. Ramsay MacDonald	Stanley Baldwin Neville Chamberlain	Neville Chamberlain	Winston S. Churchill	Winston S. Churchill
Lord Chancellor	Lord Sankey	Lord Sankey	Lord Hailsham Lord Maugham	Lord Caldecote	Lord Simon	Lord Simon
Lord President of the Council	Lord Parmoor	Stanley Baldwin	J. Ramsay MacDonald Lord Halifax Lord Hailsham Lord (W. C.) Runciman	Lord Stanhope	Neville Chamberlain Sir John Anderson C. R. Attlee	Lord Woolton
Lord Privy Seal	J. H. Thomas V. Hartshorn T. Johnston	Lord Peel Lord Snowden Stanley Baldwin Anthony Eden	Lord Londonderry Lord Halifax Lord de la Warr Sir John Anderson	Sir Samuel Hoare Sir Kingsley Wood	C. R. Attlee Sir Stafford Cripps Lord Cranborne (=Lord Salisbury) Lord Beaverbrook	Lord Beaverbrook
Chancellor of the Exchequer	Philip Snowden	Philip Snowden Neville Chamberlain	Neville Chamberlain Sir John Simon	Sir John Simon	*Sir Kingsley Wood* Sir John Anderson	Sir John Anderson
Secretary of State for the Home Department	J. R. Clynes	Sir Herbert Samuel Sir J. Gilmour	Sir John Simon Sir Samuel Hoare	Sir John Anderson	Sir John Anderson *Herbert Morrison*	Sir D. B. Somervell
Secretary of State for Foreign Affairs	Arthur Henderson	Lord Reading Sir John Simon	Sir Samuel Hoare Anthony Eden Lord Halifax	Lord Halifax	Lord Halifax Anthony Eden	Anthony Eden
Secretary of State for the Colonies	Lord Passfield	J. H. Thomas Sir P. Cunliffe-Lister (= Lord Swinton)	Malcolm Mac-Donald J. H. Thomas W. Ormsby-Gore Malcolm Mac-Donald	Malcolm Mac-Donald	Lord Lloyd Lord Moyne Lord Cranborne (=Lord Salisbury) Oliver Stanley	Oliver Stanley

Office						
Secretary of State for the Dominions	**Lord Passfield** **J. H. Thomas**	J. H. Thomas	**J. H. Thomas** **Malcolm Mac-Donald** **Lord Stanley** **Malcolm Mac-Donald** **Sir Thomas Inskip** (= Lord Caldecote)	Anthony Eden	Lord Caldecote Lord Cranborne (= Lord Salisbury) **C.R. Atlee** Lord Cranborne (= Lord Salisbury)	**Lord Cranborne** (= Lord Salisbury)
Secretary of State for India	**A. Wedgwood Benn** (= Lord Stansgate)	**Sir Samuel Hoare**	**Lord Zetland**	Lord Zetland	L. S. Amery	**L. S. Amery**
Secretary of State for Scotland	W. Adamson	*Sir A. Sinclair* **Sir G. Collins**	**Sir G. Collins** **Walter Elliot** **D. J. Colville**	D. J. Colville	A. E. Brown T. Johnston	**Lord Rosebery**
Secretary of State for War	T. Shaw	Lord Crewe **Lord Hailsham**	**Lord Halifax** **A. Duff Cooper** **L. Hore-Belisha**	L. Hore-Belisha Oliver Stanley	Anthony Eden D. H. R. Margesson Sir James Grigg	**Sir James Grigg**
Secretary of State for Air	**Lord Thompson** **Lord Amulree**	Lord Amulree Lord London-derry	**Sir P. Cunliffe-Lister** (= Lord Swinton) **Sir Kingsley Wood**	Sir Kingsley Wood Sir Samuel Hoare	Sir A. Sinclair	**Harold Macmillan**
First Lord of the Admiralty	**A. V. Alexander**	Sir Austen Chamberlain **Sir B. M. E. Monsell**	**Sir B. M. E. Monsell** **Sir Samuel Hoare** **A. Duff Cooper** **Lord Stanhope**	Winston S. Churchill	A. V. Alexander	**Brendan Bracken**
Minister (for the Co-ordination) of Defence			**Sir Thomas Inskip** (= Lord Caldecote) **Lord Chatfield**	**Lord Chatfield**	**Winston S. Churchill**	**Winston S. Churchill**
Minister of Supply			**E. L. Burgin**	E. L. Burgin	Herbert Morrison Sir Andrew Duncan **Lord Beaverbrook** Sir Andrew Duncan	Sir Andrew Duncan
Minister of Aircraft Production					*Lord Beaverbrook* J. Moore-Brabazon J. J. Llewellin Sir Stafford Cripps	A. E. Brown

BRITISH MINISTERS, 1929-1945 (*Continued*)

Office	MacDonald (1929-31) *Labour*	MacDonald (1931-35) *"National"*	Baldwin Chamberlain (1935-39) *"National"*	Chamberlain (1939-40) *"National"*	Churchill (1940-45) *Coalition*	Churchill (1945) *Caretaker Government*
President of the Board of Trade	**W. Graham**	**Sir P. Cunliffe-Lister** (= Lord Swinton) W. C. Runciman	**W. C. Runciman** **Oliver Stanley**	Oliver Stanley Sir Andrew Duncan	Sir Andrew Duncan Oliver Lyttelton Sir Andrew Duncan J. J. Llewellin Hugh Dalton	**Oliver Lyttelton**
Minister of Agriculture and Fisheries	**N. Buxton** **C. Addison** (= Lord Addison)	*Sir J. Gilmour* **Walter Elliot**	**Walter Elliot** **W. S. Morrison** **Sir R. Dorman-Smith**	Sir R. Dorman-Smith	R. S. Hudson	**R. S. Hudson**
Minister of Food				Lord Woolton	Lord Woolton J. J. Llewellin	J. J. Llewellin
President of the Board (Minister) of Education	**Sir Charles Trevelyan** **B. H. Lees-Smith**	*Sir D. Maclean* Lord Irwin (= Lord Halifax)	**Oliver Stanley** Lord Stanhope **Lord de la Warr**	Lord de la Warr H. Ramsbotham	H. Ramsbotham R. A. Butler	R. K. Law
Minister of Health	**Arthur Greenwood**	Neville Chamberlain Sir E. Hilton-Young	**Sir Kingsley Wood** **Walter Elliot**	Walter Elliot	Malcolm MacDonald A. E. Brown H. U. Willink	H. U. Willink
Minister of Town and Country Planning					W. S. Morrison	W. S. Morrison
Minister of Labour (and National Service)	**Margaret Bond-field**	*Sir H. Betterton* Oliver Stanley	**A. E. Brown**	A. E. Brown	*Ernest Bevin*	**R. A. Butler**
Minister of (War) Transport	*Herbert Morrison*	P. J. Pybus Oliver Stanley L. Hore-Belisha	**L. Hore-Belisha** **E. L. Burgin** **D. E. Wallace**	D. E. Wallace	Sir John (=Lord) Reith J. Moore-Brabazon Lord Leathers	Lord Leathers
Minister of Fuel and Power					G. Lloyd George	G. Lloyd George

Office						
Minister of Pensions	F. O. Roberts	G. C. (= Lord) Tryon	R. S. Hudson, H. Ramsbotham, Sir W. Womersley	Sir W. Womersley	Sir W. Womersley	Sir W. Womersley
Minister of National Insurance					Sir William (= Lord) Jowitt	L. Hore-Belisha
First Commissioner (Minister) of Works (and Building)	**G. Lansbury**	Lord Londonderry, **W. G. A. Ormsby-Gore**	**W. G. A. Ormsby-Gore**, **Lord Stanhope**, Sir Philip Sassoon, H. Ramsbotham	H. Ramsbotham, Lord de la Warr	Lord Tryon, Lord Reith, Lord Portal, Duncan Sandys	Duncan Sandys
Postmaster-General	H. B. Lees-Smith, C. R. Attlee	W. G. A. Ormsby-Gore, *Sir Kingsley Wood*	G. C. (= Lord) Tryon	G. C. (= Lord) Tryon, W. S. Morrison	W. S. Morrison, H. F. C. Crookshank	H. F. C. Crookshank
Paymaster-General	Lord Arnold	Sir J. Tudor-Walters, Lord Rochester	Lord Rochester, Lord Hutchison, Lord Munster, Lord Winterton	Lord Winterton	Lord Cranborne (= Lord Salisbury), Lord Hankey, Sir William (= Lord) Jowitt, Lord Cherwell	Lord Cherwell
Chancellor of the Duchy of Lancaster	Sir Oswald Mosley, C. R. Attlee, Lord Ponsonby	Lord Lothian, J. C. C. Davidson	J. C. C. Davidson, *Lord Winterton*, **W. S. Morrison**	W. S. Morrison, Lord Tryon	Lord Hankey, A. Duff Cooper, A. E. Brown	Sir Arthur Salter
Minister without Portfolio			**Anthony Eden**, **Lord Eustace Percy**	**Lord Hankey**	**Arthur Greenwood**, **Lord Beaverbrook**, **Sir William** (= Lord) Jowitt	

BRITISH MINISTERS, 1945-1963

Office	Attlee (1945–51) Labour	Churchill (1951–55) Conservative	Eden (1955–57) Conservative	Macmillan/Home (1957–63) Conservative
Prime Minister	C. R. Attlee	Winston S. Churchill	Sir Anthony Eden	Harold Macmillan Sir A. Douglas-Home (= Lord Home)
First Secretary of State				R. A. Butler
Lord Chancellor	Lord Jowitt	Lord Simonds Lord Kilmuir	Lord Kilmuir	Lord Kilmuir Lord Dilhorne
Lord President of the Council	Herbert Morrison Lord Addison	Lord Woolton Lord Salisbury	Lord Salisbury	Lord Salisbury Lord Home Lord Hailsham Lord Home Lord Hailsham (= Quintin Hogg)
Lord Privy Seal	Arthur Greenwood Lord Inman Lord Addison R. R. Stokes	Lord Salisbury H. F. C. Crookshank	H. F. C. Crookshank R. A. Butler	R. A. Butler Lord Hailsham E. Heath Selwyn Lloyd
Chancellor of the Exchequer	Hugh Dalton Sir Stafford Cripps Hugh Gaitskell	R. A. Butler	R. A. Butler Harold Macmillan	P. Thorneycroft D. Heathcoat Amory Selwyn Lloyd R. Maudling
Secretary of State for the Home Department	J. Chuter Ede	Sir D. Maxwell Fyfe (= Lord Kilmuir) G. Lloyd George	G. Lloyd George	R. A. Butler H. Brooke
Secretary of State for Foreign Affairs	Ernest Bevin Herbert Morrison	Anthony Eden	Harold Macmillan Selwyn Lloyd	Selwyn Lloyd Lord Home R. A. Butler
Secretary of State for the Colonies	G. H. (= Lord) Hall A. Creech-Jones J. Griffith	O. Lyttelton A. T. Lennox-Boyd	A. T. Lennox-Boyd	A. T. Lennox-Boyd I. N. Macleod R. Maudling D. Sandys

Secretary of State for the Dominions (Commonwealth Relations)	**Lord Addison** P. J. Noel-Baker P. Gordon Walker	**Lord Ismay** **Lord Salisbury** **Lord Swinton**	Lord Home	**Lord Home** **D. Sandys**
Secretary of State for India	**Lord Pethick-Lawrence** **Lord Listowel**			
Secretary of State for Scotland	**J. Westwood** A. Woodburn H. McNeil	**J. Stuart**	J. Stuart	**J. Maclay** M. Noble
Secretary of State for War	**J. J. Lawson** F. J. Bellenger E. Shinwell J. Strachey	A. H. Head	A. H. Head J. Hare	J. Hare C. Soames J. Profumo J. B. Godber J. E. Ramsden
Secretary of State for Air	**Lord Stansgate** P. J. Noel-Baker A. Henderson	Lord de l'Isle and Dudley	Lord de l'Isle and Dudley N. Birch	G. Ward J. Amery H. Fraser
First Lord of the Admiralty	**A. V. Alexander** **Lord Hall** **Lord Pakenham**	J. P. L. Thomas (=Lord Cilcennin)	Lord Cilcennin Lord Hailsham	Lord Selkirk Lord Carrington Lord Jellicoe
Minister of Defence	**C. R. Attlee** **A. V. Alexander** **E. Shinwell**	Winston S. Churchill Lord Alexander of Tunis Harold Macmillan	Selwyn Lloyd Sir Walter Monckton A. H. Head	**D. Sandys** H. Watkinson P. Thorneycroft
Minister of Supply (Aviation)	J. Wilmot G. R. Strauss	D. Sandys Selwyn Lloyd	R. Maudling	A. Jones D. Sandys P. Thorneycroft J. Amery
President of the Board of Trade (and Secretary of State for Industry, Trade, and Regional Development)	**Sir Stafford Cripps** J. H. Wilson **Sir Hartley Shawcross**	P. Thorneycroft	P. Thorneycroft	**Sir David Eccles** R. Maudling F. J. Erroll E. Heath
Minister of Agriculture and Fisheries (and Food)	**T. Williams**	*Sir Thomas Dugdale* D. Heathcoat Amory	D. Heathcoat Amory	**D. Heathcoat Amory** J. Hare C. Soames
Minister of Food	Sir Ben Smith J. Strachey M. Webb	*G. Lloyd George* D. Heathcoat Amory		

351

BRITISH MINISTERS, 1945–1963 (Continued)

Office	Attlee (1945–51) Labour	Churchill (1951–55) Conservative	Eden (1955–57) Conservative	Macmillan/Home (1957–63) Conservative
Minister of Education	Ellen Wilkinson G. Tomlinson	*Florence Horsburgh* Sir David Eccles	Sir David Eccles	Lord Hailsham G. Lloyd Sir David Eccles Sir E. Boyle
Minister of Health	H. A. Marquand Aneurin Bevan	H. F. C. Crookshank I. N. Macleod	I. N. Macleod R. H. Turton	D. Vosper D. Walker-Smith *E. Powell* A. Barber
Minister of Town and Country Planning (Housing and Local Government)	Lewis Silkin Hugh Dalton	Harold Macmillan D. Sandys	D. Sandys	H. Brooke Charles Hill Sir K. Joseph
Minister of Labour (and National Service)	G. A. Isaacs Aneurin Bevan A. Robens	Sir Walter Monckton	Sir Walter Monckton I. N. Macleod	I. N. Macleod E. Heath J. Hare J. B. Godber
Minister of Transport	A. Barnes	J. S. Maclay A. T. Lennox-Boyd J. A. Boyd-Carpenter	J. A. Boyd-Carpenter *H. Watkinson*	H. Watkinson E. Marples
Minister of (Fuel and) Power	E. Shinwell Hugh Gaitskell P. Noel-Baker	G. Lloyd	G. Lloyd A. Jones	Sir Percy (= Lord) Mills R. Wood F. J. Erroll
Minister of Pensions (and National Insurance)	W. Paling J. B. Hynd G. Buchanan G. A. Isaacs	D. Heathcoat Amory *O. Peake*	O. Peake J. A. Boyd-Carpenter	J. A. Boyd-Carpenter N. Macpherson R. Wood
Minister of National Insurance	J. Griffiths Edith Summerskill	O. Peake		

352

Minister of (Public Buildings and) Works	G. Tomlinson C. W. Key R. R. Stokes G. Brown	Sir David Eccles N. Birch	H. Molson J. Hope *G. Rippon*
Postmaster-General	Lord Listowel W. Paling Ness Edwards	Lord de la Warr Charles Hill	E. Marples R. Bevins
Paymaster-General (and Chief Secretary to the Treasury)	**Arthur Greenwood** H. A. Marquand **Lord Addison** **Lord MacDonald**	**Lord Cherwell** Lord Selkirk	*R. Maudling* **Lord Mills** **H. Brooke** **J. A. Boyd-Carpenter**
Chancellor of the Duchy of Lancaster	J. B. Hynd Lord Pakenham **Hugh Dalton** **Lord (A. V.) Alexander**	Lord Swinton **Lord Woolton**	Charles Hill I. N. Macleod J. Hare
Minister without Portfolio	**A. V. Alexander** A. Greenwood	Lord Munster	Lord Munster Lord Mancroft Lord Dundee **Lord Mills** **W. F. Deedes** **Lord Carrington**

BIBLIOGRAPHY

This Bibliography contains full publication data for books and articles cited in short form. Publication data for references cited only once are given in full in the footnotes.

Addison, Life of
    R. J. Minney. Viscount Addison: Leader of the Lords. London, 1958.
Addison, *Politics from Within*
    C. Addison. Politics from Within, 1911–1918, Including Some Records of a Great National Effort. London, 1924. 2 vols.
Alanbrooke
    A. Bryant. The Turn of the Tide, 1939–1943: A Study Based on the Diaries and Autobiographical Notes of Field-Marshal the Viscount Alanbrooke. London, 1957.
Amery, *Constitution*
    L. S. Amery. Thoughts on the Constitution. 2d ed. London, 1953.
Amery, *Forward View*
    L. S. Amery. The Forward View. London, 1935.
Amery, *My Political Life*
    L. S. Amery. My Political Life. London, 1953–1955. 3 vols.
Amery, *War Leaders*
    L. S. Amery. "Two Great War Leaders," in Winston Spencer Churchill, Servant of Crown and Commonwealth: A Tribute by Various Hands Presented to Him on His Eightieth Birthday. Edited by J. Marchant. London, 1954.
Anderson, *Administrative Technique*
    J. Anderson. Administrative Technique in the Public Services (Haldane Memorial Lecture). London, 1949.
Anderson, *Economic Studies*
    J. Anderson. The Organization of Economic Studies in Relation to the Problems of Government (Stamp Memorial Lecture). London, 1947.
Anderson, Life of
    John Wheeler-Bennett. John Anderson, Viscount Waverley. London, 1962.
Anderson, *Machinery*
    J. Anderson. The Machinery of Government (Romanes Lecture). London, 1946.
Anson
    W. R. Anson. The Law and Custom of the Constitution. Vol. I edited by M. L. Gwyer. London, 1922. Vol. II edited by A. Berriedale Keith, London, 1935.

Aspinall
A. Aspinall. "The Cabinet Council, 1783–1835; The Raleigh Lecture on History," *Proceedings of the British Academy*. London, 1952.

Asquith, Life of
J. A. Spender and C. Asquith. The Life of Herbert Henry Asquith, Lord Oxford and Asquith. 2 vols. London, 1932.

Asquith, *Memories*
The Earl of Oxford and Asquith. Memories and Reflections. London, 1928. 2 vols.

Attlee, *As It Happened*
C. R. Attlee. As It Happened. London, 1954.

Attlee, *Civil Servants and Ministers*
C. R. Attlee. "Civil Servants, Ministers, Parliament, and the Public," in W. A. Robson, ed., The Civil Service in Britain and France. London, 1956.

Attlee, *Labour Party*
C. R. Attlee. The Labour Party in Perspective. London, 1937.

Bagehot
W. Bagehot. The English Constitution. 2d ed. London, 1872. World's Classics ed. London, 1952.

Baldwin, Life of
G. M. Young. Stanley Baldwin. London, 1952.

Balfour, Life of
E. C. Blanche Dugdale. Arthur James Balfour, First Earl of Balfour. 2 vols. London, 1939.

Bassett
R. Bassett. Nineteen Thirty-One: Political Crisis. London, 1958.

Beaverbrook, 1914–16
Lord Beaverbrook. Politicians and the War, 1914–1916. London, 1928. 2 vols.

Beaverbrook, 1917–18
Lord Beaverbrook. Men and Power, 1917–1918. London, 1956.

Beer
S. H. Beer. Treasury Control: The Co-ordination of Financial and Economic Policy in Great Britain. 2d rev. ed. Oxford, 1957.

Beloff
M. Beloff. New Dimensions in Foreign Policy: A Study in British Administrative Experience, 1947–1959. London, 1961.

Beveridge, *Power and Influence*
Lord Beveridge. Power and Influence: An Autobiography. London, 1953.

Bevin, Life of
Alan Bullock. The Life and Times of Ernest Bevin. London, 1960. Vol. I.

Birkenhead, Life of
F. E. Smith, Earl of Birkenhead: The Last Phase. By his son, the Earl of Birkenhead. London, 1935.

Birkenhead (1960), *Life of*
The Life of F. E. Smith, First Earl of Birkenhead. By his son, the Second Earl of Birkenhead. London, 1960.

Bonar Law, Life of
R. Blake. The Unknown Prime Minister: The Life and Times of Andrew Bonar Law, 1858–1923. London, 1955.

Brabazon
Lord Brabazon of Tara. The Brabazon Story. London, 1956.

Braithwaite
Lloyd George's Ambulance Wagon, Being the Memoirs of W. J. Braithwaite. Edited by H. N. Bunbury. London, 1957.

Bridges, *Haldane*
Lord Bridges. "Haldane and the Machinery of Government," *Public Administration*, XXXV (1957), 254–65.

Bridges, *Portrait*
E. Bridges. Portrait of a Profession: The Civil Service Tradition (Rede Lecture). London, 1950.

Bridges, *Treasury Control*
E. Bridges. Treasury Control (Stamp Memorial Lecture). 2d ed. London, 1956.

Broad, *Winston Churchill*
L. Broad. Winston Churchill, 1874–1945. Revised and extended edition, London, 1946.

Bromhead
P. A. Bromhead. The House of Lords and Contemporary Politics. London, 1958.

Brundrett
F. Brundrett. "Government and Science," *Public Administration*, XXXIV (1956), 245–56.

Buck
Philip W. Buck. "M.P.'s in Ministerial Office, 1918–55 and 1955–59," *Political Studies*, IX (1961), 300–306.

Campion, *Parliamentary System*
G. Campion. "Developments in the Parliamentary System since 1918," in G. Campion *et al.*, British Government since 1918. London, 1950.

Carson, Life of
H. Montgomery Hyde. Carson: The Life of Sir Edward Carson. London, 1953.

Carter
B. E. Carter. The Office of Prime Minister. London, 1956.

Cecil
Viscount Cecil of Chelwood. The Machinery of Government (Sidney Ball Lecture). Barnett House Papers, No. 16. Oxford, 1932.

Chamberlain, *Down the Years*
A. Chamberlain. Down the Years. London, 1935.

Chamberlain, Life of Austen
C. Petrie. The Life and Letters of the Rt. Hon. Sir Austen Chamberlain. 2 vols. London, 1940.

Chamberlain, Life of Neville
K. Feiling. The Life of Neville Chamberlain. London, 1946.

Chester, *Cabinet*
D. N. Chester. "Development of the Cabinet, 1914–1948," in G. Campion *et al.*, British Government since 1918. London, 1950.

Chester, *International Social Science Bulletin*
D. N. Chester. "Introduction to the Formation of Economic and Financial Policy," *International Social Science Bulletin*, VIII (1956), 217–28.

Chester, *Machinery*
D. N. Chester. "The Central Machinery for Economic Policy," in D. N. Chester, ed., Lessons of the British War Economy. Cambridge, Eng., 1951.

Chester, *Ministerial Responsibility*
D. N. Chester. The Future of Ministerial Responsibility. Paper Presented to the Annual Conference of the United Kingdom Political Studies Association, 1956.

Chester, *Planning*
D. N. Chester. "The Machinery of Government and Planning," in G. D. N Worswick and P. H. Ady, The British Economy. London, 1952.

Chester, *Treasury*
D. N. Chester. "The Treasury, 1956," *Public Administration*, XXXV (1957), 15–23.

Chester, *Trends*
D. N. Chester. "Recent Trends in British Central Government," *Administration* (Dublin), IV (1956), 13–33.

Chester–Bowring
D. N. Chester and Nona Bowring. Questions in Parliament. Oxford, 1962.

Chester–Willson
The Organization of British Central Government, 1914–1956: A Survey of a Study Group of the Royal Institute of Public Administration. Edited by D. N. Chester. Written by F. M. G. Willson. London, 1957.

Churchill
W. S. Churchill. The Second World War. London, 1948–54. 6 vols.

Churchill, *Great Contemporaries*
W. S. Churchill. Great Contemporaries. Rev. ed. London, 1938.

Churchill, *Thoughts and Adventures*
W. S. Churchill. Thoughts and Adventures. London, 1932.

Churchill, *World Crisis*
W. S. Churchill. The World Crisis. London, 1923–29. 5 vols.

R. Churchill, *Eden*
Randolph S. Churchill. The Rise and Fall of Sir Anthony Eden. London, 1959.

Cooper, *Old Men Forget*
Viscount Norwich (Duff Cooper). Old Men Forget. London, 1953.

Crewe, Life of
J. Pope-Hennessy. Lord Crewe, 1838–1945. London, 1955.

Cripps, Life of
C. Cooke. The Life of Richard Stafford Cripps. London, 1957.

Curzon, Life of
Earl of Ronaldshay. The Life of Lord Curzon. 3 vols. London, 1928.

Dalton, *Memoirs,* I
H. Dalton. Call Back Yesterday: Memoirs 1887–1931. London, 1953.

Dalton, *Memoirs,* II
H. Dalton. The Fateful Years: Memoirs 1931–1945. London, 1957.

Dalton, *Memoirs,* III
H. Dalton. High Tide and After: Memoirs 1945–1960. London, 1962.

Dawson, Life of
J. E. Wrench. Geoffrey Dawson and Our Times. London, 1955.

Derby, Life of
Randolph S. Churchill. Lord Derby, "King of Lancashire": The Official Life of Edward, Seventeenth Earl of Derby, 1865–1948. London, 1960.

Dogan–Campbell
M. Dogan and P. Campbell. "Le Personnel Ministériel en France et en Grande Bretagne (1945–1957)," *Revue Française de Science Politique,* VII (1957), 313–45, 793–824.

Eden, *Facing the Dictators*
Lord Avon. The Eden Memoirs: Facing the Dictators. London, 1962.

Eden, *Full Circle*
Lord Avon. The Eden Memoirs: Full Circle. London, 1960.

Ehrman, *Cabinet*
J. Ehrman. Cabinet Government and War, 1890–1940. Cambridge, Eng., 1958.

Ehrman, *Strategy*
J. Ehrman. History of the Second World War. Vol. VI: Grand Strategy. London, 1956.

Encyclopaedia of Parliament
N. Wilding and P. Laundy. An Encyclopaedia of Parliament. London, 1958.

Esher, *C.I.D.*
Lord Esher. The Committee of Imperial Defence: Its Functions and Potentialities (Lecture to United Services Institution). London, 1912.

Esher Papers
Journals and Letters of Reginald Viscount Esher. London, 1934–38. 4 vols.

Evans, *Bevin*
T. Evans. Bevin. London, 1946.

Falls
C. Falls. "Haldane and Defence," *Public Administration,* XXXV (1957), 245–53.

Finer
H. Finer. Theory and Practice of Modern Government. Rev. ed. New York, 1949.

Fisher, *Memories*
Lord Fisher. Memories. London, 1919.

Fisher, *Records*
Lord Fisher. Records. London, 1919.

Fisher Correspondence
A. J. Marder. Fear God and Dread Nought: The Correspondence of Admiral of the Fleet Lord Fisher of Kilverstone. London, 1952, 1956. 2 vols.

Franks
O. Franks. Central Planning and Control in War and Peace. London, 1947.

George V, Life of King
H. Nicolson. King George the Fifth: His Life and Reign. London, 1952.

George VI, Life of King
J. W. Wheeler-Bennett. King George VI: His Life and Reign. London, 1958.

Gibbs
N. H. Gibbs. The Origins of Imperial Defence: An Inaugural Lecture. Oxford, 1955.

Gordon Walker
P. Gordon Walker. "On Being a Cabinet Minister," *Encounter,* 3 (April 1956), 17–24.

Greaves, *Civil Service*
H. R. G. Greaves. The Civil Service in the Changing State: A Survey of Civil Service Reform and the Implications of a Planned Economy on Public Administration in England. London, 1947.

Greaves, *Structure*
H. R. G. Greaves. "The Structure of the Civil Service," in W. A. Robson, ed., The Civil Service in Britain and France. London, 1956.

Grey, *Twenty-Five Years*
Lord Grey of Fallodon. Twenty-Five Years, 1892–1916. London, 1925. 2 vols.

Grigg, *Prejudice and Judgment*
P. J. Grigg. Prejudice and Judgment. London, 1948.

Guttsman, 1952
W. L. Guttsman. "The Changing Social Structure of the British Political Elite, 1886–1935," *The British Journal of Sociology,* II (1952), 122–34.

Guttsman, 1954
W. L. Guttsman. "Aristocracy and the Middle Class in the British Political Elite, 1886–1935: A Study of Formative Influences and of the Attitudes to Politics," *The British Journal of Sociology,* V (1954), 12–32.

Haig, Life of
A. Duff Cooper. Haig. London, 1935–1936. 2 vols.

Haldane, *Autobiography*
R. B. Haldane. An Autobiography. London, 1929.

Haldane, Life of
F. Maurice. The Life of Viscount Haldane of Cloan. London, 1937–1939. 2 vols.

Halifax, *Fullness of Days*
The Earl of Halifax. Fullness of Days. London, 1957.

Hall
R. Hall. "The Place of the Economist in Government" (Sidney Ball Lecture), Oxford Economic Papers (June 1955).

Halpérin
V. Halpérin. Lord Milner and the Empire: The Evolution of British Imperialism. Foreword by L. S. Amery. London, 1952.

Hancock–Gowing
W. K. Hancock and M. M. Gowing. History of the Second World War: British War Economy. London, 1949.

Hankey, *Control*
Lord Hankey. Government Control in War. Cambridge, Eng., 1945.

Hankey, *Diplomacy*
Lord Hankey. Diplomacy by Conference: Studies in Public Affairs, 1920–1946. London, 1946.

Hankey, *Science and Art*
Lord Hankey. The Science and Art of Government (Romanes Lecture). Oxford, 1951.

Hankey, *Supreme Command*
Lord Hankey. The Supreme Command, 1914–1918. London, 1961. 2 vols.

Harrison
W. Harrison. The Government of Britain. 2d rev. ed. London, 1952.

Harrod, *The Prof*
R. F. Harrod. The Prof: A Personal Memoir of Lord Cherwell. London, 1959.

Heasman
D. J. Heasman. "The Ministerial Hierarchy" and "The Prime Minister and the Cabinet," *Parliamentary Affairs*, XV (1962), 307–30, 461–84.

Hewison
R. J. P. Hewison. "The Organization of the Cabinet Secretariat," *O & M Bulletin* (The Treasury), VI, No. 6 (1951), 36–41.

Hollis
C. Hollis. Can Parliament Survive? London, 1949.

Hollis, *One Marine's Tale*
L. Hollis, One Marine's Tale. London, n.d.

Holmes-Laski Correspondence
The Correspondence of Mr. Justice Holmes and Harold J. Laski, 1916–1935. Edited by M. de Wolfe Howe. Cambridge, Mass., 1953.

Hore-Belisha Papers
R. J. Minney. The Private Papers of Hore-Belisha. London, 1960.

Howard
M. Howard. "Central Defence Organization in Great Britain, 1959," *Political Quarterly*, XXXI (1960), 66–70.

Hume
L. J. Hume. "The Origin of the Haldane Report," *Public Administration* (Australia), XVII (1958), 344–52.

Ironside
The Ironside Diaries, 1937–1940. Edited by Col. R. Macleod and D. Kelly. London, 1962.

Ismay
    Lord Ismay. The Memoirs of General Lord Ismay. New York, 1960.
Jennings, *Cabinet Government*
    I. Jennings. Cabinet Government. 3d ed. Cambridge, Eng., 1959.
Jennings, *Constitution*
    I. Jennings. The British Constitution. 3d ed. Cambridge, Eng., 1950.
Jennings, *Queen's Government*
    I. Jennings. The Queen's Government. London, 1954.
Johnson
    F. A. Johnson. Defence by Committee: The British Committee of Imperial Defence, 1885–1959. London, 1960.
Jones, *Diary*
    T. Jones. A Diary with Letters, 1931–1950. London, 1954.
Jones, *Lloyd George*
    T. Jones. Lloyd George. London, 1951.
Jones, *Prime Ministers and Cabinets*
    T. Jones. "Prime Ministers and Cabinets," *The Listener*, 13 October 1938.
Keir
    D. Lindsay Keir. The Constitutional History of Modern Britain, 1485–1951. 5th rev. ed. London, 1955.
Keith–Gibbs
    A. Berriedale Keith. The British Cabinet System. 2d ed. London, 1952. Edited by N. H. Gibbs.
Kennedy, *Business of War*
    The Business of War: The War Narrative of Maj. Gen. Sir J. Kennedy. Edited with a Preface by B. Fergusson. London, 1957.
Keynes, *Essays in Biography*
    J. M. Keynes. Essays in Biography. London, 1933.
Keynes, Life of
    R. F. Harrod. Life of John Maynard Keynes. London, 1955.
Kingsley
    J. Donald Kingsley. Representative Bureaucracy. Yellow Springs, Ohio, 1944.
Kitchener, Life of
    Philip Magnus. Kitchener: Portrait of an Imperialist. London, 1958.
Lansbury
    G. Lansbury. My England. London, 1934.
Lansbury, Life of
    R. Postgate. The Life of George Lansbury. London, 1951.
Lansdowne, Life of
    Lord Newton. Lord Lansdowne: A Biography. London, 1929.
Laski, *Cabinet Personnel*
    H. J. Laski. The British Cabinet: A Study of Its Personnel, 1801–1924. London, 1928.
Laski, *Government in Wartime*
    H. J. Laski. Government in Wartime. London, 1940.

Laski, Life of
    K. Martin. Harold Laski, 1893–1950: A Biographical Memoir. London, 1953.

Laski, *Parliamentary Government*
    H. J. Laski. Parliamentary Government in England: A Commentary. London, 1938.

Laski, *Reflections*
    H. J. Laski. Reflections on the Constitution: The House of Commons, the Cabinet, the Civil Service. Manchester, 1951.

Life of Addison
    See under *Addison, Life of.* Other biographical references are listed correspondingly.

Little
    I. M. D. Little. "The Economist in Whitehall." *Lloyds Bank Review* (new series), 44 (April 1957), 29–40.

Llewellyn Smith
    H. Llewellyn Smith. The Board of Trade. London, 1928.

Lloyd George, Life of
    F. Owen. Tempestuous Journey: Lloyd George, His Life and Times. London, 1954.

Lloyd George, *Memoirs*
    D. Lloyd George. War Memoirs. London, 1933–36. 6 vols.

Low
    S. Low. The Governance of England. 2d ed. London, 1914.

Lyman
    R. W. Lyman. The First Labour Government, 1924. London, 1957.

McCloughry
    E. J. Kingston McCloughry. The Direction of War: A Critique of the Political Direction and High Command in War. London, 1955.

MacDougall
    G. A. D. MacDougall. "The Prime Minister's Statistical Section," in D. N. Chester, ed., Lessons of the British War Economy. Cambridge, Eng., 1951.

McKenzie
    R. T. McKenzie. British Political Parties: The Distribution of Power within the Conservative and Labour Parties. London, 1955.

Mackenzie, *Administration*
    W. J. M. Mackenzie. "The Structure of Central Administration," in G. Campion *et al.*, British Government since 1918. London, 1950.

Mackenzie–Grove
    W. J. M. Mackenzie and J. W. Grove. Central Administration in Britain. London, 1957.

Mackintosh
    J. P. Mackintosh. The British Cabinet. London, 1962.

Markham, *Friendship's Harvest*
    V. R. Markham. Friendship's Harvest. London, 1956.

Markham, *Return Passage*
    Return Passage: The Autobiography of V. R. Markham. London, 1953.

Marris
R. L. Marris. "The Position of Economics and Economists in the Government Machine: A Comparative Critique of the United Kingdom and the Netherlands," *The Economic Journal*, LXIV (1954), 759–83.

Matthews
D. R. Matthews. The Social Background of Political Decision-Makers. New York, 1954.

Maurice
F. Maurice. Governments and War: A System for the Conduct of War. London, 1926.

Milne
R. S. Milne. "Britain's Economic Planning Machinery," *American Political Science Review*, LXVI (1952), 406–21.

Milner, Life of
J. E. Wrench. Alfred Lord Milner: The Man of No Illusions, 1854–1925. London, 1958.

Montgomery, *Memoirs*
The Memoirs of Field-Marshal the Viscount Montgomery of Alamein. London, 1958.

Morrison
H. Morrison. Government and Parliament: A Survey from the Inside. London, 1954.

Morrison, *Autobiography*
H. Morrison. An Autobiography by Lord Morrison of Lambeth. London, 1960.

Mosley Program
A National Policy: An Account of the Emergency Program of Sir Oswald Mosley. London, 1931.

Newsam
F. Newsam. The Home Office. London, 1954.

Parliamentary Reform
The Hansard Society for Parliamentary Government. Parliamentary Reform, 1933–1958: A Survey of Suggested Reforms. London, 1959.

Petrie
Sir Charles Petrie. The Powers behind the Prime Ministers. London, 1958.

Reading, Life of
Marquess of Reading. Rufus Isaacs, First Marquess of Reading. London, 1945. 2 vols.

Reconstruction Papers
A Collection of Memoranda, Minutes, and Other Documents Relating to the Discussions of the (Haldane) Machinery of Government Committee, 1917–18. Assembled by Mrs. Beatrice Webb and now in the British Library of Political and Economic Science, London. 4 vols.

Richards
P. G. Richards. Honourable Members: A Study of the British Backbencher. London, 1959.

Roberts, Life of
D. James. Lord Roberts. Foreword by L. S. Amery. London, 1954.

Robertson, *From Private to Field-Marshal*
W. Robertson, Bart. From Private to Field-Marshal. London, 1921.

Robinson
E. A. G. Robinson. "The Over-all Allocation of Resources," in D. N. Chester, ed., Lessons of the British War Economy. Cambridge, Eng., 1951.

Robson
W. A. Robson. "The Machinery of Government, 1939–1947," *Political Quarterly*, XIX (1948), 1–14.

Ross, *Electors and Elections*
J. F. S. Ross. Electors and Elections: Studies in Democratic Representation. London, 1955.

Ross, *Parliamentary Representation*
J. F. S. Ross. Parliamentary Representation. 2d enlarged edition. London, 1948.

Salter, *Cabinet*
A. Salter. "Cabinet and Parliament," in G. Campion *et al.,* Parliament: A Survey. London, 1952.

Salter, *Memoirs*
Lord Salter. Memoirs of a Public Servant. London, 1961.

Salter, *Personality in Politics*
A. Salter. Personality in Politics: Studies of Contemporary Statesmen. London, 1947.

Samuel, Life of
J. Bowle. Viscount Samuel: A Biography. London, 1957.

Samuel, *Memoirs*
Viscount Samuel. Memoirs. London, 1945.

Schaffer
B. B. Schaffer. "Theory and Practice in the Machinery of Government," *Public Administration* (Australia), XVII, No. 4 (1958), 353–68.

Scott–Hughes
J. D. Scott and R. Hughes. History of the Second World War: Administration of War Production. London, 1955.

Sherwood
R. Sherwood. Roosevelt and Hopkins. Bantam Books ed., New York, 1950. 2 vols.

Shinwell, *Conflict without Malice*
E. Shinwell. Conflict without Malice. London, 1955.

Simon, *Retrospect*
Retrospect: The Memoirs of the Rt. Hon. Viscount Simon. London, 1952.

Smellie
K. B. Smellie. A Hundred Years of English Government. Revised ed. London, 1950.

Snow
 C. P. Snow. Science and Government. Cambridge, Mass., 1961.
Snowden, *Autobiography*
 P. Snowden. An Autobiography. London, 1934. 2 vols.
Sommer, *Haldane*
 D. Sommer. Haldane of Cloan: His Life and Times, 1856–1928. London, 1960.
Stone
 R. Stone. "The Use and Development of National Income and Expenditure Estimates," in D. N. Chester, ed., Lessons of the British War Economy. Cambridge, Eng., 1951.
Strachey–Joad
 J. Strachey and C. F. M. Joad. "Parliamentary Reforms: The New Party's Proposals," *Political Quarterly*, II (1932), 319–36.
Strang, *Foreign Office*
 Lord Strang. The Foreign Office. London, 1957.
Strang, *Home and Abroad*
 Lord Strang. Home and Abroad. London, 1956.
Street
 A. Street. "Quasi-Government Bodies since 1918," in G. Campion *et al.*, British Government since 1918. London, 1950.
Sylvester, *Lloyd George*
 A. J. Sylvester. The Real Lloyd George. London, 1947.
Templewood, *Empire of the Air*
 Viscount Templewood (Sir Samuel Hoare). Empire of the Air. The Advent of the Air Age, 1922–1929. London, 1957.
Templewood, *Nine Troubled Years*
 Viscount Templewood (Sir Samuel Hoare). Nine Troubled Years. London, 1954.
Thomas, *My Story*
 J. H. Thomas. My Story. London, 1937.
Tivey–Rendel
 P.E.P. Advisory Committees in British Government, 1960. A Report Drafted by L. Tivey and M. Rendel. London, 1960.
Tizard
 H. Tizard. A Scientist in and out of the Civil Service (Haldane Memorial Lecture). London, 1955.
Trend
 B. S. Trend, "The Formation of Economic and Financial Policy, Great Britain," *International Social Science Bulletin*, VIII (1956), 239–52.
Vansittart, *The Mist Procession*
 The Mist Procession. The Autobiography of Lord Vansittart. London, 1958.
Vernon–Mansergh
 R. V. Vernon and N. Mansergh. Advisory Bodies; A Study of their Uses in Relation to Central Government; with a Preface by A. Salter. London, 1940.

Wade–Phillips
E. C. S. Wade and G. Godfrey Phillips. Constitutional Law: An Outline of the Law and Practice of the Constitution, including Central and Local Government and the Constitutional Relations of the British Commonwealth and Empire. 4th ed. London, 1952.

Beatrice Webb's Diaries, 1912–24
Beatrice Webb's Diaries, 1912–1924. Edited by M. I. Cole. London, 1952.

Beatrice Webb's Diaries, 1924–32
Beatrice Webb's Diaries, 1924–1932. Edited by M. I. Cole. London, 1956.

Webb Memorandum
S. Webb. "The First Labour Government," *Political Quarterly*, XXXII (1961), 6–36.

Wells, *Autobiography*
H. G. Wells. Experiment in Autobiography: Discoveries and Conclusions of a Very Ordinary Brain (since 1866). London, 1934. 2 vols.

Wells, *The New Machiavelli*
H. G. Wells. The New Machiavelli. London, n.d.

Williams, *Bevin*
F. Williams. Ernest Bevin: Portrait of a Great Englishman. London, 1952.

Williams, *Science*
E. C. Williams. "Science and Defence." *Public Administration,* XXXIV (1956), 257–66.

Williams, *Triple Challenge*
F. Williams. The Triple Challenge: The Future of Socialist Britain. London, 1948.

Willson, *Ministries and Boards*
F. M. G. Willson. "Ministries and Boards: Some Aspects of Administrative Development since 1832," *Public Administration*, XXXIII (1955), 43–58.

Willson, *Routes of Entry*
F. M. G. Willson. "The Routes of Entry of New Members of the British Cabinet, 1868–1958," *Political Studies,* VII (1959), 222–32.

Willson, *Supplement*
F. M. G. Willson. "The Organization of British Central Government: 1955–1961," *Public Administration*, XL (1962), 159–200. (See also Chester–Willson.)

Wilson, *Haldane*
C. H. Wilson. Haldane and the Machinery of Government (Haldane Memorial Lecture). London, 1956.

Wilson, Life of Henry
C. E. Callwell. Field-Marshal Sir Henry Wilson: His Life and Diaries. London, 1927. 2 vols.

Winterton, *Orders of the Day*
Earl Winterton. Orders of the Day. London, 1953.

Wiseman
H. V. Wiseman. "Cabinet Government," *Telescope* (Official Journal of the Joint Committee of Students' Societies of the Institute of Municipal Treasurers and Accounts), V (1953), 138–42, 168–72.

Woolton, *Memoirs*
The Memoirs of the Earl of Woolton. London, 1959.

Yu
Wangteh Yu. The English Cabinet System. Westminster, 1939.

INDEX

Names set in boldface are those of ministers whose careers between 1914 and 1963 may be traced by consulting the Appendix (pp. 341–53).